The Complete Guide to
Blender Graphics

Blender™ is a **free Open-Source 3D Computer Modeling and Animation Suite** incorporating Character Rigging, Particles, Real World Physics Simulation, Sculpting, Video Editing with Motion Tracking and 2D Animation within the 3D Environment.

Blender is **FREE** to download and use by anyone for anything.

The Complete Guide to Blender Graphics: Computer Modeling and Animation, Eighth Edition is a unified manual describing the operation of the program, updated with reference to the Graphical User Interface for **Blender Version 3.2.2**, including additional material covering **Blender Assets, Geometry Nodes, and Non-Linear Animation**.

Divided into a two-volume set, the book introduces the program's Graphical User Interface and shows how to implement tools for modeling and animating characters and created scenes with the application of color, texture, and special lighting effects.

Key Features:

- The book provides instruction for New Users starting at the very beginning.
- Instruction is presented in a series of chapters incorporating visual reference to the program's interface.
- The initial chapters are designed to instruct the user in the operation of the program while introducing and demonstrating interesting features of the program.
- Chapters are developed in a building block fashion providing forward and reverse reference to relevant material.

Both volumes are available in a discounted set, which can also be purchased together with **Blender 2D Animation: The Complete Guide to the Grease Pencil**.

Abut the author

John M. Blain has become a recognised expert in Blender having seven successful prior editions of this book to date. John became enthused with Blender on retirement from a career in Mechanical Engineering. *The Complete Guide to Blender Graphics* originated from personal notes compiled in the course of self-learning. The notes were recognized as an ideal instruction source by Neal Hirsig, Senior Lecturer (Retired) at Tufts University. Neal encouraged publication of the First Edition and in doing so is deserving of the author's gratitude. Gratitude must also be extended to the author's wife Helen for her continuing encouragement and patience as new editions of the book are compiled.

The Complete Guide to
Blender Graphics
Computer Modeling
& Animation

EIGHTH EDITION

Volume 2

JOHN M. BLAIN

CRC Press
Taylor & Francis Group
Boca Raton London New York

CRC Press is an imprint of the
Taylor & Francis Group, an **informa** business

AN A K PETERS BOOK

Eight edition published 2024
by CRC Press
2385 Executive Center Drive, Suite 320, Boca Raton, FL 33431

and by CRC Press
4 Park Square, Milton Park, Abingdon, Oxon, OX14 4RN

CRC Press is an imprint of Taylor & Francis Group, LLC

© 2024 John M. Blain

First edition published by AK Peters 2012
Second edition published by AK Peters 2014
Third edition published by AK Peters 2016
Fourth edition published by AK Peters 2017
Fifth edition published by AK Peters 2019
Sixth edition published by AK Peters 2020
Seventh edition published by AK Peters 2022

ISBN: 978-1-032-51056-9 (hbk)
ISBN: 978-1-032-51055-2 (pbk)
ISBN: 978-1-003-40431-6 (ebk)

DOI: 10.1201/9781003404316

Publisher's note: This book has been prepared from camera-ready copy provided by the authors.

Contents

Introduction

The Complete Guide to Blender Graphics - 8th Edition provides instruction in the use of the Computer Graphics 3D Program **Blender.** The book has been compiled in two separate volumes with Volume 1 being inclusive of all material which will allow a new user to obtain, install and operate the program. Volume 2 is complimentary to Volume 1 encompassing some of the more advanced aspects of the program. The books are an operation manual for those who wish to undertake a learning experience and discover a wonderful creative new world of computer graphics. The books also serves as a reference for established operators.

Instructions throughout the book demonstrate Blender with examples and diagrams referenced to the **Graphical User Interface (GUI).**

In selecting **Volume 2** of **The Complete guide to Blender Graphics** it is assumed you are conversant with Blender and its interface and the fundamentals of operating the Blender Program as described in Volume 1.

Volume 2 provides an introduction to Blenders features which expand on the basics of Modeling and Animation. Knowing that these features exist and where to find them will significantly improve the working experience and enhance your ability to produce fantastic effects.

The Complete Guide to Blender Graphics originated when Blender's Graphical User Interface was transformed with the release of Blender version 2.50. Subsequent editions of the book have kept pace with developments to the program and have included new material.

The **8th Edition of The Complete Guide to Blender Graphics** is applicable to:
Blender Version 3.2.2

The Blender program is maintained by the **Blender Foundation** and released as **Open Source Software** which is available for download and **FREE** to be used for any purpose.

The program may be downloaded from: <u>www.blender.org</u>

The Complete Guide to Blender Graphics provides a fantastic learning experience in **Computer Graphics** using **Blender,** by introducing the operation of the Blender program through the use of its' Graphical user Interface. The book is intended to be read in conjunction with having the program in operation, with the interface displayed.

Instruction is presented using the tools displayed in the Graphical User Interface, with basic examples demonstrating results. Understanding where features are located, their uses and how they are implemented will allow the reader to more easily follow detailed instruction in the many written and video tutorials available on the Internet.

Instruction provided on the internet in the form of written and video tutorials is integral to the compendium of Blender learning material. Although comprehensive, **The Complete Guide to Blender Graphics** is limited by the number of pages in a volume. The internet vastly expands the knowledge base of learning material.

Important: The Blender Program is continually being developed with new features being added and improvements to the interface and operation procedures being amended. When reading instructions or viewing video tutorials the version of the Blender program for which the instruction is written should be considered.

Program Evolution

Blender is continually evolving. New versions of the program are released as additions and changes are incorporated, therefore, it is advisable to check the Blender website, from time to time for the latest version.

At each release of Blender a different **Splash Screen Image** is displayed in the interface.

Blender Version 3.2.2

Earlier versions of the program and documentation may be obtained which provide valuable information when you are conversant with the current release of the program. Video tutorials available on the internet may not strictly adhere to the current user interface or work flow. Major transformations occurred when the program changed from version 2.49 to 2.50 and again at the change from version 2.79 to version 2.82. Since 2.82 development has continued.

Previous Versions of Blender

As previously stated, Blender is continually evolving with new versions being released. To fully utilise internet material you may find it advantageous to study older tutorials by installing previous Blender versions. Previous versions of the program can be obtained at:

https://download.blender.org/release/

Index of /release/

../		Blender2.93/	03-Aug-2022 08:58	-
Blender1.0/	11-Jul-2020 07:17	Blender3.0/	26-Jan-2022 13:21	-
Blender1.60/	05-Jul-2020 16:22	Blender3.1/	01-Apr-2022 08:23	-
Blender1.73/	20-Aug-2003 11:13	Blender3.2/	03-Aug-2022 08:58	-
Blender1.80/	20-Aug-2003 11:13	BlenderBenchmark1.0/	17-Aug-2018 12:31	-
Blender2.04/	20-Aug-2003 11:13	BlenderBenchmark2.0/	20-Jan-2020 14:19	-
Blender2.26/	20-Aug-2003 11:13	Publisher2.25/	20-Aug-2003 11:13	-
		plugin/	23-Nov-2004 12:56	-
		yafray.0.0.6/	03-Feb-2004 22:31	-
		yafray.0.0.7/	05-Aug-2004 10:33	-
		GPL-license.txt	19-Aug-2013 11:54	17997
		GPL3-license.txt	19-Aug-2013 11:54	35147
		blender2.04-ipaq.zip	20-Aug-2003 11:14	2048262

Installation

Note: You may install multiple versions of Blender on you PC.

Blender Features

A comprehensive display of the Blender features is available at:

www.blender.org/features**?**

Modeling   Animation

The Author

John M. Blain

John was born in Swindon, Wiltshire in England in 1942. At the time of writing this makes him a pretty old dude. He emigrated to Canada with his family in 1952 and now lives in Coffs Harbour, New South Wales in Australia.

Drawing and painting were skills John developed from an early age and while attending school on Vancouver Island he became interested in wood sculpture inspired by the work of the indigenous west coast people. Artistic pursuits were curtailed on graduating from high school when he returned to England to undertake a technical engineering apprenticeship. Following his apprenticeship, he worked for a short period in England and then made the decision to return to Vancouver, Canada. On the voyage between Southampton and Vancouver, he met his wife to be and Vancouver became a stopover for a journey to Sydney Australia. In this new country, he began work as an engineering draughtsman, married, had children and studied engineering. The magic milestone of seven years saw John with his young family move out of the city to the coastal town of Coffs Harbour, New South Wales.

Coffs Harbour was a center for sawmill machinery and John became engaged in machinery design and manufacture. He acquired a sound knowledge of this industry acting as installation engineer then progressing to sales. This work afforded travel throughout Australia, Canada, the United States and New Zealand.

On retirement, artistic pursuits returned with additional interests in writing and computing. Writing notes whilst learning computer animation using Blender resulted in **The Complete Guide to Blender Graphics**. The first edition, published in 2012, was well received and encouraged John to compile a second edition inline with the latest version of the Blender program. This afforded the opportunity to include new material. Subsequent editions have followed until this newly reformatted eighth edition.

Preamble

The **Preamble** will walk you through the method of reading this book in conjunction with operating the Blender program. It is assumed that you are conversant with the Blender program and its Graphical User Interface as described in Volume 1 of The Complete Guide to Blender graphics.

Formats Conventions and Commands

In writing this book the following formatting conventions have been adopted:

Paragraphs are separated by an empty line and have not been indented.

Key words and phrases are printed in **bold text** with the first letter of a component name specific to Blender capitalised.

Headings are printed in Bold Olive Green.

The following conventions will be used when giving instructions.

When using a Mouse connected to a computer, the commands will be:

Click or **Click LMB** – In either case this means make a single click with the left mouse button with the Mouse Cursor positioned over a control on the computer Screen.

In some instances it is explicit that the left mouse button should be used.

Note: Computer Screen and Monitor are synonymous.

Mouse Over: Place the Mouse Cursor over a control.

A **Control** is a specific area of the Computer Screen.

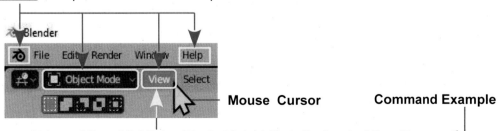

Mouse Cursor   Command Example

Mouse Over on **View** (Highlights Blue). Click LMB to display the **View Menu**.

The View Menu contains a selection of text annotations which are button controls for selecting functions affecting the 3D Viewport.

A Control: Is a designated area on the computer Screen represented by an icon in the form of a button or bar, with or without text annotation.

Double Click – Make two clicks in quick succession with LMB (the left mouse button).

Click, Hold and Drag – Click the left mouse button, hold it depressed while moving the mouse. Release the button at the end of the movement.

Click RMB – Click the right mouse button.

Click MMB – Click the middle mouse button (the middle mouse button may be the scroll wheel).

Clicking is used in conjunction with placing the Mouse Cursor over a button, icon or a slider which is displayed on the Screen.

Scroll MMB – Scroll (rotate) the scroll wheel (MMB).

The Graphical User Interface (GUI)

When Blender is first opened what you see on the computer Screen is the **Graphical User Interface (GUI)** for the program. This arrangement of panels is the interface which allows you to communicate with the program by entering commands (data) using the Keyboard and Mouse previously described. The panels that you see are called **Editors** or **Headers** with one exception, the **Splash Screen**.

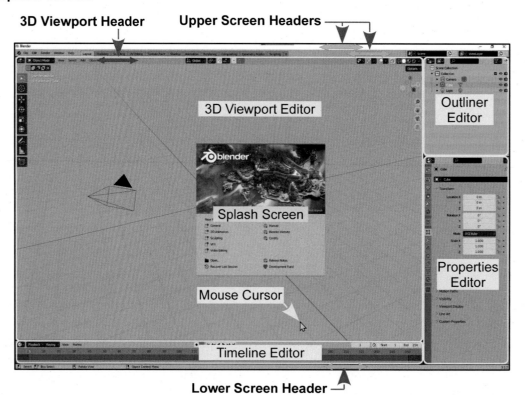

VIII

Note: In the preceding diagram the different Editors have been colored to distinguish one from the other. Changing Editor background colors, in affect, modifies the color scheme or Theme of the GUI. The Theme of the GUI in the diagram is not what you see when you first run Blender.

The very first time Blender runs the Graphical User Interface displays on the computer Screen with a default Theme or color scheme named **Blender Dark**. You will see this as one of the **Quick Setup options** in the **Splash Screen**.

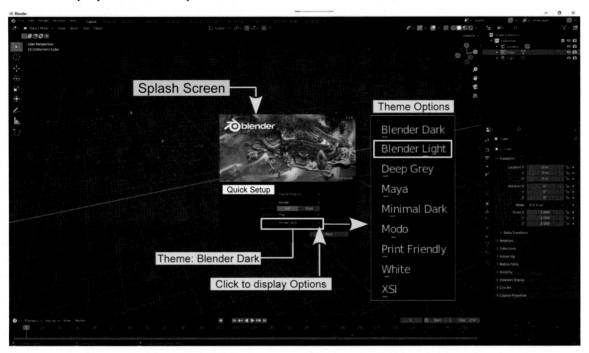

Clicking the **Theme button** displays a menu with alternative **Theme Options**. You may select any option depending on your preference. Having made a selection click the **Next button** to apply your Theme. The color scheme changes and the **Splash Screen** is replaced.

The Graphical User Interface with **Theme: Blender Light** selected.

What! You want to try a different Theme!

Logically, you would think, reinstating the Splash Screen would provide the **Quick Setup** controls previously employed.

To reinstate the Splash Screen click the little Blender Logo in the Screen Header and select **Splash Screen** in the menu that displays.

Click the Blender Logo.

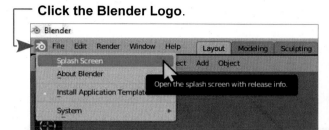

The Splash Screen is reinstated but it is different from the initial display containing the Quick Setup options.

To try a different Theme, in fact, to customise Blender to your personal choice you go to the **Preferences Editor** by clicking **Edit, Preferences** in the Screen Header..

In the **Preferences Editor**, select **Themes** in the left hand column and click on **Presets** to display the list of color schemes.

Click Presets

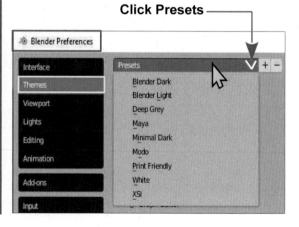

The assumption has been made that you are conversant with the Blender GUI, therefore, you may be aware of the **Preferences Editor** and the procedure for selecting Themes. The forgoing instruction is provided to familiarise you with the method of presenting instruction in the book which incorporate references to Editors, Headers, Panels and Tabs.

The following diagram will recap on these terminologies when viewing the interface.

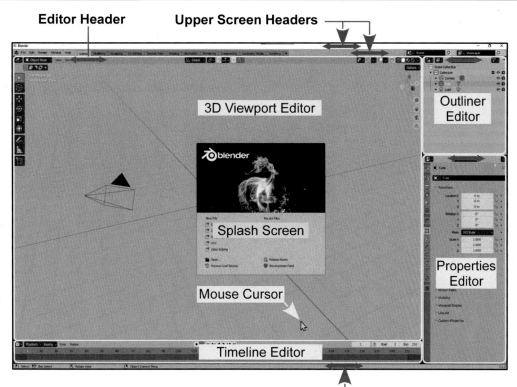

Editor Header   **Upper Screen Headers**

3D Viewport Editor

Outliner Editor

Splash Screen

Properties Editor

Mouse Cursor

Timeline Editor

Lower Screen Header

Editors

There are four **Editors** displayed when Blender is first opened. The Editors are; the **3D Viewport Editor**, the **Outliner Editor**, the **Properties Editor** and the **Timeline Editor**. In the center of the display you see the **Splash Screen** showing you which version of Blender you have opened and containing buttons for selecting a variety of functions.

Traditionally the Splash Screen image is changed at each new release of the Blender Program.

At the top and bottom of the Screen you see **Screen Headers**. At the top of each Editor Panel there is also an **Editor Header**. Headers contain Button Controls for selecting functions pertaining to the Screen or the Editor as the case may be.

Note: Clicking the Left Mouse Button with the Mouse Cursor in the 3D Viewport Editor cancels the display of the Splash Screen (Reinstate as previously described)**.**

Note: In the preceding diagram the default background colors of the different Editors have been altered to distinguish the panels.

Controls - Buttons, Icons and Sliders

Each **Editor** in the **GUI** is a separate panel with a **Header** at the top of the panel. The Headers contain buttons which activate functions or display sub menus with buttons for activating functions.

A button may be a text annotation which highlights blue on Mouse Over or an icon representing a function or a bar with text annotation. Clicking a button relays data to the program to perform an action.

Example 1 : The 3D Viewport Editor (the default Screen display – **Upper LH Side**)

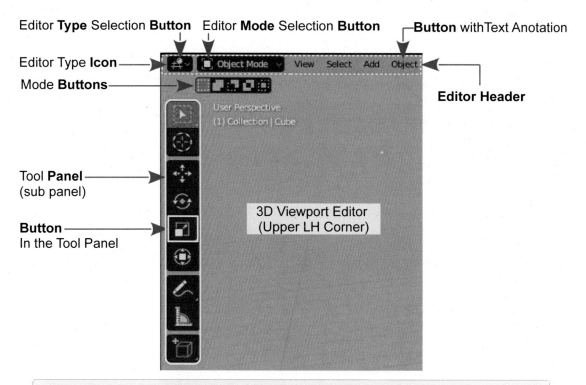

Editor **Type** Selection **Button**   Editor **Mode** Selection **Button**   **Button** withText Anotation

Editor Type **Icon**

Mode **Buttons**

Editor Header

Tool **Panel**
(sub panel)

Button
In the Tool Panel

Note: The buttons shown in the diagram can be seen in the panel at the upper left hand side of the **default** Blender Screen arrangement.

Note: In giving instructions, **Default** means, that which is displayed on the computer Screen before any action is taken.

Example 2 : The Properties Editor (the default Screen display – **Lower RH Side**)

The default display shows the content of the **Properties Editor** with the **Object Properties** active. In this state the controls affect the default **Cube Object** in the 3D Viewport Editor.

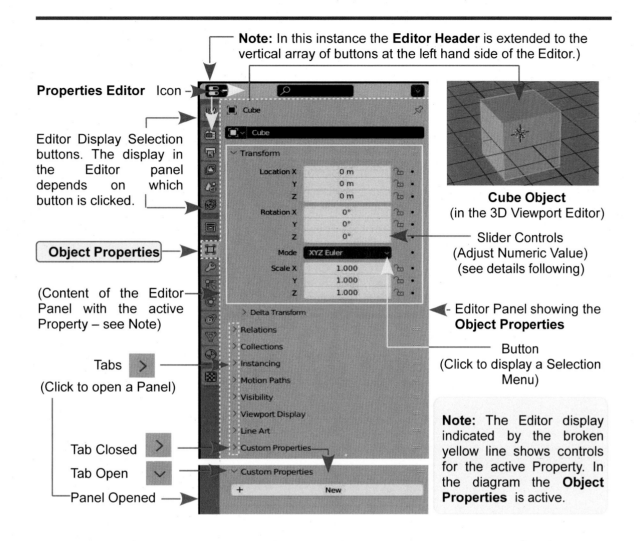

Properties Editor Icon

Note: In this instance the **Editor Header** is extended to the vertical array of buttons at the left hand side of the Editor.)

Editor Display Selection buttons. The display in the Editor panel depends on which button is clicked.

Object Properties

(Content of the Editor Panel with the active Property – see Note)

Tabs >
(Click to open a Panel)

Tab Closed >
Tab Open ∨
Panel Opened

Cube Object
(in the 3D Viewport Editor)

Slider Controls
(Adjust Numeric Value)
(see details following)

- Editor Panel showing the **Object Properties**

Button
(Click to display a Selection Menu)

Note: The Editor display indicated by the broken yellow line shows controls for the active Property. In the diagram the **Object Properties** is active.

A Button in Blender can be a small square or rectangular area on the screen or an elongated rectangle in which case it may be referred to as a bar. Some buttons display with icons.

An Icon is a pictorial representation of a function. In the diagram the icon in the upper left hand corner indicates that the **Properties Editor** is displayed.

A Slider is an elongated area, usually containing a numeric value, which is modified by clicking, deleting and retyping the value, or clicking, holding and dragging the Mouse Cursor that displays on **Mouse Over**, left or right to decrease or increase the value. Some sliders have a small arrow at either end which display when the Mouse Cursor is **positioned over the Slider** (Mouse Over).

Click on an arrow to incrementally alter the value. Some sliders directly alter the display on the computer Screen.

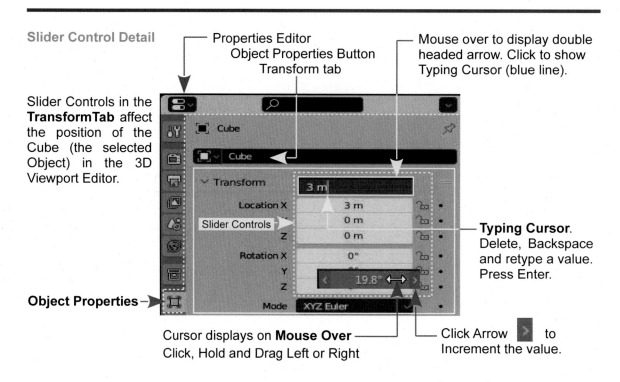

Slider Control Detail

Properties Editor
Object Properties Button
Transform tab

Mouse over to display double headed arrow. Click to show Typing Cursor (blue line).

Slider Controls in the **TransformTab** affect the position of the Cube (the selected Object) in the 3D Viewport Editor.

Cube

Cube

∨ Transform

3 m

Location X · · · · 3 m

Slider Controls · · · · 0 m

Z · · · · 0 m

Rotation X · · · · 0°

Y

Z · · · · 19.8° ⟷

Mode · · · · XYZ Euler

Typing Cursor. Delete, Backspace and retype a value. Press Enter.

Object Properties →

Cursor displays on **Mouse Over** Click, Hold and Drag Left or Right

Click Arrow [>] to Increment the value.

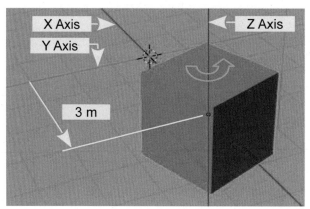

X Axis

Y Axis

Z Axis

3 m

With the Cube Object selected in the 3D Viewport Editor, altering the **X Location Slider** value to 3m and the **Z Axis Rotation Slider** to 19.8° moves the Cube forward along the X Axis (Red Line) and rotates the Cube about the vertical Z Axis.

For Keyboard input, a command is; to press a specific Key or a series of Keys. Press **Shift + Ctrl + T Key** means, press and hold both the **Shift** and **Ctrl** Keys simultaneously and tap the **T Key**. **Num Pad** (Number Pad) Keys are also used in which case the command is Press **Num Pad 0** to **9** or **Plus** and **Minus**.

Command Instruction Example:

> Go to the **Blender Screen Header, Render Properties,** click **Render Image:**

Remember: A control button, icon or slider which is displayed, indicates a specific location on the computer Screen. Positioning the Mouse Cursor at this location and clicking the Mouse button or depressing a keyboard button, inputs a signal to the computer. The interpretation , made by by the computer is; signal received at specific location = perform explicit computation and export result.

The example above means; in the **Blender Screen Header,** position the **Mouse Cursor** over the **Render Properties** button and click the left mouse button, clicking once. In this case the signal received by the computer with the Mouse Cursor at the position of the Render Properties button tells the computer to display the **Render Options Sub Menu**. Positioning the Mouse Cursor over **Render Image** in the sub menu and clicking once renders an image of **Camera View** (what the camera sees). The Rendered Image is displayed in a new Editor panel, the **Image Editor**. The image may be saved from this location but for the time being press **Esc** on the Keyboard to cancel the render and return to the 3D Viewport Editor.

┌── Mouse Cursor over the Render Button   **Camera View**

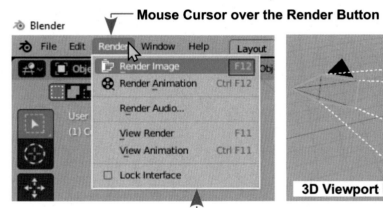

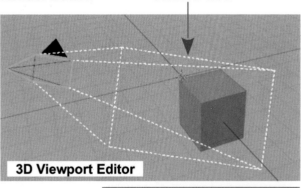

3D Viewport Editor

Render Options Sub Menu ┘

Pressing **Num Pad 0** on the Keyboard shows a preview in the 3D Viewport Editor of what will be **Rendered** in an image (What the Camera sees).

Rendered Image
As seen in the Image Editor

Render Preview ──▶

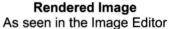

Note: The annotation **F12** adjacent to **Render Image** is a **Keyboard Shortcut**. Pressing **F12** on the Keyboard will also Render the Camera View.

Remember: The purpose of exercises in this preamble are to familiarise you with commands and diagrams not to provide instruction an any particular task. Full instruction will be provided as you progress.

Objects in the 3D View Editor

1.1	Object Primitives	1.5	Blender Assets
1.2	Additional Objects	1.6	The Assets Library
1.3	The Add Cube Tool	1.7	BlenderKit Add-on
1.4	Objects from Add-ons		

Objects in the 3D Viewport Editor are the Models and Characters you create as components of a Scene. They also include the Lights that illuminate the Scene and Cameras which capture that part of a Scene you wish to Render. In fact, pretty much everything entered in a Scene is considered an Object in Blender.

One starting point for Modeling is the base **Object Primitives** that are entered in a Scene. Primitives are then modified or edited to create new shapes which is the basis of Modeling. Besides Object Primitives there are other sources for obtaining Objects as a starting point.

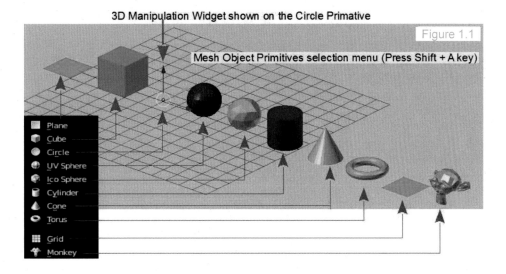

3D Manipulation Widget shown on the Circle Primative

Figure 1.1

Mesh Object Primitives selection menu (Press Shift + A key)

Plane
Cube
Circle
UV Sphere
Ico Sphere
Cylinder
Cone
Torus
Grid
Monkey

1

1.1 Object Primitives

Object Primitives are entered in a Scene by selecting from the **Add, Mesh** menu in the **3D Viewport Editor Header**. ⎯⎯

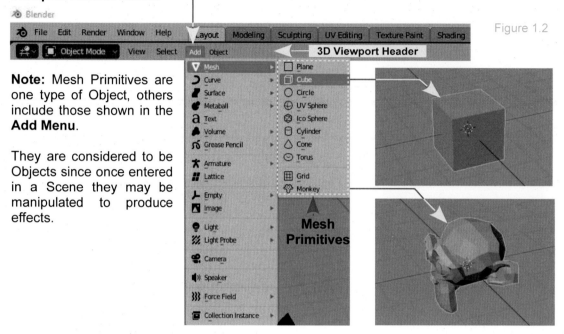

Figure 1.2

Note: Mesh Primitives are one type of Object, others include those shown in the **Add Menu**.

They are considered to be Objects since once entered in a Scene they may be manipulated to produce effects.

1.2 Additional Objects

Besides **Mesh Primitive** Objects there are a variety of additional Object Types available from the **Add Menu** in the **3D Viewport Editor Header**.

Curve - Bezier Curve

Figure 1.3

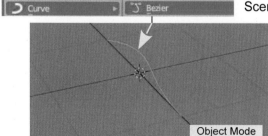

Curve Object Types are used when creating Models and ancillary to the modeling process or for creating Scene effects.

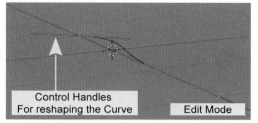

Control Handles
For reshaping the Curve

Object Mode

Edit Mode

Note: The Bezier Curve is one of five Curve Types; Bezier, Circle, Nurbs Curve, Nurbs Circle and Path.

Surface - Nurbs Torus

Figure 1.4

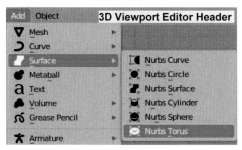

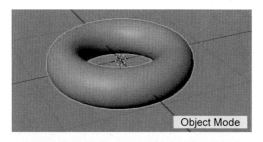

Object Mode

The **Nurbs Torus** has a cage surrounding the mesh, in Edit Mode, which is used for shaping. After shaping, go to Object Mode, RMB click and select **Convert To – Mesh.**

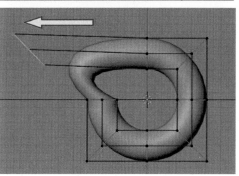

Edit Mode

Select Cage vertices and Drag

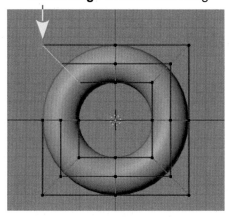

Surface - Nurbs Cylinder

Figure 1.5   **Select Cage** vertices and Drag

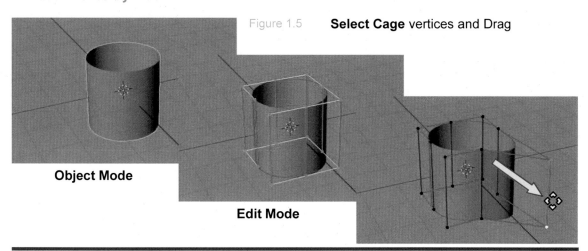

Object Mode

Edit Mode

Note: Not all Object Types selected from the Add menu Render. The Bezier Curve does not Render while the Surface – Nurbs Torus will Render.

1.3 The Add Cube Tool

The **Add Cube Tool** in the 3D Viewport Editor, Object Mode, Tool Panel, also provides a means of adding Objects to a Scene.

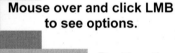

Mouse over on the Tool, click LMB to see the Tool Options. Hold LMB, drag the Mouse over an option (highlights blue) and release LMB to select the option.

With an option selected the Mouse Cursor in the 3D Viewport Editor displays as a grid which you position in the Scene by dragging the Mouse.

Figure 1.6

**Mouse over and click LMB
to see options.**

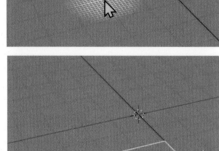

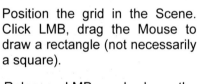

Position the grid in the Scene. Click LMB, drag the Mouse to draw a rectangle (not necessarily a square).

Release LMB and drag the Mouse up to draw a cuboid (Figure 1.7).

Click LMB to set the shape.

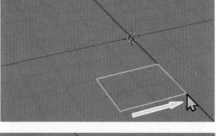

Figure 1.7

Figure 1.8

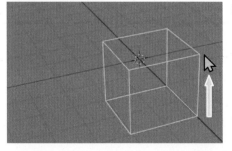

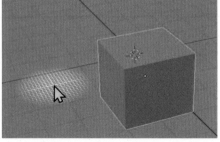

Clicking LMB reverts the Mouse to the Cursor with the grid attached. You may repeat the procedure to construct more cuboids (figure 1.8).

To cancel the process click the **Box Select Tool** in the Tool Panel (upper Tool).

Note: The Add Cube Tool may be employed in Object Mode and Edit Mode. To enter Edit Mode you must have a Mesh Object existing in the Scene. Constructing a new Object using the Add Cube (shape) Tool in Edit Mode will see the new shape joined to the original Mesh Object.

1.4 Objects from Add-ons

The default selection from the Add Menu in the 3D Viewport Editor includes Mesh Objects and other Object Types. You should, however, be aware that there are other Mesh Objects available in Blender. To access these you have to activate **Add-ons** in the **Preferences Editor**.

The **Preferences Editor** is opened by clicking **Edit** in the **Blender Screen Header** and selecting **Preferences**.

Figure 1.9

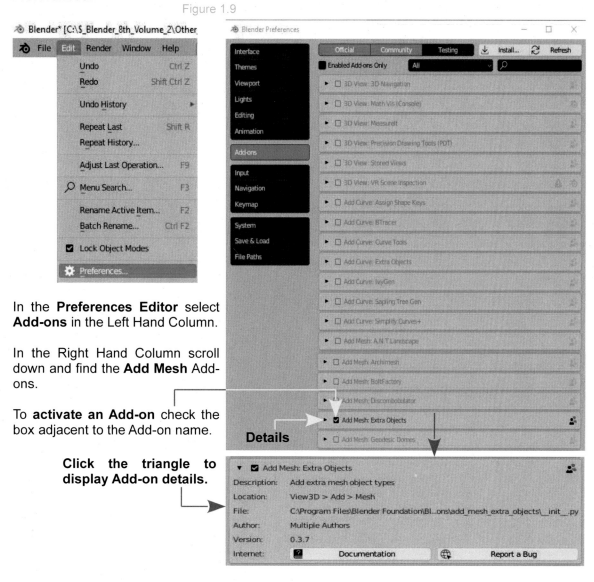

In the **Preferences Editor** select **Add-ons** in the Left Hand Column.

In the Right Hand Column scroll down and find the **Add Mesh** Add-ons.

To **activate an Add-on** check the box adjacent to the Add-on name.

Details

Click the triangle to display Add-on details.

Add Mesh: Default   Figure 1.10   Add Mesh: Extra Objects

Extra Objects

Experiment with the different Add-ons to discover new Objects.

Add Mesh: Archimesh   Figure 1.11

Archimesh provides a selection of Architectural components.

Gear   **Worm**

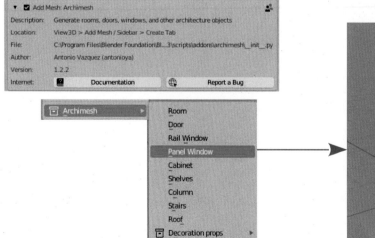

Add Mesh: BoltFactory

BoltFactory allows you to generate different configurations of **Bolts and Nuts**. Figure 1.12

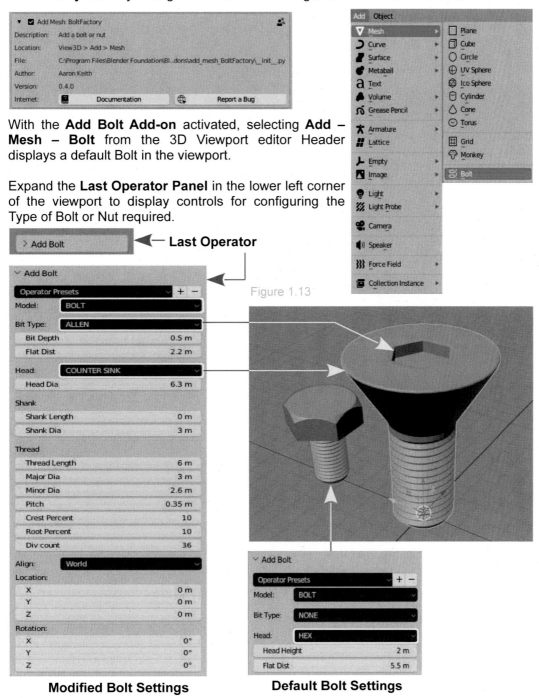

With the **Add Bolt Add-on** activated, selecting **Add – Mesh – Bolt** from the 3D Viewport editor Header displays a default Bolt in the viewport.

Expand the **Last Operator Panel** in the lower left corner of the viewport to display controls for configuring the Type of Bolt or Nut required.

Figure 1.13

Modified Bolt Settings   **Default Bolt Settings**

Add Mesh: Discombobulator

Figure 1.14

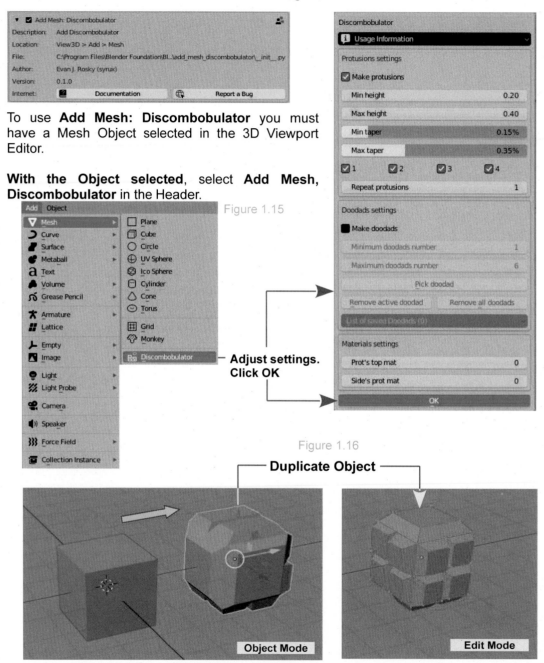

To use **Add Mesh: Discombobulator** you must have a Mesh Object selected in the 3D Viewport Editor.

With the Object selected, select **Add Mesh, Discombobulator** in the Header.

Figure 1.15

Adjust settings. Click OK

Figure 1.16

Duplicate Object

Object Mode

Edit Mode

Discombobulating produces a duplicate of the selected Object, subdivided and reconfigured into a confused shape according to the settings entered in the Discombobulator panel.

1.5 Blender Assets

In blender an **Asset** is a Pre-Constructed Model, a Material (color), or a Material Texture or anything that is useful.

Objects are Assets in that they provide a starting point for Modeling and creating the components of a Scene.

Computer Graphics Artists often draw on **Assets** to embellish their work or to save time. There are many sources on the internet where Assets may be downloaded, therefore, Blender incorporates an **Assets Browser** in the program which links to an **Assets Library.** There are also **Add-ons** which may be installed in Blender to provide additional Asset Resources.

The **Assets Library** is a Folder you create on your hard drive which, initially, will be empty. You add Assets to the Library which may be viewed and selected in the Assets Browser, then entered in the Scene in the current Blender File. The Assets Browser is, therefore, a special Editor.

One **Add-on** is named **BlenderKit** which provides a selection of Models, Materials, Scenes, HDR Images and Brushes. The Add-on has to be downloaded and installed in Blender where it provides links to on-line resources. To obtain **BlenderKit** you have to register as a user then select a Free or Paid option.

Many on-line sources for Assets provide Free Assets and Paid Assets.

The Assets Browser

As previously stated the **Assets Browser** links to the **Assets Library**. At the time of writing this feature is under development, therefore, the procedure of operation will depend on your version of the Blender program. Initially access to the Assets Browser is obtained by clicking the Editor Type Icon and selecting **Assets Browser** in the selection menu (Figure 1.17).

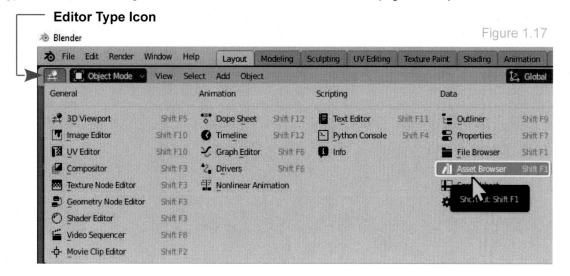

Figure 1.17

For convenience divide the 3D Viewport Editor vertically and make one half the **Assets Browser**.

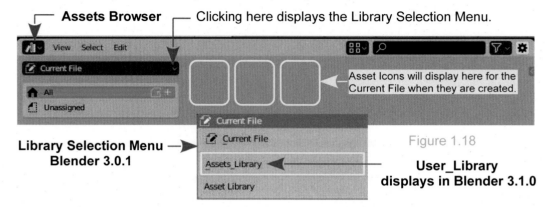

Assets Browser — Clicking here displays the Library Selection Menu.

Asset Icons will display here for the Current File when they are created.

Library Selection Menu → Blender 3.0.1

Figure 1.18

User_Library displays in Blender 3.1.0

Selecting **Assets Library** or **User Library** results in the following message being displayed.

Figure 1.19

No Asset Icons display when **Current File** is selected since Assets haven't been created (Marked). The **Path to Asset Library** message displays because the File Path to the Library hasn't been set or the Library hasn't been created.

Asset Libraries are Folders created on your hard drive in which you save Blender Files containing content **Marked as Assets**.

The **Assets Library** is simply a Folder that you create on your hard drive. The Folder may include sub Folders to categories your Assets.

Windows File Explorer   Figure 1.20

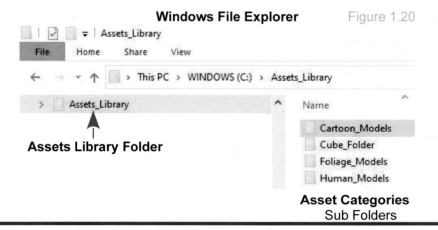

Assets Library Folder

Asset Categories
Sub Folders

To enable the **Assets Browser** to find the **Assets_Library Folder** you set the **File Path** in the **Preferences Editor**.

Figure 1.21

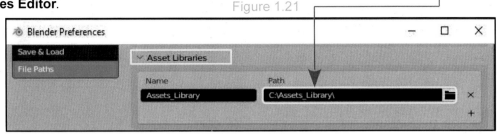

Before creating a Library, Assets may be generated when **Current File** is selected.

For example; A modified default Cube Object can be an Asset. With the Modified Cube selected in the 3D Viewport Editor, go to the Outliner Editor, select Cube, RMB Click and select **Mark as Asset** in the menu that displays. An Icon depicting the Modified Cube appears in the Asset Browser when **Current File** is Selected).

Asset Browser   Figure 1.22   **Outliner Editor**

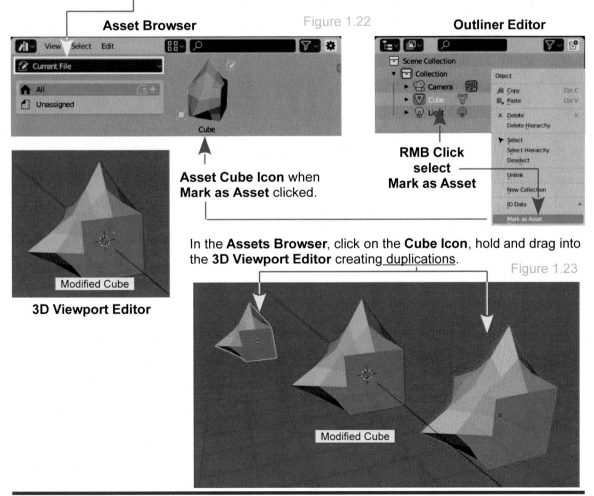

Asset Cube Icon when
Mark as Asset clicked.

**RMB Click
select
Mark as Asset**

3D Viewport Editor

In the **Assets Browser**, click on the **Cube Icon**, hold and drag into the **3D Viewport Editor** creating duplications.

Figure 1.23

Modified Cube

Add a **Material** to the Original Modified Cube in the Properties Editor, Material Properties. In the Outliner Editor, select Material under Cube. RMB Click and select **Mark as Asset**.

Assets Browser   Figure 1.24   **Outliner Editor**   Figure 1.25

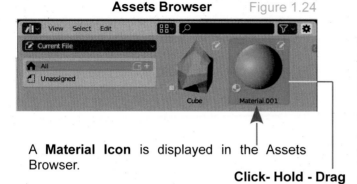

A **Material Icon** is displayed in the Assets Browser.

Click- Hold - Drag

Select one of the duplicated Modified Cubes in the 3D Viewport Editor. Click, hold and drag the Material Icon over to the selected Cube to apply the material to the Cube.   Figure 1.26

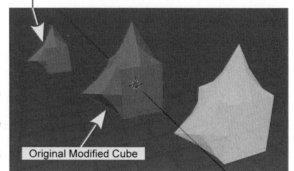

The foregoing has created and applied **Assets** with the **Assets Browser** in **Current File mode**. Saving the Blender File saves the Assets. The Assets are available when the File is reopened. When a new Blender File is opened the Assets created are not available in a new Blender File.

Original Modified Cube

To make Assets available for all Blender Files you create the **Assets Library**.

1.6 The Assets Library

Figures 1.24 and 1.25 show the Assets Library Folder created with Sub Folders categories. For convenience the Assets Library Folder has been created in the C: Drive of the computer. You can create a Folder and name it anything you like to be used as an Assets Library, providing you enter the **File Name** and **File Path** to the Folder in the **Preferences Editor**.

Figure 1.27

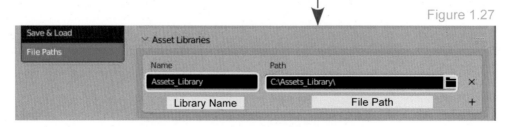

Preferences Editor – Asset Libraries Tab

Adding Assets to the Library

Assets are added to the Library as previously explained when adding to the Current File. The only difference being; you select **Assets_Library** instead of Current File.

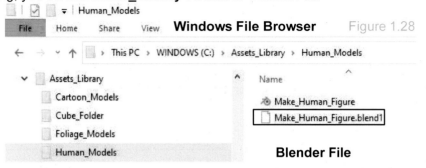

Windows File Browser   Figure 1.28

Blender File

The caveat for adding Assets is; you must have Blender Files containing what you wish to be an Asset saved in your Assets Library Directory.

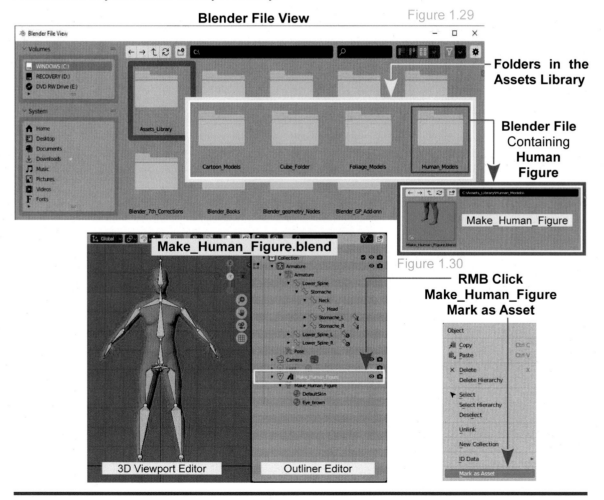

Blender File View   Figure 1.29

Folders in the Assets Library

Blender File Containing **Human Figure**

Make_Human_Figure

Figure 1.30

RMB Click Make_Human_Figure Mark as Asset

Make_Human_Figure.blend

3D Viewport Editor   Outliner Editor

Clicking **Make_Human_Figure** in the Outliner Editor and **Mark as Asset** places an Icon in the Assets Browser (Figure 1.31). Click the Icon in the Assets Browser, hold and drag into the 3D Viewport Editor to place the Model in the 3D Viewport Editor. You will have to Rotate and Scale to suit the Scene.

Blender Assets Browser

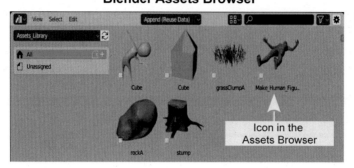

Figure 1.31

Assets Packs

Assets Packs are collection of Blender Files containing pre-constructed Models. Models can sometimes be very complex which means they are time consuming to create. There are numerous websites which offer Assets Packs which will save you time when creating Scenes. Some Packs are free, others require payment.

One free Asset Pack is named **Ground Foliage Pack** which may be downloaded from:

https://www.motionblendstudio.com/blender-vfx-assets

Figure 1.32

This particular **Assets Pack** downloads as a **ZIP file** named **blenderGroundFoliage.zip** Unzipping the file produces two Folders; **MACOSX** and **blenderGroundFolige**.

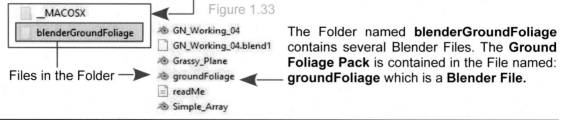

Figure 1.33

Files in the Folder →

The Folder named **blenderGroundFoliage** contains several Blender Files. The **Ground Foliage Pack** is contained in the File named: **groundFoliage** which is a **Blender File.**

Opening **groundFoliage.blend**, in Blender, displays a selection of models which may be **Appended** into other Blender File.

Figure 1.34

You may also select each Model in the **Outliner Editor** and **Mark as Asset** which adds the Model to your **Assets Library**.

Figure 1.35

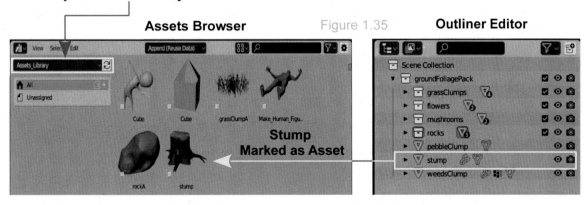

You may add as many Assets as you like to the Assets Library, providing you have Blender Files saved on your PC containing the Assets. The saved Assets will be available when you open a new Blender File.

As you can imagine, over time, the Assets Library could become heavily populated and you will accumulate many Blender Files.

An alternative is to use **on-line resources**. One resource is the **BlenderKit Online Assets Library**.

1.7 BlenderKit

BlenderKit as an Add-on to Blender. Download: https://www.blenderkit.com/get-blenderkit/

Figure 1.36

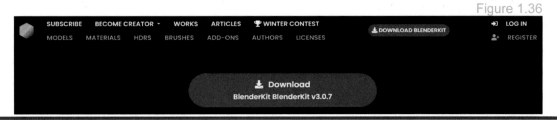

Download BlenderKit v3.0.7

Figure 1.37

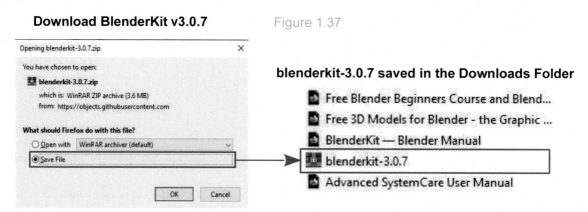

blenderkit-3.0.7 saved in the Downloads Folder

The **blenderkit-3.0.7** File is a compressed ZIP File. **Do NOT unzip the File**.

Go to the **Preferences Editor, Add-ons**. Click on **Install.** Navigate to the Downloads Folder in **Blender File View** and select **blenderkit-3.0.7**. Click **Install Add-on** at the bottom of the panel.

Don't forget to **activate the Add-on** once installed.

Install blenderkit-3.0.7 in Blender

Activate the Add-on

Figure 1.38

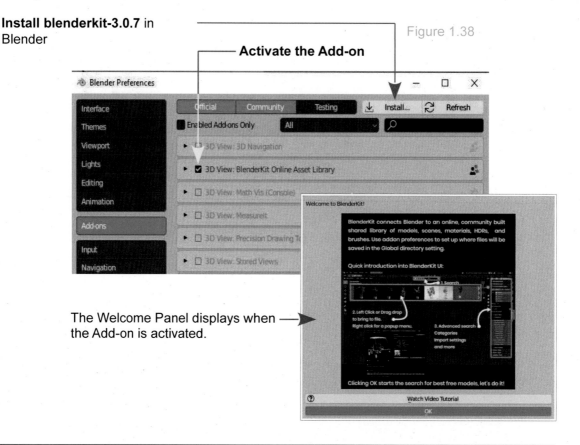

The Welcome Panel displays when the Add-on is activated.

With **BlenderKit** installed **and Activated** the Properties Panel in the 3D Viewport Editor (press N Key to toggle display) includes a **BlenderKit Tab**.

Figure 1.39

With **Search** highlighted, clicking on one of the categories opens **selection panels** for choosing an Asset.

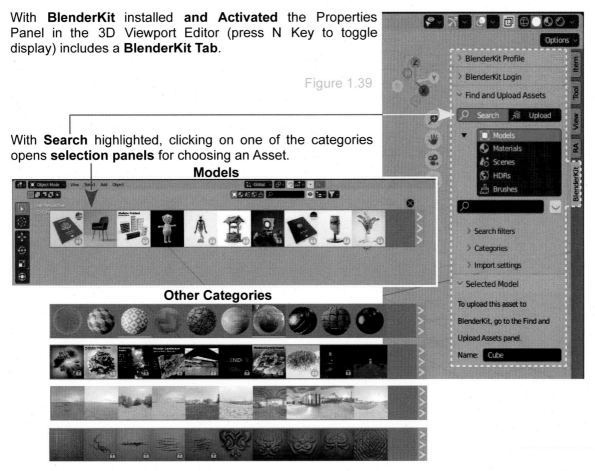

Models

Other Categories

BlenderKit is linking Blender to an on-line Assets Library, therefore, Assets are not stored on your PC.

Note: There are Locked and Unlocked Assets. Unlocked Assets are free, Locked Assets, you have to pay for.

Figure 1.40

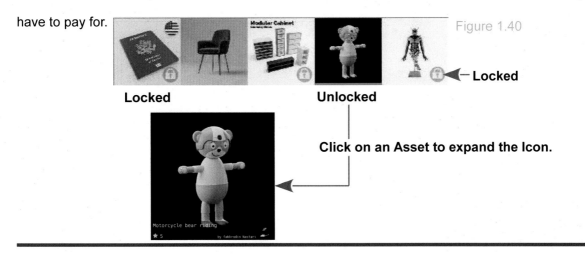

Locked

Locked   **Unlocked**

Click on an Asset to expand the Icon.

Mouse over on an Asset, <u>click, hold and drag into the 3D Viewport Editor</u>. Zoom in and rotate the View.

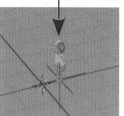

Figure 1.41

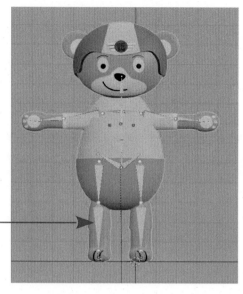

In Figure1.41 the **Motorcycle bear riding** Model is imported into the Blender File complete with **Materials** and has a **Metarig** for posing an Animation.

To use **Material Assets**, have a Model in the 3D Viewport Editor selected. Click, hold and drag the Material Asset over the selected Model.

Figure 1.42

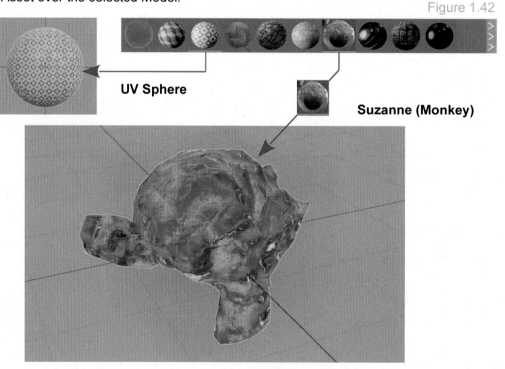

UV Sphere

Suzanne (Monkey)

Note: Some Materials take a while to load and only display with the 3D Viewport Editor in Material Preview or rendered Viewport Shading Mode.

18

2

Editing & Add-Ons

Editing Objects is the precursor to Modeling. Basic Primitives (Mesh Objects) are Edited (Modeled) to create characters and components of a Scene. Editing is performed in Object Mode and Edit Mode by the basic procedures of Translating, Rotating and Scaling an Object as a whole or manipulating the Vertices of the Object's Mesh Surface.

The 3D Viewport provides Editing Tools in the form of Widgets and procedures to assist in the Modeling process. The Editing Tools are self evident in the Tool Panels displayed in the Editor Panel in Object Mode and Edit Mode but it is not always clear how to select the various options available. Besides Editing Tools, there are numerous **Add-ons** to assist in the Editing process located in the **Preferences Editor**.

This chapter will provide instruction in how to access Editing Tools and Add-ons.

Basic Modeling Process

Editing a Sphere to create a humanoid character for Animation.

 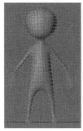 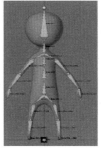 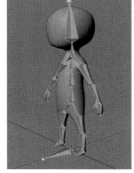

The Character is Rigged to allow Animation.

2.1 Object Mode and Edit Mode

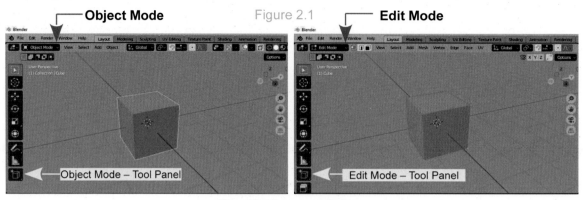

The 3D Viewport Editor

Tool Panels are displayed by default in the 3D Viewport Editor in Object Mode and Edit Mode. The Tool Panels may be hidden from view by pressing the **T Key** on the Keyboard (T Key toggles hide / show).

2.2 Object Mode Tool Panel

The **Object Mode Tool Panel** contains Tools for the basic Translation, Rotation and Scale operations.

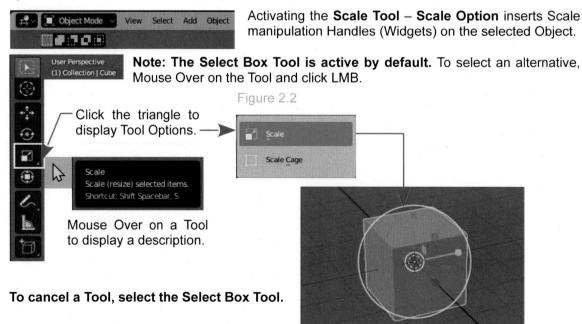

Activating the **Scale Tool – Scale Option** inserts Scale manipulation Handles (Widgets) on the selected Object.

Note: The Select Box Tool is active by default. To select an alternative, Mouse Over on the Tool and click LMB.

Figure 2.2

Click the triangle to display Tool Options.

Scale
Scale (resize) selected items.
Shortcut: Shift Spacebar, S

Mouse Over on a Tool to display a description.

Scale

Scale Cage

To cancel a Tool, select the Select Box Tool.

Experiment with the various Tools to become familiar with each operation.

2.3 Edit Mode Tool Panel

The **Edit Mode Tool Panel** contains a comprehensive selection of Tools for manipulating Mesh Objects when in Edit Mode. Note: The first nine Tools are identical to Object Mode.

A detailed instruction of a sample of Editing Tools has been given Volume 1. Further explanation will not be provided here except for the reminder that when performing Mouse Over on a Tool and holding LMB will display Tool Options. Also, do not forget the **Last Operator Panel** in the lower left of the 3D Viewport Editor. Expanding the Panel with a Tool selected allows you to enter values and refine the Editing.

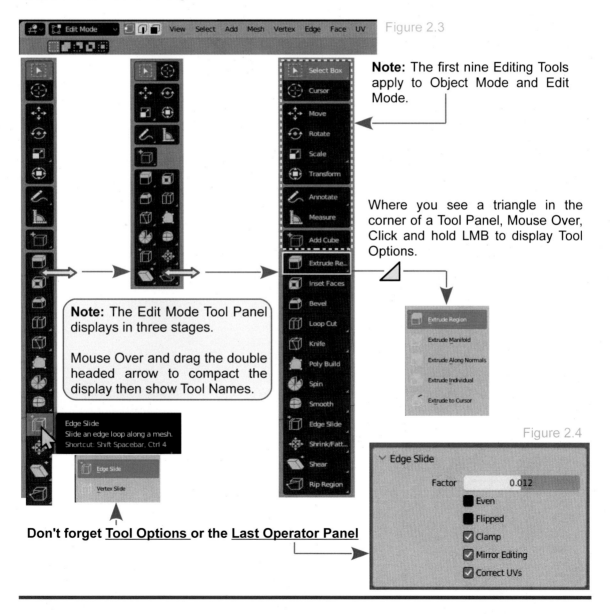

Figure 2.3

Note: The first nine Editing Tools apply to Object Mode and Edit Mode.

Where you see a triangle in the corner of a Tool Panel, Mouse Over, Click and hold LMB to display Tool Options.

Note: The Edit Mode Tool Panel displays in three stages.

Mouse Over and drag the double headed arrow to compact the display then show Tool Names.

Figure 2.4

Don't forget Tool Options or the Last Operator Panel

2.4 Add-ons for Editing

In addition to the editing Tools provided in the 3D Viewport Editor Tool Panel, Blender incorporates several useful Add-ons for adding basic Objects to a Scene and for Editing Objects.

Add-ons are located in the Preferences Editor which is located in the Blender Screen Header by selecting Edit then Preferences at the bottom of the menu that displays. To see Add-ons select the Add-ons category in the left hand column.

Add-ons are listed alphabetically and are categorised to some extent. To demonstrate implementing Add-ons for Editing the following are offered.

Add-on Add Mesh Extra Object

Add Mesh extra Object is located near the top of the listing (scroll down in the Preferences Editor).

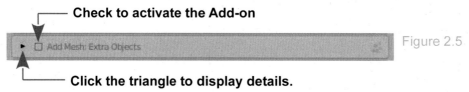

Check to activate the Add-on

Figure 2.5

Click the triangle to display details.

By default the Add-on is **not active**. To activate the Add-on check (tick) the ☐ box preceding the Add-on name.

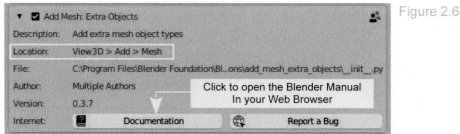

Figure 2.6

With the Add-on details displayed you will see the Location of the controls (View 3D > Add > Mesh).

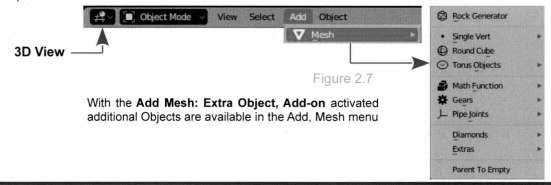

3D View

Figure 2.7

With the **Add Mesh: Extra Object, Add-on** activated additional Objects are available in the Add, Mesh menu

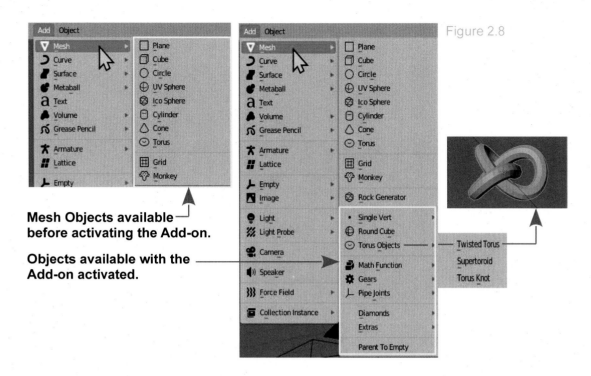

Figure 2.8

Mesh Objects available before activating the Add-on.

Objects available with the Add-on activated.

Note: Some Add-ons controls are accessed in the 3D Viewport Editor Header while others display in the Object Properties Panel in the 3D Viewport.

Add-on Mesh: Edit Mesh Tools

Click to Activate

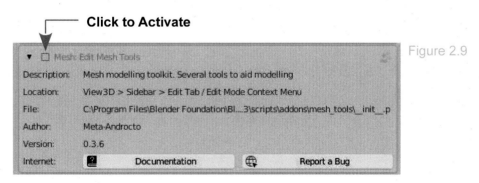

Figure 2.9

In this instance note the **Location:** View 3D > Sidebar > **Edit Tab / Edit Mode** Context Menu.

With an Object selected in the 3D Viewport, **Tab into Edit Mode** to display controls for the Add-on, **Mesh: Edit Mesh Tools** press the **N Key** on the Keyboard to display the <u>**Object Properties Panel**</u> (Side Panel - Context Menu) in the upper RHS of the 3D Viewport Editor.

Note different terminologies

Object Properties Panel
Figure 2.10

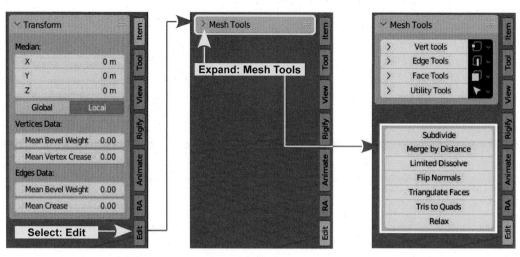

Withe the Object in the 3D Viewport selected (the Cube) in Object Mode, using the **Subdivide** tool sees the Cube Mesh **Subdivided in Edit Mode**.

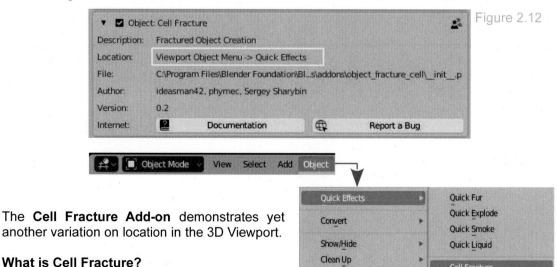

Figure 2.11

Add-on Object : Cell Fracture

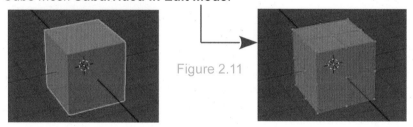

Figure 2.12

The **Cell Fracture Add-on** demonstrates yet another variation on location in the 3D Viewport.

What is Cell Fracture?

Clicking Cell Fracture in the Quick Effects menu opens the Cell Fracture control panel in the 3D Viewport Editor. The controls are applicable to the Object that is selected. Cell Fracture divides (Fractures) a mesh into parts depending on the options selected in the control panel.

Note: In the diagram the default **Point Source** option has been changed to **Own Verts**.

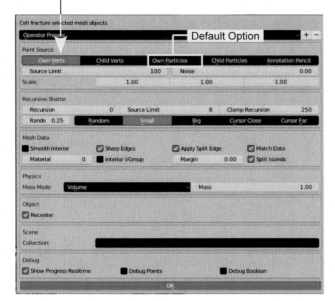

With an Icosphere selected in the 3D Viewport Editor the Icosphere will be divided (Fractured) into parts determined by the arrangement of its Vertices.

Note: Other settings also have an effect on the number of Cells produced.

Figure 2.13

Icosphere with Cell Fracture applied showing one cell removed.   Figure 2.14

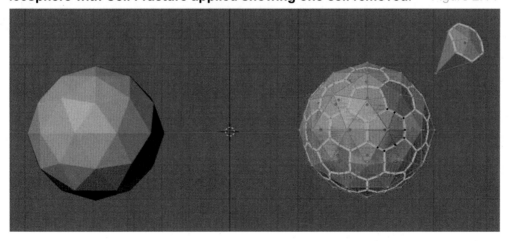

Editing with Generate Modifiers

Modifiers are automatic operations that affect an Object in a non-destructive way allowing effects to be generated which would otherwise be tedious to do manually. Modifiers work by changing how an Object is displayed and rendered in the Viewport. The underlying geometry of the mesh is maintained until the Modifier is Applied. This means that the underlying geometry of the mesh may be edited to suit, before permanently applying the Modifier.

3.1 Accessing Modifiers

Figure 3.1

Properties Editor

Modifiers are accessed in the **Properties Editor, Modifiers Properties**.

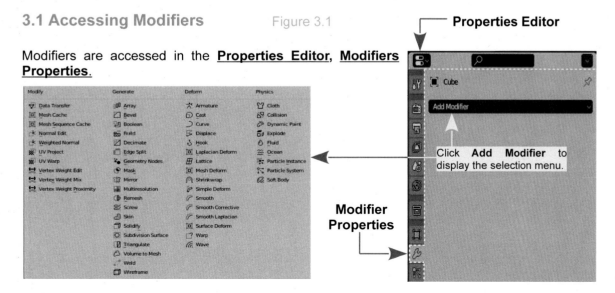

Click **Add Modifier** to display the selection menu.

Modifier Properties

3.2 The Modifier Selection Menu

The **Modifier Selection Menu** is divided into four categories as shown in Figure 3.2.

Modifiers listed under **Modify** add a procedural / operation effect to the selected Object in the 3D Viewport Editor. This category does not physically edit or modify the shape of the Object.

Generate and Deform Modifiers physically affect the shape of the selected Object while **Physics Modifiers** apply real world physical attributes to an Object.

Figure 3.2

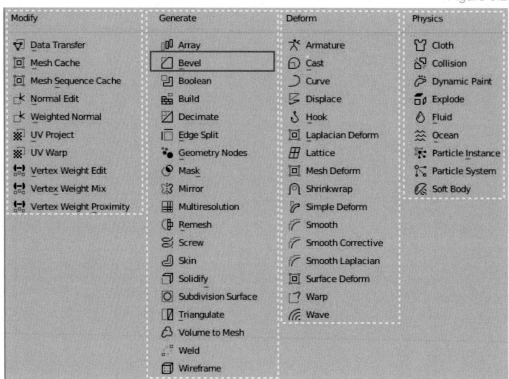

You can add several modifiers to a single Object combining effects. This forms a **Modifier Stack**.

3.3 Modifiers – Generate

The **Generate** group of Modifiers are building tools that change the general appearance of, or automatically add new geometry to an Object.

The **Bevel Modifier** falls in this category and is the second Modifier in the alphabetical listing .

3.4 The Bevel Modifier

Figure 3.3

Properties Editor

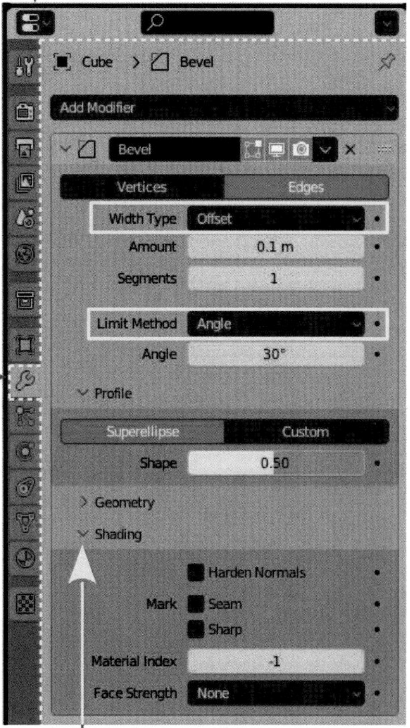

The Bevel Modifier is reasonably simple to understand and is, therefore, suitably for demonstrating the application of a Modifier. To use a Modifier, select the Object to be modified in the 3D Viewport Editor. The Modifier will be specific to the selected Object.

In the Properties Editor, Modifier Properties, click the **Add Modifier** button to display the selection menu (Figure 3.1).

In the **Generate** category select **Bevel**. The Bevel Modifier panel displays in the Properties Editor, Modifier Properties.

Figure 3.4

Modifier Properties

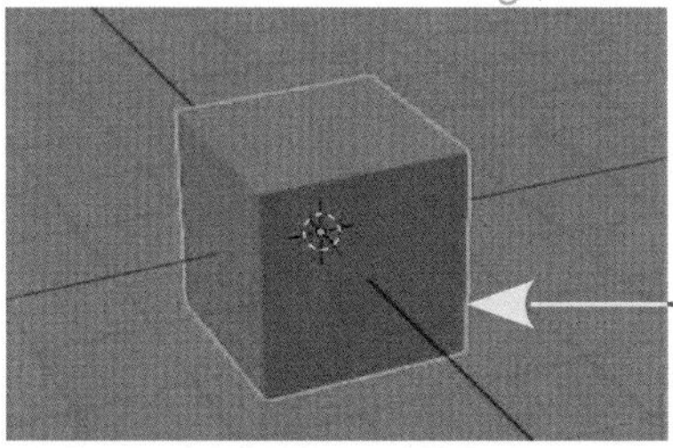

Note: The settings in the Bevel Modifier Panel are specific to the Object selected in the 3D Viewport.

Figure 3.5

When the Bevel Modifier is added the selected Object displays with its Edges Bevelled (Object Mode).

In Edit Mode you will see the Bevel but with only eight Vertices.

Click the chevron to expand / collapse Tabs.

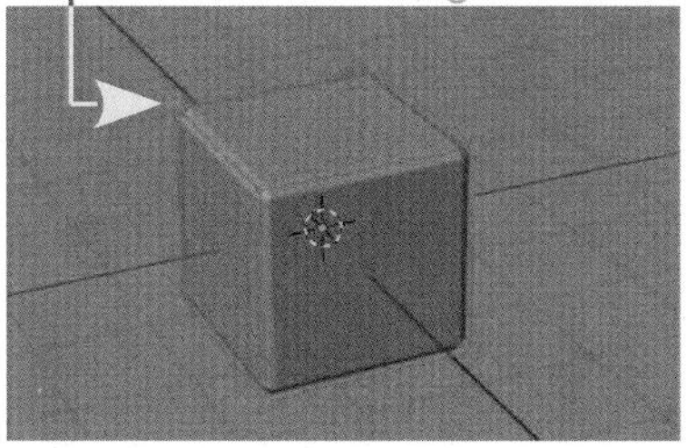

Click and select **Apply** in the menu.

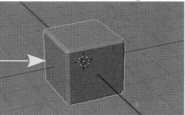

Figure 3.6

Figure 3.7

The Modifier has been Added but not Applied

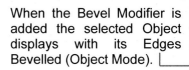

With the **Modifier Applied** Vertices are added to the selected Object permanently affecting the shape.

Figure 3.8

Sub Menu in the Properties Panel

Figure 3.9

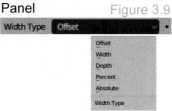

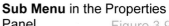

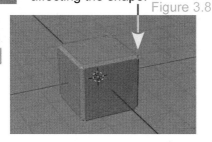

Sub Menu in the Properties Panel

Figure 3.10

3.5 Array Modifier

Figure 3.11

The **Array Modifier** creates copies of an Object, placing the copies in an array with each copy offset from the original. Figure 3.11 shows a **Monkey** Object in **Front Orthographic** view duplicated using an Array Modifier. To add the modifier select the Monkey in the 3D Viewport Editor then in the **Properties Editor, Modifier Properties** click on **Add Modifier** and select **Array** from the menu.

To produce the arrangement shown in Figure 3.12 enter the **Relative Offset** values shown in Figure 3.11. The **Count: 3** value tells Blender to produce three Monkeys in the array (the original plus two).

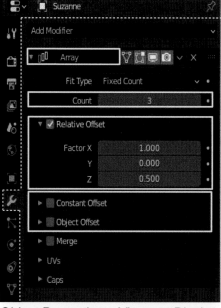

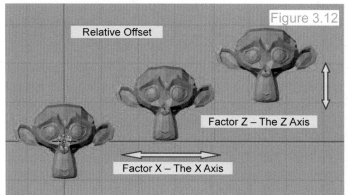

Figure 3.12

Relative Offset

Factor Z – The Z Axis

Factor X – The X Axis

The Offset is calculated using the **Object's Bounds**. Every Object has a **Bounding Volume** which encapsulates its shape. You may view the Bound Volume by checking (tick) **Bounds** in the **Properties Editor, Object Properties, Viewport Display Tab**.

Object Properties – Viewport Display

Check **Bounds**

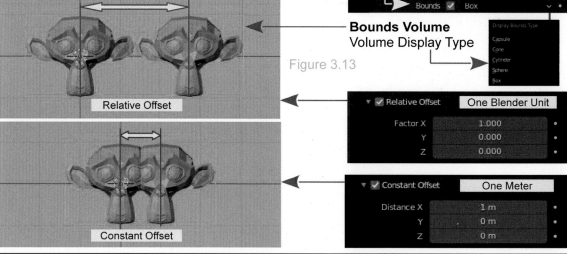

Relative Offset

Constant Offset

Bounds Volume
Volume Display Type

Figure 3.13

One Blender Unit

One Meter

The difference between relative and constant offset is shown in Figure 8.6. Constant offset one (1) means offset one Blender unit irrespective of the Object's size. The Monkey's center is offset one Blender unit which overlaps the display. Relative offset uses the **Bound** size (overall size) of the Object.

Object Offset: Uses the relative displacement of one Object to influence the displacement of another.

To use **Object Offset** position the **Control Object** (UV Sphere) in the 3D Viewport Editor (you can Translate, Rotate and Scale after adding the modifier if you wish). By default **Relative Offset** is checked (ticked) in the **Properties Editor, Modifier Properties**. Change to **Constant Offset** and check **Object Offset**. Click in the bar below Object Offset and select your **Offset Object** (the Sphere) from the menu that displays (Figures 3.14, 3.15).

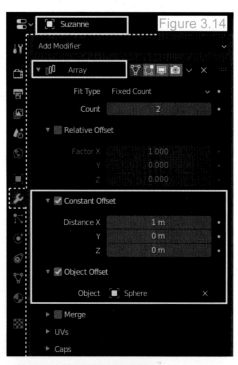

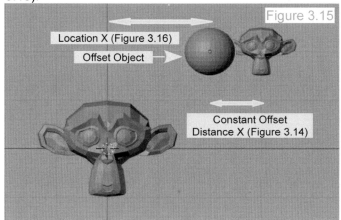

In Figure 3.15 **Suzanne** (Monkey) has an Array Modifier added (Figure 3.14) with Constant Offset and Object Offset checked. The Viewport shows Front Orthographic View. A UV Sphere has been placed in the Scene and positioned plus two (2) meters on the X Axis and plus two (2) meters on the Z Axis (Figure 3.15). The Sphere is Scaled down 0.500.

With Count 2 set in the Array Modifier for Suzanne and Object Offset selected with Object Offset, Object: Sphere, a duplicate is generated half size and positioned plus one meter offset on the X Axis away from the Sphere.

The position of the Object Offset control Object is set in the **Object Properties** for the Sphere (Figure 3.16).

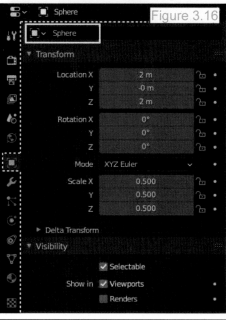

Note: When a Control Object is used in the Array Modifier it will Render even though you cancel the display in the 3D Viewport Editor by clicking the Eye Icon adjacent to Sphere in the Outliner Editor. To prevent the Control Object from Rendering, select it in the 3D Viewport then in the Properties Editor, Object Properties, Visibility Tab, uncheck **Renders**.

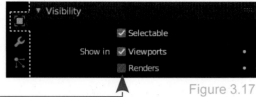

Figure 3.17

Increasing the Count Value in the Array Modifier panel duplicate Objects. As demonstrated, when using Object Offset, the duplicated Object is positioned and Scaled accordingly. Increasing the Count Value in the Modifier will replicate the original Object, repositioning and Scaling exponentially. Any modification made to the Control Object will be reflected in the duplications. (Figure 3.18).

Figure 3.18

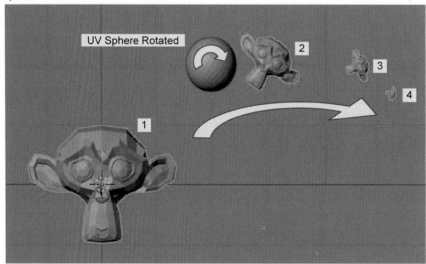

Figure 3.18 shows the Array with the **Count Value** in the Modifier increased to 4 and with the UV Sphere Control Object Scaled and Rotated.

3.6 Boolean Modifier

Figure 3.19

Boolean Modifiers are used to create shapes by adding or subtracting one Object from another. In the Modifier panel there are three options: **Difference**, **Intersection**, and **Union.**

To demonstrate the different operations position a UV Sphere Object with the default Cube as shown in Figure 3.19. Scale the sphere down to fit inside the top face of the cube.

The arrangement of cube and sphere will be used for all three Boolean operations.

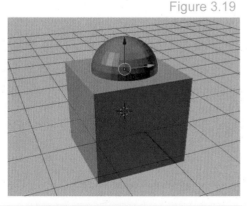

The procedure for a Boolean Operation is as follows; Select the Cube. Add the Modifier. Select the Operation Type. Enter the Boolean Object. Click Apply (Figure 3.20)

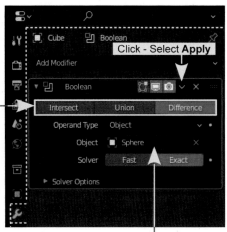

Boolean Difference

Figure 3.20

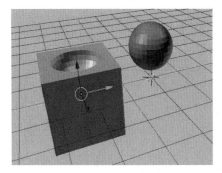

Select an **Operation**

Difference:
The part of the Boolean Object (the Sphere) overlapping the Cube forms a dish in the surface of the Cube.

Enter the **Boolean Object**

Boolean Intersect

Figure 3.21

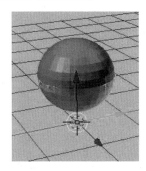

The part of the Cube intersected by the Boolean Object (the Sphere) is separated as a New Object

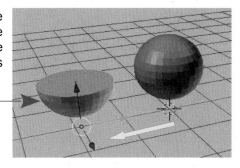

Boolean Union

Figure 3.22

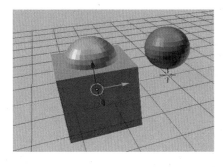

Union: The surfaces of the two Objects are joined. **Note:** The lower part of the Sphere <u>inside</u> the Cube does not exist after Union.

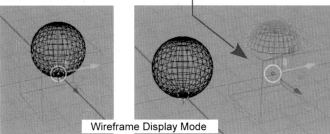

Wireframe Display Mode

3.7 Build Modifier

The **Build Modifier** creates the effect of something building linearly over a period of time. Any Object can have a build modifier, but to see a nice effect, a high vertex count is required.

In the 3D View Editor, Scale the default Cube on the Y axis, Tab to **Edit mode** and Subdivide the surface (Number of Cuts 10).

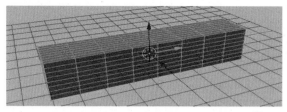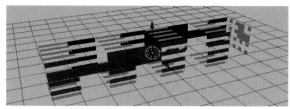

Figure 3.23

Tab back to **Object mode** and add a **Build Modifier** (Figure 5.19). **The Object disappears from view**.

When adding a Build Modifier you have, in effect, created an Animation of the Object building over time. The Animation is controlled in the **Timeline Editor** at the bottom of the Screen.

Figure 3.24

Timeline Cursor

Frame Numbers — The Play Button — Animation End Frame

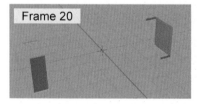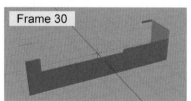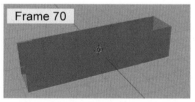

Timeline Editor

You may click, hold and drag the **Timeline Cursor** to the right to see the Object in the 3D Viewport Editor reconstruct in sections.   Figure 3.25

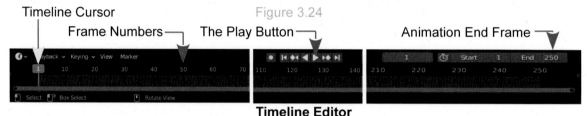

Frame 20   Frame 30   Frame 70

By pressing the **Play Button** in the Timeline Editor you play the Animation showing reconstruction.

Note: The Object is fully reconstructed at Frame 100 due to the **Length** setting in the Properties Editor, Build Modifier (Figure 3.26).

For a more dramatic reconstruction (Figure 3.27), check **Randomize** in the Modifier.

Figure 3.26

Figure 3.27

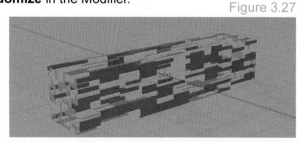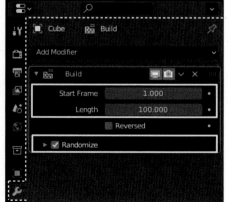

3.8 Decimate Modifier

When a mesh Object has been created using complex modeling, you may well have an Object with many vertices and , therefore, a high Vertex Face count. Blender uses the Vertex/Face count to calculate such things as shading effects. This should not be confused with the Vertices and mesh Faces in the actual construction of a model. The Vertex/Face count is, in effect, triangulation within mesh Faces.

Using the Decimate Modifier is a quick and easy way of reducing the Vertex/Face count.

To demonstrate Decimation start with the default blender Scene, delete the Cube Object and add a **Monkey**. The Monkey is a reasonably complex shape consisting of numerous Faces and Vertices.

Figure 3.28   Figure 3.29

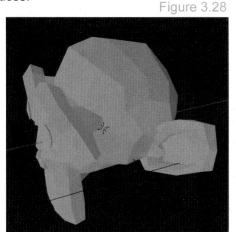
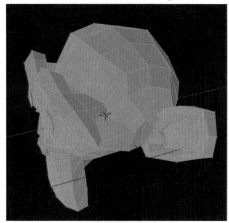

Object Mode   **Edit Mode**

In Object Mode the shape of the Monkey is representative of the Vertices you see in Edit Mode.

Figure 3.30   Figure 3.31

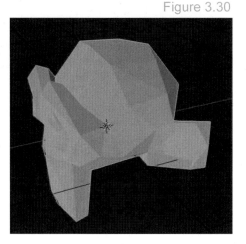
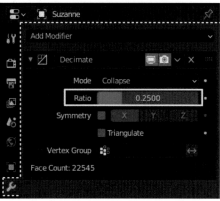

Applying a Decimate Modifier and reducing the Ratio value to approximately 0.25 (Figure 3.31) significantly alters the shape in the 3D View Editor (Figure 3.30).

Starting over with the original Monkey Object and Subdividing with Count 10 in Edit Mode produces many Vertices (Figure 3.32). With this increased number of Vertices Applying a Decimate Modifier and reducing the Ratio value to 0.25 has no appreciable effect on the display in the 3D Viewport Editor (Figure 3.33) or in a rendered View.

Figure 3.32

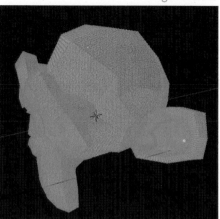

Figure 3.33

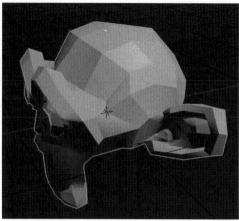

Reducing the Ratio Value to 0.255 in the Decimate Modifier when there are many Vertices reduces the Face Count for generating Shading Effects.

3.9 Edge Split Modifier

Figure 3.34

Although named **Edge Split** the **Edge Split Modifier** allows you to split an Object apart by selecting **Vertices**, **Edges**, or **Faces**.

To demonstrate: Select the Cube Object in the default 3D Viewport Editor in Object Mode and **Add and Apply** an **Edge Split Modifier** (Figure 3.34). The Modifier panel in the Properties Editor disappears when the Modifier is Applied. Tab to Edit Mode after Applying the Modifier.

Remember the selection options in the Viewport Header.

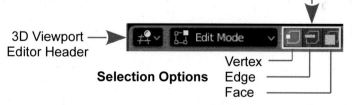

3D Viewport Editor Header

Selection Options

Vertex
Edge
Face

Figure 3.35

Choosing one of the Selection Options determines how the Edge Split Modifier operates.

After Applying the Modifier in Object Mode the Modifier is operable in Edit Mode.

Edge Split – Vertex   Figure 3.36

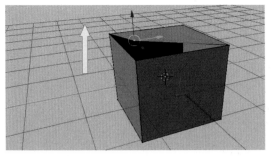

Selecting a **Vertex** will allow a corner to be lifted (moved.

Edge Split - Edge   Figure 3.37

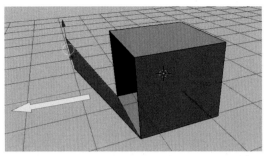

Selecting an Edge will open a face like the lid on a box (see also: **Rip Region Tool**).

Edge Split - Face   Figure 3.38

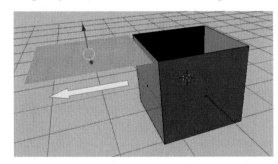

The Face remains part of the Object even though it is separated.

Select a **Face**. Use the **Move Tool Widget** to pull the Face away from the Cube.

3.10 Mask Modifier

Figure 3.39

The **Mask Modifier** allows you to limit what part of a mesh displays in the 3D View Editor or what part Renders. The part of the mesh is defined by a **Vertex Group.** Add a **UV Sphere** to the Scene. In **Edit Mode** select Vertices (Figure 3.40). Leave the Vertices selected and create a Vertex Group. By default the Vertex Group will be named **Group**.

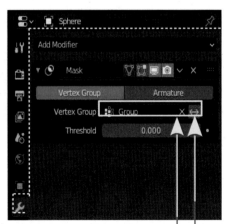

Figure 3.40

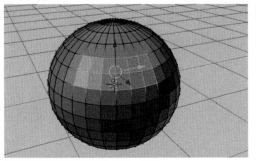

While remaining in Edit Mode, Add a **Mask Modifier** to the Sphere and enter **Group**.

Click the double headed arrow to reverse the display (Figure 3.39)

Tab into **Object Mode** to see only the part of the Sphere defined by the Vertex Group displayed (Figures 3.40, 3.41). No need to Apply the modifier unless you want this to be permanent.

To reverse the display, that is, display the whole Sphere less the section defined by the Vertex Group, click the double headed arrow in the Modifier panel (Figures 3.41. 3.42).

Figure 3.41

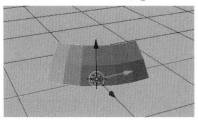

Figure 3.42

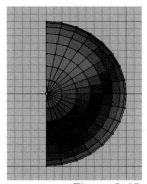

By using the modifier, visibility can be controlled without removing any Vertices from the UV Sphere.

3.11 Mirror Modifier

The **Mirror Modifier** allows the construction or deformation of a mesh on one side of a centre point to be duplicated (mirrored) on the opposite side.

Add a **UV Sphere** to the Scene in **Top Orthographic View**. Tab to **Edit Mode**, deselect the Vertices. **Have Toggle X Ray on,** then B key (Box Select) and drag a rectangle to select one half of the Sphere's Vertices (Figures 3.43, 3.44). Press **X Key** to delete the selected Vertices (Figure 3.45).

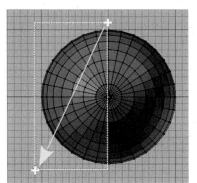
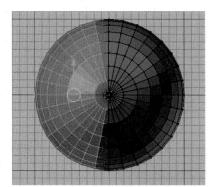
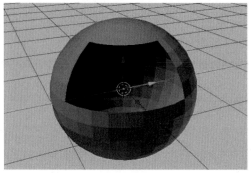

Figure 3.43   Figure 3.44   Figure 3.45

Tip: Don't forget to turn **Toggle X-Ray** on in the 3D Viewport Editor Header before dragging the rectangle.

In **Object Mode** (with the half sphere selected), in the **Properties Editor, Modifier buttons** add a **Mirror Modifier** (Figure 3.46 over).

The deleted half of the UV Sphere will be reinstated in the 3D View Editor (Figure 3.47).

Figure 3.46

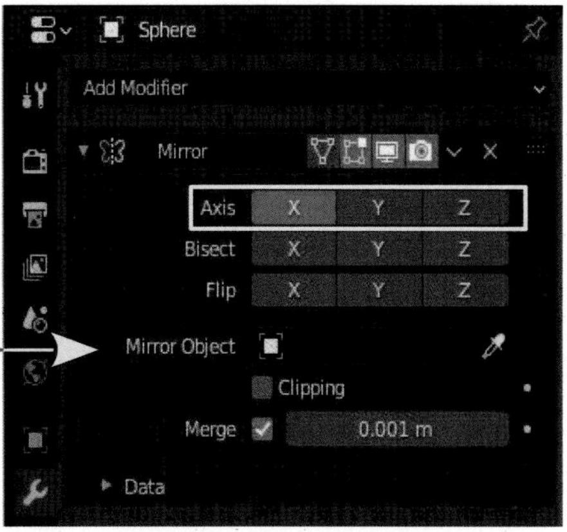

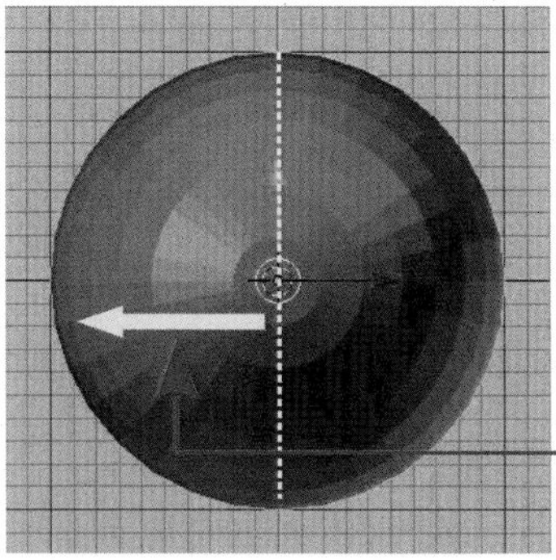

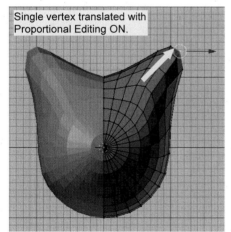

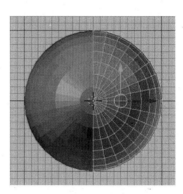

Figure 3.47

Note: In the Modifier panel, by default, **Axis X** is selected, therefore, the Mirror takes place **along the X Axis.**

Mirror Object Figure 8.43

In **Edit Mode** you will see that vertices exist only on one side of the sphere (Figure 8.41).

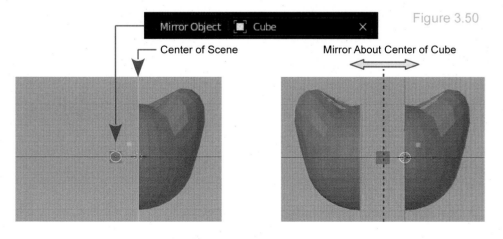

Figure 3.48   Figure 3.49

Select and Translate a single Vertex and you see that the mesh on the opposite side is duplicated (mirrored) (Figure 3.49).

When the Modifier is applied (click **Apply** in the Modifier Panel) Vertices are created on the mirrored side.

Single vertex translated with Proportional Editing ON.

In the center of the Mirror Modifier panel you will see **Mirror Object**. Placing an Object in the Scene and entering the name of this Object in the Mirror Object Bar causes the mirror to be about the centerline of the new Object instead of the centerline of the original Object (Figure 3.50).

Figure 3.50

Mirror Object   Cube   X

Center of Scene

Mirror About Center of Cube

3.12 Multiresolution Modifier

The **Multiresolution Modifier** is designed to be used with the **Sculpt Tool**.

3.13 Remesh Modifier

The **Remesh Modifier** allows you to recalculate how a Mesh Surface is constructed. Some basic mesh shapes do not provide sufficient Vertices, Edges and Faces to allow detailed modeling.

To demonstrate, use a Cylinder Object to cut a hole through the default Cube Object by applying a **Boolean Difference Modifier (to the Cube Object)**.

Figure 3.51

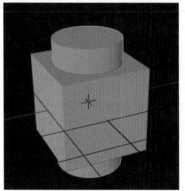 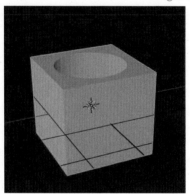 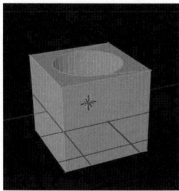

| Cylinder scale down and extended on the Z Axis. | The Boolean Difference Modifier Applied. | Edit Mode showing the Mesh construction |

When the Boolean Modifier is applied you see a minimal mesh construction which limits any detailed modeling. To increase the Vertex count apply a **Remesh Modifier.**

Remember: To apply a Modifier to an Object it must be in Object Mode.

Figure 3.52

With the Cube selected in Object Mode add a **Remesh Modifier.** In **Object Mode** you see a deformation at the rim of the hole. **Note: The default Remesh Mode is Voxel. Change the Mode to Sharp.**

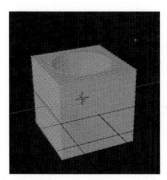

Note: In the Modifier Panel the default **Octree Depth** value is **4** and the **Scale** is **0.900.**

Figure 3.53

With the default values, when the Modifier has been Applied (click the Apply button) the Mesh surface of the Cube in Edit Mode shows a significant increase in the number of Vertices, Edges and Faces (Figure 3.53).

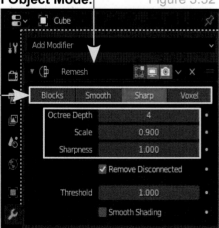

When the **Remesh Modifier** is Applied the Modifier Panel is cancelled. To adjust the Octree and Scale values press Ctrl + Z Key to undo and step back through the operations until the panel is reinstated. Increasing the Octree Depth significantly increases the number of Vertices on the Mesh. Even increasing from 4 to 5 has a dramatic effect.

Be Warned: Increasing to 6 - 7 - 8 will exponentially increase the Vertex Count and seriously affect computer speed.

Figure 3.54

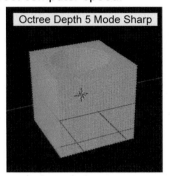
Octree Depth 5 Mode Sharp

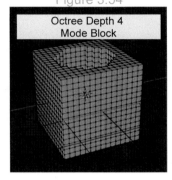
Octree Depth 4
Mode Block

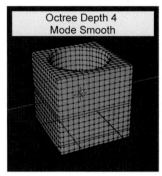
Octree Depth 4
Mode Smooth

3.14 Screw Modifier

The **Screw Modifier** generates a spiral shape by revolving a profile or an Object around an Axis defined by an Axis Object. To demonstrate, construct a spiral from the a Plane Object revolved around an Axis defined by a Cylinder.

The Plane, by default is entered into the Scene in the horizontal plane. Rotate (R Key + X Key + 90) to stand the Plane on edge then move it back along the X Axis of the Scene. Enter a Cylinder Object, scaled down and scaled up on the vertical Z Axis (Figure 3.56).

Figure 3.55

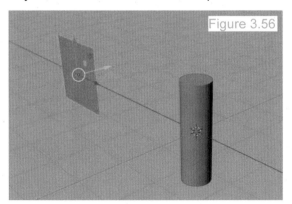
Figure 3.56

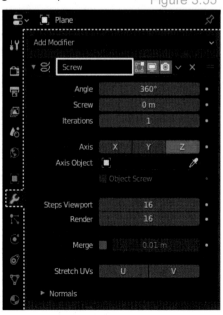

With the Plane selected Add a Screw Modifier in the Properties Editor, Modifier buttons (Figure 3.55).

When the Screw Modifier is Added the Plane displays as a flat circular shape in the XZ Plane (Figure 3.56).

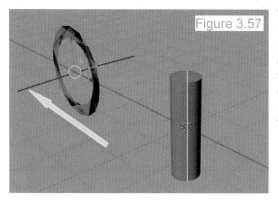
Figure 3.57

Without an Axis Object being entered in the Modifier panel the Plane is duplicated and revolved 360° about its own Y Axis (Figure 3.57). The degrees of revolution are defined by the Angle value in the Modifier panel. The number of duplications are defined Steps value in the Modifier panel (**Note:** there are different Steps values for the Viewport and Render. The default values are 16).

Figure 3.58 depicts the revolution of the Plane duplications.

This effect may be usefull but it is not the Screw that is intended.

Enter **Axis Object: Cylinder** in the Modifier panel.

Axis Object 　■ Cylinder 　　　　　×

Change the 3D Viewport Editor to **Edit Mode**.

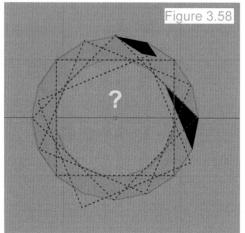
Figure 3.58

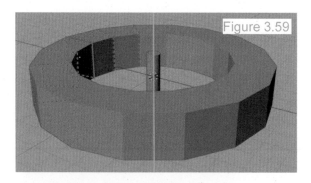
Figure 3.59

In Edit Mode you see the Vertices of the Plane duplicated in a circle about the vertical Axis (blue line) of the Cylinder Object (Figure 3.59) .

The circle is determined by the **Angle 360°** value in the Modifier panel.

By increasing the Screw value the last duplication is displaced vertically forming a Screw effect (Figure 3.60).

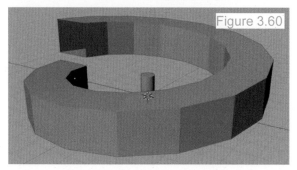
Figure 3.60

Increase the Iterations value in the Modifier panel to increase the number of coils.(Figure 3.61)

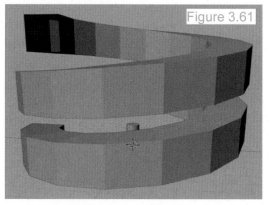
Figure 3.61

3.15 Skin Modifier

The **Skin Modifier** allows you to create a three dimensional shape from a basic stick arrangement consisting of a minimal number of Vertices. To demonstrate how this is achieved have a Plane Object in the 3D Viewport Editor. The Plane is a simple Object with four Vertices, four Edges and one Face.

Rotate the Plane about the Z Axis. This simply moves the Edges of the Plane away from the background grid lines to improve visibility when in Edit Mode.

Figure 3.62

Background Grid Line

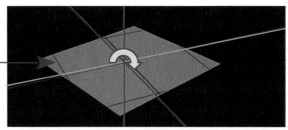

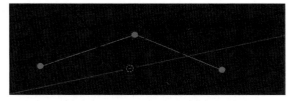

In **Edit Mode** delete one Vertex leaving two Edges (the basic stick arrangement).

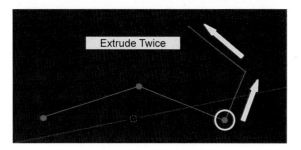

Extrude Twice

Select one Vertex and extrude twice. Remember; the original Edges are located on the X – Y Axis of the Scene. The two new Edges will be drawn in a plane passing through the center of the Scene normal to the computer Screen.

Figure 3.63

In Object Mode, with the stick figure selected, add a **Skin Modifier** (Figure 3.63) and **click Apply** to produce the solid shown in Figure 3.64.

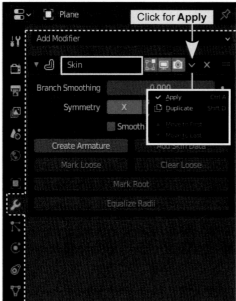

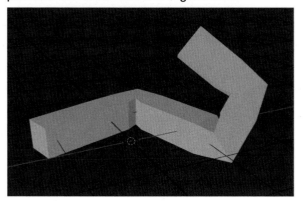

Figure 3.64

The Skin Modifier procedure, in essence, entails Extruding Vertices from a simple Object to form a rudimentary stick shape in Edit Mode. The Skin Modifier is then added to the shape in Object Mode. The Modifier creates a cage around the stick which converts to a Mesh Object when the Modifier is Applied.

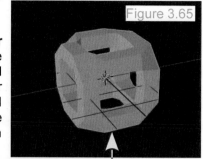
Figure 3.65

At this point, note the distinction between **Adding the Modifier** and **Applying the Modifier**. You add the Modifier in the Properties Editor, Modifier Properties by clicking the Add Modifier button and selecting from the menu. The Modifier panel displays where you adjust values to affect the selected Object in the 3D Viewport Editor. When adjustments are complete you Apply the Modifier by clicking the Apply button in the Modifier panel.

Skin Modifier Applied to the default Cube

3.16 Solidify Modifier

Figure 3.66

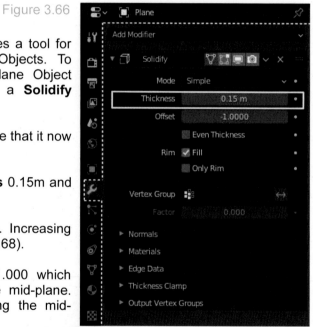

The **Solidify Modifier** (Figure 3.66) provides a tool for creating solid Objects from thin-walled Objects. To demonstrate this, begin with a simple Plane Object selected in the 3D Viewport Editor. Add a **Solidify Modifier** in the **Properties Editor.**

Look closely at the plane and you will observe that it now has a thickness (Figure 3.67).

In the Modifier panel you will see **Thickness** 0.15m and **Offset** -1.0000.

Thickness is the thickness of the surface. Increasing this to 10 cm will give a better view (Figure 3.68).

The Offset value range is -1.0000 to +1.000 which places the Thickness below or above the mid-plane. Offset 0.0000 has the Thickness straddling the mid-plane.

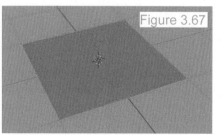
Figure 3.67

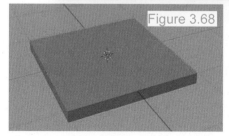
Figure 3.68

Tab to **Edit mode** and see that the original vertices of the plane object remain on the mid-plane of the Scene.

For a practical demonstration of how to use the **Solidify Modifier**, create a new Scene with a **Cylinder** object instead of the default Cube. **Delete the upper face of the Cylinder**. You now have a thin-walled container (Figure 3.69). In Object mode add a **Solidify Modifier** and change the thickness value 0.1m. The container will have wall thickness (Figure 3.70).

> **Note:** Dimensions in Blender are proportional. A wall thickness of 0.01m (1.0cm) gives a thin wall thickness considering that the default overall dimensions of the Cylinder are 2m in diameter by 2m high (press the N Key to see Dimensions).

With Offset -1.0000 the wall thickness is created inside the original surface of the Cylinder. Offset +1.0000 creates the thickness outside the original surface.

In Edit Mode you see the original Vertices, Edges and Faces are unchanged until you click Apply in the Modifier Panel with the Cylinder in the 3D View Editor in Object Mode

Figure 3.69   Figure 3.70

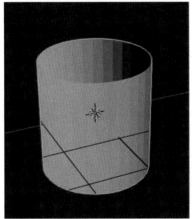 

Original Cylinder – Top Face Deleted   Cylinder – Solidify Modifier Added Thickness 0.1m (10cm)

3.17 Subdivision Surface Modifier

The Subdivision Surface Modifier subdivides the surface of an Object adding Vertices, Edges and Faces giving the surface of the Object a smoother and rounded appearance. The additions also allow more detail to be modeled.

To demonstrate, use the container created in the previous exercise (Figure 3.70) with the Solidify Modifier Added but **NOT Applied,** add a **Subdivision Surface** (Subserf) Modifier.

When the Subdivision Surface Modifier is Added it is placed in the Modifier Stack in the Properties Editor below the Solidify Modifier. Remember; The Modifier at the top of the Modifier Stack takes precedence over Modifiers lower down. Therefore, the Solidify Modifier has precedence over the Subdivision Surface Modifier (Figure 3.71).

In the Subserf Modifier panel adjust the Subdivisions – **Level** values (Figure 3.71, 3.72).

Subdivision – Levels Figure 3.72

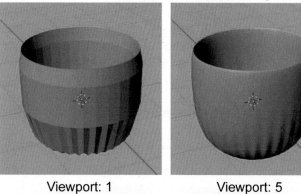

Viewport: 1   Viewport: 5

Render: 0   Render: 6

Note: Render Figures are Rendered Views (Press F12)

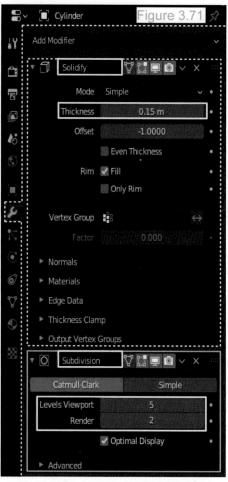

Blue outline indicates active Modifier

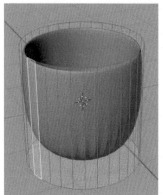

At this point neither the Solidify Modifier or the Subserf Modifier have been Applied. The Apply button, in both cases, has **NOT** been activated. The Modifiers display their effects in the 3D Viewport Editor but placing the Cylinder Object in Edit Mode shows that the original Vertices, Edges and Faces remain (Figure 3.73).

Figure 3.73

Another simple example using the **Subsurf Modifier** forms a whale's tooth (Figure 3.74).

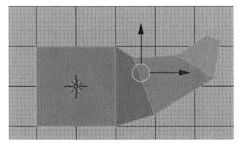

Cube Extruded – Edit Mode

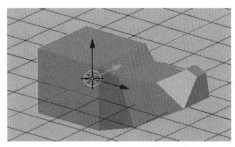

Object Mode – 3D View Rotated

Figure 3.74

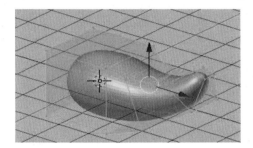

Object Mode – Subserf Added
Edit Mode – Show Original Mesh

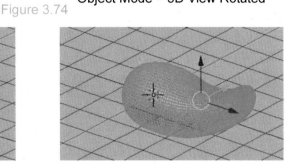

Modifier Applied – New Mesh Created
Levels Viewport Value : 4

3.18 Triangulation and Weld Modifier

A **Triangulation Modifier** is added when a mesh model has been subdivided and Vertices added producing fine detail in a model. The Modifier ensures that triangulation will remain consistent when exporting or rendering.

If the model is animated using armatures the modifier should be placed in the modifier stack before (above) the armature modifier.

The Triangulation Modifier is also used when **Baking** prior to exporting and importing.

Baking is the process of pre-calculating and storing data to save time when converting data in the Viewport into an Image or Video file. The conversion is called **Rendering**.

The **Weld Modifier** is used to merge Vertices in a non destructive manner. At this point the definition is probably meaningless, therefore a simple explanation is required.

In complex modeling, Vertices will occasionally be duplicated, that is, two Vertices will be generated at the same point in the same 3D Space. It is advisable that the number of Vertices be kept at a minimum especially when Animation is involved and also to create the correct visual appearance.

To demonstrate, a shape will be generated from a Plane Primitive using Modifiers.

Figure 3.75

In the default 3D Viewport Editor delete the Cube Object and add a Plane. Scale the Plane three times on the X Axis and add a **Bevel Modifier** (Figure 3.75).

Important: While in Object Mode, press **Ctrl + A and select Apply – Scale** (Apply Object Transform to Scale).

In the **Properties Editor, Bevel Modifier**, check **Vertices**. Change the **Segments** to 5 then adjust the **Amount** value to 1 m to produce a complete rounded end on the Plane (Figure 3.76).

Figure 3.76

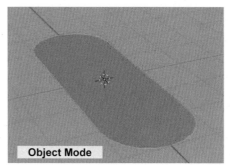

Object Mode

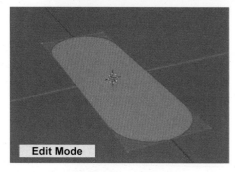

Edit Mode

Note: In Edit Mode the original geometry is retained

Add a **Solidify Modifier** (Figure 3.77)   **Solidify Modifier →**

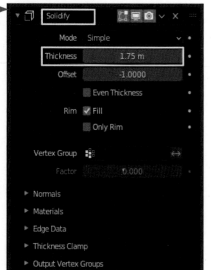

Figure 3.77

In the Properties Editor, Solidifier Modifier increase the **Thickness** value to 1.75.

Figure 3.78

At this point, in Edit Mode you can see the results of the **Offset** value and **Segments** set in the Bevel Modifier.

Offset

Segments

In Object Mode RMB Click and select **Shade Smooth**.

Selecting **Shade Smooth, smooths the display**.

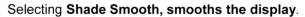

Figure 3.79

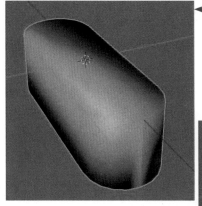

Figure 3.80
In the **Properties Editor, Object Data Properties, Normals Tab** check **Auto Smooth**

Figure 3.81

In Object Mode and Edit Mode you see the shape with round smooth ends. In Edit Mode you see that the original geometry (Four Vertices) is retained.

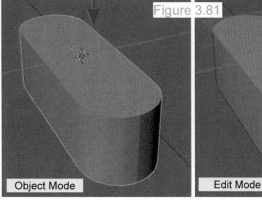

Object Mode

Edit Mode

Although the ends of the shape are smooth there is a shadow line caused by a seam.

Remember: The shape is generated using the Bevel Modifier. At this point the Modifier **has not** been applied as seen in Edit Mode but were the Modifier to be applied there would be a duplication of Vertices where the seam displays.

Figure 3.82

One Vertex selected and moved aside.

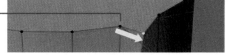

Since the Modifier is **NOT** applied you can **NOT** manually merge Vertices (remove the doubles).

Remember: In complicated models it is advisable not to apply the Modifiers to minimise the number of Vertices.

Figure 3.83

To clean up the seam add the **Weld Modifier**.

Note: Each Modifier Added has been placed at the bottom of the Modifier Stack.

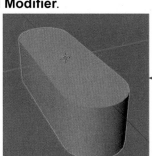

Figure 3.84

3.19 Wireframe Modifier

The **Wireframe Modifier** converts a solid display as seen in **Solid Viewport Shading** to **Stick** or **Wireframe** display.

With the modifier added to a **Cube** object, instead of a solid Cube, you see a frame where the edges of the Cube have thickness (Figure 3.85).

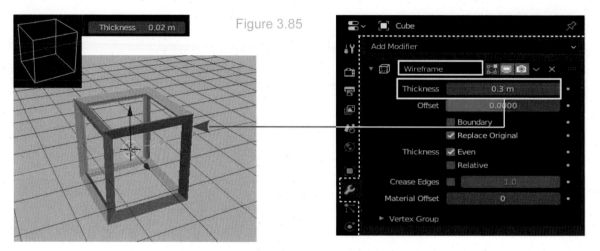

Figure 3.85

Figure 3.86 shows the Whale's Tooth from the previous example (Figure 3.74) with a Wireframe Modifier added.

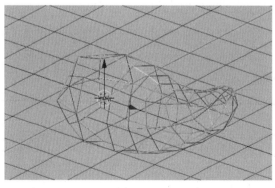

Figure 3.86

4

Editing with Deform Modifiers

The Deform group of Modifiers change the shape of an Object without adding new geometry, and are available for meshes, texts, curves, surfaces and/or lattices. The Mesh Deform modifier allows an arbitrary mesh (of any closed shape) to act as a deformation cage around a mesh Object.

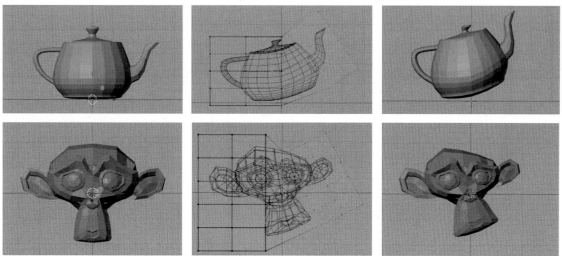

4.1 Modifiers for Editing - Deform

Figure 4.1

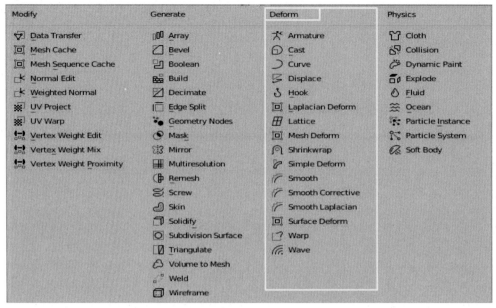

The Deform group of Modifiers generally provide tools for modifying or deforming a mesh Object as a whole. Some of these modifiers require a knowledge of other Blender features and will, therefore, be described as those features are encountered.

4.2 Armature Modifier

Armatures in Blender are Objects used for manipulating and posing other Objects such as models of characters. Posing is the technique used when animating figures. The **Armature Modifier** is discussed in conjunction with Armatures and Character Rigging in Chapter 10.

4.3 Cast Modifier

Figure 4.2

The **Cast Modifier** is used to deform a primitive Object such as the Cube Object in the default Scene.

Select the Cube Object. In **Edit Mode,** Subdivide (number of Cuts 4) then **Tab** back to **Object Mode**.

In the **Properties Editor, Modifier Properties** add a **Cast Modifier** (Figure 4.2). By changing the **Cast Type**, altering the **Factor**, **Radius** and **Size** values and or limiting the effects to the X,Y and Z axis the deformation of the cube is controlled.

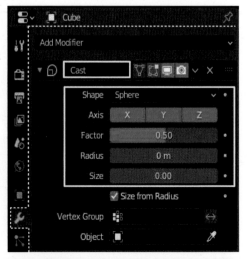

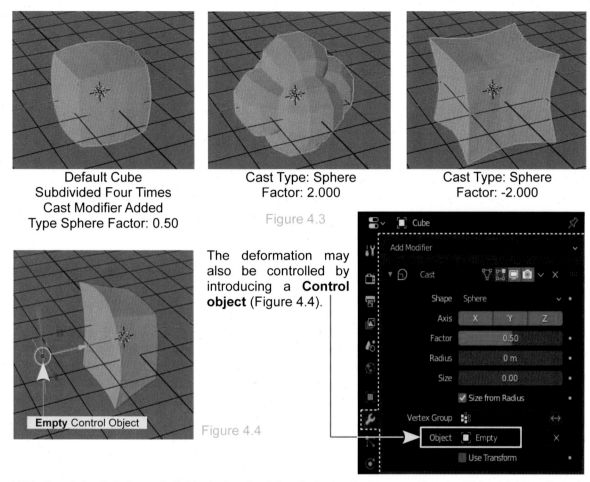

Default Cube
Subdivided Four Times
Cast Modifier Added
Type Sphere Factor: 0.50

Cast Type: Sphere
Factor: 2.000

Cast Type: Sphere
Factor: -2.000

Figure 4.3

The deformation may also be controlled by introducing a **Control object** (Figure 4.4).

Empty Control Object

Figure 4.4

With the default Cube subdivided, deselect the Cube and place an **Empty Object** in the Scene. Add a **Cast Modifier** to the **Cube** and then click on the **Control Object** (cube icon) and select **Empty** from the menu to enter the **Empty** as the **Control Object**.

Move the Empty in the Scene to see the Cube being deformed.

Experiment with the Cast Type, the X,Y and Z axis settings and Factor, Radius and Size values. Keep in mind that the Empty Object may be animated to move in the Scene thus animating the deformation of the Cube.

4.4 Corrective Smooth Modifier

The **Corrective Smooth Modifier** is primarily designed to smooth incorrect mesh deformation which can occur when Armatures are used to deform a mesh.

4.5 Curve Modifier

The **Curve Modifier** uses the shape of a Curve to deform a mesh. Figure 4.5 shows the default Blender Scene with the Cube Scaled down, then Scaled along the Y Axis (S Key + Y Key) and Subdivided in Edit Mode with Number of Cuts = 10.

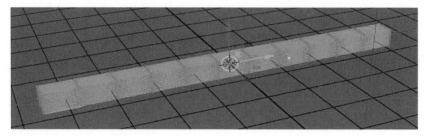

Figure 4.5

In **Object Mode** the elongated Cube is deselected and a **Bezier Curve** added. The **Curve** is rotated and scaled up to match the length of the Cube (Figure 4.6).

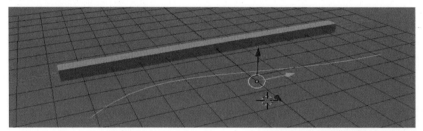

Figure 4.6

Deselect the Curve and **select the Cube**. Be in **Object Mode** and add a **Curve Modifier.** Enter **BezierCurve** as the name in the **Object** panel (Figure 4.7).

Click and select **Bezier Curve** in the menu.

Figure 4.7

Manipulate the Curve in **Edit Mode**. Change its shape and position to affect the shape of the Cube (Figure 4.8).

Figure 4.8

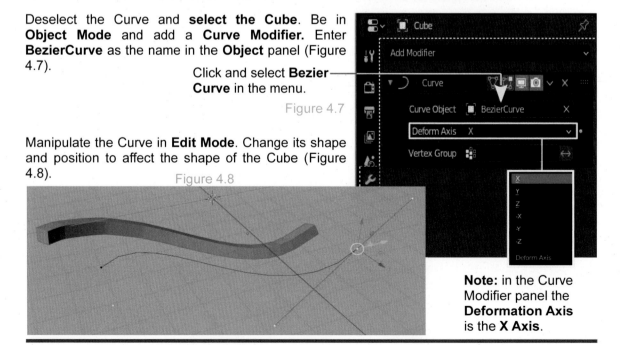

Note: in the Curve Modifier panel the **Deformation Axis** is the **X Axis**.

4.6 Displace Modifier

The **Displace Modifier** manipulates the Vertices of a Mesh Object. If Vertices are assigned to a **Vertex Group** and the group is entered in the Modifier, only the Vertices belonging to the group will be affected. Incorporating a **Texture** displaces Vertices according to the dark and light values in the Texture.

Start with the default Blender Scene and replace the **Cube** with a **Plane**. Have the Plane selected in **Edit Mode** and subdivide sixteen times. Select a group of Vertices and create a **Vertex Group** in the Properties Editor, Object Data buttons (Figure 4.9, 4.10).

Figure 4.9

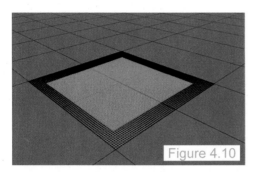

Figure 4.10

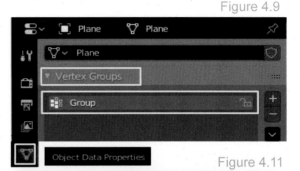

Figure 4.11

Tab back to **Object Mode.** Add a Material (default gray is OK) then in the **Texture Type** add a **Noise Texture**. Click the **Texture button**, click **New** and where you see **Type: Image or Movie**, click the bar and select **Noise** in the menu that displays. **Note** the Texture Name in this example is: Texture) (Figure 4.11).

Figure 4.12

In the Properties Editor, with the Plane selected , go to the Modifier buttons and add a **Displace Modifier** (Figure 4.12).

In the Displace Modifier panel enter the Texture and the Vertex Group to <u>displace the Vertices</u> (Figure 4.13).

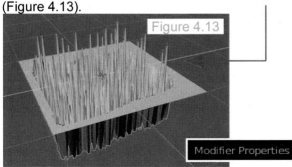

Figure 4.13

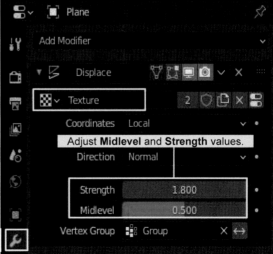

4.7 Hook Modifier

The **Hook Modifier** allows you to manipulate or animate selected vertices of a mesh while in Object mode. Vertices are assigned (hooked) to an **Empty** Object which is moved in Object Mode pulling the selected vertices with it. This can be used for a static mesh deformation or the movement can be animated.

Start with the default Scene with the Cube Object selected. Tab to **Edit mode** and select one Vertex (corner) only.

Press **Ctrl + H key** and select **Hook to New Object**. An **Empty Object** is added to the Scene. In the **Properties Editor, Modifiers Properties**, you will see that a **Hook Modifier** has been added named **Hook-Empty** (Figure 4.14).

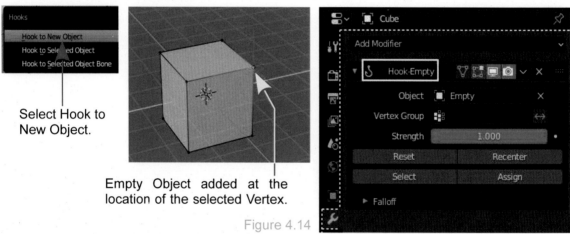

Select Hook to New Object.

Empty Object added at the location of the selected Vertex.

Figure 4.14

Select and move the **Empty** in **Object Mode** to move the Vertex (Figure 4.15, 4.16).

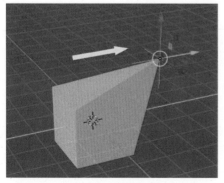

In **Edit Mode** you will see the Empty in the new location but the selected Vertex remains in its original position.

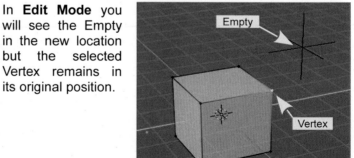

Object Mode Figure 4.15

Edit Mode Figure 4.16

In Object mode click **Apply** in the Modifier panel and the Cube deformation is made permanent. You may delete the Empty Object.

With the default **Cube Object** in the default Scene, **Tab** to **Edit Mode** and select one Vertex only. In the **Properties Editor, Object Data Properties, Vertex Groups Tab** click on the plus sign to add a Vertex Group and click **Assign.** This creates a Vertex Group consisting of the one Vertex.

In **Object Mode** deselect the Cube and add an **Empty Object**. Position the **Empty** away from the Cube (Figure 4.17).

Figure 4.17

Figure 4.18

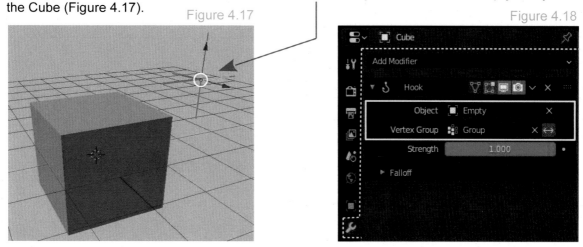

Deselect the Empty and select the Cube. In the **Properties Editor, Modifiers Properties** add a **Hook Modifier**. In the **Hook Modifier** panel click on the **Vertex Group panel** and select **Group**. This is assigning the Vertex Group consisting of one single Vertex to the Modifier. Click on the **Object panel** and select **Empty** to assign the Empty Object to the Modifier (Figure 4.18).

By selecting the **Empty** Object in the 3D Viewport Editor and moving it, the single Cube's Vertex in the Vertex Group will follow the movement (Figure 4.19).

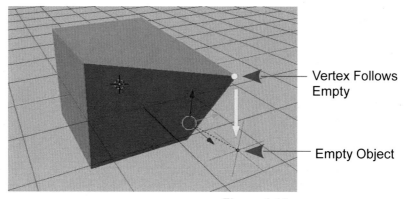

Vertex Follows Empty

Empty Object

Figure 4.19

4.8 Laplacian Deform Modifier

The **Laplacian Deform Modifier** allows you to pose a mesh while preserving geometric details of the surface. This means, you may alter the shape of an Object as seen in Object Mode while the original mesh is retained in Edit Mode.

The process is performed by assigning a **Hook-Empty** to a Vertex or group of Vertices and anchoring part of the mesh in place. The Hook-Empty pulls the mesh out of shape against the anchored Vertices.

Edge Vertices Anchored

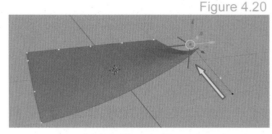

Figure 4.20

Hook-Empty assigned to corner Vertex   Hook-Empty Translated

To replicate the example shown in Figure 4.20 perform the following procedure paying attention to the sequence of operations.

Figure 9.20 shows a **Plane** Object with its mesh subdivided ten times in Edit Mode.

While in Edit Mode select the single corner Vertex, press **Ctrl + H Key** and select **Hook to New Object** in the menu that displays. This assigns a **Hook** in the form of an **Empty Object** to the Vertex. In Object Mode you will see that a Hook-Empty Modifier has been automatically added in the Properties Editor, Modifier Properties.

Have the Plane in the 3D Viewport Editor in **Edit Mode** and with the single Vertex and Hook-Empty remaining selected, select the Vertices forming the two Edges of the Plane opposite the single Vertex with the Hook-Empty.

With the Vertices selected, in Edit Mode, go to the **Properties Editor, Object Data Properties** (Figure 4.21) and create a **Vertex Group** and Assign the Vertices to the Group.

Note: The single Vertex with the Hook-Empty attached and the Edge Vertices are all selected when assigning Vertices to the Vertex Group. By default the Vertex Group is named **Group**.

Tab to Object Mode and select the Plane.

Figure 4.21

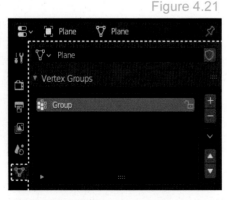

In the **Properties Editor, Modifier Properties**, Add a **Laplacian Deform Modifier**. Enter **Group** (the Vertex Group previously created) in the **Anchor Weights** panel and click Bind (changes to Unbind).

Figure 4.22

By selecting the **Hook-Empty**, pressing the G Key and dragging the Mouse you can move the corner of the Plane with the two opposite Edges remaining in situ.

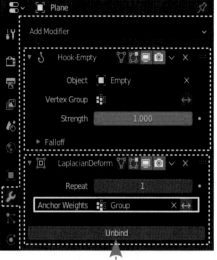

Bind / Unbind

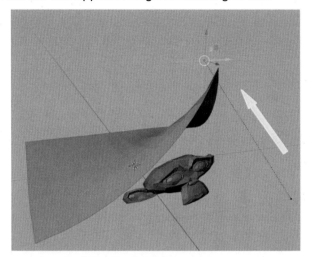

You could use this to reveal something previously hidden below the Plane.

Animate the Hook-Empty

Figure 4.23

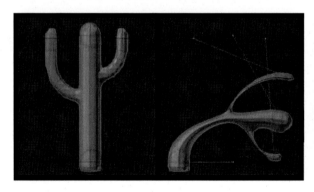

4.9 Lattice Modifier

The **Lattice Modifier** is used to deform a mesh Object or to control the **movement of Particles** (Chapter 12). By using the Modifier, it is easy to shape a mesh Object that has many Vertices.

When deforming a Mesh Object there are two components in the Scene; the Object which is to be deformed and a **Lattice**. The Lattice is a special non-renderable Object or, if you like, a non-renderable grid of Vertices. You can use the same Lattice to deform several Mesh Objects by giving each Object a Modifier pointing to the Lattice.

The basic procedure is to surround the Mesh Object or Objects with the Lattice then add a Lattice Modifier to each Object pointing to the Lattice. Bear in mind the Lattice does not necessarily have to encapsulate an Object.

To demonstrate a **UV Sphere** Object will be deformed using a **Lattice Modifier.**

The Object which is to be deformed must have a reasonable number of Vertices for the Modifier to be effective.

In the default Scene, delete the Cube Object and add a UV Sphere. Remember, when Objects are added to a Scene they are located at the position of the 3D Cursor. By default the 3D Cursor is located at the center of the Scene.

Move the UV Sphere to one side. Moving the sphere is purely for demonstration purposes.

Add a **Lattice** to the Scene (Figure 4.25).

When the Lattice is added it is located at the center of the Scene, the position of the 3D Cursor (Figure 4.26).

Figure 4.24

Figure 4.25

In the Properties Editor you will find a **Lattice Object Properties** button.

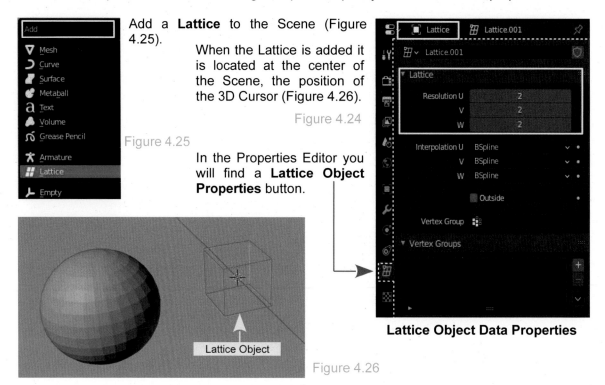

Lattice Object Data Properties

Lattice Object

Figure 4.26

Note that the UV Sphere and the Lattice are entered at default Scale: 1.000 although the Lattice displays at half the size of the Sphere.

In this example a Lattice will encapsulate the Object being deformed, therefore, scale the Lattice up and position it around the UV Sphere (Figure 4.27).

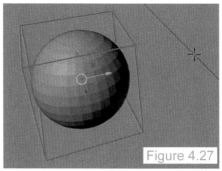

Figure 4.27

Tab into Edit Mode. You may subdivide the Lattice by increasing the **Resolution U, V and W** values in the **Lattice Object Data Properties** panel (Figure 4.23 Resolution values all: 2). How many subdivisions depends on the detailed control required in the deformation. Change the Resolution to: U, V and W = 3.

In Object Mode, select the UV Sphere and Add a **Lattice Modifier** in the Properties Editor (Figure 4.28). Enter Lattice in the Object panel of the Modifier to point to the Lattice.

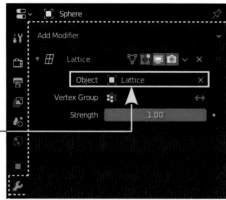

Figure 4.28

Enter **Lattice**

Deselect the UV Sphere, select the Lattice and Tab to Edit Mode (Figure 4.29). Select a single Vertex. Press G Key (Grab) and Translate the Vertex to see the UV Sphere deform (Figure 4.29).

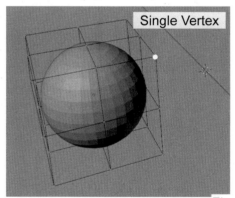

Single Vertex

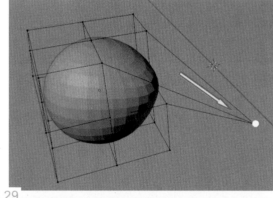

Figure 4.29

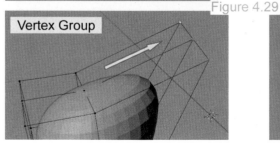

Vertex Group

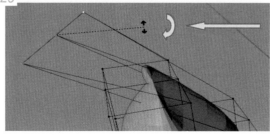

You may select multiple Lattice Vertices to achieve the deformation required. You will have to experiment with different configurations to become proficient in the use of the Lattice Modifier. Figure 4.30 (over page) shows a single Lattice at the center of the Scene with two Objects either side to which Lattice Modifiers have been Added. Selecting a single Vertex on the LH Side of the Lattice affects the LH Object and vice versa.

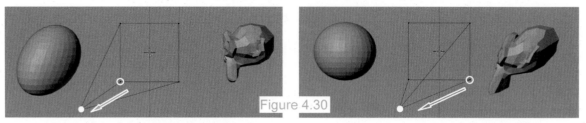

Figure 4.30

LH Vertex – LH Object (Sphere)   **RH Vertex – RH Object (Monkey)**

4.10 Mesh Deform Modifier

The **Mesh Deform Modifier** deforms a mesh with **Cage Mesh**. This is similar to a Lattice Modifier but instead of being restricted to the regular grid layout of a lattice, the cage can be modeled to fit around the mesh Object being deformed. The Cage Mesh must form a closed cage around the part of the mesh to be deformed, and only vertices within the cage will be deformed. Typically the cage will have far fewer Vertices than the mesh being deformed.

Model a UV Sphere Object by scaling on the Y Axis as shown in Figure 9.31, surround it with a simple cage mesh by scaling a Cube to fit around the elongated Sphere, then select Vertices in **Edit Mode** and extrude (Figure 4.31).

Figure 4.31

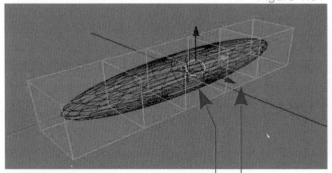

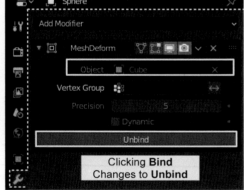

UV Sphere Scaled on the Y Axis
Cube Extruded to form a Cage

Figure 4.32

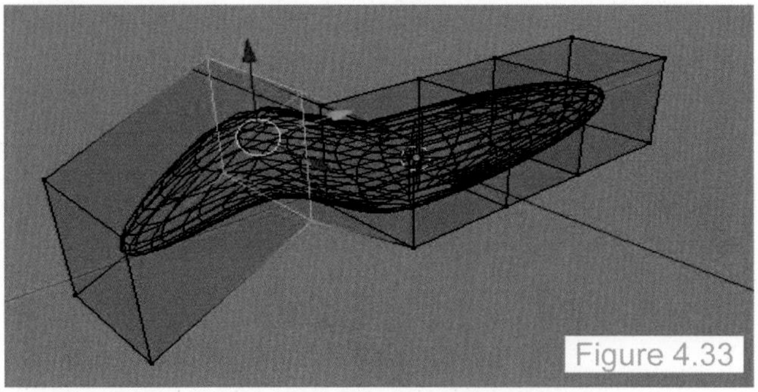

Add a **Mesh Deform Modifier** to the scaled **UV Sphere**. Enter the name of the cage mesh (Cube) in the **Object panel** and press **Bind** (Figure 4.32) to link the two meshes. The Bind operation may take several seconds to calculate depending on the complexity of your model. Wait until **Bind** changes to **Unbind** before selecting Vertices on the cage (Figure 4.32). By Moving, Scaling and Rotating the selected Vertices, the

Figure 4.33

Sphere mesh will be deformed (Figure 4.33). The proximity of the cage to the original Object has an influence on how the deformation reacts.

Note: The Cage Mesh will render in the Scene; With the **Sphere** selected in Object Mode **Apply the Modifier and delete the Cage.**

Click and select **Apply** in the menu.

Figure 4.34

Properties ▶
Editor
Modifier

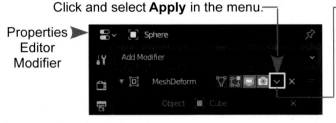

4.11 Shrinkwrap Modifier

Figure 4.35

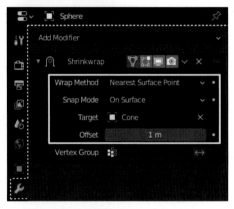

The **Shrinkwrap Modifier** takes a mesh and shrinks it down, wrapping the mesh around another Object. The deformed mesh can then be **Offset** to produce shapes in between the original shape and the deformed shape.

Delete the Cube in the default Blender Scene and add a **UV Sphere** and a **Cone** mesh Object. The Cone should be located inside the UV Sphere (Figure 4.36), which is easy to see when both Objects are viewed in **Wireframe Mode**. Add a **Shrinkwrap Modifier** to the UV sphere, and enter **Cone** in the **Target panel** (Figure 4.35).

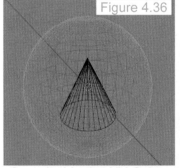

Figure 4.36

Figure 4.37

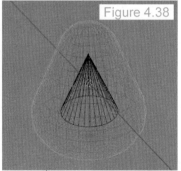

Figure 4.38

Cone inside the UV Sphere in Wireframe Display Mode.

Shrinkwrap Modifier added to the UV Sphere. **Target: Cone**

Altering the **Offset** value in the Modifier panel changes the size of the modified UV Sphere.

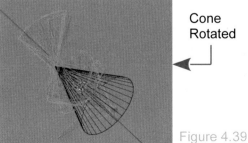

Cone Rotated

Experiment with the **Wrap Method** and **Snap Mode** values.

Figure 4.39

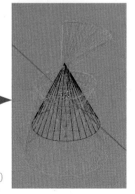

Figure 4.40

4.12 Simple Deform Modifier

The **Simple Deform Modifier** deforms a mesh by changing values in the Modifier and having a second Object with an influence. To see this Modifier in action, add a UV Sphere in the default Scene with a scaled down Cube located in the center of the Sphere (Figure 4.41). Activate **Wireframe Display Mode** and add the **Simple Deform Modifier** to the UV Sphere with Cube entered as the **Origin** (Figure 4.42). When the Modifier is Added you immediately see the Sphere's mesh skew. **Note:** By default **Twist** is selected in the Modifier (highlighted blue).

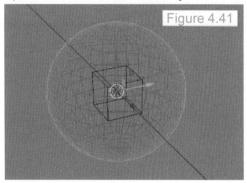

Figure 4.41

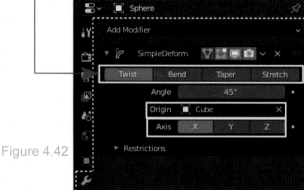

Figure 4.42

Try the options: **Twist, Bend, Taper** and **Stretch**.   Adjust the **Angle** slider to change the skew.

Experiment with the different settings in the Modifier panel. With any setting combination, Translating, Rotating or Scaling either the Cube or the UV Sphere affects the result. Deleting the Origin also affects results.

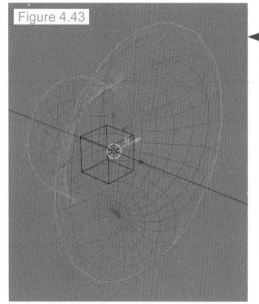

Figure 4.43

Stretch – Factor: 0.785 – Origin: Cube – Axis X

The result when the **Cube Origin** is removed.

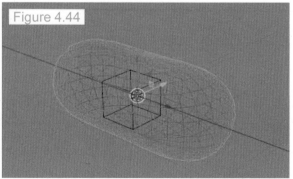

Figure 4.44

There are more settings in the Modifier, Restrictions Tab

4.13 Smooth Modifier

Figure 4.45

The **Smooth Modifier** smooths the mesh Object by softening the angles between adjacent Faces; this shrinks the size of the original Object at the same time. **Note:** The smoothing effect is only applied to how the Object's surfaces are drawn in the 3D Viewport . In smoothing, no additional Vertices, Edges or Faces are added to the Object. To use the Smooth Modifier select an Object in the 3D Viewport then Add the Modifier in the **Properties Editor, Modifier Properties (**Figure 4.45**).**

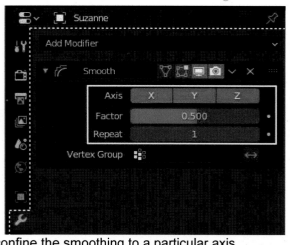

Adjust the **Factor slider** to increase or decrease smoothing. The **Repeat value** multiplies the Factor value. The **X, Y** and **Z** axis confine the smoothing to a particular axis.

Figure 4.46

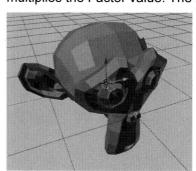 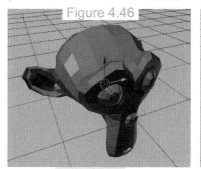 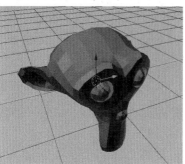

| Factor: 0.500 – Repeat: 1 | Repeat: 5 | Repeat: 10 |

In applying the **Factor** and **Repeat** values the logic of the operation is to first set a value (the Factor) then perform the calculation (repeat) several times to achieve the desired smoothing. When the desired smoothing is achieved Apply the Modifier.

Note: An Object should have a reasonable number of Faces before the Modifier is effective. For example; the Monkey Object with its default Faces will shrink in size as **Repeats** are applied. When subdivided three or four times it will show a completely different effect.

Figure 4.47

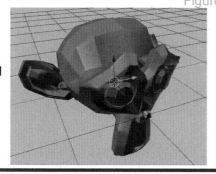 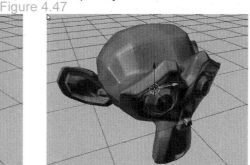

Repeat: 1   Repeat: 10

4.14 Smooth Corrective Modifier

Figure 4.48

The **Smooth Corrective Modifier** is used to Smooth and Correct imperfections in a model which occur when the surface is deformed. Figure 4.48 shows a model of an arm which has been posed and in doing so creates an imperfection .

Imperfection

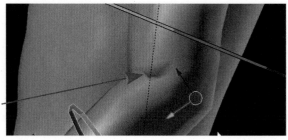

4.15 Smooth Laplacian Modifier

The **Laplacian Smooth Modifier** is used to smooth a mesh which has become irregular when Vertices have been manipulated during detailed modeling (Figures 4.49, 4.50).

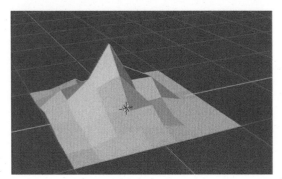

Object Mode   Figure 4.49

Object Mode   Figure 4.50

Plane Object, Subdivided – Number of Cuts: 7 One Vertex moved up with Proportional Editing enabled and Random Falloff.

Smooth Laplacian Modifier added in Object Mode. Repeat Value: 5, Lambda Factor: 1.100.

With the Modifier added (NOT Applied) Edit Mode shows the Vertices in their original state (Figure 4.51).

Figure 4.51

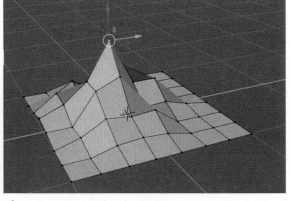

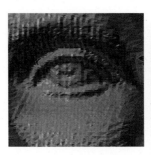

Practical application of the Smooth Laplacian Modifier.

To permanently set the surface smooth, Apply the Modifier.

4.16 Surface Deform Modifier

The Surface Deform Modifier is similar to the Mesh Deform Modifier in that one mesh is used to shape another. The difference being, the controlling mesh does not have to surround the Object being shaped.

Figure 4.52

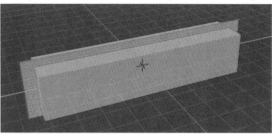

In Figure 4.52 a Cube Object has been Scaled along the Y Axis in Object Mode. In Edit Mode the Cube has been Subdivided with Number of Cuts: 10. A Plane Object has been added to the Scene, Rotated on the Y Axis and Scaled to bisect the elongated Cube. The Plane has also been Subdivided in Edit Mode, Number of Cuts: 10.

Figure 4.53

In Object Mode select the elongated Cube and add a **Surface Deform Modifier** (Figure 9.53). Enter **Plane** in the **Target Panel** as the controlling Object. **To set the Plane as the control click on Bind**.

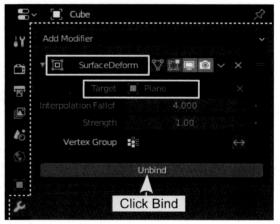

Deforming the Plane will deform the elongated Cube (Figure 4.54 over).

Proportional Editing Circle of Influence
(see Chapter 5 – 5.10)

Figure 4.54

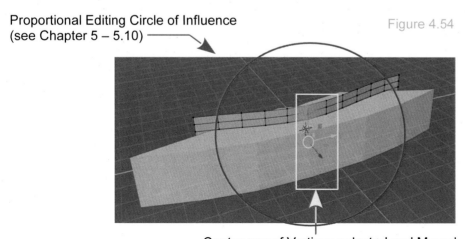

Center row of Vertices selected and Moved

In Figure 4.54 the center row of Vertices of the Plane is selected (in Edit Mode) and Moved forward deforming the Cube. In performing this operation Proportional Editing has been activated with Smooth Falloff and a Circle of Influence expanded to encapsulate the entire Plane.

After using this method to shape the Cube, Apply the Modifier and delete the Plane.

Animating the vertices of the Plane to move is an effective way of introducing lifelike characteristics to a Model. Figure 4.55 shows a Plane being animated to make the tail of a fish model move. (Reference: YouTube Video by yojigraphics)

https://www.youtube.com/watch?v=EJLIaNhoSSs

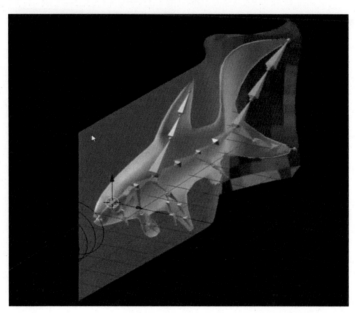

Figure 4.55

4.17 Warp Modifier

The **Warp Modifier** allows you to deform a mesh surface in Object mode by manipulating Target Objects. If you do not want the Targets to render in the Scene use Empty Objects. The deformation of the mesh takes place in a gradient between the two Targets.

This description requires clarification by a simple exercise.

In a new Blender Scene add a **Plane** Object, zoom in and **Subdivide** in Edit Mode (Cuts 10).

In Object Mode add two **Empty objects** and position as shown in Figure 4.56. Make note of the Empty names in the **Outliner Editor**; **Empty** and **Empty.001** (you may rename if you wish).

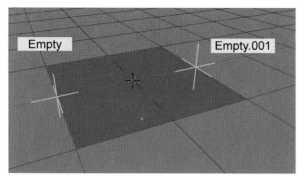

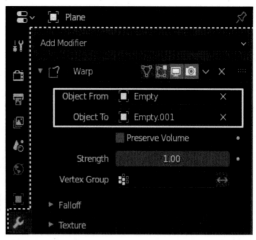

Figure 9.56

Select the Plane and in the Properties Editor, Modifier buttons add a **Warp Modifier** (Figure 4.57).

Figure 4.57

In the Modifier panel enter the names of the Empty Target Objects in the **From** and **To** panels (From: Empty and To: Empty.001). You will immediately see the Plane deform in the 3D View Editor (Figure 4.58).

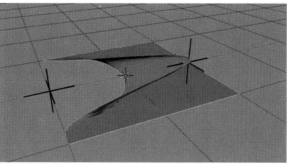

Figure 4.58

You may consider the Modifier as saying; deform the mesh From Empty to Empty.001.

By selecting either Empty in the 3D View Editor and translating the deformation of the Plane is affected (Figure 4.59).

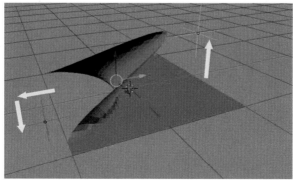

Figure 4.59

In the Modifier panel you may choose a different **Falloff Type** by opening the Falloff Tab (Figure 4.57). Adjust the **Strength** and **Radius** sliders to modify the deformation (Figure 4.60).

When the Modifier is Applied the shape of the Plane is permanently set.

Figure 4.60

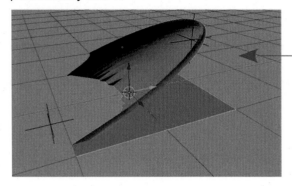

Figure 4.61
Spherical Falloff

Note: In Figures 4.61 and 4.62 the position of the Empty target objects have NOT been moved.

Figure 4.62

Radius and Strength Sliders Adjusted ——

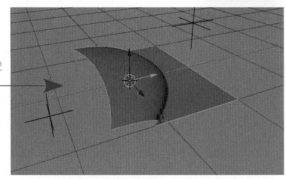

4.18 Wave Modifier

The **Wave Modifier** applies a deformation and creates an animation in a wave form. To demonstrate, in the default Blender Scene, delete the Cube and add a **Plane**. Scale the Plane up six times, Tab into **Edit mode**, and Subdivide the Plane by clicking **RMB - Subdivide** in the **Mesh Context** menu. In the **Subdivide** panel, make **Number of Cuts** 15. **Tab** back to **Object Mode**.

Figure 4.63

With the Plane selected, in the **Properties Editor, Modifiers Properties** add a **Wave Modifier** (Figure 4.63).

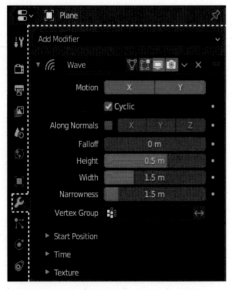

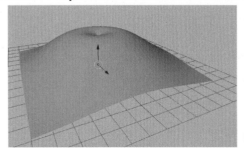

Figure 4.64

You immediately see the plane deform in the 3D Viewport Editor, pulled up in the middle and punched in at the top of the bulge (Figure 4.64).

The Wave Modifier has been applied on both the **X** and **Y** axis. In the Modifier panel you see **X**, **Y**, and **Cycli**c selected. **X** and **Y** refer to the axis and **Cyclic** means that an animation of the wave will repeat over and over.

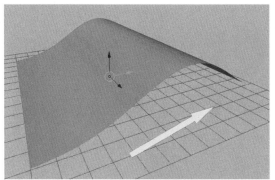

Figure 4.65

Press the **Play** button in the **Timeline Editor Header** to see the animation play.

Deselect the **X Axis** in the Modifier panel and play again. A wave along the **Y** axis results (Figure 4.65).

By expanding the **Start Position** and **Time** Tabs in the Modifier you have full control over the wave motion (Figure 4.66).

Figure 4.66

Frame 1

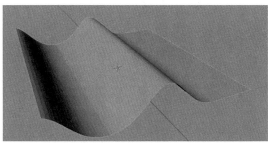

Frame 53

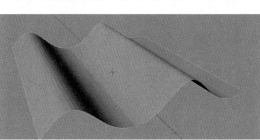

Frame 96

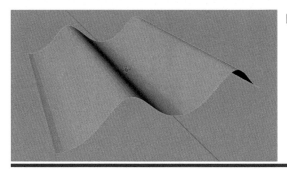

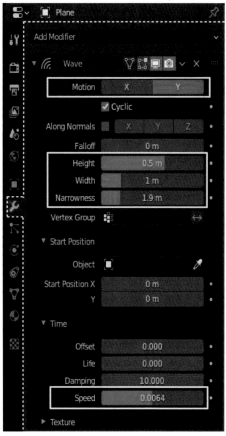

Editing Using Curves

Introduction

3D Viewport Header ——▶ Add (Alternativ: Press Shift + A Key)

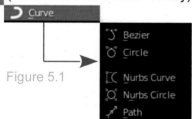

Figure 5.1

In Blender a Curve is a line or a path used to control the shape of a mesh in modeling or the movement of an Object in animation.

In Blender there are five types of curves: **Bezier** (Bezier Curve)**, Circle** (Bezier Circle), **Nurbs Curve, Nurbs Circle** and **Path**.

Each type of Curve is entered in the Blender Scene in Object Mode as a basic line. Control Handles display in Edit Mode which allow the shape of the Curve to be modified. The Curve may be Scaled and Extruded and additional control handles may be added.

A Curve does not Render. It merely acts as a control for editing a Mesh Object. The Object renders but the curve is invisible to the Render process.

Bezier and Nurbs Curves can be circular (circles) in which case they form a closed loop.

5.1 Curves Circles and Paths

Figure 5.2

In Blender, **Curves, Circles and Paths** are lines, giving a graphical representation of data or a line representing a path which controls direction or movement. Do not be confused with the Circle Object.

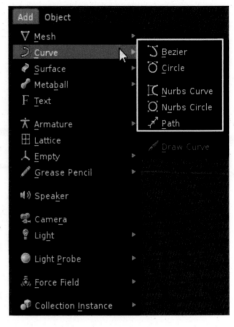

Curves are editable, which means that the shape of the curve may be altered to suit a particular application. An Object can be made to follow a Curve in an animation or it can be extruded along a Curve to affect its shape or it can be duplicated along a Curve. **Curve Circles** are merely circular Curves joined at the ends forming a continuous loop.

In Blender there are five basic Curve options which are accessed in the **Add menu in the 3D Viewport Editor Header** (Figure 5.2) or by pressing the **Shift + A Key** with the Mouse Cursor in the 3D Viewport Editor.

To examine the options place the 3D Viewport Editor in **Top Orthographic View** and delete the default Cube.

Note: Curves are entered in the 3D Viewport Editor in the XY Plane (Top Orthographic View).

Path: To understand Curves, Circles and Paths begin with the **Path** option. Select **Path** from the **Add – Curve** menu.

A **Nurbs Path** is entered in the 3D Viewport Editor in **Object Mode (Top Orthographic View).**

Figure 5.3

Edit Mode: In Edit Mode the Path displays yellow with **Control Point**

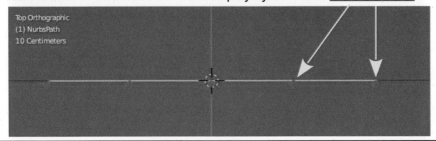

In Edit Mode, deselect the Path and click LMB on a **Control Point** (turns white).

Press G Key (Grab), move the Mouse or activate the Translate Tool in the Tool Panel to move the Control Point reshaping the Path.

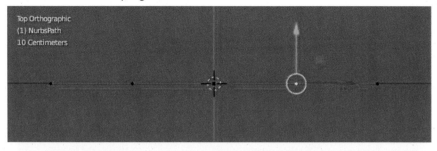

Figure 5.4

Top Orthographic
(1) NurbsPath
10 Centimeters

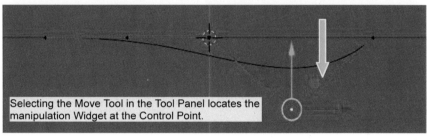

Selecting the Move Tool in the Tool Panel locates the manipulation Widget at the Control Point.

One application for a **Path,** is to animate an Object to move, following the Path. In this case, checking **Normals** in the **Edit Mode, Viewport Overlays**, displays chevrons along the Path.

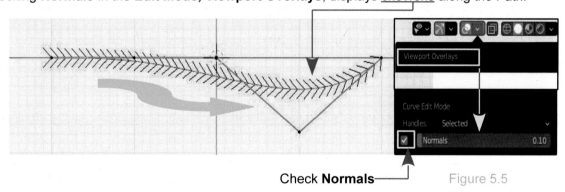

Check **Normals**

Figure 5.5

The **chevrons** indicate the direction of travel when the Object is Animated to follow the Path.

Remember: The Path may be Scaled, Rotated and Translated like any Object but it does NOT Render when an Image or Animation is created.

5.2 Bezier Curve

In some respects the **Bezier Curve** appears to be similar to a **Curve Path** when reshaped as shown in the previous example (Figure 5.5). Inspection in Edit Mode reveals a more refined control for shaping the curve.

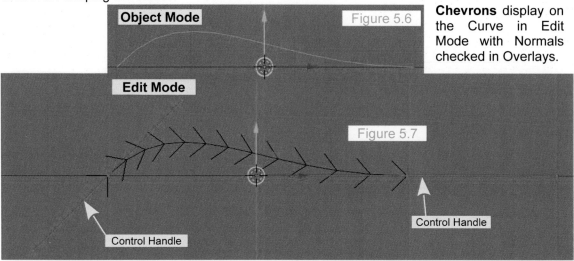

Object Mode

Figure 5.6

Edit Mode

Chevrons display on the Curve in Edit Mode with Normals checked in Overlays.

Figure 5.7

Control Handle

Control Handle

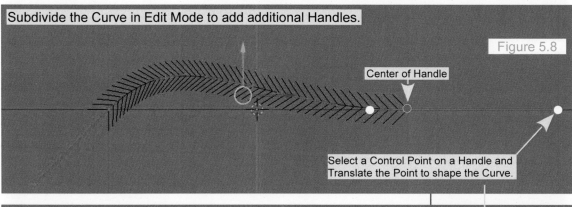

Subdivide the Curve in Edit Mode to add additional Handles.

Figure 5.8

Center of Handle

Select a Control Point on a Handle and Translate the Point to shape the Curve.

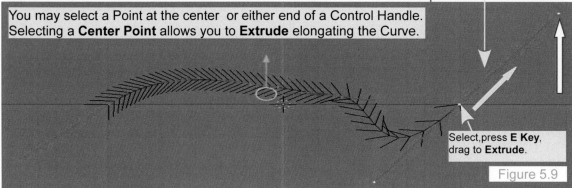

You may select a Point at the center or either end of a Control Handle. Selecting a **Center Point** allows you to **Extrude** elongating the Curve.

Select, press **E Key**, drag to **Extrude**.

Figure 5.9

5.3 Bezier Circle

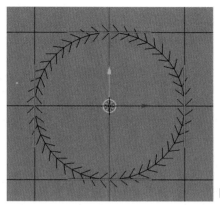

The **Bezier Circle** is similar to the Bezier Curve with control handles at the four cardinal points.

Click RMB to select a handle. **G Key** to grab and move to reshape the path. **R Key** to rotate and flatten the curve.

> **Note: The Bezier Circle, Nurbs Path and Nurbs Circle are shown in Edit Mode.**

Figure 5.10

5.4 Nurbs Path

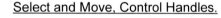
Select and Move, Control Handles.

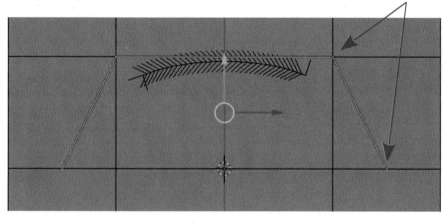

Figure 5.11

5.5 Nurbs Circle

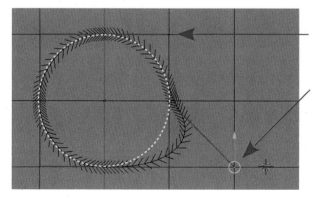

The **Nurbs Circle** with Control Handles external to the Path.

Control Handle Moved reshaping the Circle Curve.

> **Note:** The diagrams serve only to show you what the different Curves look like and how to Edit their shape.

Figure 5.12

5.6 Modeling from a Curve

Any Curve Path or Circle may be used to create a Mesh Object by Extrusion.

Enter a **Bezier Curve** in **User Perspective View,** zoom in and **Tab into Edit Mode**.

Note: The following is **NOT** the way to create a Mesh Object but to demonstrate what happens when the Curve is Extruded in Edit Mode. When Edit Mode is entered the Control Handles at both ends of the Curve are selected. Extrude down on the Z Axis (E Key +Z Key, drag the Mouse).

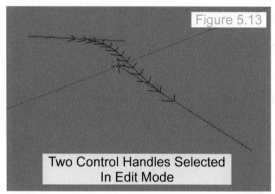

Figure 5.13

Two Control Handles Selected
In Edit Mode

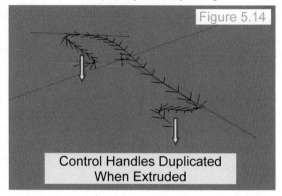

Figure 5.14

Control Handles Duplicated
When Extruded

To create a Mesh from a Curve be in **Object Mode** with the default **Bezier Curve** selected (**NOT Extruded**). In the **Properties Editor, Object Data Properties, Geometry Tab** change values as shown (Figure 5.15). Rotate the 3D Editor Viewport (Figure 5.16)

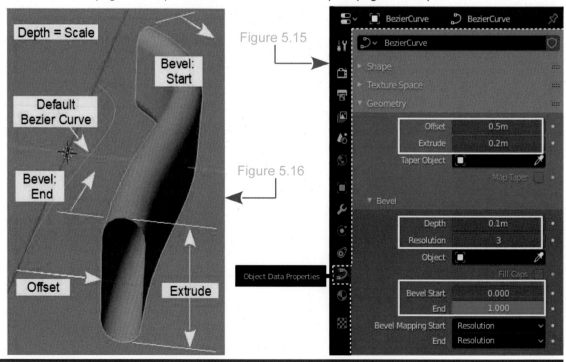

With the shape of the Mesh created, in Object Mode, go to the **3D Viewport Editor Header**, click on **Object** and select **Convert - Mesh** . In Edit Mode you will see that Vertices, Edges and Faces have been created.

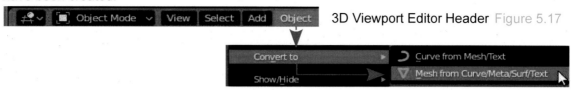

3D Viewport Editor Header Figure 5.17

Note: Before converting to a Mesh, in Edit Mode, you can select the Control Handles on the original Bezier Curve and reshape the Object. Once converted to a Mesh the original Curve is deleted.

Figure 5.18

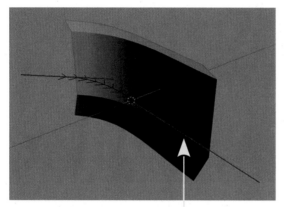

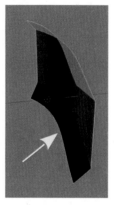

Select Control Handles and reshape before converting   Original Curve Shape

5.7 Closed Loops

Bezier and Nurbs Circles are Closed Loops which means they can be used to create tubular Objects or form a continuous path for an animation. Any Curve or Path may be converted to a Closed Loop.

The following shows a **Curve Path** entered in **Edit Mode** with the RH Control Point Moved then Extruded three times. **In Edit Mode**, click **Curve** in the Header and select **Toggle-Cyclic** to form a closed loop.

Figure 5.19

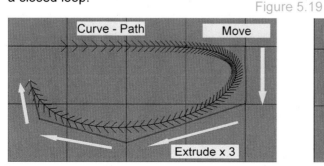

5.8 Using Nurbs Curves

Nurbs Curves are entered in the 3D Viewport Editor by pressing **Shift + A Key** or clicking **Add** in the 3D Viewport Header and selecting from the menu that displays. There are two options; **Nurbs Curve** and **Nurbs Circle** (Figure 10.20). **Place the 3D Viewport Editor in Top Orthographic View**.

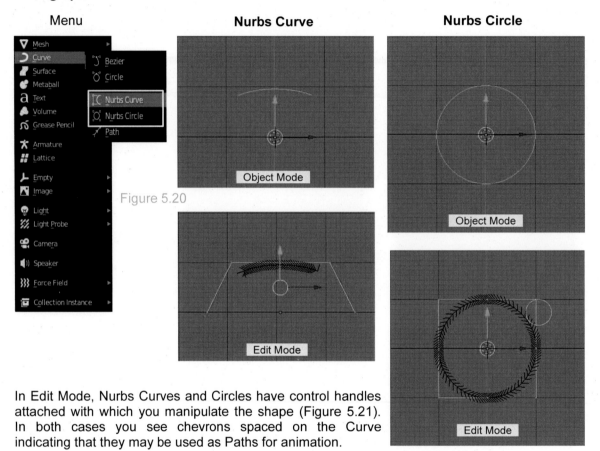

Figure 5.20

In Edit Mode, Nurbs Curves and Circles have control handles attached with which you manipulate the shape (Figure 5.21). In both cases you see chevrons spaced on the Curve indicating that they may be used as Paths for animation.

Figure 5.21

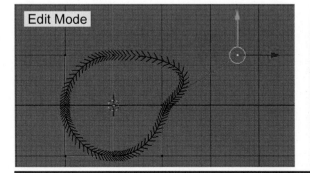
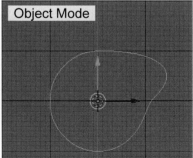

5.9 Nurbs Circle

Figure 5.22 shows a **Nurbs Circle** with a Control Point selected and Moved on the X Axis.

With the Nurbs Circle selected in **Object Mode** the shape may be expanded by changing settings in the **Properties Editor, Object Data Properties, Geometry Tab** (Figure 5.22). To demonstrate, skew the 3D Viewport into a User Orthographic View as shown in Figure 5.22

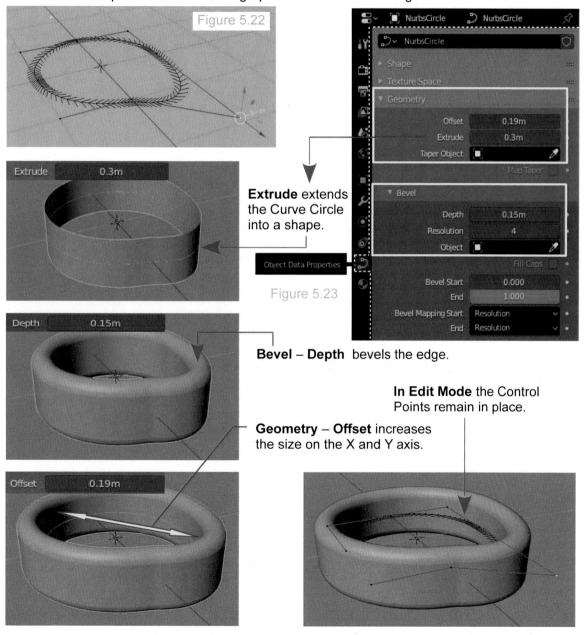

Figure 5.22

Extrude extends the Curve Circle into a shape.

Object Data Properties

Figure 5.23

Bevel – Depth bevels the edge.

In Edit Mode the Control Points remain in place.

Geometry – Offset increases the size on the X and Y axis.

81

With the Circle expanded then selected in **Object Mode** you may convert the shape into a **Mesh Object** (in the Header, click Object, select Convert to – Mesh from Curve). You see the Object in Edit mode with vertices, edges and faces (Figure 5.24).

Note: When you convert to a Mesh Object the ability to use the settings in the Properties Editor, Data buttons, Geometry tab is no longer available.

Deselect the Vertices then select individual vertices for manipulation.

A key - Deselect

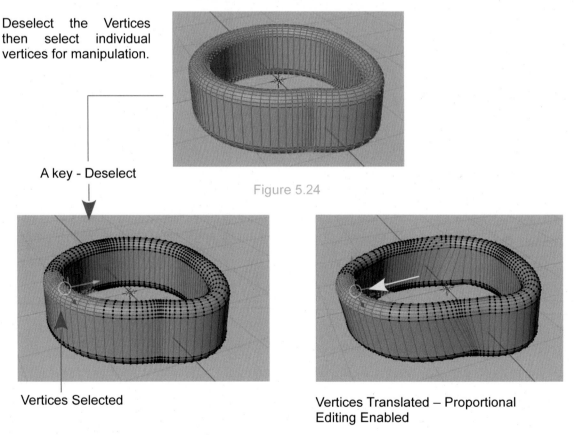

Figure 5.24

Vertices Selected

Vertices Translated – Proportional Editing Enabled

This procedure shows that by converting one type of object to another, you have different options for shape manipulation.

5.10 Nurbs Curve Figure 5.25

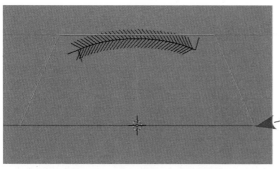

The **Nurbs Curve** is another starting place for creating shapes, objects or animation paths.

Edit mode shows the Curve surrounded by Control Handles (orange lines) with control points (orange dots)

You may select a single point or multiple points then Move, Rotate or Scale to shape the Curve.

In **Object Mode** settings in the **Properties Editor, Object Data Properties, Geometry Tab** control the shape.

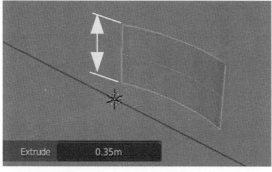

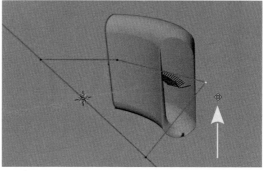

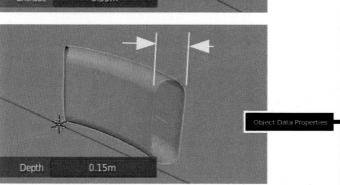

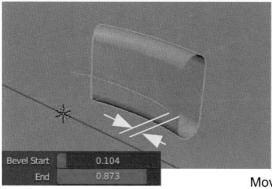

Move Control Handles to alter the shape in **Edit Mode**.

5.11 Lofting

Lofting is sometimes referred to as **Lathing** which is the process of generating shapes using Curves. The shape is generated then converted to a Mesh Object.

To demonstrate the process a **Bezier Circle** will be used in conjunction with a **Bezier Curv**e.

Begin a new Blender Scene, delete the default Cube then add a Bezier Circle. Deselect the circle and add a Bezier Curve. Zoom in on the 3D Viewport Editor (Figure 5.26).

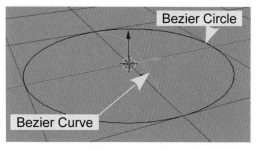

Figure 5.26

Figure 5.27

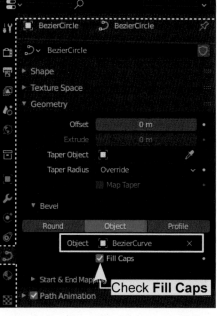

Deselect the Curve and select the Circle. In the **Properties Editor, Object Data Properties, Geometry Bevel Tab,** click on **Taper Object** and select **Bezier Curve** (Figure 5.27). Check **Fill Caps**.

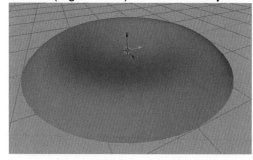

Figure 5.28

A shape is generated in the 3D Viewport Editor (Figure 5.28).

To understand what has occurred place the 3D Viewport Editor in **Wireframe Viewport Shading** Mode (Figure 5.29). Select the **Bezier Curve** by clicking on the name in the **Outliner Editor** (Figure 5.30). To see more clearly turn off the grid and floor display in the **Overlays**.

Figure 5.29

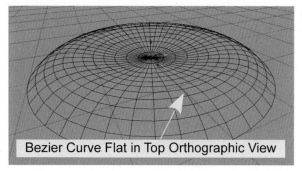

Bezier Curve Flat in Top Orthographic View

Figure 5.30

The profile of the Bezier Curve is presented flat in **Top Orthographic View** (Figure 5.26). With the curve selected press R + X + 90 + Enter to flip it on edge. Go into **Front Orthographic View** and translate the Curve to align with the profile of the generated shape (Figures 5.31, 5.32).

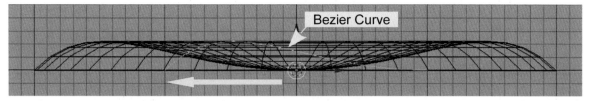

Bezier Curve

Figure 5.31

Bezier Curve Aligned with Shape Profile

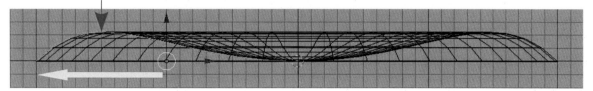

Figure 5.32

By skewing the 3D View Editor you will see that the shape has been generated by extruding the Curve profile through 360° (Figure 5.33).

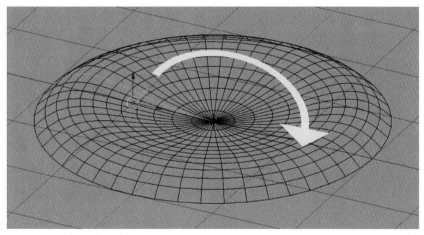

Figure 5.33

With the Bezier Curve still selected Tab to Edit Mode to see the **Control Handles** at each end of the Curve (Figure 10.33).

By selecting the Control Handle at the center of the shape and translating it along the **X Axis** towards the outside, you will see that it increases the inner diameter of the shape. Similarly translating the Control Handle at the outer diameter alters the outer diameter (Figure 5.34).

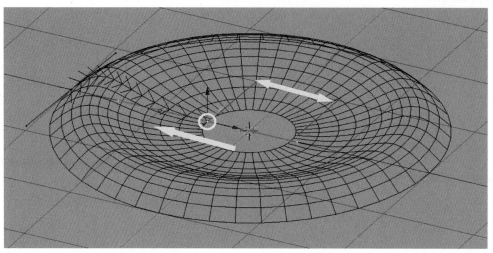

Figure 5.34

Shift select both Control Handles then press **R + Y + 90**. Doing this flips the Bezier Curve up on edge and changes the shape into something resembling a pot (Figure 5.35).

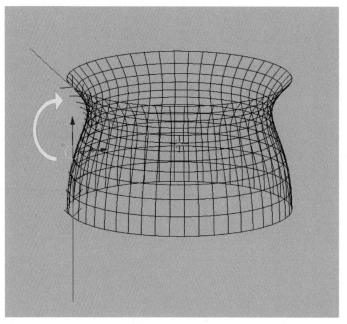

Figure 5.35

By manipulating the Control Handles you can modify the shape. Selecting both Control Handles and Subdividing (Click RMB in the Editor and select Subdivide in the Curve Context Menu) adds a third Control Handle (Figure 5.36). With the Control Handle selected, press the **V Key** to display the Handle type menu. Type **Vector** allows you to produce sharp corners when the handle is rotated.

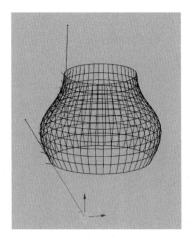 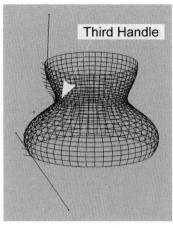

Third Handle

Figure 5.36

When you have completed shaping, Tab to Object Mode, deselect the **Bezier Curve** and select the shape itself. Change to **Solid Viewport Shading Mode** (Figure 5.37).

In the **Properties Editor, Object Properties (NOT Object Data), Viewport Display Tab** check (tick) **Wireframe** to view to see the subdivisions that will be created when the shape is converted to a Mesh Object (Figure 5.38). You may modify the subdivisions by altering values in the **Properties Editor, Object Data buttons, Shape Tab, Resolution.**

 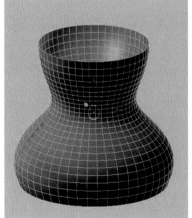 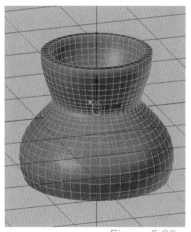

Figure 5.37   Figure 5.38   Figure 5.39

Finally, with the shape completed, click Object in the Header and select Convert to Mesh from Curve.

Add a **Solidify Modifier** and increase the **Thickness value** to give the shape **wall thickness** (Figure 5.39).

Material Assignment

Facts and Definitions

A **Material,** in Blender, is how the surface of an Object displays on the computer Screen. In its simplest form a Material is the color of an Object which is how the visible spectrum of light reflects from the Object's surface. In the real World this reflection is influenced by the **Base Color** of the Object, the **Texture** of the Object's surface and **Lighting Effects** (Ambient Lighting).

Materials, Texture and Lighting are the three **Properties** which determine how an Object displays in a Scene in the 3D Viewport Editor but the Viewport itself has four different display modes. The display modes are intended to simplify what you see in the Editor depending on the procedure being performed i.e. Modeling, Previewing a color scheme or viewing what will be Rendered (converted to image or video).

How Materials (colors) display in the 3D Viewport Editor depends on the **Viewport Shading Mode** being employed.

Solid Viewport Shading Mode is the default display when Blender is first opened which is primarily used for Modeling. Material (color) is not considered necessary for basic Modeling.

Also by default, Materials are controlled by the **Blender Material Node System** which provides a versatile and comprehensive control for producing fantastic effects. When Blender first opens the Node System is active.

Note: With the 3D Viewport Editor in **Solid Viewport Shading Mode,** Materials (colors) do NOT display in the 3D Viewport Editor when the Node System is active.

The Node System may be disabled to allow the color to display with the 3D Viewport in Solid Viewport Shading Mode.

6.1 Material Assignment

Coloring an Object may be considered to be Assigning a Material. To understand the procedure for doing this, in relation to the Graphical User Interface, start with the default Blender Screen with the default Cube Object displayed in the 3D Viewport Editor. Have the **Properties Editor, Material Properties** opened.

Properties Editor

The default Cube Object displays with a gray Material (color).

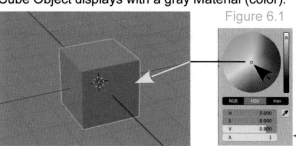

Figure 6.1

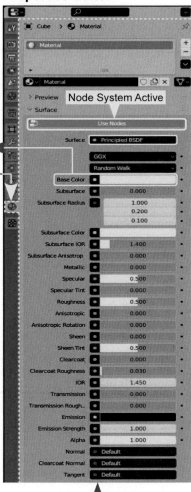

Node System Active

Material Properties

The Properties Editor, Material Properties show that the **Blender Material Node System** is controlling the Material. This is indicated by the **Use Nodes** button in the Surface Tab being highlighted blue and **Principled BSDF** entered in the Surface bar. The **Base Color bar** shows a white color which is actually the gray color of the Cube. Clicking on the Base Color bar displays a color picker circle where you click in the circle to select a different color (different Material).

In the default Screen, selecting a new color will **NOT** see any change in the 3D Viewport Editor. The Cube remains gray since the Node System is in control and the 3D Viewport is in **Solid Viewport Shading Mode** (explanation to follow).

You should also understand that the default Cube Object has a Material (color) pre-applied. This is indicated by the Properties Editor, Material Properties display with its controls.

When a new Object is entered in a Scene the controls do not display. Only the New button displays.

Figure 6.2

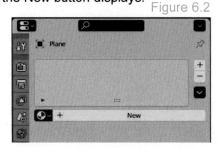

With a new Object in the 3D Viewport Editor and selected, click the **New button** to display the Material Properties for the new Object.

The display will be identical to that for the default Cube and the default gray material will be applied.

6.2 Viewport Shading Modes

The 3D Viewport Editor displays in four **Shading Modes** which you select, depending on the operation you are performing. The default Shading Mode is **Solid** which will be used to demonstrate **Material Assignment**.

Solid Viewport Shading Mode ⎯⎯⎯⎯⎯⎐ Figure 6.3

3D Viewport Editor Header
Upper Right Hand Side

Only the default gray Material (color) displays in Solid Viewport Shading Mode.

Figure 6.4

To enable a different Material (color) display in the 3D Viewport Editor, in Solid Viewport Shading Mode, **cancel the Node System** by clicking the **blue Use Nodes button** in the **Properties Editor, Surface Tab** (Use Nodes will change from blue to white.) ⎯⎯▲

6.3 Material Properties   Figure 6.5 **Properties Editor**

The application of Materials is primarily controlled in the **Properties Editor, Material Properties** but may also be controlled using the Blender Material Node System.

Figure 6.5 shows the default Material Properties control for the display of the Material (color) of the default Cube Object in the 3D Viewport Editor.

Figure 6.6

Material Properties⎯⎯⎯

The Base Color is the Material color of the selected Object in the 3D Viewport Editor.

Color is one of many Properties   Figure 6.7

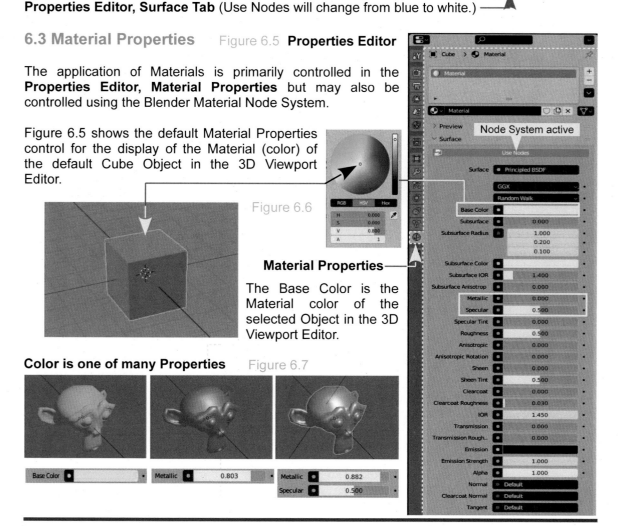

Note: The default 3D Viewport is in **Solid Viewport Display Mode.** The Material (color) of the default Cube Object is set in the **Base Color bar** in the Material Properties but if you click the bar and select a different color in the color picker circle you will NOT see the color change in the 3D Viewport until you **click the blue Use Nodes button to cancel the Node System**.

Although new Objects do **NOT** have a Material applied, Blender displays them with the default gray color.

6.4 Material Node System

The **Blender Material Node System** is a graphical representation of computer data or instruction which is arranged in a **pipeline** producing the display of color. Think about mixing colors. The primary colors are Red, Green and Blue, which when mixed in equal proportions produce White In a **Node System** this would look like:

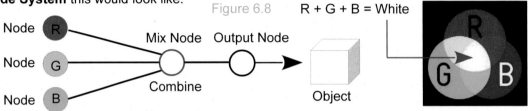

Figure 6.8   R + G + B = White

The Blender Node system looks like this: Figure 6.9

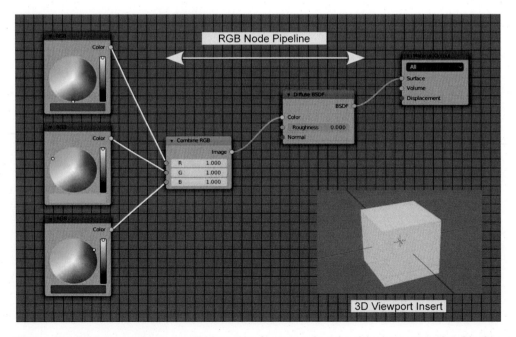

Note: Nodes are used to control many features but in this instance the Nodes control **Material Color**. Nodes may be connected and disconnected and rearranged in the pipeline to create effects.

The Default Material Node System

The **Blender Material Node** system displays in the **Shader Editor**.

Shader Editor   Figure 6.10

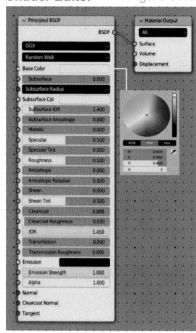

With the default Cube Object selected in the 3D Viewport Editor the Shader Editor displays with a **Principled BSDF Node** connected to a **Material Output Node** (Figure 6.9).

Nodes do not automatically display when a new Object is entered and selected in the 3D Viewport.

The Base Color bar in the Principled BSDF Node controls the Material (Color) of the Cube Object in the 3D Viewport (the selected Object).

To see Material (color) changes in the 3D Viewport **using the Node System** the Viewport must be in **Material Preview** or **Rendered Viewport Shading Mode**.

Properties Editor

Figure 6.11

Surface Tab

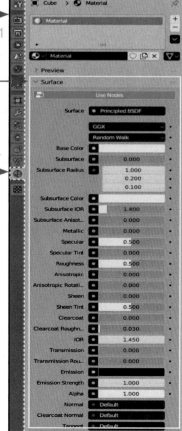

You have probably noticed that the controls in the Principled BSDF Node are replicated in the Properties Editor, Material Properties. Yes; you may adjust settings in either to affect the Material display in the 3D Viewport Editor.   **Material Properties →**

As you see there are many controls which produce a multitude of effects. Knowing where the controls are located in the GUI will enable you to research and follow detailed tutorials.

At this point an explanation will be provided outlining how the settings in the Material Properties are organised and how they relate to the display in the 3D Viewport.

The basic philosophy is; The settings in the Material Properties, Surface Tab, create a Material Index. The Index is stored in a Datablock in a Material Cache and may be retrieved to be used on Objects in the 3D Viewport.

6.5 Material Properties Expanded

For simplicity Material may be considered as color. The color of an Object in the 3D Viewport Editor is determined (controlled) by a set of Data called a **Material Index**. In the default Blender Scene, in the 3D Viewport Editor, the color of the default Cube Object is determined by a **Material Index** which displays the Cube with the default gray color.

The default Cube is said to have the default gray Material Index pre-applied. This is indicated by the display of controls in the Properties Editor, Material Properties as shown in Figure 6.5. The pre-application of the Material Index only takes place for the default Cube.

All additional Objects entered in a Scene do NOT have a Material Index. The controls in the Properties Editor, Material Properties only consist of the New Button.

Figure 6.12

Prior to you clicking the New Button, Blender uses the default Material Index, behind the scenes, to give you a display in the 3D Viewport Editor (default gray) (Figure 6.6).

When you click the New Button, controls in the Properties Editor display indicating that the default Material Index has been applied. Note; the Blender Node System is active. **Use Nodes** is highlighted blue (Figure 6.5).

Cancel the Node System by clicking Use Nodes (displays white) (Figure 6.4).

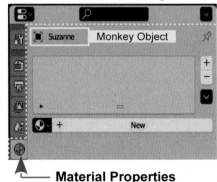

Material Properties

In Figure 6.12 you will see that **Suzanne (Monkey Object)** is a new Object entered in the Scene. To understand the components of the Material Properties start a new Blender File with only the default Cube in the 3D Viewport.

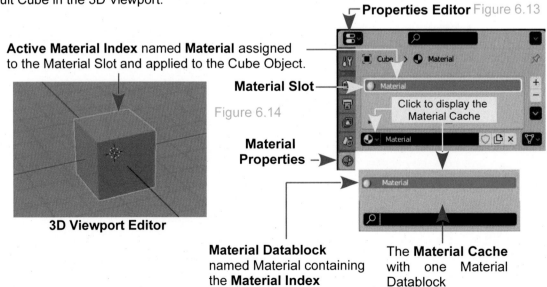

Active Material Index named **Material** assigned to the Material Slot and applied to the Cube Object.

Properties Editor Figure 6.13

Material Slot

Click to display the Material Cache

Figure 6.14

Material Properties →

3D Viewport Editor

Material Datablock named Material containing the **Material Index**

The **Material Cache** with one Material Datablock

6.6 Properties Assignment Components

Properties Assignment Components are shown in Figure 6.13.

The Data controlling the Material display of the selected Object in the 3D Viewport Editor is called the **Material Index**. The Material Index is contained in a **Material Datablock** which is stored in a **Cache** (the Material Cache). In the default Scene there is a single Datablock stored in the Cache which contains the Material Index. Selecting the Datablock in the Cache (click to highlight blue) enters the Datablock in the Material Properties assigning the Material Index to the **Material Slot** which in turn is assigned the Datablock / Material Index to the selected Object in the 3D Viewport.

Note: This analogy may not be strictly correct in terms of programming but explains the assignment of data in terms of the Graphical User Interface. The term **Material Slot** is derived from the fact that clicking the **plus sign** adjacent to where you see the Active Material Index, adds a new Material Slot.

Figure 6.15

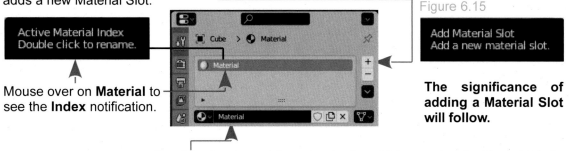

Active Material Index
Double click to rename.

Mouse over on **Material** to
see the **Index** notification.

Add Material Slot
Add a new material slot.

The **significance of adding a Material Slot will follow.**

Datablock selected from the Cache which contains the **Material Index**.

6.7 Adding Materials (Datablocks)

Figure 6.16

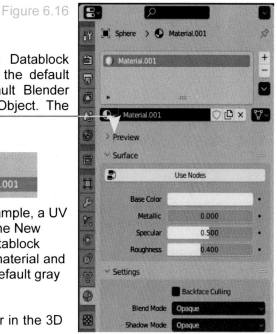

Adding a Material is in effect adding a new Datablock containing a Material Index. Figure 6.14 shows the default Material Datablock which exists when the default Blender Scene is opened containing the default Cube Object. The Datablock is named **Material**.

Material Cache

Material
Material.001

When a new Object is added to the Scene, for example, a UV Sphere, the Material Properties display with only the New Button. Clicking the New Button creates a new Datablock named Material.001. Both the Datablock named material and the Datablock named Material.001 produce the default gray color.

Remember: Cancel the Node System to see color in the 3D Viewport when in Solid Viewport Shading Mode.

The foregoing has demonstrated that, when a new Object is added to the Scene and the New Button in the Material Properties is pressed a new Material Datablock is automatically created.

You may manually create new Material Datablocks by having either the Cube or the UV Sphere selected in the 3D Viewport.

Note: You must have an Object selected in the 3D Viewport to display Material Properties in the Properties Editor.

Figure 6.17

To simplify manually creating new Datablocks, have the default Cube Object selected in the 3D Viewport. The Properties Editor, Material Properties will display with the default Material Datablock named Material assigned to the Material Slot. This produces the default gray color of the Cube.

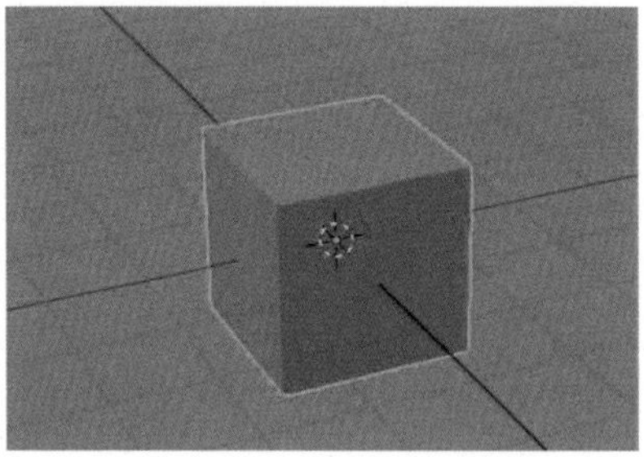

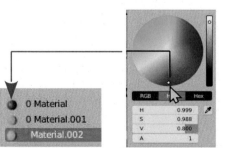
Figure 6.18

Click the **New Material Button** to manually create a new Material Datablock.

Datablock Material.001 is created and assigned to the Material Slot.

Figure 6.19

The Material Cache will show two Datablocks, Material and Material.001 which produce the default gray color (Figure 6.19).

Click the New Material Button a second time to create a third Datablock named Material.002 (Figure 6.20).

Material Cache →

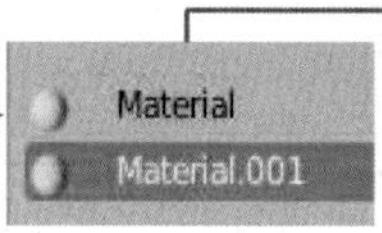

Datablock Material.002 again produces the default gray.

Figure 6.20

Cancel the Node System. Select each Datablock in turn from the Material Cache, click the Base Color bar and select a color from the color picker (Figure 6.21).

Material Cache

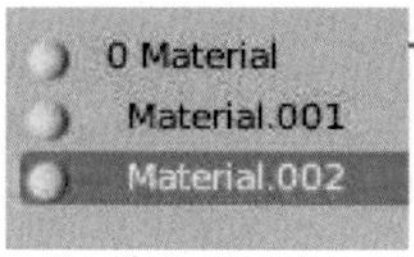

Figure 6.21

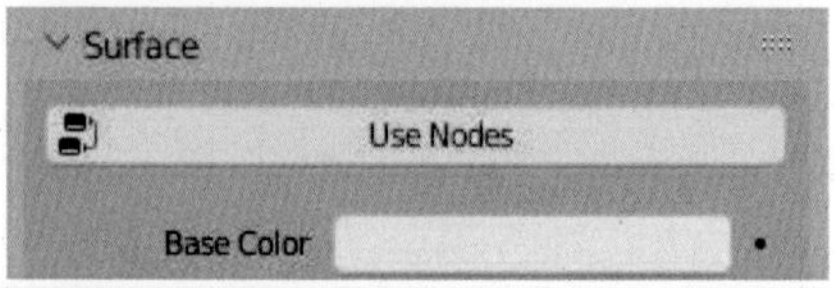

As colors are assigned to each Datablock the Cube Object in the 3D Viewport displays with the corresponding color.

New Objects entered in the Scene display in the 3D Viewport with the default gray and the Properties Editor, Material Properties will only have the New Button.

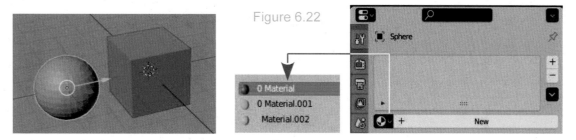

Figure 6.22

Instead of clicking **New**, select a **Datablock** from the **Material Cache** (0 Material - red).

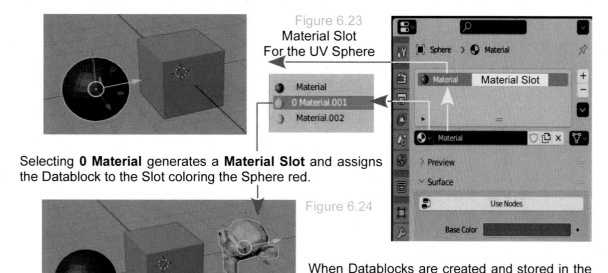

Figure 6.23

Material Slot
For the UV Sphere

Selecting **0 Material** generates a **Material Slot** and assigns the Datablock to the Slot coloring the Sphere red.

Figure 6.24

When Datablocks are created and stored in the Material Cache they may be assigned to new Objects entered in the Scene via the Material Slot.

Remember: The Material Cache is only applicable to the Blender File being worked.

Also Remember: Each Object has a single Material Slot. Selecting a Datablock from the Cache assignes that Datablock to the Slot hence to the selected Object.

6.8 Multiple Datablock Assignment

Material Datablocks stored in the Material Cache can be assigned to any Object or to a part of an Object. For example, the Faces of a Cube can be colored differently.

Per the preceding instruction, the Cube Object has been assigned the Material Datablock, Material.002 coloring it blue. The Material Cache containd Datablocks named, **Material** (red), **Material.001** (green) and **Material.002** (blue).

Multiple Material Slots

Datablocks, when selected from the Cache, are assigned to a **Material Slot** which is associated with the selected Object. To employ multiple Datablocks for multiple colors you use multiple Material Slots.

Figure 6.25

As an example, start a new Blender File. Select the default Cube in the 3D Viewport. The Properties Editor, Material Properties will show the Datablock named Material from the Cache entered in the Material Slot coloring the Cube gray.

Click the **New Material Button** and create new Material Datablocks selecting a different Base Color for each.

As each Datablock is created and given a Base Color it is assigned to the Material Slot changing the color of the Cube.

In the Cache select **0 Material** (gray). Colors the Cube gray.

Tab to Edit Mode in the 3D Viewport Editor.

With the Cube selected in the 3D Viewport deselect all Vertices (click LMB in the Viewport). In the Viewport Header change to **Face Select Mode**.

Figure 6.26

3D Viewport Header (upper RHS)   **Click + to add a Material Slot**

In the **Properties Editor, Material Properties** create a new **Material Slot** and with the **Slot** selected open the **Cache** and select a **Datablock.**

Figure 6.27

Select a Face on the Cube   **Select the new Slot**

Click Assign

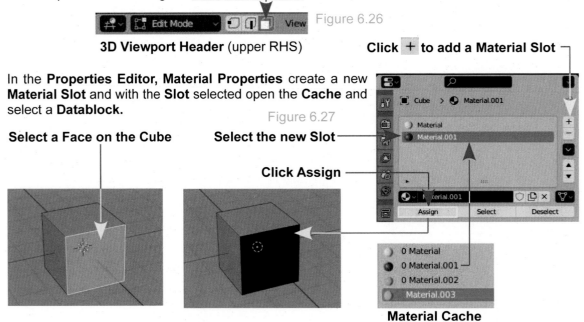

Material Cache

Multiple Material Slots may be used to color areas on the surface of an Object defined by **Vertex Groups.**

As an example, in a new Blender file, delete the default Cube Object and add a UV Sphere.

Properties Editor   Figure 6.28

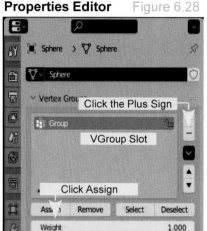

In Edit Mode, Face Select, select Faces on the UV Sphere (Figure 6.28). In the Properties Editor, Object data Properties click the **Plus Sign** to create a VGroup **Slot** and click **Assign**.

Figure 6.29

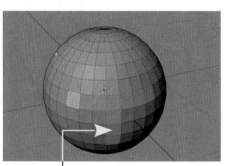

Faces Selected   Object Data Properties →

Properties Editor   Figure 6.30

In Object Mode with the UV Sphere selected go to the Properties Editor, Material Properties and add a Material with a new Base Color (Figures 6.30, 6.31).

Figure 6.31

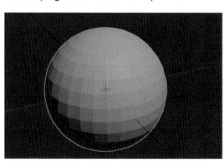

Object Mode – Rendered Viewport Shading

Remember: To see color in the 3D Viewport be in Material Preview or Rendered Viewport Shading Mode or cancel the Node System.

Material Properties →

Create a new **Material Slot** and assign a new Material with a different Base Color.

Tab to Edit Mode and with the Vertex Group selected in the **Object Data Properties** and the **new Material Slot** selected in the Material Properties click the **Assign Button** to apply the Material from the new Slot to the Vertex Group.

Edit Mode – Vertex Group Selected

Figure 6.33

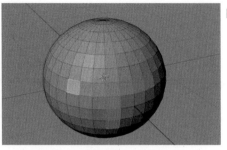

Properties Editor   Figure 6.32

Edit Mode – Material Assigned

Figure 6.34

Figure 6.35

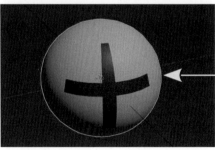

In **Object Mode** Shade the UV Sphere Smooth.

6.9 Material Nodes

Note: To simplify the forgoing instruction and allow colors to display in the 3D Viewport Editor with the Editor in **Solid Viewport Shading Mode**, in some cases, the Node System was cancelled.

You can follow the same procedure for creating new Material Datablocks with the Node System active but to see the change in color in the 3D Viewport you will have to be in **Material Preview Mode or Rendered Mode.**

To demonstrate, since you are only concerned with the **Base Material Color**, the default **Principled BSDF Node** in the Shader Editor may be replaced with the **Diffuse BSDF Node.**

Note: When the Principled BSDF Node is replaced by the **Diffuse BSDF Node**, Base Color in the Surface Tab, becomes simply Color.

Rendered Viewport Shading Mode

Figure 6.36

3D Viewport

Material

Shader Editor

Properties Editor Materials

Diffuse BSDF Node

Material Cache

Material.001

Material.002

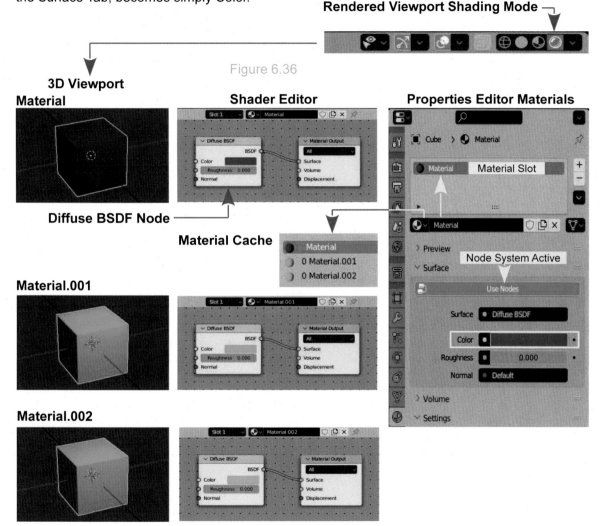

Constraints

Constraints control an Object's properties such as its Location, Rotation and Scale by Targeting the Object to a secondary Object or connecting Objects in a Scene together, such that they act as a single entity while maintaining individual characteristics. Another way to define Constraints is to say they define relationships between Objects.

For example, the **Track To Constraint** applied to a **Camera** Object, with a **Target** set as another Object in the Scene, causes the Camera to always point to the second Object no matter where it moves.

Another example is a **Child Of Constraint** which when applied to one Object (the child) with a **Target** set as a second Object (the parent) causes the child to follow the parent. Using a Child Of Constraint creates what is termed a **Child / Parent Relationship.** This has a particular application in animating characters (see Chapter 10 Armatures & Character Rigging).

Constraints are applied to Objects in the **Properties Editor, Object Constraint Properties** by clicking on **Add Object Constraint** then selecting a Constraint from the menu that displays.

Constraints in Blender are listed in four categories as shown in Figure 9.2 on the following page.

In this chapter, Constraints are briefly defined and several examples provided which will allow you to understand their application.

7.1 Introduction to Constraints

Constraints are accessed in the **Properties Editor, Object Constraint Properties** (Figure 7.1).

Clicking **Add Object Constraint** displays the Constraint selection menu listing Constraints in four categories (Figure 7.2).

Note: Not all constraints work with all Objects.

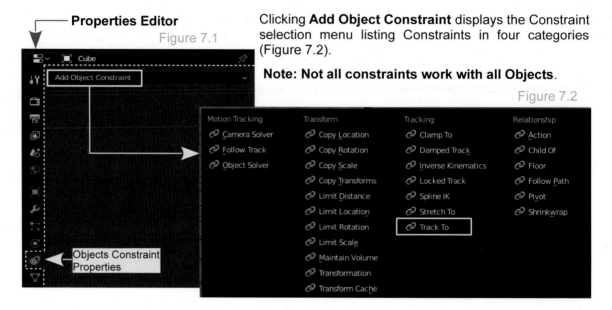

7.2 Track to Constraint

The **Track To Constraint** provides an introduction demonstrating what a Constraint is, in practical terms and how Constraints are used.

In the default Blender Scene a Camera Object is directed towards the Cube Object such that it captures the Cube in Camera View (Num Pad 0). When the Cube is animated to move across the Screen the Cube can move in and out of Camera View. If you want the Cube to remain in view no matter where the Cube is in the Scene, you track the Camera to the Cube by employing the **Track To Constraint** (add the Constraint to the Camera).

Note: The default camera has been rotated and locked in position to point towards the center of the Scene (default position of the Cube). The rotation of the default Camera has to be unlocked to use the Track To Constraint. This only applies to the default Camera. A new camera entered in the Scene is not locked.

To unlock the default Camera have it selected then press **Alt + R Key**. The rotation is cleared and the Camera points down in the Scene. **Note:** The **Clear Rotation Panel** displays in the lower LH corner of the Editor.

Figure 7.3

If **Delta Transform Rotation** values have been entered in the **Properties Editor, Object Properties, Delta Transform Tab**, check **Clear Delta** in the Clear Rotation Panel.

With the Camera selected click **Add Object Constraint** (Figure 7.1) and select **Track To** in the menu (Figure 7.2).

Figure 7.4

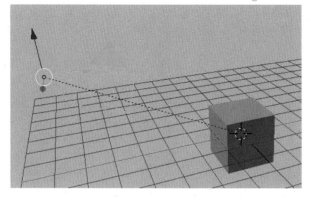

In the **Track To** panel click on **Target** and select the **Target Object** (Cube) in the menu (Figure 7.5).

Note: On entering the **Target** (Cube) the Camera swings around pointing to the Cube. There is a broken line connecting the Camera to the Cube indicating that a Constraint is applied. Note the **Track Axis** and **Up** directions in the Constraint Panel (Track Axis:-Z and Up: Y**)** (Figure 7.5). With the Cube animated to move in the Scene the Camera always points to the Cube.

Constraints are associated with an Object by selecting the Object in the 3D Viewport Editor then clicking on **Add Object Constraint** in the **Properties Editor, Object Constraints Properties** and selecting the Constraint from the menu that displays (Figure 7.2).

7.3 Constraint Stack

Figure 7.6

It should be noted, in some cases, it is appropriate to apply more than one Constraint to an Object. When this is done the Constraints are placed in a stack in order of priority. The priority can be changed by moving a constraint up or down in the stack (Figure 7.6).

In Figure 7.6 a **Follow Path** and a **Track To** Constraint are applied to the same Object. The **Track To** takes precedence over the **Follow Path**. To reverse the

precedence click, hold and drag the **dimple button** up or down.

Figure 7.5

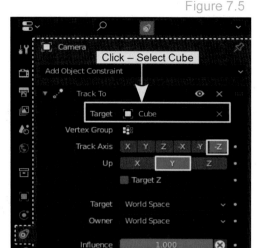

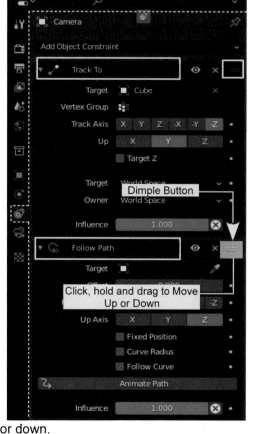

In many cases, when using Constraints, there are control values to be inserted in the Constraint Panel to regulate the functions. The following pages in this chapter contain a brief description of Constraint functions. Most Constraints are self explanatory, therefore a detailed explanation will only be given for a few common Constraints, or where it is not self evident.

7.4 Transform Constraints List

- **Copy Location.** Forces the Object with the constraint added to take up the location of the Target Object.

- **Copy Rotation.** Forces the Object with the constraint added to copy the rotation of the Target Object. When the target rotates, the Object rotates.

- **Copy Scale.** Forces the Object with the constraint added to copy the scale of the Target Object

- **Copy Transforms.** Similar to the copy location constraint.

- **Limit Distance.** Constrains the Object to remain within a set distance from the Target Object. The distance is a spherical field surrounding the target and the Object is constrained within or outside the spherical field.

- **Limit Location.** Constrains the Object's location between a minimum and maximum distance on a specific axis. The distance is relative to either the world center or a parented Object.

- **Limit Rotation.** Constrains an Object's rotation about a specific axis between limits.

- **Limit Scale.** Constrains the scale of an Object between limits on a specified axis.

- **Maintain Volume.** Constrains the dimensions of a side on a specified axis.

- **Transformation.** See Section 9.5. Note: In 9.5 the Properties Editor is shown using the Blender Light, Preset Theme.

- **Transform Cache.** Look up the transform Matrix from an external file.

7.5 The Transformation Constraint

The **Transformation Constraint** allows you to control the Location, Rotation or Scale of one Object or part of an Object by adjusting the Location, Rotation, or Scale of another Object. The Location, Rotation or Scale values in either case can be set to operate within a specific range.

The Object to be controlled is called the **Source** and has the **Constraint** applied to it, while the other Object (the controlling Object), is called the **Target object**.

To demonstrate have a Cube Object and a UV Sphere in the 3D Viewport Editor in Top Orthographic View (Figure 7.7)

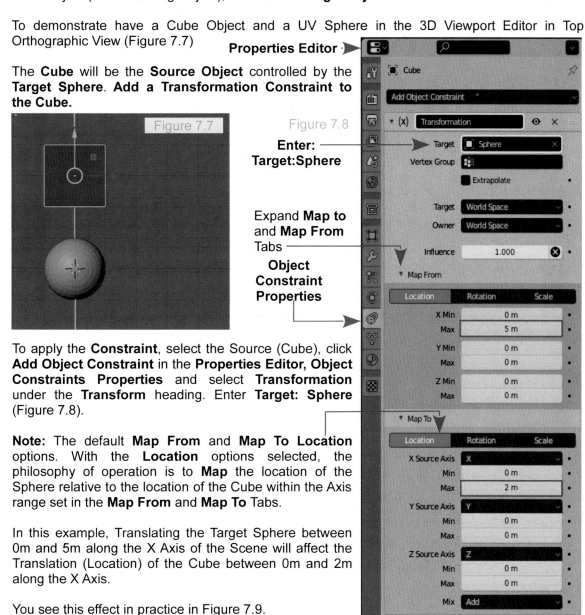

Properties Editor

The **Cube** will be the **Source Object** controlled by the **Target Sphere**. **Add a Transformation Constraint to the Cube.**

Figure 7.7

Figure 7.8

Enter:
Target:Sphere

Expand **Map to** and **Map From** Tabs

Object Constraint Properties

To apply the **Constraint**, select the Source (Cube), click **Add Object Constraint** in the **Properties Editor, Object Constraints Properties** and select **Transformation** under the **Transform** heading. Enter **Target: Sphere** (Figure 7.8).

Note: The default **Map From** and **Map To Location** options. With the **Location** options selected, the philosophy of operation is to **Map** the location of the Sphere relative to the location of the Cube within the Axis range set in the **Map From** and **Map To** Tabs.

In this example, Translating the Target Sphere between 0m and 5m along the X Axis of the Scene will affect the Translation (Location) of the Cube between 0m and 2m along the X Axis.

You see this effect in practice in Figure 7.9.

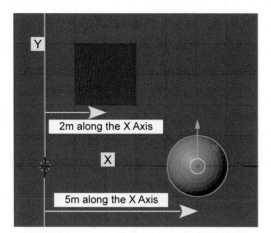

2m along the X Axis

X

5m along the X Axis

Figure 7.9

As the Sphere is Translated along the X Axis the Sphere is Constrained such that it follows. The Translation only occurs when the Sphere is translated between 0m and 5m on the X Axis and the Cube only moves between 0m and 2m.

By configuring the Map From and Map To values in the Constraint Properties the movement of one Object is used to affect the movement of another.

Consider the following example.

Figure 7.10

With the initial arrangement as shown in Figure 7.7 and with values revised in the **Map From** and **Map To** Tab as shown in Figure 7.10, when the Target Sphere is Translated between 0m and 5m along the X Axis the Source Cube moves in a negative direction towards the X Axis of the Scene.

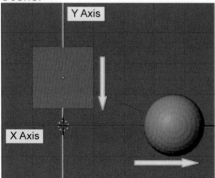

Y Axis

X Axis

When the Sphere is Translated the Cube moves towards the X Axis of the Scene.

Figure 7.11

Note: Negative Max value (-2).

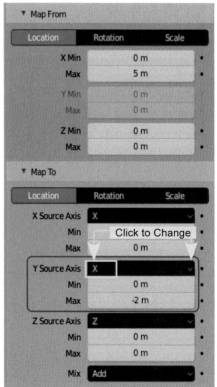

The **Map From**, Location values are retained per the previous example but **Note: the Map To, Location values are changed**. In particular **Note:** the **Y Source Axis Y is changed to X (Min 0m and Max -2m)**.

To apply a logical thought process to the procedure think of the Map From values controlling the **Map To** values.

Figure 7.12

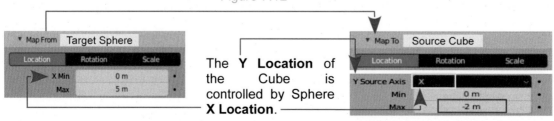

▼ Map From Target Sphere

Location	Rotation	Scale
X Min	0 m	
Max	5 m	

The **Y Location** of the Cube is controlled by Sphere **X Location**.

▼ Map To Source Cube

Location	Rotation	Scale
Y Source Axis	X	
Min	0 m	
Max	-2 m	

Location, Rotation or Scale Min – Max range values have to be entered in a Map From Axis channel and a Map To Axis channel, for a constraint to take effect.

As seen in Figure 7.12 the Range: Min 0 – Max 5m is entered in the Map From, Location channel. In the Map To the Range: Min 0m – Max **-2m** is entered in the Y Source Axis channel and, importantly, the **Y Source Axis** is set to be controlled by the **X Location channel**.

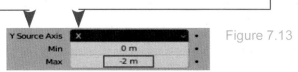

Figure 7.13

To reinforce the concept of the procedure, the **Translation** of the Sphere will control the **Rotation** of the Cube.

Figure 7.14

Important: Figure 7.15 shows the Objects in Top Orthographic View, therefore, the Z Axis of the Scene is normal to the computer Screen. The Axis of Rotation of the Cube is about the Z Axis.

The **Target Object** is the **Sphere**.

The Map From (Target Sphere) Location Range is set for the Y Axis (Min 0m – Max 3m) which means that the Sphere must be Translated on the Y Axis of the View.

The Map To (Source Cube) Range is set for Rotation about the Z Axis (Z Source Axis) being controlled by the values set in the Map From Y Axis Range.

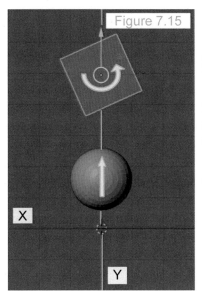

Figure 7.15

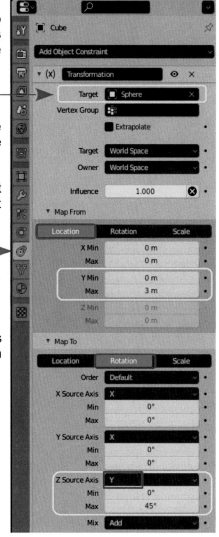

Properties Editor

Object Constraint Properties

Rotation: 0° to 45°

Note: The use of Plus and Minus Values when setting Range limits.

Translation: 0m to 3m

7.6 Tracking Constraints

- **Clamp To:** Clamps or locks the position of the Object to a target curve. Figure 7.16

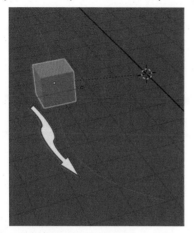 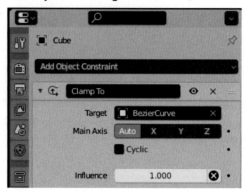

G Key, drag the Mouse moves the Cube along the Curve.

- **Damped Track:** Constrains one local axis of the Object to always point towards the target Object. Figure 7.17

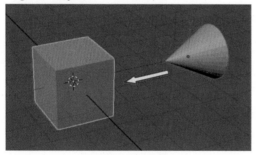 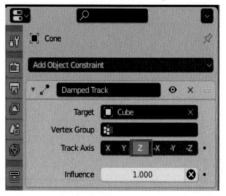

The Local Z Axis of the Cone points to the Cube.

- **Locked Track:** Similar to a Damped Track Constraint with more axis control.

- **Stretch To:** Stretches the Object towards the Target Object or compresses the Object away from the Target Object.

- **Track To:** As seen in the introduction to Constraints the Track To Constraint causes the Object to always point towards the Target Object no matter where either the Object or the Target is positioned (Figure 7.4 Camera points to the Cube).

7.7 Relationship Constraints

- **Action:** See Section 7.8.
- **Child Of:** Causes the Object to follow the Object designated as it's Parent
- **Floor:** Allows the Target Object to obstruct the movement of the Object. For example, a Sphere animated to descend in a Scene will not pass through a Plane that has been set as a Target Object.
- **Follow Path:** Causes the Object to be animated to follow a Curve Path nominated as the Target. This Constraint also has the feature to follow the Curve, which means that the Object will rotate and bank as it follows the Curve. This constraint can also be employed to duplicate Objects along a Curve Path.
- **Pivot:** Causes the Object to leapfrog to the opposite side of the Target Object along an axis between the Object and the Target Center. The location can be offset on either side of the axis by inserting offset values.
- **Shrinkwrap:** Locks an Object to the surface of another mesh Object that is set as the Target.

7.8 The Action Constraint

Figure 7.18

The **Action Constraint** allows you to control the action of one Object by manipulating the action of another. An action may be the Translation, Rotation, or Scale of an Object. To demonstrate, the **Rotation of a Sphere Object will control the Translation of a Cube.**

The location of the UV Sphere in the Scene is not important.

Animate the Cube to move from minus three Blender units to plus three units on the X Axis in 100 Frames (see Chapter 20 Volume 1 for Animation). Place the animation at Frame 1.

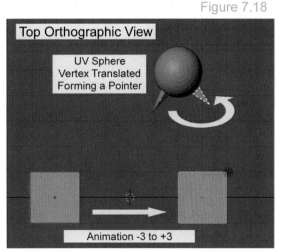

Select the **Cube** then in the **Properties Editor, Constraints Properties,** Add **Relationship Constraint** type **Action**. In the Constraint panel set the values as shown in Figure 7.9 (over).

Note: On entering the **Action** as; **CubeAction** in the **Action Tab** the Cube jumps from position minus three to minus six. When the Animation is played the Cube moves from minis six to the center of the Scene. Rotating the Sphere about the Z Axis will Translate the Cube

The Z Rotation of the Target (UV Sphere) controls the Action of the Cube within the limits of the Animation (the movement set in 100 Frames).

The Z Rotation (Target Range) is limited to: 0 to 90° (see Figure 7.19 over).

The Action Range is between Frame 1 and frame 100 of the animation. **Note:** When the Action Constraint is applied the Cube Animation changes to minus 6 to 0 in the 3D Viewport Editor?

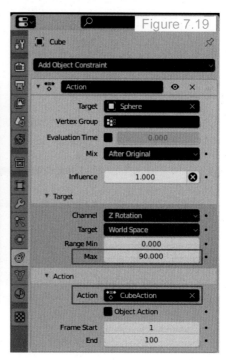

Figure 7.19

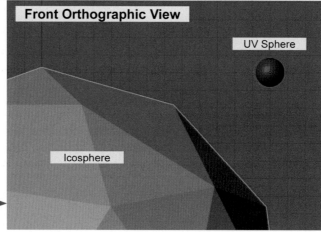

Figure 7.20

Sphere Rotated 90°

Movement Minus 6 to 0

Cube Animation

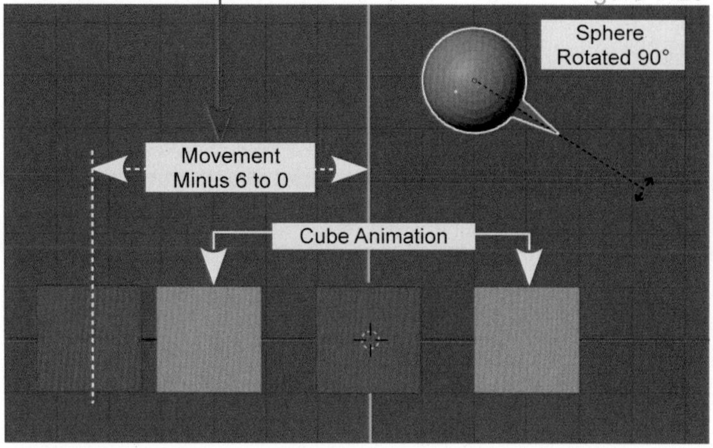

You may set an Animation to rotate the UV Sphere in which case when the Cube is Translated (Moved) the Sphere Rotates.

7.9 The Shrinkwrap Constraint

The **Shrinkwrap Constraint** could be more aptly named the **Mesh Surface Lock** since the constraint locks an Object to the surface of another mesh Object that is set as the **Target**.

Do not confuse this constraint with the **Shrinkwrap Modifier**. To demonstrate how the constraint operates; In the default Blender Scene, in Front Orthographic view, add a **UV Sphere** and an **Icosphere.** Scale the **UV Sphere** way down, and arrange the objects as shown in Figure 7.21.

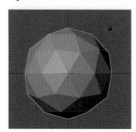

Figure 7.21

Zoom in on the View to see a close up of the UV Sphere and the surface of the Icosphere

Figure 7.22

Front Orthographic View

UV Sphere

Icosphere

Select the **UV Sphere** and in the **Properties Editor, Object Constraints Properties**, add a **Shrinkwrap Constraint** (Figure 7.23).

Figure 7.23

In the **Shrinkwrap Constraint panel**, click in the **Target selection bar** and select **Icosphere** as the Target (Figure 7.23).

In the default Shrinkwrap panel make note **that the Mode** is **Nearest Surface Point**.

Figure 7.24

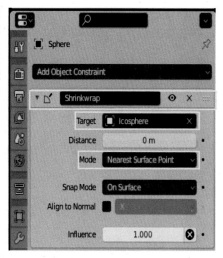

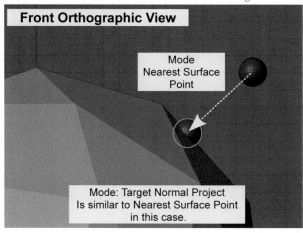

Figure 7.25

Nearest Surface Point

Project

Nearest Vertex

Target Normal Project

Shrinkwrap Type

With the **Mode: Nearest Surface Point** and the **Target** set as **Icosphere** the UV Sphere relocates to the surface of the Icosphere at the nearest point to the original position of the UV Sphere (Figure 7.24). **Mode: Nearest Surface Point** is one of four options (Figure 7.25).

Mode: Project. Figure 7.26   Figure 7.27

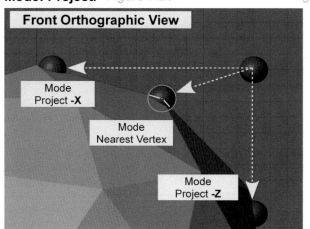

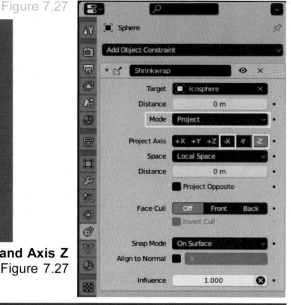

With **Mode: Project** selected, **Axis X, Axis Y, and Axis Z** buttons are present in the **Constraints panel** (Figure 7.27 **Note** there are positive and negative values).

Note: In the Shrinkwrap Constraint Properties, the **Mode is: Project** and **Space is: Local Space**

Local Space means that the **Projection** is determined by the **Local Axis** of the selected Object.

Figure 7.28   Figure 7.29

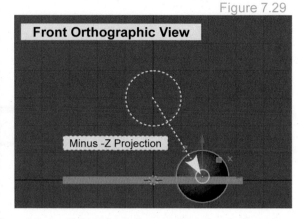

Figures 7.28 shows the difference between the Local Axis of the UV Sphere when the Sphere is Rotated. Since the Local Minus -Z Axis is set as the Project Axis in the Constraint Properties the Sphere is projected to the nearest point on the Target Projection Plane along its **Minus Z Axis**.

Pressing the **R Key** and Rotating the Sphere alters the direction of the Minus Z Axis causing the Sphere to be moved along the surface of the Target Projection Plane. (Figure 7.30).

Figure 7.30

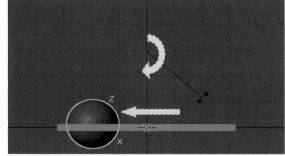

7.10 Follow Path – Extrude/Bevel

The **Follow Path Constraint** causes an Object to follow a **Curve Path** set as the **Target when the Object is Animated to move**. The constraint incorporates a **Follow Curve** setting which make the Object rotate and bank as it moves along the Path in the Animation. This has been demonstrated in Chapter 20 - Volume 1 **Animation Follow Path**.

The **Follow Path Constraint** may also be used to **Generate** shapes by extruding a profile along the length of a Curve Path. Consider that a three dimensional regular shape is defined by its cross section profile and the curvature of its length.

Review Chapter 5 and in particular Modeling from a Curve where a Bezier Curve was manipulated to generate a Mesh Object. The Mesh Object created was a regular shape. The following procedure will demonstrate how **irregular shapes** may be created by generating a profile along a Curve Path.

The Cross Section Profile and Length

Figure 7.31 shows a Cross Section Profile and a Length Curve

Figure 7.31

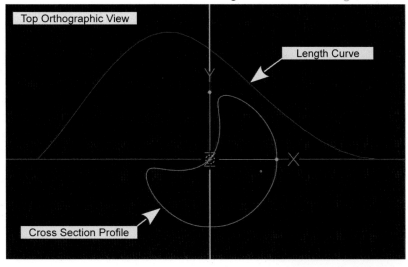

The Cross Section Profile is a **Nurbs Circle** reshaped in Edit Mode and the Length Curve is a **Bezier Curve**, Scaled up and reshaped in Edit Mode. (see Chapter 5). The Length Curve (Bezier Curve) will be the centerline of the Extrusion.

Figure 7.32

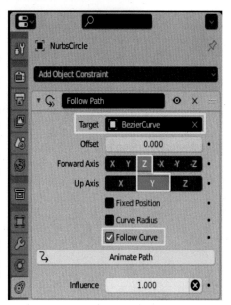

To Extrude the Cross Section along the Length Curve, the Cross Section has to be orientated and positioned at the start of the Length Curve. Note: Figure 7.31 shows the 3D Viewport Editor in Top Orthographic View, therefore, the Local Axis of the Profile coincides with the Global XY Axis of the Scene.

To orientate and position the Cross Section for Extrusion, select the Cross Section (Nurbs Circle – Modified) and in the **Properties Editor, Object Constraint Properties** add a **Follow Path Constraint** (Figure 7.32). Enter **Target** as **BezierCurve**.The Cross Section relocates to the start of the Bezier Curve (Figure 7.33).

Figure 7.33

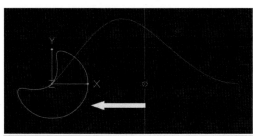

In the Follow Path Constraint the default Forward Axis is Y (highlighted blue) and the Up Axis is Z. This corresponds to the Local Axis of the Cross Section. To Extrude the Cross Section along the Length Curve the Cross Section is required to be at right angles to the Length Curve.

115

To Rotate the Profile, in the Properties Editor, Follow Path Constraint, change the Forward Axis to **Z** and the Up Axis to **Y. No change occurs** in the orientation until you check **Follow Curve** in the Constraint panel.

Figure 7.34

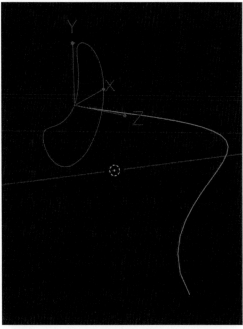

With **Follow Curve** checked you will see the Profile at the end of the Curve Path with its Local Axis; Y Up and Z Forward pointing approximately in line with the Curve Path (Figure 7.34).

Extruding the Profile along the Curve to generate the 3D Shape is an anomaly since the operation is a Bevel operation carried out in the **Bezier Curve's Object Data Properties** in the **Properties Editor.**

Object Data Properties

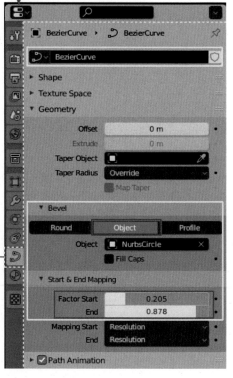

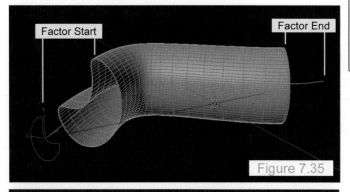

Factor Start

Factor End

Figure 7.35

Rendered Camera View

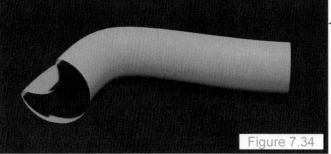

Figure 7.34

Scale the Nurbs Circle down before applying the Bevel to the Bezier Curve.

Note: The difference in orientation between the Nurbs Circle Profile and the profile of the final Object.

8

Shape Keys & Action Editors

The **Shape Key** and **Action Editors** provide a method of quickly controlling the shape of an Object or the pose of a Character. This is accomplished by inserting **Keyframes** in an Animation Timeline.

Armature Control Handles allow the posing of the character as a whole but when detail is animated, such as facial expression or finger movement, a more refined control is desirable. If you think about an Object or a character model and all the Vertices contained in its mesh surface you will realise the impossibility of individually manipulating Vertices between the Frames of an Animation.

The **Shape Key** and **Action Editor** allow you to set up **Slider Controls** for manipulating the Mesh shape or posing the Character or Model.

The **Shape Key Editor** controls the manipulation and animation of Vertices

The **Action Editor** allows you to set up an animation of an Object's movement and scale.

8.1 Shape Key Editor

The **Shape Key Editor** allows you to control the manipulation of Vertices or Vertex Groups.

The **Shapes Key Editor** is located in the **Dope Sheet Editor Header**.

To demonstrate, start with the default Blender Scene, delete the Cube, and add a simple **Plane Object** which contains four Vertices. Place the Scene in **Top Orthographic View** and zoom in.

Below the 3D Viewport Editor is the **Timeline Editor**. Change the Timeline to the **Dope Sheet Editor**.

In the Dope Sheet Editor, click on the drop down in the Header where you see **Dope Sheet** and select **Shape Key Editor**.

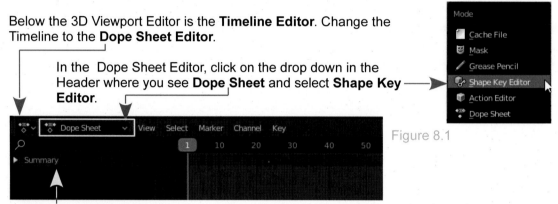

Figure 8.1

Summary only displays if you change from the Shape Key Editor back to the Dope Sheet.

With the **Shapes Key Editor** selected, the Editor has become a simple Animation Timeline (Figure 8.2) with **Frame** numbers in the horizontal bar along the top of the Editor. There is also a vertical blue line in the Editor which is the **Timeline Cursor**.

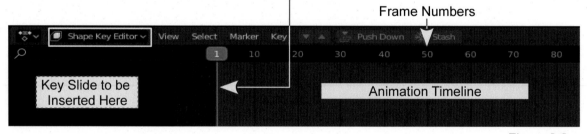

Figure 8.2

Key Sliders will be added in the **Shape Key Editor** which will allow you to control the shape of an Object in the 3D Viewport Editor. The movement of the Object's Vertices will be set within minimum and maximum limits. By moving the Vertices, via the Key Sliders, to different positions within the limits, at different Frames of the Animation Timeline you create an animation of the change in shape of the Object.

The Key Sliders to be created are applicable only to the selected Object. The first step in the process is to enter a **Basis Key** in the **Properties Editor, Object data Properties, Shape keys Tab**.

The **Basis Key** is a **Master Key** (Datablock) for subsequent Keys, for the selected Object.

Add a Basis Key

Figure 8.3 **Properties Editor**

Select the Plane in the 3D Viewport Editor. In the **Properties Editor, Object Data Properties, Shape Keys Tab** click on the **Plus sign** (Figure 8.3).

The Tab expands, showing a **Basis Key** inserted.

Dope Sheet Summary displays in the **Shape Key Editor.**

Figure 8.4

Object Data Properties →

Add a Key Slider

Figure 8.5

In the **Properties Editor, Shape Keys Tab** click on the plus sign again and **Key 1** will be added.——————

In the **Dope Sheet Summary, Key 1** is displayed.

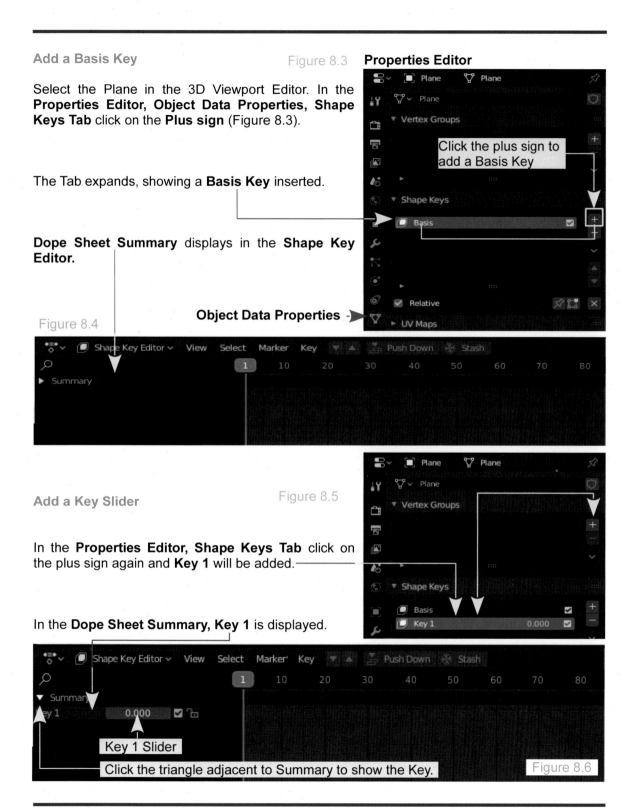

8.2 Set Limits of Movement   Figure 8.7

With a Key Slider in place you set limits for what is to be controlled.

With the Mouse Cursor in the 3D Viewport Editor, in Top Orthographic View, **Tab to Edit Mode**. Deselect the Vertices (LMB Click in the Viewport). Select a single Vertex and drag it (press the G Key and drag the Mouse) to where you want it to move to (maximum movement Limit - Figure 8.7). Tab back to **Object Mode.** The Vertex reverts to its original position. Moving the vertex in Edit Mode has **set the limits** for the movement.

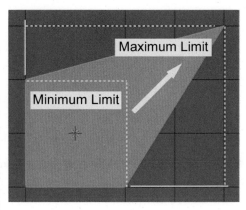

With the 3D Viewport Editor In Object Mode drag the **Key 1 Slider** in the Dope Sheet, Shape Key Editor all the way to the right (0.000 – 1.000 Figure 8.8) then return to 0.000. The Plane changes shape in the 3D Viewport Editor.

Figure 8.8

8.3 Inserting Keyframes

Dragging the slider in the **Shape Key Editor** and returning it to 0.000 automatically sets a **Keyframe** in the **Timeline**. The Keyframe is placed at the location of the Timeline Cursor (the blue line at Frame 1) and displays as little orange diamonds (Figure 8.8). The Keyframes display in the Shape Key Editor and in the Timeline Editor.

> **Note:** Dragging the slider moves the selected Vertex only within the limits that were set. The slider value is from 0.000 to 1.000, that is from the initial position to the maximum limit of the movement.

Inserting a Second Keyframe

To insert a second Keyframe move the blue line **Cursor** in the **Shapes Key Editor** to another Frame (Frame 50). Move **Key 1 Slider** until the Vertex in the 3D Viewport Editor is where you want it (0.759). Release the mouse button (Figure 8.8). Leave the Slider at the chosen value of the second Keyframe. Return the blue line Cursor to Frame 1.

When you drag the blue line Cursor, the shape of the Plane in the 3D window changes with the corner (Vertex) moving from its initial rest position to where you positioned it at Frame 50.

Maybe you didn't get the position of the Vertex exactly where you intended. Dragging the Key Slider is a bit touchy when you want an exact location.

Deleting a Keyframe

Figure 8.9

To delete a Keyframe and start over, place the blue Cursor in the Shape Key Editor at the Frame in the Timeline where you want to remove Keyframes. **RMB click on Value bar** (Figure 8.9) in the **Properties Editor, Object Data Properties, Shape Keys Tab** and select **Delete Keyframe**.

Note: The relative Value Bar replicates the Key 1 Slider.

Add a New Keyframe

You may add a new Keyframe by moving the Key 1 slider again. If you want an exact value double click the slider and type in a value.

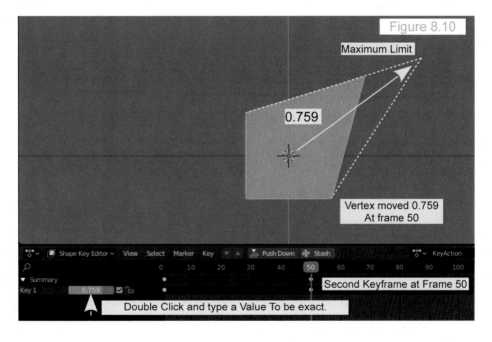

After placing a Keyframe you do not have to return the Timeline Cursor to frame 1. Move it to another Frame. Move the Key 1 Slider. Another Keyframe is added. Repeat the process for multiple Keyframes (Figure 8.11).

Figure 8.11

8.4 The Animation

To this point Keyframes have been added in the **Shape Key Editor Timeline**. You may scrub the Timeline (drag the blue line Cursor) to see the shape change in the 3D Viewport Editor. To see an animation play open the **Timeline Editor** and press the **Play** button (Figure 8.12).

Figure 8.12

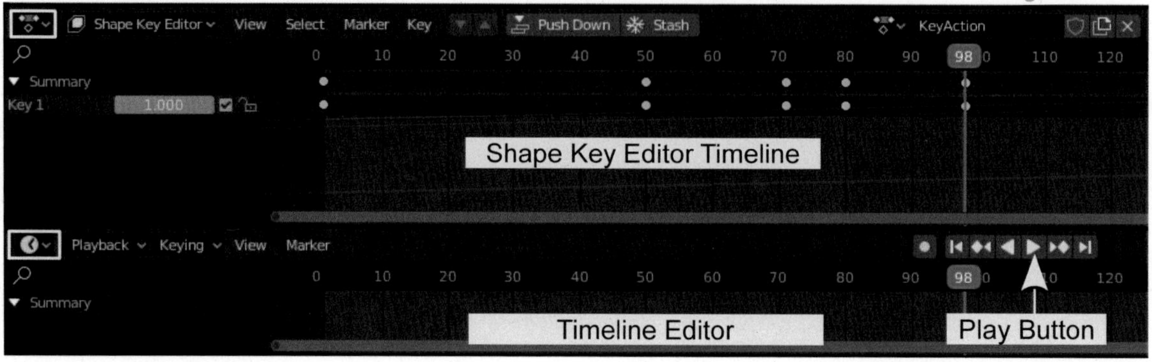

8.5 Additional Keys

Additional **Keys** are added to the Dope Sheet Summary for Animating other parts of the Mesh (other Vertices).

Move the cursor in the Shapes Key Editor Timeline to Frame 1. In the Properties Editor, Object Data Properties, Shape Key Tab, click on the plus sign again to add Key 2 (Figure 8.13). In the 3D Viewport Editor, Tab to Edit Mode, select a different Vertex, and move it somewhere to set the limit of movement. Tab back to Object Mode and you'll see that Key 2 has been added to the Dope Sheet Summary (Figure 8.13). Repeat the Keyframing process using Key 2 for the new Vertex.

Figure 8.13

Drag the Slider to see the Limit of Movement for the new Vertices.

After inserting Keyframes for the new Vertex controlled by Key 2, scrubbing the Timeline Editor Cursor or playing the Animation will show both Vertices moving as the animation plays.

8.6 Action Editor

Click to display the Menu

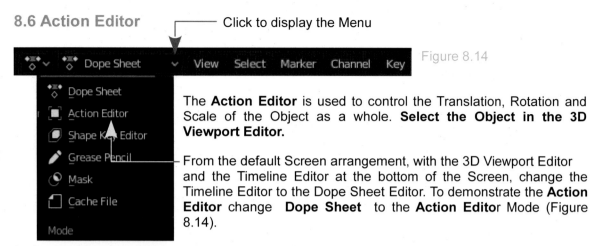

Figure 8.14

The **Action Editor** is used to control the Translation, Rotation and Scale of the Object as a whole. **Select the Object in the 3D Viewport Editor.**

From the default Screen arrangement, with the 3D Viewport Editor and the Timeline Editor at the bottom of the Screen, change the Timeline Editor to the Dope Sheet Editor. To demonstrate the **Action Editor** change **Dope Sheet** to the **Action Edito**r Mode (Figure 8.14).

In the **3D Viewport Editor** select the default **Cube**. With the Mouse Cursor in the 3D Viewport Editor press the **I Key** and select **Location, Rotation & Scale**. This inserts a **Keyframe at Frame 1** and enters an **Object Transforms Summary** in the Action Editor. Click on the triangle preceding **Object Transforms** to display the Keyframe entries for **X,Y and Z, Location Rotation and Scale** (Figure 8.15).

Figure 8.15

In the **Action Editor Header**, click on **View** and check **Show Sliders**; sliders display for each Keyframe component (Figure 8.16).

Figure 8.16

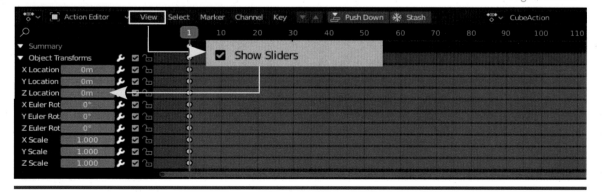

By repositioning the Cursor (blue line) in the Action Editor to a new Frame and moving the Sliders, you manipulate the Cube in the 3D Viewport Editor (Figure 8.17). After moving the Slider, **RMB click** on the new value and select **Replace Keyframe**. When the Cursor is positioned at a different Frame and slider values are changed, Keyframes are inserted, which produces an Animation.

Figure 8.17

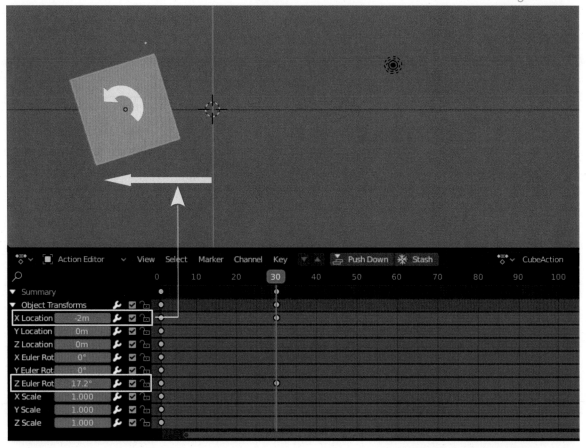

8.7 Shape Keys and Action Editor in Practice

The forgoing examples show you the fundamentals of the tools but they are not very exciting and you could be left wondering what to do with them in some practical application. To expand on the topics perform the following exercise:

In a new Blender Scene delete the Cube and add a Monkey Object. Place the Scene in Front Orthographic view and zoom in to fill the 3D Viewport Editor with Suzanne's head. Tab to Edit Mode and select the Vertices in the face as shown in Figure 8.18.

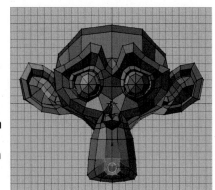

Figure 8.18

Change the Timeline Editor to the **Dope Sheet Editor** then to the **Shape Key Editor Mode**. In the **3D Viewport Editor** position Monkey to have the mouth visible (Figure 8.18 ,8.19).

Tab to Object Mode.

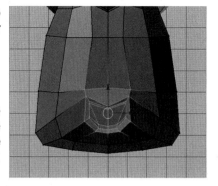
Figure 8.19

In the **Properties Editor, Object Data Properties, Shape Key Tab** click on the plus sign to add a **Basis Key**. In the **Action Editor Header** click **New** to enter a **Summary** in the Dope Sheet. Click the plus sign again in the Properties Editor, Object Data Properties Shape Keys Tab to insert **Key 1**.

You are about to make Suzanne laugh. Suzanne's lips will move but you will have to use your imagination as far as sound is concerned.

In the **3D Viewport Editor** change to **Right Orthographic View** . Tab to **Edit Mode**. Use the widget and move the selected Vertices to the left making Suzanne's lips protrude slightly (Figure 8.20). Change to **Front Orthographic View** . Scale the selected Vertices up on the Z Axis and a little bit on the X Axis (Figure 8.21). Using the widget move the Vertices up. **Tab to Object Mode**. The Vertices revert to their original location.

Figure 8.20

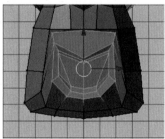

Figure 8.21

In performing the scaling and location operations you have set the limits of movement for **Key 1** for each of the Vertices that were selected.

Change the Dope Sheet Action Editor to Shape Key Editor.   In the Header click **View** and check **Show Sliders**.

Expand the Summary and Move the Key 1 Slider to see Suzanne's mouth move. Remember, moving the Slider inserts a Keyframe at the Frame number in the Animation Timeline where the Timeline <u>Cursor is positioned (Frame 1)</u> (Figure 8.22).

Figure 8.22   Figure 8.23

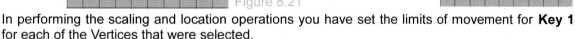

If you don't want Suzanne to start laughing at the start of the animation move the cursor down the track in the Timeline before moving the Slider (Frame 30 – Figure 8.23).

Remember; by default, Blender has a 250 Frame animation set in the Timeline. If you place the Shape Key Editor Cursor beyond this it will have no effect unless you change the End Frame value in the Timeline Editor Header.

Place a series of Keyframes in the animation. Move the Cursor to Frame 40. Move the Key slider leaving it in position. This inserts a Keyframe at frame 40. Move the Cursor to frame 50. Move the slider. Repeat the operation as many times as you like (Figure 8.24).

In the Timeline Editor, go back to Frame 1 and play the animation. Monkey's mouth moves as the animation plays.

Figure 8.24

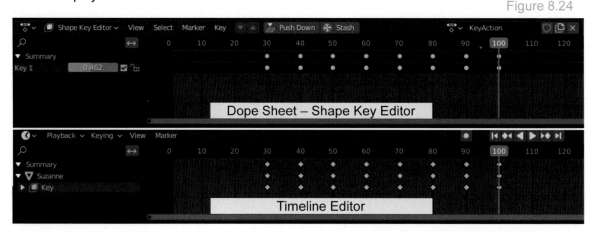

To create more action in the Animation have Suzanne turn her head as she laughs.

Figure 8.25

Zoom out on the 3D Viewport Editor. Change to User Perspective View. In the Action Editor Header click the New button. With the Timeline Cursor at Frame 1, Press I Key and select Location, Rotation & Scale to place action Keyframes (Figure 8.25).

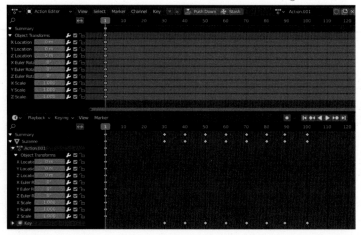

Move the Cursor to Frame 100 to coincide with the end of the **Shape Key** animation and move the **Z Euler Rotation slider to 45 degrees** (Rotation in Blender is measured in Euler units).

Place the 3D Viewport Editor in Camera View and play the animation. Suzanne's mouth moves while turning to face the Camera.

Particle Systems

Particle Systems are used to simulate effects like fire, dust, clouds and smoke and for creating hair, fur, grass and other strand based Objects. When a Particle System is applied to an Object it causes the Object to generate and emit Particles which may be configured to display in a multitude of ways creating static and animated patterns or as Models of Characters. For example, an army of solders or a swarm of insects.

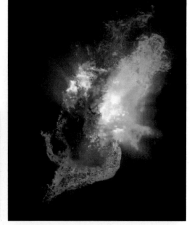

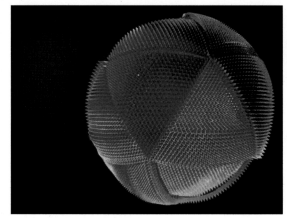

The preceding examples are screen captures from a YouTube video created by:

 Iago Mota   https://www.youtube.com/watch?v=UHmRP3iLztU

In Blender, **Particles** appear as small spheres on the computer screen, being emitted from an Object. To Emit Particles from an Object a **Particle System** is added to the Object then an animation sequence is run.

Adding a Particle System to an Object creates a system with default settings which is ready to run by itself. To create Particle effects you modify the settings.

Particles are simply points on the computer Screen which can be configured to display in different ways. **The Particles (points) do not render when the Scene is Rendered**. The Particles are reconfigured to display as other Objects in the Scene which will Render.

A single Particle being emitted from the Face of the Cube Object   Figure 9.1

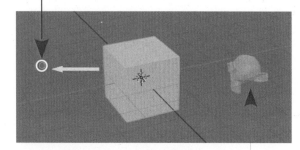

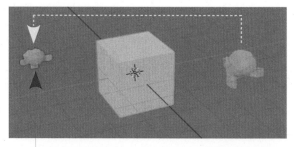

Monkey Object in the Scene   The Particle displaying as the Monkey

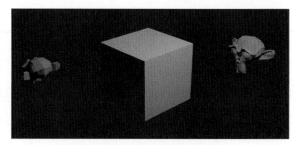

Render of Camera View
Before reconfiguring the Particle
To display as the Monkey

Rendered of Camera View
After configuring the Particle
To display as the Monkey

Usually a Particle System will be used to generate more than one Particle. In fact, it is usual to create thousands of Particles and possibly from multiple Objects in a Scene.

To see how this is accomplished follow a few simple instructions and run a Particle System.

9.1 The Default Particle System

To set up a default **Particle System** open a new Scene in Blender. Delete the default Cube Object and add a **UV Sphere**.

Particles are emitted from the Vertices, the Faces or from the Volume of a mesh. Using a UV Sphere provides a reasonable number of Vertices and Faces from which to emit the Particles. Leave the default values for the Sphere as they appear in the Properties Editor. With the UV Sphere selected, go to the **Properties Editor, Particles Properties**. Click on the **plus sign** to add a **Particle System** (Figure 9.2).

The **Particles Properties** open displaying the **Tabs** (panels)   that control the system. Blender has automatically created a default Particle System for the UV Sphere (Figure 9.3).

Figure 9.2

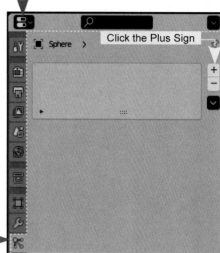

Particle Properties ⟶

Figure 9.3

Note the default **Type: Emitter** under **Particle Settings.**

The alternative system is **Hair**. Type: Hair is a unique system which will be discussed later in this chapter.

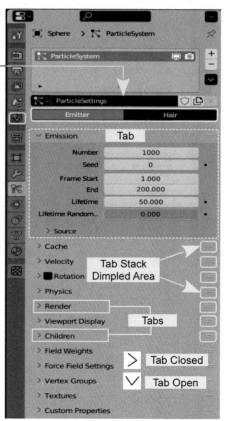

Note:
When a Particle System is created it is unique to the selected Object in the 3D Viewport Editor.

The arrangement of the **Tabs** (see Emission Tab panel) in the **Properties Editor** is purely a matter of convenience. There is no order of priority. The Properties Editor is arranged with the Tabs in a vertical stack at the LHS of the panel. The Tabs (panels) may be moved up or down by clicking and dragging the dimpled area in the upper RH corner of each Tab.

Particles only display in the 3D Viewport Editor when an animation sequence is run by activating Play in the Timeline Editor or scrubbing (dragging) the Timeline cursor (vertical blue line) to a Frame in the animation.

The default Particles display as small white spheres.

The default **Particles** display as small **Spheres**.

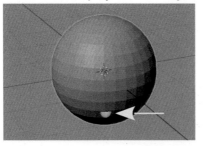

Figure 9.4

Figure 9.5

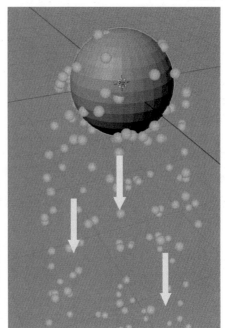

To see the default **Particle System** in action, press the **Play button** in the **Timeline Editor** to run an animation sequence showing Particles being generated (Figure 9.5).

Note: The **Timeline Editor** is displayed across the bottom of the Screen (Figure 9.6). The blue line (Timeline Cursor) moves as the animation plays. With the Emitter Object selected (the UV Sphere), the animation will play showing Particles as small white spheres being emitted and falling towards the bottom of the Screen (Figure 9.5).

Timeline Editor   Figure 9.6   Play Button

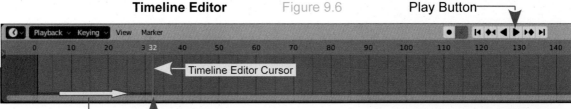

Timeline Editor Cursor

Frame 32

Animation Frames Generated (red line)

Figure 9.7

The animation plays for 250 frames then repeats. Press **Esc** to stop the animation. Advance the animation to Frame 32 by pressing the right arrows on the Keyboard (**with the Mouse Cursor in the Timeline Editor**) or by clicking RMB, holding and dragging the blue line Cursor in the Timeline Editor or by RMB clicking on frame 32 in the Timeline Editor. The Particles will be displayed as they occur at Frame 32.

The example has demonstrated a simple Particle System being applied. The Particles emitted from the UV Sphere cascade down; this occurred since there is a **gravitational effect** applied (see the **Scene Properties** in the Properties Editor).

In the **Properties Editor, Scene Properties, Gravity Tab,** click on the tick next to **Gravity** (removes the tick) to remove the gravitational effect (Figure 9.7).

Set the animation in the Timeline Editor back to Frame 1 and replay the animation. Replaying the animation shows Particles Emitted from the UV Sphere disperse in all directions away from the Sphere (Figure 9.8).

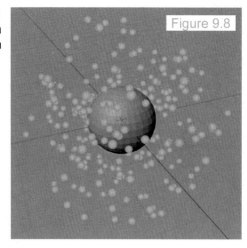

Figure 9.8

Figure 9.9

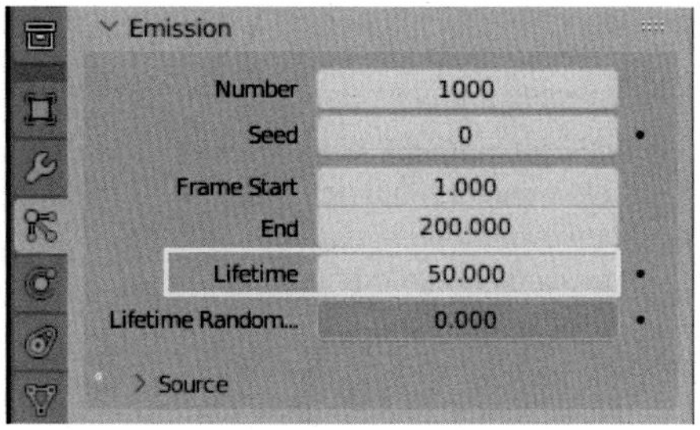

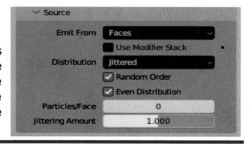

Note: The Particles move for a certain time (Lifetime) and disappear before the end of the animation. The time that the Particles display is set in the **Emission Tab** (Figure 9.9).

9.2 The Emissions Tab (Figure 9.9)

Number: The total number of Particles to be Emitted over the length of the animation.

Seed: Sets a randomized **Emission** variation.

Frame Start: The Frame number in the animation to start emitting.

End: The Frame number to stop Emitting Particles.

Lifetime: The number of Frames in the animation that Particles, **which have been Emitted**, will display. The default number of Frames is 50.

Lifetime Randomness: Gives **Lifetime** a random variation.

With the default settings, 1000 Particles will be emitted over the length of the animation. The default animation length is 250 Frames (see the Timeline Editor). The Particles will begin Emitting at Frame 1 and end at Frame 200. The Particles display for a Lifetime of 50 Frames, therefore, the last Particle to be emitted (at Frame 200) displays for 50 frames, that is, to the end of the animation.

9.3 The Emission Source Tab

Figure 9.10

Emit From: Faces. The Particles Emit from the Faces of the Object's **Mesh**. The alternatives are from the **Vertices** or from **Volume** (the body of the mesh - See Section 9.7). The remainder of the settings in the Source Tab govern the order in which Particles are emitted (Figure 9.10).

9.4 The Cache Tab

Figure 9.11

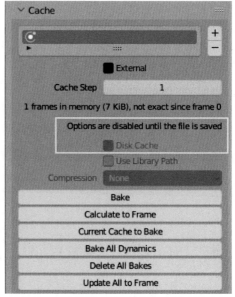

When a Particle System is played for the first time in the default Blender Scene the computer calculates the information required to display each Frame in the simulation (animation) and stores it in RAM (memory). When the simulation is played a second time the computer recalculates the information with any changes made to the settings and again stores the information in RAM. If the Blender file is closed without being saved the information is lost.

With a complicated Particle Simulation, writing data to RAM can use a considerable amount of memory which in turn can influence the performance of the computer. It is, therefore, advisable to save the Blender file as early as possible. With the file saved you have the option to save the simulation to a Cache which frees up memory.

Note the statement in the Cache Tab: Options are disabled until the file is saved. This is basically saying, you can't save to the Cache until you have saved the Blender file. With the file saved check **Disk Cache** which will save the data to the Cache using the Library (Lib) Path.

Playing the simulation with **Disk Cache** checked creates a **blendcache_Cache** file and places it in the same directory as the **.blend file**. When Disk Cache is checked after saving the file you will see a red line at the bottom of the Timeline Editor indicating the data that has been saved. Playing the simulation with the default settings creates a solid line since data is recorded for each Frame of the default 250 Frames. In the directory where the Blender file is saved you will find the **blendcache_Cache folder** containing 250 BPHYS files.

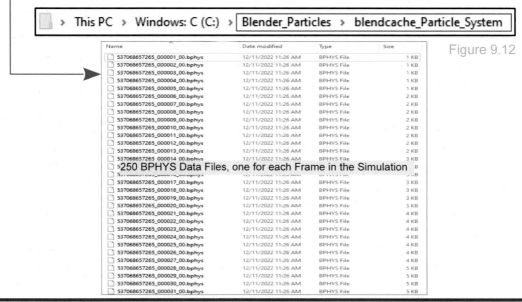

Figure 9.12

With the default simulation (250 Frames) there are 250 BPHYS Files. The longer the simulation the more files are created. To save space in the Cache, when you have a lengthy simulation, you may elect to only save data for some of the Frames. To do this increase the Cache Steps value. Increasing the value to 10 means every tenth frame is recorded, therefore, the number of BPHYS files in the Cache for the default 250 frame simulation would be 26 (25 divisions – Frame at each end). Increasing the Cache Steps saves space on the Hard Drive at the expense of a lesser quality in the simulation.

9.5 The Velocity Tab

Figure 9.13

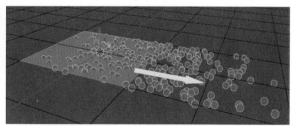

The settings in the **Velocity Tab** control the direction and speed of the Particle Emission (Figure 9.13).

Normal: Gives the Particles an initial Velocity normal (at right angles) to the point of origin.

Figure 9.14

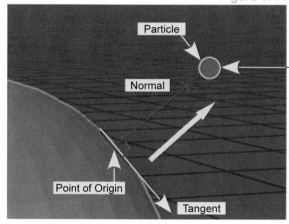

The Particle is being emitted from the point of origin on the Face, **Normal to the Face** (at right angles to the Face).

Tangent: Parallel to the Face.

Tangent Phase and Object Alignment: Both Control the Emission direction between Normal and Tangent.

Tangent: 1m/s – Tangent Phase +0.5

Figure 9.15

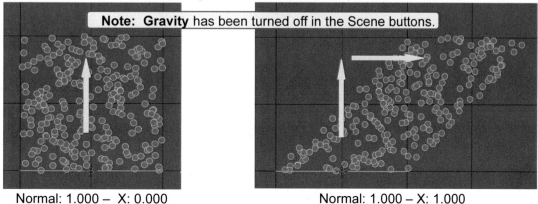

Note: Gravity has been turned off in the Scene buttons.

Normal: 1.000 – X: 0.000   Normal: 1.000 – X: 1.000

Understanding Tangent Phase

To assist in understanding **Tangent Phase** study the following diagrams (Figure 9.16, 9.17)

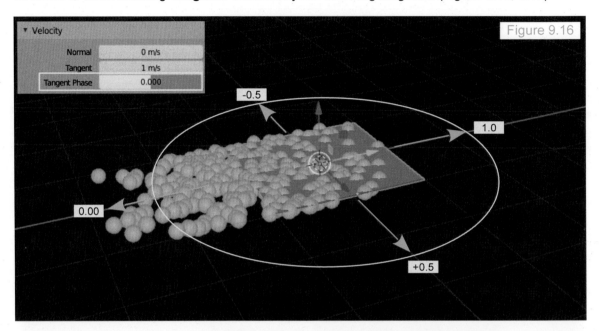

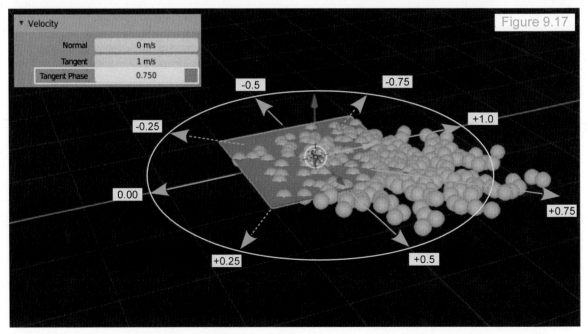

By adjusting the **Tangent Phase** values in the Properties Editor, Particle Properties the direction of Particle Emission is controlled. Pay attention to positive and negative value.

Emit From Vertices

Figure 9.18

Figure 9.14 shows a Particle being emitted from the single Face of the Plane Object. By changing Face to **Vertices** in the **Source Tab**, with the default values (Normal: 1.000 – X: 0.000) the Particles are emitted from the four **Vertices** of the Plane, normal to the face of the Plane (Figure 9.18).

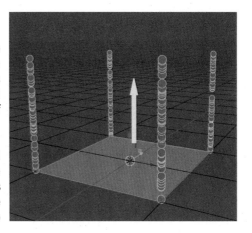

At this point you have just enough information to control the Emission of Particles but they are just Particles, little white spheres, which do not Render. The spheres represent positions on the computer Screen for the display of other Objects with the objective being, to create visual displays.

9.6 Particle Display

Figure 9.19

A Particle will display as an Object which has been added to a Scene.

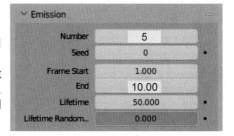

To demonstrate; have a Plain Object and a Monkey Object in a Scene. Scale the Monkey way down and park it off to one side (Figure 9.20).

Have the Plane selected in the 3D Viewport Editor and apply a Particle System. **Turn off Gravity in the Scene buttons.** Figure 9.21

In the **Emission Tab** (Figure 9.19) in the Particles buttons for the Plane decrease the Number to 5 (Emit 5 Particles only) and change the End value to 10 (the 5 Particles will be Emitted in 10 Frames).

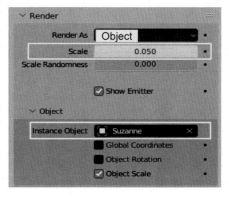

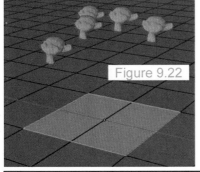

In the **Render Tab** (Figure 9.21) change **Render As** to Object. Selecting Object introduces an Object Tab. Click where you see **Instance Object** and select **Suzanne** (Monkey).

Play the animation in the Timeline Editor (you may stop at Frame 50 since the Particles will only display for 50 Frames). Position the Timeline Cursor at Frame 45 then zoom in on the Plane. If you look closely you will see five tiny Monkeys sitting above the Plane. In the **Render Tab** increase the **Scale**.

9.7 Particle Emission Options

The options for Particle Emission have been briefly mentioned when discussing the Source Tab in 9.3 and Emission from Vertices demonstrated in 9.5 - Figure 9.17. To clarify the options look at the default Cube Object in the default 3D Viewport Editor. Have the Cube displayed in **Wireframe Display Mode**. Click the button in the Header (upper RH side of Screen) (Figure 9.22).

Wireframe Display ——————— Figure 9.22

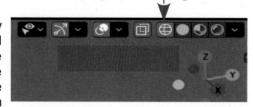

Figure 9.23

The Particle Emission options are accessed in the Properties Editor, Particle buttons, Source Tab (Figure 9.23).

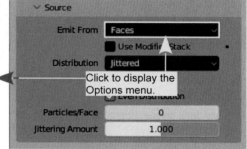

———— Single Particle at Frame 1

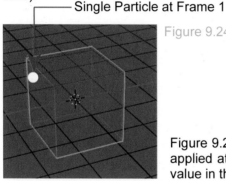

Figure 9.24

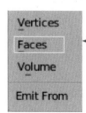

Vertices
Faces
Volume
Emit From

Click to display the Options menu.

Figure 9.24 shows the default Cube with the default Particle System applied at Frame 1 (One Particle Showing). The default **Emit From** value in the **Source Tab** is: **Faces** (Figure 9.23).

Wireframe Display Mode

Figure 9.25

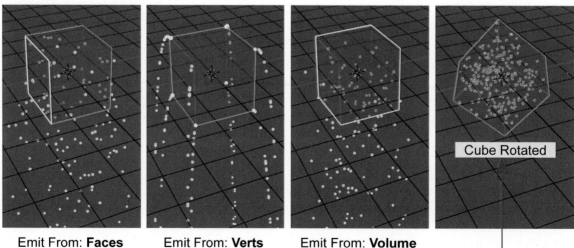

Emit From: **Faces**   Emit From: **Verts**   Emit From: **Volume**

Cube Rotated

Figure 9.25 shows particles being Emitted with the different options selected.

Emit From: Volume with Velocity Normal = 0.00 and Gravity turned off. The Particles accumulate inside the Volume of the Cube.

9.8 Particle Emission

Figure 9.26

To demonstrate Emission options, replace the default Cube in the 3D Viewport Editor with a UV Sphere. The Sphere has significantly greater number of Vertices and Faces from which to Emit Particles.

Disable Gravity in the Scene buttons.

The Order Of Particle Emission is controlled in the Properties Editor, Particle buttons, **Emission Source Tab** (the Source Tab only displays when the Emission Tab is opened).

By default Particles are set to **Emit From: Faces** in a **Random Order** (Distribution).

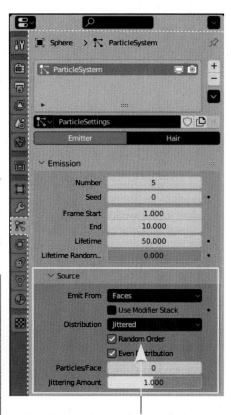

Figure 9.27

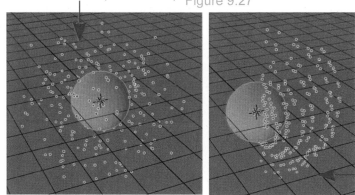

In the Source Tab **uncheck Random Order** and replay the animation.

The 3D Viewport Editor, by default, is in **User Perspective View**, therefore, it is difficult to see what has been achieved by removing the Random tick. Change the view to **Top Orthographic View** (Figure 9.28) then to **Front Orthographic View** (Figure 9.29). With the Timeline Editor Cursor, advanced to Frame 50, you will see an ordered array of Particles.

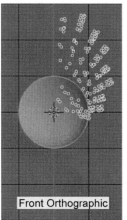

Figure 9.28

Figure 9.29

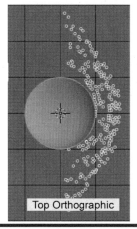

Front Orthographic

Top Orthographic

Note: In both views the Particles are being Emitted from Faces.

By changing Emit From to **Verts** in the **Source Tab** (figure 9.30) the array of Particles is even more ordered (Figure 9.31 over).

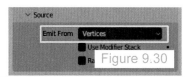

Figure 9.30

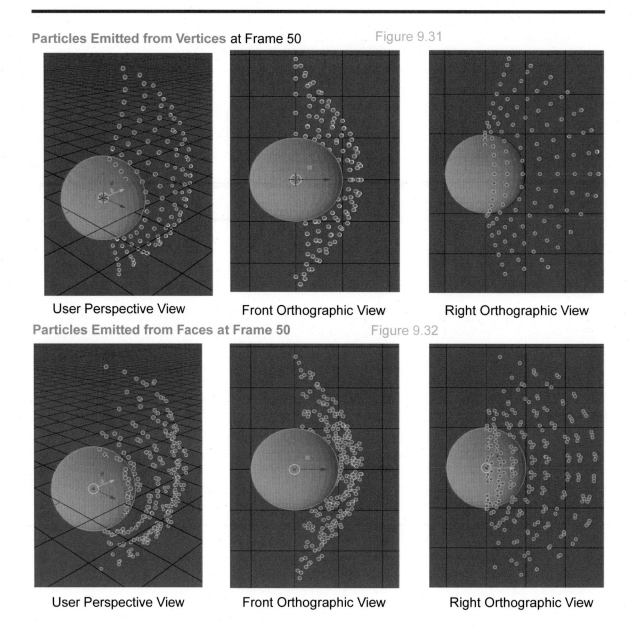

Particles Emitted from Vertices at Frame 50   Figure 9.31

| User Perspective View | Front Orthographic View | Right Orthographic View |

Particles Emitted from Faces at Frame 50   Figure 9.32

| User Perspective View | Front Orthographic View | Right Orthographic View |

The preceding emission examples have been with the assumption that the selected Object in the 3D Viewport Editor, in its entirety, is the **Emitter** and that the options to emit from **Faces**, **Vertices** and **Volume** are selected.

On occasion you may wish to confine the Particle Emission to a specific area of an Object's surface. In this case the Particles would be emitted from an area defined by a **Vertex Group.**

9.9 Normals

Figure 9.37

Particle Effects may be created by using different shaped Objects as Particle Emitters and manipulating **Normal** values in the Particle Properties (see 9.5 The Velocity Tab – Normals). Understanding how to control Normals is a key factor.

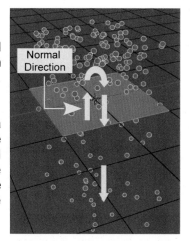

Have a Plane Object in the 3D Viewport Editor and apply a Particle System. When the animation is played in the Timeline Editor, Particles are emitted from the Face of the Plane and descend in the Scene due to the Gravitational force. In the **Velocity Tab** increase the Normal value to 5.000 and replay the animation. You will observe that the Particles rise from the surface of the Plane before descending (Figure 9.37).

Figure 9.38   **Screen Header** ➝

The Particles are emitted from the surface, Normal to the Face. In the default   Particle System the direction of the Normal is upwards. Rotate the Plane 45° about the X Axis (R Key + X Key + 45).

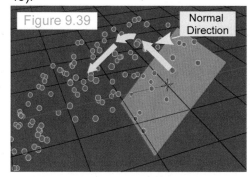

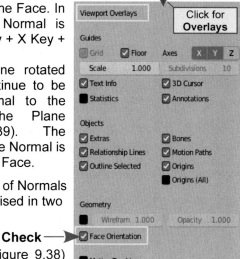

With the Plane rotated Particles continue to be emitted Normal to the Face of the Plane (Figure 9.39). The direction of the Normal is relative to the Face.

The direction of Normals may be visualised in two ways.

Check ➝

In **Object Mode** click on **Overlays** in the Header (Figure 9.38) and check **Face Orientation**. In the default Scene the upper surface of the Plane displays blue indicating the positive direction for Emission. By rotating the view you will see the underside of the Plane is displayed red (negative) (Figure 9.39). Bear in mind that you can enter positive and negative values in the **Velocity Tab** which changes the direction of Emission. This does not change the color display on the surface.

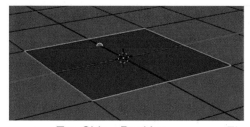

Top Side - Positive   Figure 9.39   Bottom Side - Negative

In **Edit Mode Overlays** (at the bottom of the panel) you will find **Normals** (Figure 9.40).

Figure 9.40

3D View Editor – Edit Mode　　　**Edit Mode - Overlays Panel**

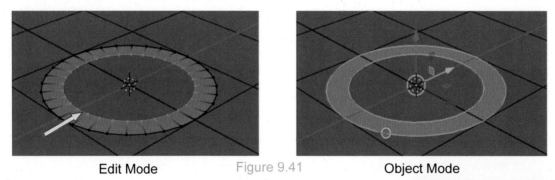

Click to toggle hide and display of Normals in the 3D View Editor. Adjust the Size slider to increase or decrease the Normal display.

Note: Adjusting the Size value does not change the Velocity for emission.

Knowing how Particles will be Emitted from an Object allows you to set up a Particle Display.

As an example, construct a flat disk Object as shown in Figure 9.41 by selecting a Circle Object in Edit Mode. Press the E Key (Extrude – DO NOT Move the Mouse). The Vertices are duplicated. Scale the duplicated Vertices in.

Edit Mode　　　Figure 9.41　　　Object Mode

Turn off **Gravity** in the **Properties Editor, Scene buttons, Gravity tab**.

With the Disk Object selected in the 3D Viewport Editor, in Object Mode, add a **Particle System** leaving the default values in place. Play the animation in the Timeline Editor.

Particles will be Emitted from the Faces of the Disk and **fall** towards the bottom of the Screen despite Gravity being turned off. (Figure 9.42).

Figure 9.42

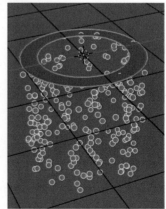

Particles are Emitted with a default starting velocity of **Normal = 1**. The velocity value is seen in the **Particle Properties, Velocity Tab**.

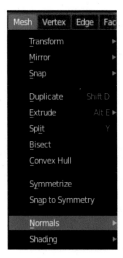

By turning on Normal visualisation as previously described you can see that the Normal direction is down, hence the descent (Figure 9.44).

Figure 9.43   Figure 9.44

You may quickly change direction in the Edit Mode Screen Header, Mesh Button by selecting **Normals, Flip** (Figure 9.43).

Note: You can Not play the Animation in Edit Mode.

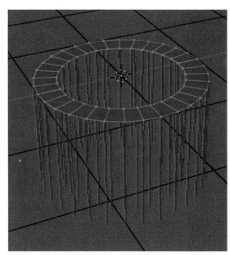

An example of creating a Particle Effect is as follows:

With the disk as shown in Figure 9.44, flip the Normals into the upward direction. In Object Mode change the Emit From: Faces to **Vertices** in the **Source Tab** and **uncheck Random Order**. Change the **Lifetime** value in the Emission Tab to 200.

When the animation is replayed the Particles are Emitted progressively around the disk from the mesh Vertices and rise up forming a spiral configuration (Figure 9.45). The Particles are grouped in short columns.

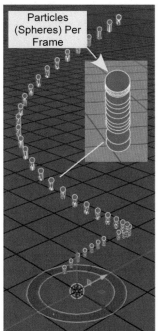

Figure 9.45

In the **Velocity Tab** make the Emitter Geometry, **Normal: 0.000** and the **Object Alignment Y: 1.000**.

When the animation is replayed the Particles spiral on the Y Axis in the Scene (Figure 9.46).

Up to this point Particles have been displayed in the 3D Viewport Editor as little white spheres in Object mode.

Figure 9.46

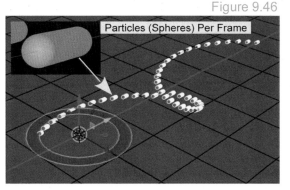

9.10 Particle Modifiers

In the **Properties Editor, Modifier Properties**, selection menu you will find the **Particle System Modifier** and the **Particle Instance Modifier**. Having gained a little knowledge in respect to the Particle System it is appropriate to mention these two Modifiers.

Particle System Modifier

Adding a **Particle System Modifier** to a selected Object merely adds a default Particle System. This is the same as going to the Particle Properties and clicking the **Plus Sign**. With the Modifier added you manipulate settings to achieve the desired result.

Particle Instance Modifier

Figure 9.47

The **Particle Instance Modifier** allows you to create an array of Objects mimicking the array of Particles which are being Emitted.

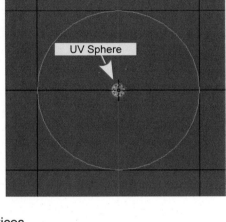

To demonstrate, set up a Scene in **Top Orthographic View** containing a Circle Object and a UV Sphere Object (scaled down) positioned as shown in Figure 9.47.

Turn Gravity off.

Have the Circle selected and add a Particle System with values as follows: In the Emissions Tab:— Number: 10
Lifetime: 200
In the Source Tab ——— Emit From: Vertices
Uncheck Random Order
In the Velocity tab:——— Normal: 0.25 m/s

Do not play the animation at this point.

Deselect the Circle and select the UV sphere.

In the Properties Editor, Modifier Properties, Add a **Particle Instance Modifier** and enter **Circle** as the Object (the Circle being the Object with the Particle System applied).

Figure 9.48

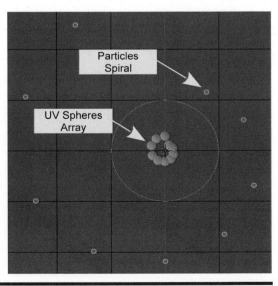

Play the animation in the Timeline window to see an array of Spheres generated in a spiral configuration mimicking the spiral of the Particles (Figure 9.48).

9.11 Particles Array

With the control of Particle Emission and the display of Particles as other Objects you can create arrays for effect when combined with the application of Materials and the addition of lighting . The following is an example.

In the default Blender Scene delete the Cube and add a UV Sphere. The default Scene has a single Point Light. Add a second Point Light and a Sun Light and position above and spaced around the UV Sphere.

Add an **IcoSphere**, set to smooth shading and scale 0.500. **Add a Material Color**. Park the Ico Sphere to one side of the Screen. You may hide the IcoSphere from view by clicking the eye icon in the Collection in the Outliner Editor.

Select the UV Sphere (the Emitter Object) and add a Particle System. Increase the Emission Number to 30 000. In the Render Tab, Render as Object with the IcoSphere as the Instance Object in the Object Tab. Deselect the UV Sphere.

Turn Gravity Off.

Add a Turbulence Force Field to the Scene (Shift + A Key – Force Field – Turbulence - Strength 5) (set the Strength value in the Properties Editor, Physics Properties, Settings Tab).

Figure 9.49

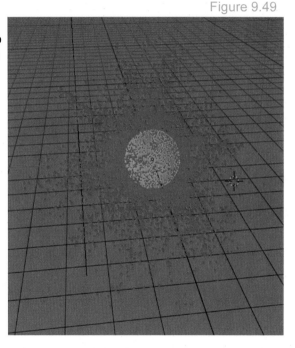

Play the animation to see the flow of Objects. Figure 9.49 shows the flow in **Material Preview Viewport Shading Mode** with the 3d Viewport Editor background (Gradient High/Off) color modified).

Note: The effect you generate in the 3D Viewport will depend on the Material applied to the Ico Sphere, the Lights, their strength value and their position in the Scene and the orientation of the 3D Viewport.

In the Particle Properties change Lifetime to 999 (forever) and the End value to 100. In the render Tab leave Scale: 0.050 but change Scale Randomness to 0.800.

Move the Timeline editor Cursor to frame 120 and rotate the Viewport to see the scatter of Ico Spheres.

Divide the 3D View Editor in two and have one in **Material Preview Viewport Shading Mode** and the other as **Rendered Viewport Shading** (Figure 9.50).

Figure 9.50

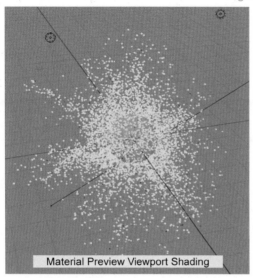

Material Preview Viewport Shading

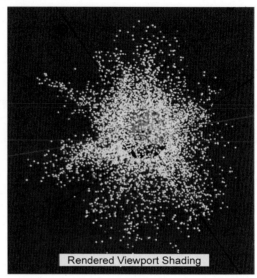

Rendered Viewport Shading

Select the UV Sphere and add a Material and set to Smooth Shading. Select the Ico Sphere and add a Material using the Node Arrangement shown in Figure 9.51.

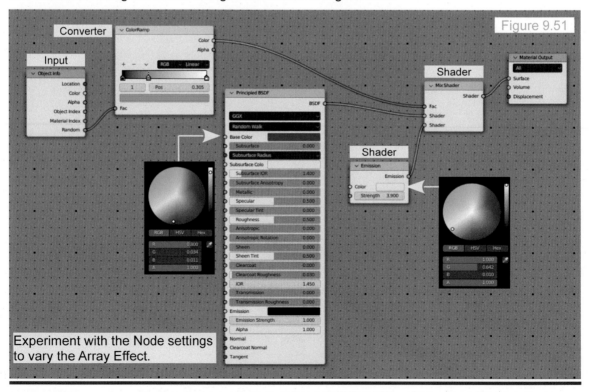

Figure 9.51

Experiment with the Node settings to vary the Array Effect.

Viewport Displays - See the results in different Viewport Displays (Figure 9.52).

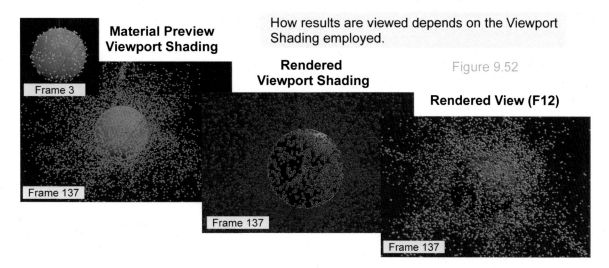

Material Preview Viewport Shading

How results are viewed depends on the Viewport Shading employed.

Rendered Viewport Shading

Figure 9.52

Rendered View (F12)

Frame 3

Frame 137

Frame 137

Frame 137

9.12 The Viewport Display Tab

How Particles display is controlled in the **Properties Editor, Particle Properties Viewport Display Tab**.   Figure 9.53

When multiple Particle Systems are in play it is advantageous to display Particles from one system differently to another. This is not to be confused with what takes place in a

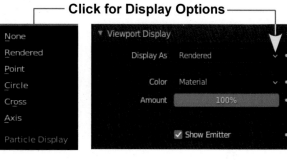

Click for Display Options

Rendered Image of a Scene. Particles themselves do not Render. In Figure 9.52 above, the Particles are Rendered as the IcoSphere (the Instance Object). In the default 3D Viewport Editor the Particles display as white spheres with the Display set as Rendered. They also display as spheres with **Display As: Poin**t is set. Alternative displays are shown in Figure 9.54.

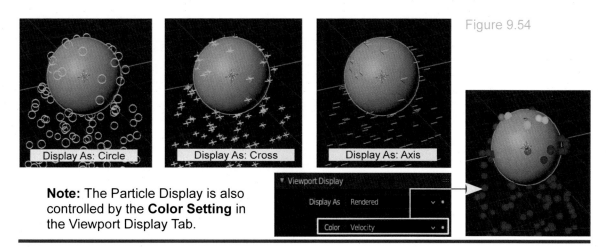

Figure 9.54

Display As: Circle

Display As: Cross

Display As: Axis

Note: The Particle Display is also controlled by the **Color Setting** in the Viewport Display Tab.

9.13 Particle Interaction

Figure 9.55

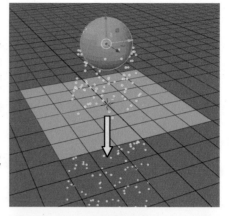

Particles can interact with other Objects and be affected by Forces like Wind, Turbulence and Drag. Particles can bounce off other Objects and act like sparks or droplets. To show how these features work, set up a Scene with a UV Sphere positioned above a Plane as shown in Figure 9.55 (the Plane is scaled up three times).

With the UV Sphere selected, go to the **Properties Editor, Particle Properties** and add a **Particle System** (to the UV Sphere).

In the **Emission Tab**, set the **End** value to 100 and in the **Velocity Tab**, set the **Object Aligned: Z value** to –3.000 (Emitter Object gives the Particles a starting velocity -3 down).

Figure 9.56

In the **Timeline Edito**r press the Play button . You will see the Particles fall and pass through the Plane (Figure 9.55).

To stop the Particles passing through the Plane, select the **Plane** and go to the **Properties Editor, Physics Properties** (Figure 9.56). Select **Collision** and replay the animation (**Remember** you must be at frame 1 before you replay).

The Particles bounce up from the surface of the Plane (Figure 9.57).

Physics Properties

By increasing the **Particle Damping: Factor** value in the **Particles Tab** to 1.000 (Figure 9.56), the Particles will land on the Plane but they will no longer bounce; they will just slide on the surface (Figure 9.58).

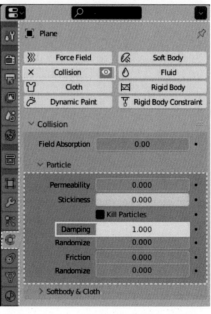

Figure 9.57   Figure 9.58

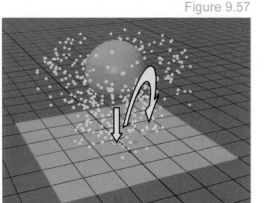

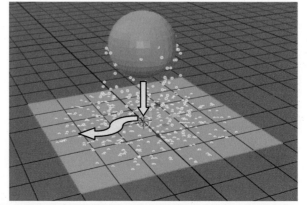

9.14 Force Effects

Particles can be influenced by a simulated **Force Field Effect**. Effects are in the **Add Menu** in the 3D Viewport Header (Figure 9.59).

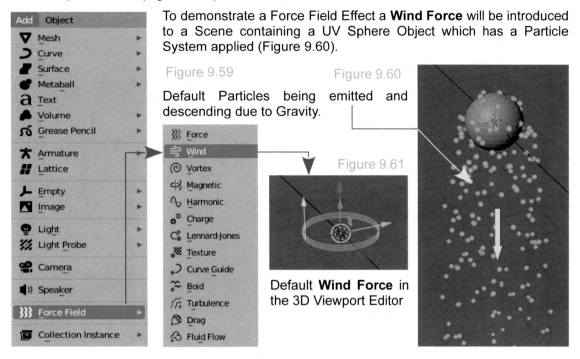

To demonstrate a Force Field Effect a **Wind Force** will be introduced to a Scene containing a UV Sphere Object which has a Particle System applied (Figure 9.60).

Figure 9.59

Figure 9.60

Default Particles being emitted and descending due to Gravity.

Figure 9.61

Default **Wind Force** in the 3D Viewport Editor

Properties Editor, Physics Properties

Figure 9.62

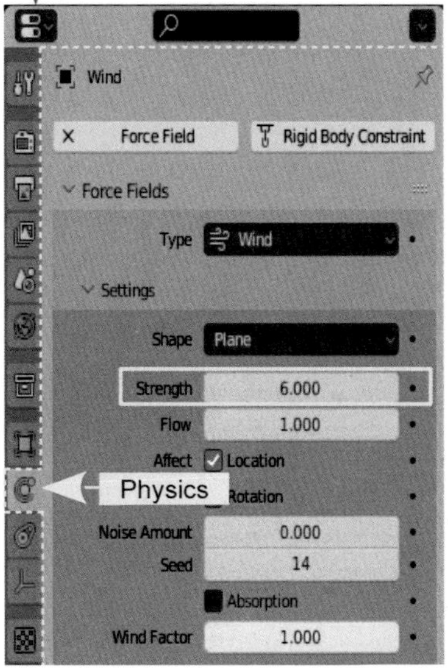

Figure 9.63

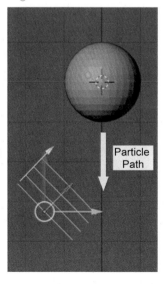

Adding a Force Field places the Graphical Display of the Wind Force at the location of the 3D Viewport Cursor. To have the Wind Force influence the Particles relocate it to the side and below the Particle path (Figure 9.63).

Controls for the Wind Force are found in the Properties Editor, **Object Properties** and **Physics Properties** (with the Force selected in the 3D Viewport Editor). Object Properties basically control the position and scale of the Force in the 3D Viewport which are identical to controls in the Transform Panel (press **N Key** to display).

Remember: Physics Properties control how the Force influences Particles.

Wind Force positioned below the UV Sphere and Rotated 45°. **Wind Force: Strength** = 6.000

When the Animation is played, Particles are emitted from the UV Sphere and descend and are blown to the side by the Wind Force.

Experiment with the controls in the Properties Editor, Physics to discover how the Force influence is affected.

Note: The Wind Force **Strength** is indicated by the separation of the orange rings and the affect on the descending Particles is influenced by the **Min/Max Distance** values set in the Falloff Tab.

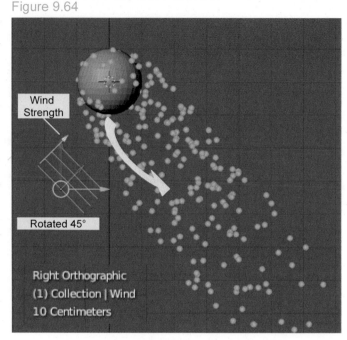

Figure 9.64

Wind Strength

Rotated 45°

Right Orthographic
(1) Collection | Wind
10 Centimeters

Add a **Force Field Vortex** into the mix. You will have to experiment to determine where best to locate the Force.

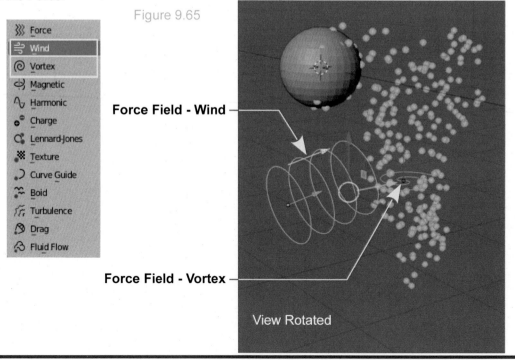

Figure 9.65

Force Field - Wind

Force Field - Vortex

View Rotated

9.15 Boids Particles

Boids Particle Systems are used to simulate flocks, swarms, herds and schools of various kinds of animals or anything that acts with similar behaviour. **Boids** Particle Systems are of **Type: Emitter** with **Boids Physics** applied. **Note:** The Physics is applied in the Properties Editor, Particle Properties NOT in the Physics Properties.

Boids Particles in one Particle System can react to Particles in another system or they can react to Particles within their own system. Boids are given **rules of behaviour**, which are listed in a Stack. The rules at the top of the Stack take precedence over rules lower down, but the Stack may be rearranged once it is written.

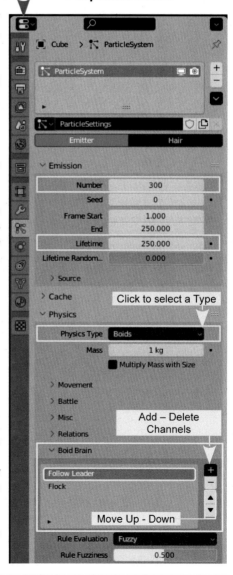

Properties Editor

Since only a certain amount of information is evaluated, if the memory capacity is exceeded, rules lower down the Stack are ignored.

Figure 9.66

The procedure for setting up **Boids Particle Systems** will be demonstrated with the following examples.

Example 1: A Flock of Birds

In this example the Particles will act like a flock of birds but won't actually look like birds.

Open a new Blender Scene with the default Cube. The Cube will be the **Particle Emitter**. In the **Properties Editor, Particles Properties**, add a new **Particle System**. Leave all the settings with their default values, except for the following:

- **Emission Tab**
    Number: 300 (Have a small flock.)
    Lifetime: 250 (The default animation
                length in the timeline.)
- **Physics Tab**
    Select Physics Type: **Boids**.
- **Boid Brain Tab** (in the Physics Tab)

With **Separate** highlighted, hit the **minus** sign to delete it. Click on the **plus** sign at the RH side of the window to display a selection menu for **Boids Rules**
 and select **Follow Leader**. Click on the up arrow below the minus sign to move Follow Leader to the top of the Stack.

You have instructed the Particles to follow the leader while flocking together. Give the Particles a leader to follow.

Deselect the Cube in the 3D Viewport and add an **Empty.**

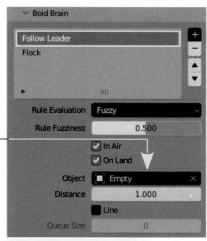

The **Empty** is a location point that can be animated to move in the Scene but does not render. Select the Empty and move it to the side. Animate the Empty to move across the Screen (see Chapter 20 for a refresher on Animation) Say 11 grid spaces in 140 Frames (gives PS time to catch up). Deselect the Empty and select the Cube.

Figure 9.67

In the **Boid Brain Tab** , make sure **Follow Leader** is highlighted (gray) (Figure 9.66).

Below the stack panel Click in the <u>panel</u> and select **Empty** from the menu that displays. You have instructed the Particles to follow the Empty. When the animation is played Particles Emitted from the Cube, head towards the Empty, and attempt to follow it as it moves across the Screen (Figure 9.68).

Figure 9.68

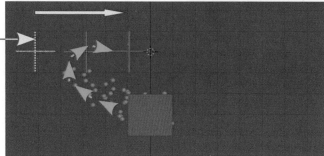

Empty in start position
Particles emitted from the Cube follow the Empty .

Figure 9.69

The Particles clump into a swarm and chase the Empty.

Particles continue being emitted and follow the swarm

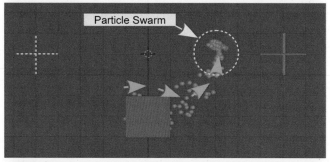

The Empty stops moving at Frame 140 but Particles continue to be emitted and join the swarm.

Note: With a high Particle count your computer may crash if the computer lacks power.

Figure 9.70

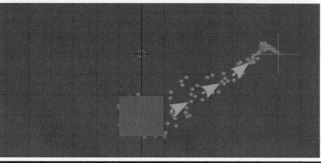

Empty Animation Timeline

Empty stops at Frame 140 ——

Figure 9.71

Animation continues while Particles Swarm

Example 2: Directing Movement

Particles will be directed to move from one Object to another. Start a new Scene and add a second Cube Object. Note that the default Cube is named **Cube** (see the upper left side of the 3D Viewport Editor) and the new Cube is named **Cube.001**.

Figure 9.72

Position the Cubes as shown in Figure 9.73, scaling the new Cube down.

Figure 9.73

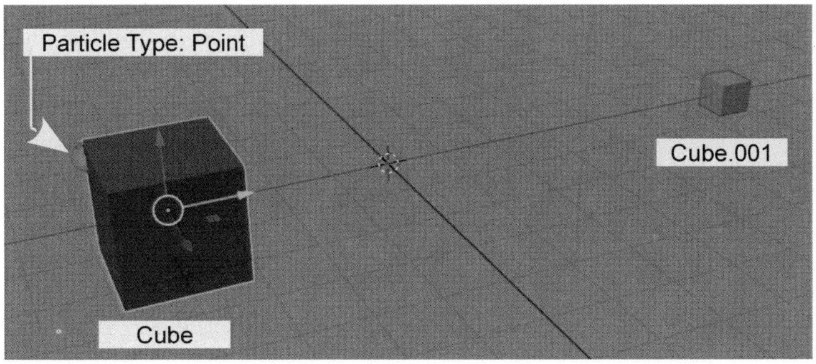

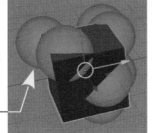

Particle Type: Point

Cube.001

Cube

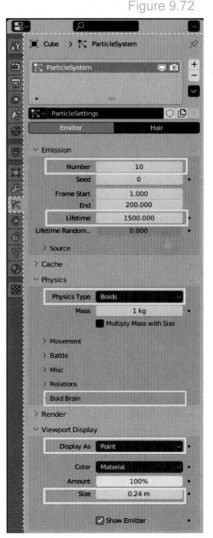

Select **Cube** and add a **Particle System** with **Physics, Boids Physics**. In the **Emission Tab**, reduce the **Number** value to **10** and set the **Lifetime** value to **1500**; you want to keep the number of Particles low and have them visible for a fair amount of time in the animation.

Set the **Viewport Display** for the Particles as **Point**.

Setting the Display Type as Point shows Particles in the 3D Viewport Editor as Spheres. The **Size** of the Point (Sphere) may be adjusted in the Viewport Display Tab. Increase the Size to 0.8.

Figure 9.74

Playing an Animation at this point will see 10 Particles generated sticking to the surface of the Cube.

Particle Size: 0.80 ——

Instructions directing the Particles to migrate from **Cube** to **Cube.001** are entered in the **Boids Brain Tab** (Figure 9.75).

By default two channels display in the Tab (Separate and Flock). Select (Click) each channel in turn (highlight gray) and click the minus button to delete.

Enter a new channel by clicking the plus (+) button and select **Goal** from the menu. Click the Object bar and select Cube.001.

Entering **Cube.001** as the Goal instructs the Particles emitted from **Cube** to migrate to **Cube.001.**   (Figure 9.76)

Figure 9.75

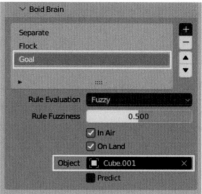

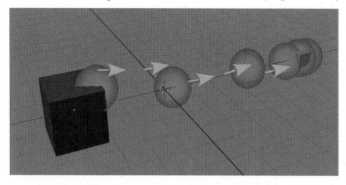

Be aware that the location of either or both of the Cubes in the Scene may be animated at the same time. Animating the target Cube can cause the Particles confusion. They may head over to where the target Cube was originally located , have a think, then chase the target. Some Particles may take off in a completely different direction but in letting the animation play on they will eventually find out they have made a mistake and discover where they should be going.

Emission Number 3000, Viewport Display – Color Velocity and Acceleration

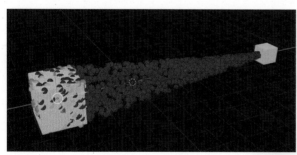

Experiment with different values to discover the possibilities.

Figure 9.77

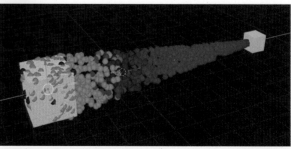

9.16 Hair Particles

Hair Particles are used to create such things as grass, fur, hair, or anything that has a surface with fibrous strands.

Figure 9.78

Examples from the Blender Wiki

Note: As previously stated, **Particles do not Render** to an Image or Video file unless they have been configured to display as an **Instance Object**. Hair Particles are the exception. Hair Particles Render as you see them in the 3D Viewport Editor.

To demonstrate the creation of Hair Particles, in the 3D Viewport Editor, delete the default Cube object, add a Plane, and zoom in.

Properties Editor ──▶

With the Plane selected, go to the **Properties Editor, Particles Properties** and add a **Particle System.**

Figure 9.79

In the top panel of the Particles Editor select **Hair** (Figure 9.79).

Figure 9.80

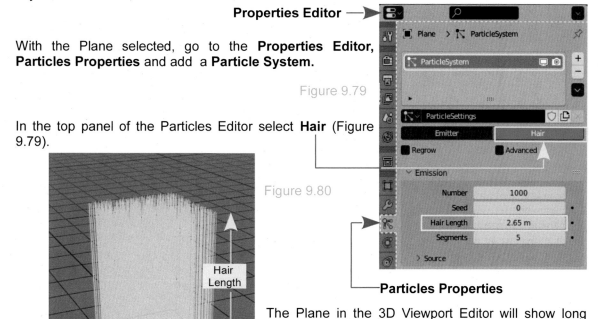

Hair Length

Particles Properties

The Plane in the 3D Viewport Editor will show long strands sticking up from the surface. The **Hair Length** value in the **Emission Tab** (Figure 9.79) allow you to adjust the length of the strands.

Note: Hair Particles Render in the 3D Viewport Editor and take on the color of the Emitter Object.

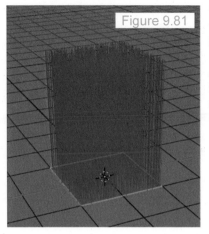

Figure 9.81

Hair Particles Emitted From Plane with Material Added to the Plane in **Material Preview Viewport Shading Mode**

Adding a Hair Particle System to a Plain Object would be suitable for generating a surface with fibrous strands such as a door mat or a patch of grass but a more interesting affect is to add Hair to a characters head.

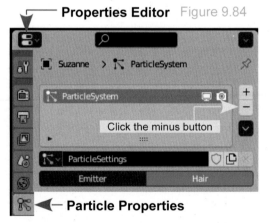

Figure 9.82

Adding Hair to a Character

To demonstrate Hair will be added to a monkeys head (Suzanne the Monkey Mesh Object). In a new Blender file delete the default Cube an add a Monkey Object (Suzanne). With Suzanne selected in the 3D Viewport Editor add a **Hair Particle System**.

Adding a **Hair Particle System** to **Suzanne** creates a hairy-headed Monkey with hair sticking out in every direction.

Figure 9.83

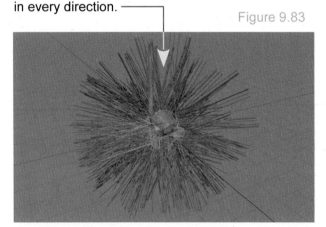

Properties Editor Figure 9.84

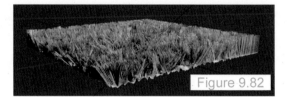

Particle Properties

At this early stage make note that the **Particle System** is named **ParticleSystem** with settings named **ParticleSettings** linked (Figure 9.84). This is unimportant just now but will have significance as you progress.

Try for a more clean-cut look. **Remove the Particle System** by clicking the minus button (Figure 9.84). You designate specifically where the hair is to grow by selecting a **Vertex Group.**

In **Edit Mode** create a **Vertex Group** on the top of Suzanne's head. **Name the Vertex Group - Hair.**

Figure 9.85

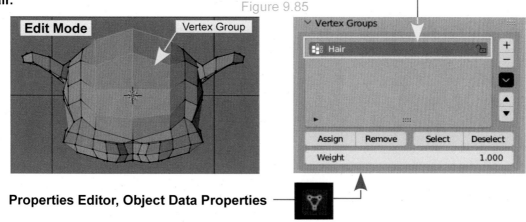

Properties Editor, Object Data Properties ⎯⎯⎯⎯⎯

At this point you have nominated an area on the head by selecting a group of Vertices. **You do not have hair.** While remaining in **Edit Mode** go to the **Particles Properties** and add a new **Particle System.** Change **Type: Emitter to Type: Hair.** There is no change in the **3D Viewport Editor** because you are in **Edit Mode.**

Figure 9.86

Note: Blender has named the new Particle System, **ParticleSystem** as before, but since you are working in the same Blender file, new Particle Settings named **ParticleSettings.001** are linked (Figure 9.86).

Tab to **Object Mode** in the 3D Viewport Editor and you will see plenty of hair. In fact, there is hair everywhere.

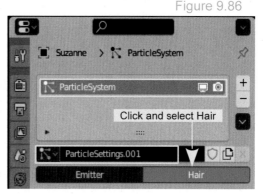

To correct this look, in the **Hair Length bar** in the **Emission Tab,** decrease the value until the hair strands look reasonable; say, about 0.820.

Figure 9.87

Remain in the Particles Properties, go down to the **Vertex Groups Tab** and in the panel next to **Density** click and select **Hair** from the menu that displays (Figure 9.87).

Hair only displays on the area selected (the Vertex Group). Press Num Pad 3 to get a side view (Figure 9.88). To fix the scrawny look, go to the **Children Tab** in the **Particle Properties** and click on **Simple** to get a bushy, Mohawk (Figure 9.89).

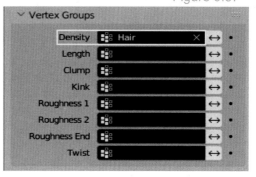

Suzanne is beginning to look like some cool dude in a cartoon feature but needs a little more character. A beard could do the trick.

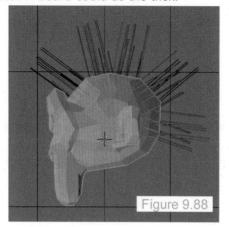

Figure 9.88

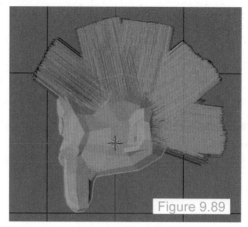

Figure 9.89

Suzanne is beginning to look like some cool dude in a cartoon feature but needs a little more character. A beard could do the trick.

Adding a Beard

To add a Beard you create a new second **Vertex Group** and apply a new **Hair Particle System** to the group.

The **Hair Vertex Group** was created by selecting Vertices in Edit Mode. To vary the procedure create the new Vertex Group using the **Weigh Paint Method**.

Hair Particles assigned to **Vertex Group** named **Hair**   Figure 9.90

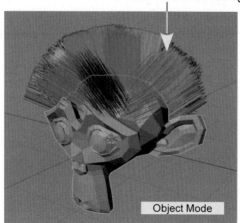

Object Mode

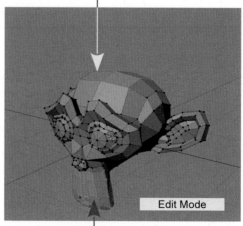

Edit Mode

New Second Vertex Group to be created

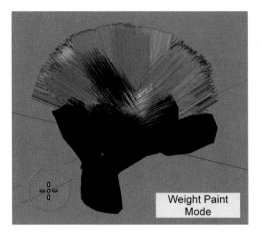

Weight Paint Mode

With Hair Particles assigned to Vertex Group Hair, placing the 3D Viewport Editor in Weigh Paint Mode sees Suzanne blue in the face with a splash of colored scalp in amongst the hair. The color represents the Hair Vertex Group that has been created.

In Weigh Paint Mode the 3D Viewport Editor Cursor becomes a **Paint Brush**.

Figure 9.91   Figure 9.92

To select Vertices for a new Vertex Group you drag the Paint Brush (Cursor) over the surface of the Object (Suzanne). As you drag the surface changes color indicating the selection. The color is graduated showing the strength of the selection (Light Blue , Partial – Red, Full).

Warning: At this point Suzanne is selected in Object Mode with the Vertex Group named Hair activated in Edit Mode. The Hair Particle System with ParticleSettings.001 is applied.

Dragging the Brush over Suzanne's chin will assign new Vertices to the Hair Vertex Group and consequently apply the Hair Particle System. This adds Hair to the chin with the same properties as the scalp. Ideally you want different properties, therefore, a different Vertex Group.

Create a New Vertex Group   Figure 9.93

Before select Vertices by painting Suzanne's chin, place the 3D Viewport Editor in Edit Mode and deselect all Vertices.

Go to the Properties Editor, Object Data Properties (for Suzanne), At this point you see the Vertex Group previously created named **Hair**.

Click the plus sign to create a new Vertex Group slot (The default name will be Group, rename Beard).

At this point you create a new Particle System to be applied to the Beard Vertex Group. This will provide full control over the properties of the Beard.

Create a New Particle System

Figure 9.94

In the **Properties Editor, Particle Properties**, click the plus sign to enter a new Particle System and set **Type: Hair.**

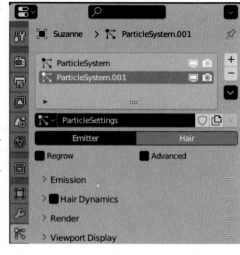

The new system is named **ParticleSystem.001**. You could rename the Particle Systems, Hair Particles and Beard Particles.

When you set the new Particle System to Type: Hair, Suzanne again takes on a completely hairy look. Hair everywhere. Head down to the **Vertex Group Tab** and in the **Density Slot** enter **Vertex Group Beard**. The hairy look disappears. Its time to Paint to select Vertices.

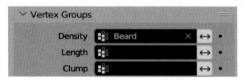

Figure 9.95

Change the 3D Viewport Editor to **Weight Paint Mode** and paint over Suzanne's chin.

In the **Properties Editor, Particle Properties, Emission Tab** reduce the **Hair Length** (0.33m). In the **Children Tab** change from type **None** to type **Simple**.

Figure 9.96

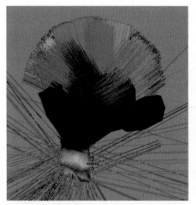
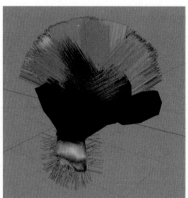
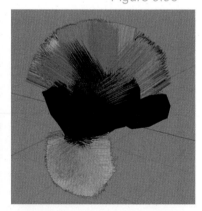

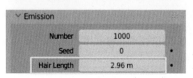
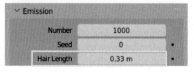

In Object Mode in the 3D Viewport Editor you have a gray Monkey with a grey beard and gray hair (Figure 9.97). This is fine, but it isn't all that exciting. Jazz it up by adding different **Materials** to Suzanne's surface creating **Skin and Hair Colors** (Figure 9.98).

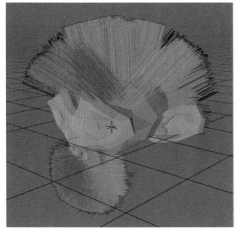

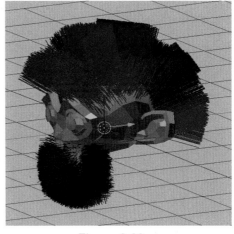

Figure 9.97　　　　　　　　　　　　　Figure 9.98

Hair Color

In Object Mode Suzanne displays complete with hair with the default gray color (Figure 9.97). The Hair Particles (Strands) take on the Material color of the Emitter Object which, in the case, is Suzanne with the default gray.

To color the Hair you create **Material Datablocks** (colors) and **assign the Datablocks to the Vertex Groups.**

Remember: A Datablock is a block of data containing information. In the case of a Material Datablock the information produces the Material (color) that displays in the 3D Viewport Editor.

You are about to generate new Material Datablocks but you should be aware that in a Blender file you will probably already have Material Datablocks pre-existing. For example, a new Blender file opens with a Cube Object in the 3D Viewport Editor which displays with a gray color (the default gray). In the Properties Editor, Material Properties you will see a Material Datablock named **Material**. This datablock produces the default gray color.

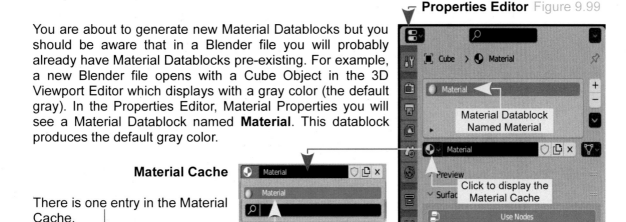

Properties Editor Figure 9.99

Material Datablock Named Material

Click to display the Material Cache

Material Cache

There is one entry in the Material Cache.

Material Properties →

If you have other Objects in the 3D Viewport you will have corresponding Material Datablocks.

Remember; In creating the current Blender file, the default Cube Object was deleted and Suzanne was added. When Suzanne was added or when any new Object is added, Blender automatically creates a new Material Datablock and assigns the default data which produces the gray color. At this point you modify the data to produce a color of your choice.

Default Cube Object   **Properties Editor, Material Properties**

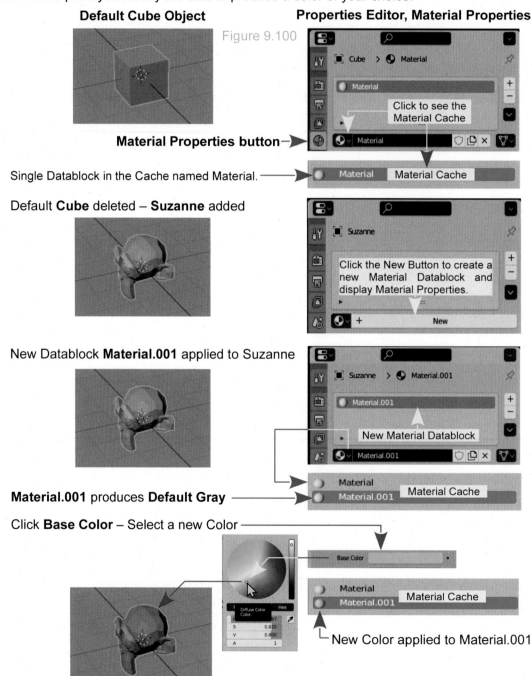

Figure 9.100

Material Properties button→

Single Datablock in the Cache named Material. ──────

Default **Cube** deleted – **Suzanne** added

Click to see the Material Cache

New Datablock **Material.001** applied to Suzanne

Click the New Button to create a new Material Datablock and display Material Properties.

New Material Datablock

Material.001 produces **Default Gray** ──────

Click **Base Color** – Select a new Color ──────

New Color applied to Material.001

Figure 9.100 depicts the sequence of commands applied when modifying a Material Datablock to color an Object which is selected in the 3D Viewport Editor.

Note: This procedure is described with the Blender Node System deactivated to allow Materials (colors) to display in the 3D Viewport Editor in **Solid Viewport Shading Mode**.

Material Datablocks may be created independent of Objects in the 3D Viewport Editor. The Datablocks created can then be applied to any Object entered in the Scene or to Vertex Groups on an Object's surface. There is, however, one caveat. Before you can see Material Properties in the Properties Editor there must be an Object in the 3D Viewport Editor.

Figure 9.101

Material Properties – Object Mode

The assumption will be made that you have Suzanne selected in the 3D Viewport, that you have applied a Material to color her face and have created Vertex Group where you want to place hair and beard.

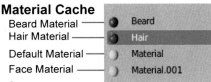

Material Cache

Beard Material —— Beard
Hair Material —— Hair
Default Material —— Material
Face Material —— Material.001

Create Material Datablocks

With Suzanne selected in Object Mode create two new Material Datablocks naming them Hair and Beard and assigning a Material (color) to each. When creating Datablocks don't forget to disable the Node System so that Materials will display in the 3D Viewport Editor when in Solid Viewport Shading Mode.

Material Properties – Edit Mode

Assign Material Datablocks to Vertex Groups Figure 9.102

With Suzanne selected in **Edit Mode** and with Vertex Group Hair selected in the Properties Editor, Object data Properties, go to the Material Properties. Select the Hair Datablock and click the Assign button.

Repeat the procedure for the Beard Datablock and the Beard Vertex Group.

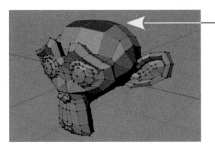

Hair Particles adopt the Material (color) assigned to the Vertex Group. (Figure 9.98).

9.17 Particles for Arrays

Particles emitted from an animated Object may be used to create interesting Arrays such as a spiral (Figure 9.103).

To create the spiral, have a Plane Object in the Scene as the Emitter Object with an IcoSphere as the Rendered Object.

When you add the IcoSphere, the **Add Ico Sphere panel** displays in the lower LH corner of the Screen. Click on the panel and you will see Subdivisions: 2 as the default setting. Reduce this to Subdivisions: 1. This reduces the Vertex count on the surface of the Ico Sphere. This is not necessary here but is good practice when creating simulations where it's advisable to use a minimum number of Vertices.

Figure 9.103

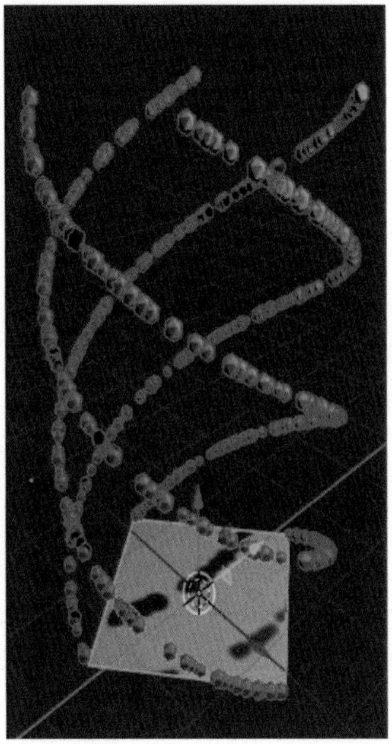

Park the IcoSphere off to the side of the Screen or you may place it in a separate Collection to hide it from view. Give the Ico Sphere a nice bright Material. Have the 3D Viewport Editor in **Material Preview Viewport Shading Mode**.

Animate the Plane to Rotate

Select the Plane. Follow these cook-book instructions.

With the Timeline Editor Cursor at Frame 1, turn **ON** Auto Keyframing.

Press **I Key** . Select **Rotation** in the Keyframe menu. A Keyframe is manually entered at frame 1 in the Timeline Editor.

With the Timeline Cursor at frame 30 and the Mouse Cursor in the 3D Viewport Editor, press R Key + Z Key + 90 + Enter. Repeat this for Frames 60, 90 and 120 (Automatic Keyframes Insertion). When completed TURN OFF Auto Keyframing.

With the mouse Cursor In the Graph Editor press **Shift + E Key** and select **Linear Extrapolation** to smooth the rotation.

Playing the animation will show the Plane continually rotating about the Z Axis.

Add a Particle System

Add a Particle System to the Plane with Particles being Emit from **Verticies** (Source Tab) and **Rendering as** the **Ico Sphere** Object (Render Tab – Render as Object – Object Tab – Instance Object - Icosphere). Play with the Scale and Randomness settings. Increase the **Lifetime to 250** and in the **Source Tab** uncheck **Random Order. Turn off Gravity.**

Playing the simulation (animation) in the Timeline Editor show Particles displayed as Ico Spheres being emitted and rising in spirals as the Plane rotates (Figure 9.103).

This is a relatively simple exercise demonstrating how an effect is created by combining the different Particle settings. There are no hard and fast rules which have to be obeyed. The way to create something is to experiment and when you produce a worthwhile result, save the file and record results for future use. The following example incorporates more combinations.

9.18 More Arrays

Particle Arrays are only limited by your imagination and your knowledge of what tools to use and where the tools are located. This example will help you on your way.

In the default Blender Scene replace the default Cube with a **UV Sphere** as a **Particle Emitter** and add an **Ico Sphere** to be used as a Rendered Object (Instance Object).

Give the Ico Sphere Smooth Shading and park it to one side of the Scene. Scale down to approximately 0.250. The Ico Sphere will be what is termed the **Instance Object**. When Particles are generated by the UV Sphere they will display as this Object.

Add Lamps to improve illumination in the Scene.

Figure 9.104

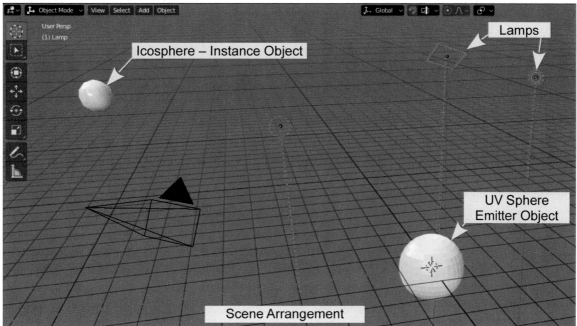

The objective in the exercise is to create an array of small Objects that could represent a swarm of insects hovering around the UV Sphere or a cloud of stars in a far off galaxy. This is where your imagination comes into play. For realism you would create a small model of what the Objects in the Array were to be but for simplicity, the Ico Sphere will be used.

Turn off **Gravity** in Scene buttons to make the Particles disperse in 3D Space. Select the UV Sphere and add a Particle System.

Playing an animation in the Timeline Editor at this point with the default Particle System would see particles being emitted as small circles which float away from the UV Sphere and disappear after 50 Frames from their point of creation (Lifetime 50.000). To generate something a little more exciting modify the Particle System.

In the Emission Tab
Increase **Number** to 30 000.
Change Lifetime to 999 (i.e. Forever).
Leave Start: 1 and End: 200.000.
Change Lifetime Randomness to 0.800
In the Render Tab
Change Render As from Halo to Object.
Leave Scale at 0.050
Change Scale Randomness to 0.080.
In the Render, Object Tab
Click where you see **Instance Object** and select **Ico Sphere.**

In the Timeline Editor play the animation then move the Timeline Cursor to Frame 120 and rotate the Viewport.

Figure 9.105 shows the Array generated in Rendered Viewport Shading Mode. The Array is ordered as seen by the Particles radiating out from the UV Sphere as scattered lines. By zooming in on the 3D Viewport Editor you will see that each Particle is an Instance (copy) of the Ico Sphere parked in the Scene.

Figure 9.105

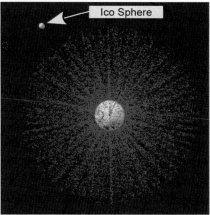

From this point you make further modifications to settings to alter the appearance of the Array.

Add a Material to the Ico Sphere. Figure 9.106

Figure 9.107

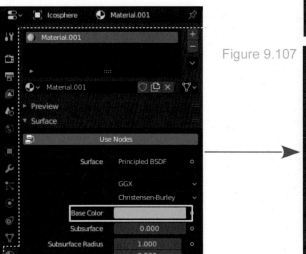

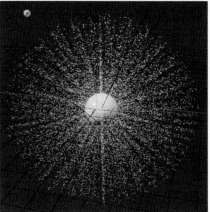

To see the Material be in **Material Preview Viewport Display Mode**.

Deselect the UV Sphere and add an **Empty Object** and activate a **Force Field, Type Turbulence**, Strength 5 in **Physics Properties** (Figure 9.108).

Figure 9.108

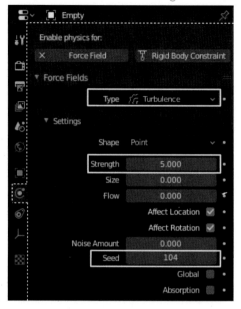

Particles Dispersed by Force Field   Figure 9.109

Play animation to see flow of Particles.

Figure 9.109 shows a Screen Capture taken while playing the animation at approximately Frame 120.

Select the **UV Sphere** and change the **Particle System to Emitter Type: Hair**. With the animation in the Timeline Editor at Frame 1 the UV Sphere displays as a speckled   orange / yellow disk.

In the **Particle System, Render Tab**, change **Render As** to **Path**. In the Children Tab select Simple for a different sort of Array (Figure 9.110).

The possibilities are endless, therefore, experiment and record settings or save Blender files for future use.

Figure 9.110

9.19 The Assignment Panel

When a **Particle System** is first added to a Scene by clicking on the plus sign in the Particles Properties, Blender introduces data to the Scene that creates a default Particle System. Blender names this data block **ParticleSettings**, as seen in the **Settings panel**. The data block named **ParticleSettings** is automatically linked to the default Particle System that is named **ParticleSystem**. ParticleSystem is placed in the Assignment Panel where it is assigned to an Object in the 3D Viewport Editor.

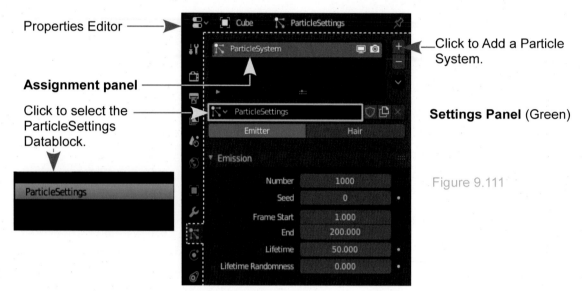

There is no **Assignment Tab** or **Assignment Panel** as such, but for the purpose of this discussion consider the **Settings Panel** marked in green as the **Assignment Tab** and the panel displaying **ParticleSystem** as the Assignment Panel (Figure 9.111).

Below the Settings panel there is a Particle Type selection menu with the two options, **Emitter** and **Hair**.

Type: Emitter is the default selection, which means that with the Particle System assigned to an Object in the Scene, that Object becomes the emitter of the Particles. In either case, the Object becomes an emitter with a Particle System assigned. **Type: Hair** may be viewed as a specialised static emitter which generates Particles that Render.

In Figure 9.111, Particle System, Type: Emitter is selected with the ParticleSettings Datablock. assigned to the ParticleSystem which in turn is assigned to the Object which is selected in the 3D Viewport Editor.

Note that the names **ParticleSettings** and **ParticleSystem** may be renamed by double clicking in the panels, deleting the name and retyping a new name. This is useful when there are multiple Objects, Data Blocks and Particle Systems. Multiple Objects in the 3D Viewport Editor can each have a different Particle System assigned, and each Object may have more than one Particle System.

When a new Particle System Data Block is added to the Scene, Blender creates a new name for the Data Block. The default particle settings Data Block is named **ParticleSettings** as previously stated. When a second Data Block is added, it is named **ParticleSettings.001**, a third would be named **ParticleSettings.002**, etc.

Renaming Data Blocks to something more relevant to Objects in the Scene would be an advantage. When new Data Blocks are created, they are stored in a cache for reuse by other Particle Systems.

When a new Particle System is added to the Scene, Blender assigns that system to the Object selected in the 3D Viewport Editor. If no Objects are selected, the new Particle System is assigned to the last Object that was introduced to the Scene. Particle Systems added to a Scene initially have the default ParticleSettings Data Block linked and a new name applied as described previously. At this point, the Data Block settings may be altered to create a new unique Data Block or a previously created Data Block may be selected and linked to the new Particle System. Clicking on the icon in front of the Particle Settings panel reveals a drop down menu showing the Cache, mentioned previously, with Data Blocks for selection.

The forgoing statements may seem confusing and not easily related to what has been labelled the **Assignment Tab.** The following exercise will attempt to clarify the statements and at the same time demonstrate the application of Particle Systems in practical terms.

9.20 Particle Exercises

Open a new Scene in Blender and delete the Cube from the 3D Viewport Editor. Add three separate Plane Objects and position them at the center of the Scene so that they are all visible in Camera View . Add a diffuse Material color to each of the Planes. Make the colors red, green and blue. (Figure 9.112). To see Materials in the 3D Viewport Editor be in Material Preview Viewport Shading Mode.

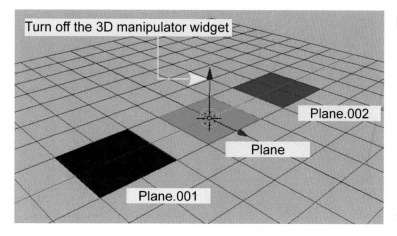

Figure 9.112

Turn off the 3D manipulator widget

Plane.002

Plane

Plane.001

Turn off the **Gravity** setting in the Properties Editor, Scene Properties, Gravity tab (untick).

Turn off the 3D Manipulator Widget in the 3D Viewport Editor.

At this time, the three Plane Objects have been named **Plane**, **Plane.001**, and **Plane.002** by Blender, as seen in the upper left-hand corner of the 3D View Editor when each is selected. In the diagram the green Plane was entered first followed by the red Plane then the blue Plane.

This automatic naming is not all that relevant to what is in the Scene, therefore, the Planes will be renamed.

In the 3D Viewport Editor, select the red Plane and go to the **Properties Editor, Object Data Properties**. At the top of the Editor you will see **Plane.001** in the Data Block ID name panel (Figure 9.113).

Figure 9.113

Click on the name (displays typing cursor), hit delete, type in **Red_Plane** and press Enter. Select the green plane in the 3D Viewport Editor and rename it **Green_Plane**, and then similarly for the blue Plane.

> **Note:** Renaming may be done in the Properties Editor, Object Properties, Datablock ID name panel or in the Outliner Editor (upper RH of the Screen).

Add **Particle Systems** to the Planes. Select the red Plane and click on the **Particles Properties** in the **Properties Editor**. Click **the plus sign** to add a Particle System. The Particle System panel displays with all the tabs and buttons for controlling the settings and has been set up with default values. Leave all the values as they are displayed except for the **Lifetime** and **Number** value in the **Emission Tab**. Change the value as shown in Figure 9.114. This will give you a better view of Particles being generated.

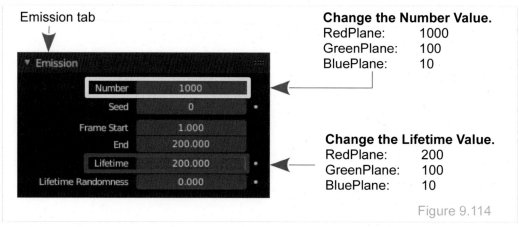

Emission tab

Change the Number Value.
RedPlane: 1000
GreenPlane: 100
BluePlane: 10

Change the Lifetime Value.
RedPlane: 200
GreenPlane: 100
BluePlane: 10

Figure 9.114

Do the same for the other two Planes. Play the animation in the Timeline Editor to show Particles being generated.

Cycle through the animation in the Timeline Editor (drag the Timeline Cursor) to frame 170 and observe the Particles (Figure 9.115). You have three different Planes with three different Particle Systems—RedPlane: 1000 Particles, GreenPlane: 100 Particles, BluePlane: 10 Particles.

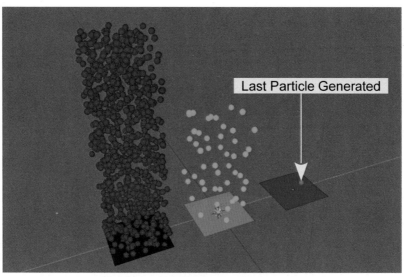

Figure 9.115

Last Particle Generated

3D Viewport Editor at Frame 170

Blender generates Particles beginning at Frame 1. The number of Particles set for each Plane is generated and spread over 200 Frames (200 is the End value in the Emission tab). The actual length of the Animation is 250 Frames. In Figure 9.115 BluePlane is showing the last of the 10 Particles being generated. For BluePlane the Particle Lifetime is set at 10 Frames, therefore, the first Particle disappears at Frame 11, the next appears at Frame 21 and disappears at Frame 31. For the BluePlane the last Particle appears at Frame 161 and disappears at Frame 171.

In the 3D Viewport Editor select each Plane separately and note the names that display in the panels in the **Properties Editor, Particles Properties , Assignment tab**, (Figure 9.116).

Figure 9.116

- **Red_Plane**
  - Name: ParticleSystem
  - Settings: ParticleSettings
- **Green_Plane**
  - Name: ParticleSystem
  - Settings: ParticleSettings.001
- **Blue_Plane**
  - Name: ParticleSystem
  - Settings: ParticleSettings.002

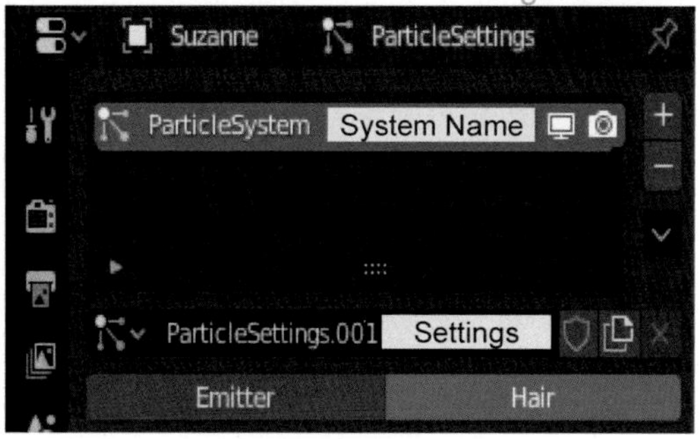

Entries for the Red_Plane

It was previously stated that there were three separate Particle Systems, however, you see that the three names are all **ParticleSystem**, but each one has a different **Settings** name. At this stage it's probably a good idea to do some renaming.

Change the names to the following:

- **Red_Plane**
  - Name: RedPSystem
  - Settings: RedPSettings
- **Green_Plane**
  - Name: GreenPSystem
  - Settings: GreenPSettings
- **Blue_Plane**
  - Name: BluePSystem
  - Settings: BluePSettings

After renaming, proceedings should be easier to follow.

To continue; In the 3DView Editor select the **Green Plane** to reassign some settings.

In the **Properties Editor, Particles Properties, Assignment Tab**, click on the button just in front of the name panel and next to Settings.

Figure 9.117

Browse Particles Settings to be linked menu

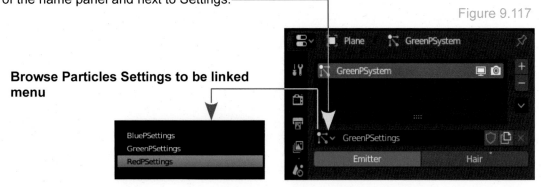

The menu that displays has the names of the three **Particle Settings Data Blocks** (Figure 9.118). Whenever a new group of Particle Settings is created, Blender puts it into a cache for reuse. You can see these **Data Blocks** in the **Outliner Editor** in **Data API Mode**.

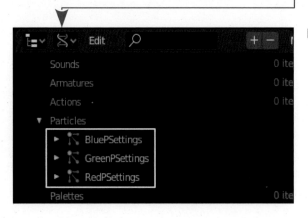

Figure 9.118

With the **BluePlane** selected in the 3D Viewport Editor, click on **GreenPSettings** in the **Browse Particles to be linked menu.**

You will have the **BluePSettings** assigned to the **GreenPSystem**.

If you replay the Particle generation animation, the green and blue Planes generate the same number of Particles.

Note that in the **Settings panel** for the green and the blue Planes, a number 2 has appeared; this tells you that **BluePSettings** is being used by two systems. The number of Particles Emitted is set by the Particle System settings.

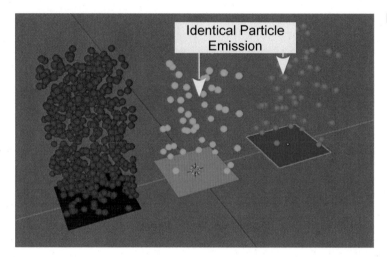

Identical Particle Emission

Figure 9.119

The forgoing has demonstrated that any Settings Data Block can be assigned to any Particle System.

Continue by clicking on the number 2, which makes the Data Block a single user. Blender does this by leaving the original as it is and creating a new Data Block, however, the new Data Block is identical to the original.

Figure 9.120

You can see that the settings name is **BluePSettings.001** (Figure 9.120).

In the **Emission tab** change the **Number** value to 10 and the **Lifetime** value to 30.

In the 3D Viewport Editor, add a **UV Sphere** to the Scene and give it a yellow Diffuse Material color.

Note: Blender has named the Sphere simply, **Sphere**. Make sure it is off to one side in the Scene away from the planes.

Select the Green Plane in the 3D Viewport Editor and then go back to the **Particle Properties** in the **Properties Editor**.

Change data in this new Data Block (BluePSettings.001) which is assigned to the GreenPSystem for the green Plane.

In the **Render Tab** in the **Particles Properties** (scroll down a bit). In the bar labelled **Render as** click and select Type: **Object** (Figure 9.121). Selecting **Type: Object** instructs Blender to Render (Display) Particles as an Object entered in the Scene .

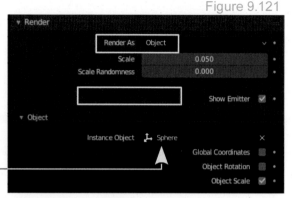

Figure 9.121

In the **Object Tab** that displays, click where you see **Instance Object** and select **Sphere** (the yellow UV Sphere).

You are telling Blender to display and Render the Particles as replicas of the yellow Sphere entered in the Scene. Play the particle generation animation and you will see yellow Spheres being generated (Figure 9.122). (increase the Render Scale Value).

Yellow Sphere (Instance object) entered in the Scene Parked to one side

Figure 9.122

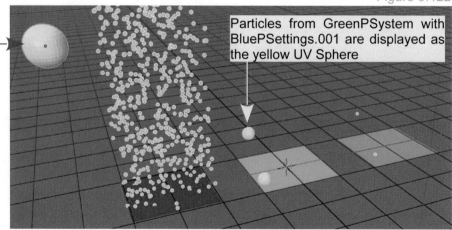

Particles from GreenPSystem with BluePSettings.001 are displayed as the yellow UV Sphere

The size of the Spheres generated is determined by the size of the yellow Sphere entered in the Scene and the Scale value in the Particle Properties, Render Tab .

This exercise has demonstrated how manipulating values in the Properties Editor controls the Emission of Particles in the 3D Viewport Editor. This can be used to create visual effects in a Scene. **Note:** An Object can have more than one Particle System in operation at the same time.

9.21 Multiple Particle Systems

Work through the following exercise to see how to apply **Multiple Particle Systems**. A Plane Object is entered in the 3D Viewport Editor with a blue Material applied. The 3D Viewport Editor is in Material Preview Viewport Shading Mode.

A Particle System is added to the Plane in the Properties Editor, Particle Properties with the Emission values as shown in Figure 9.124 (default settings except Lifetime 200). Gravity has been turned off in the Scene buttons.

Playing the animation in the Timeline Editor produces the array of Particles shown in Figure 9.123.

Figure 9.123

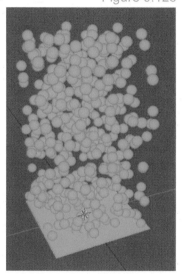

Figure 9.124

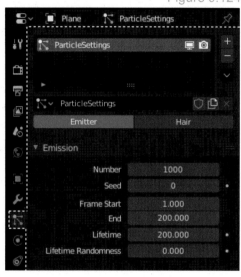

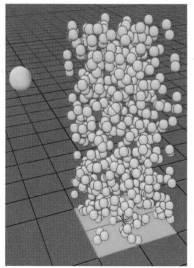

You may have the Particles display as another Object. Add a UV Sphere to the Scene. Give the Sphere a nice bright Material (color) and park it off to the side. **Select the Plane.**

In the **Particle System, Render Tab** change **Render As** to **Object** (Figure 9.125) then in the Object Tab select Sphere as the **Instance Object**.

Figure 9.125

Replay the animation For a colorful display (Figure 9.126).

Figure 9.126

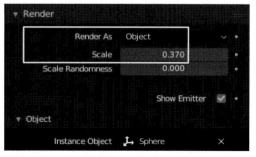

To add a second Particle System to the Plane click on the Plus icon adjacent to the Assignment Panel.

ParticleSystem.001 is entered in the Assignment Panel. **Note;** Settings: **ParticleSettings.001**.

Change the **Lifetime** in the Emission Tab to 200 so that the Particles remain visible when the animation is played.

Add a **Monkey Object** to the Scene with a Material and park it to one side.

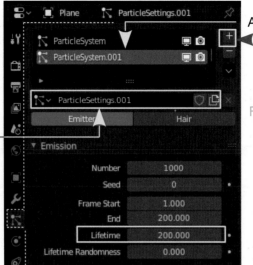

Assignment Panel
Click to add a
second
Particle System

Figure 9.127

At this point a second Particle System is applied to the Plane with **Settings: ParticleSettings.001**. The Settings (at this point) are identical to the original ParticleSettings (Figure 9.127), therefore, playing the animation will produce two identical Particle displays (yellow spheres) and appear as if nothing has changed. To make it obvious that two systems are in play modify the settings for ParticleSettings.001.

Figure 9.128

With **ParticleSettings.001** selected (highlighted) change the values in the **Render Tab** as shown in Figure 9.128.

Change values in the **Velocity Tab** (Figure 9.130) as shown to change the direction of emission of the second set. Play the animation.

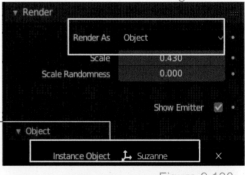

Instance Objects

Figure 9.129

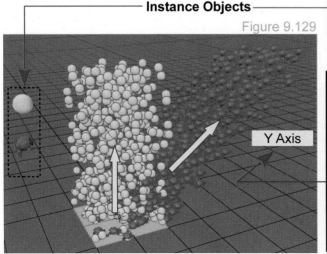

Y Axis

Figure 9.130

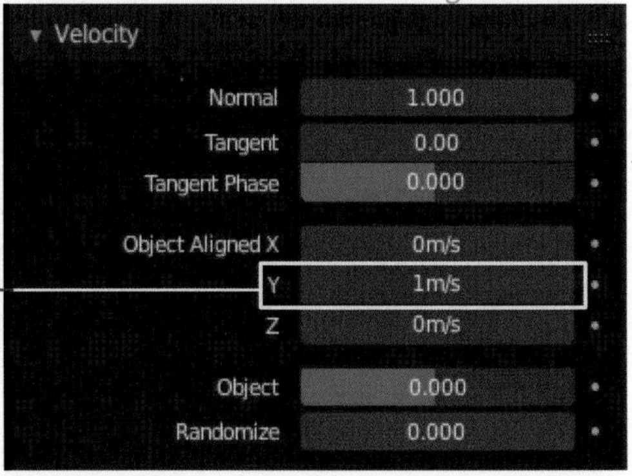

174

9.22 Keyed Particles

Keyed Physics is a way of controlling the movement of particles by directing them from the original Emitter Object to a second Target Object and onto subsequent Target Objects. The flow of Particles may be used as an animation or used to create a static image. The following procedure for setting up a keyed system will demonstrate the principles involved.

Open a new Scene in Blender and delete the default Cube. Add three separate Plane Objects and position them as shown in Figure 9.131. Note that in the **Outliner Editor** under **Collection** the first Plane (red) will be named **Plane**. The second Plane (blue) named **Plane.001** and the third (green) **Plane.002**.

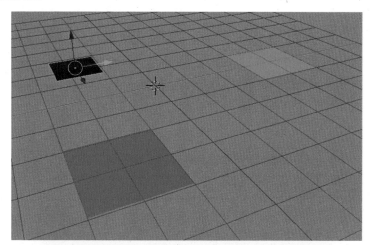

Figure 9.131

Figure 9.132

In the **Outliner Editor** rename the Planes, **Red_Plane**, **Green_Plane** and **Blue_Plane.**

> **Note:** You can go to the Properties Editor – **Object Data Properties** and edit the name in the **Name box** at the top of the panel or you can edit the names in the **Outliner Editor**. You could use any name you like but since the Planes are colored it's best to name per the colors assigned.

Select the first plane, **Red_Plane** and in the **Properties Editor, Particles Properties**, add a Particle System. In the **Physics Tab** change Physics Type: Newtonian to **Keyed.**

Figure 9.133

Deselect **Red_Plane** in the 3D Viewport Editor and select **Green_Plane** and **Blue_Plane** in turn, repeating the procedure for adding a **Keyed** type particle system.

Go back and select **Red_Plane**. At this point you are about to tell the Particles emitted from Red_Plane to migrate to Blue_Plane then on to Green_Plane. This is done by designating Blue_Plane and Green_Plane as **Targets** in the **Physics, Keys, Relation Tab**.

Click on the plus sign at the RHS of the Relations panel. This enters a Target Channel and inserts **Invalid target**. Below the relations panel click in the **Target Object** panel and select **Red_Plane**.

With Red_Plane selected click the plus sign a second time and repeat the process, this time entering **Green_Plane** as the Target. Repeat for **Blue_Plane**.

OK! You have the objects, **Red_Plan, Green_Plane** and **Blue_Plane** each with a **Keyed** particle system and you have told the particles generated from **Red_ Plane** to assemble.

Figure 9.134

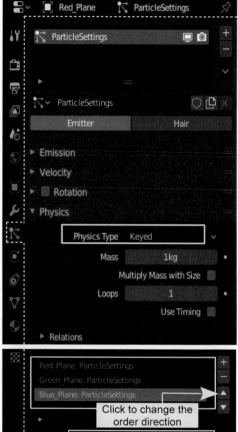

When the animation is played Particles emitted from Red_Plane travel towards Blue_Plane then turn and head over to Green_Plane. To alter the direction, select one of the channels in the relations Panel then click a Up or Down Arrow to change the order.

Figure 9.135

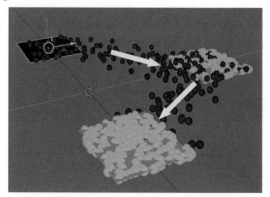

Remember: All the rules for number of particles, Lifetime, Start, End, and Normal velocity apply.

Physics and Simulation

Simulation refers to Animation where dynamic events which take place in the real world are simulated in an Animated Sequence. When physical actions occur in the real world they obey the laws of Physics.

Characters and Objects in a Computer Animation are made to move and interact as if they were complying with Real World Physics. Characters jump up and fall down obeying the law of gravity. They collide with and bounce off each other and with obstacles in the Scene. These actions may be exaggerated to create effect and, therefore, do not strictly adhere to the laws of physics, depending on the story being depicted. Blender incorporates Modifiers to simulate how Characters and Objects behave as if following these laws.

In the preceding chapter describing Particles and Particle Effects, Wind Force and Gravity have been encountered. When an Objects emits Particles they descend in the Scene as if under the influence of the real world force of **Gravity** and are affected by a **Wind Force** when applied. Gravitational Force is treated as a separate force with controls for cancelling the effect and applying the strength in the **Properties Editor, Scene Properties**. The Wind Force is found, with several other Physics simulation effects in the **Properties Editor, Physics Properties**.

Physics Properties are **Modifiers** (coding that produces an effect) and are applied to an Object which is selected in the 3D Viewport Editor, much the same as a Modifier is applied. When Physics is applied to an Object, controls for Physics display in the **Properties Editor, Physics Properties** (Figure 10.2).

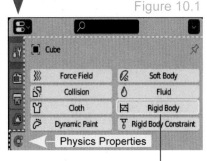

Properties Editor

Figure 10.1

Physics Properties

Figure 10.2

Physics – Ridged Body Controls

10.1 Applying and Cancelling Physics

To apply Physics, select the Object in the 3D Viewport Editor then click on the **Physics Type** in the **Properties Editor, Physics Properties**. You will see that the icon preceding the Physics Type name changes to a cross indicating that Physics has been applied and controls for the Physics Type display in the Editor.

Should you wish to cancel the Physics for the Object, click on the cross.   Figure 10.3

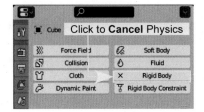

Physics may also be applied (in some cases) in the **Properties Editor, Modifier Properties**.

Note: Some Modifiers display in both the Physics Properties and the Modifier Properties.

Figure 10.4

Note: When applying a Physics Property from the Modifier Properties, a panel displays directing you to the Physics Properties for the controls.

Figure 10.5

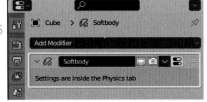

Modifier Properties→

Properties Editor

10.2 Real World Physics   Figure 10.6

In Chapter 9, you will have observed that Particles being generated from a default Object descended in the Screen when an animation sequence is played. The Emitter Object remains stationary unless it is animated to move.

The default Blender Scene may be considered to be a view of a 3D World. There is a gravitational force in existence, but generally, Objects placed in the Scene will not react to Gravity until **Physics** is applied to the Object. Particles are an exception since they have **Newtonian Physics** applied by default (Figure 10.6).

Particle Properties→

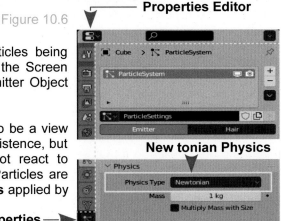

New tonian Physics

Real World Physics is referred to as; **Rigid Body Physics** (Rigid Body Constraint). The Object is said to be a Rigid Body.

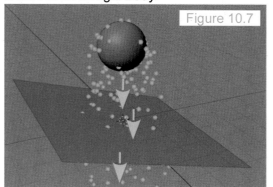

Figure 10.7

Figure 10.7 shows a UV Sphere positioned above a Plane which is rotated on the X Axis to form an incline. The Sphere has a Particle System applied.

When an animation is played in the Timeline Editor, Particles are Emitted from the Sphere and fall through the Plane. The Sphere and Plane remain stationary (Figure 10.7).

Figure 10.8

By selecting the **Plane** and **Enabling Physics** for: **Collision**, in the Properties Editor Physics Properties (Figure 10.8), the Particles will bounce off the Plane when the animation is replayed (Figure 10.9).

Properties → Editor

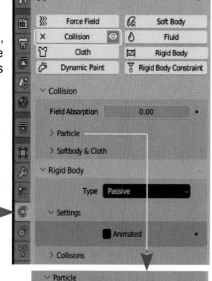

Physics → Properties

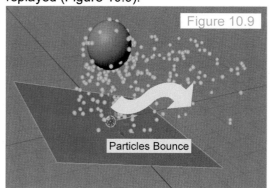

Figure 10.9

Particles Bounce

Controls display when Physics is enabled ⟶

Adjust controls in the Properties for effects (Figures 10.10, 10.11)

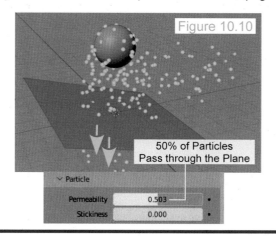

Figure 10.10

50% of Particles Pass through the Plane

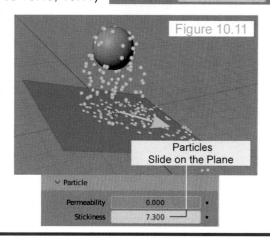

Figure 10.11

Particles Slide on the Plane

You are probably wondering why Particles fall due to the Gravitational affect but the UV Sphere and Plane remain stationary. By default a Particle System has a **Physics Type: Newtonian** applied hence they act as if in the Real World due to Gravity.

You see Newtonian Physics for Particles in the Properties Editor, Particle Properties, Physics Tab. Gravity is in the Properties Editor, Scene Properties.

Particle Properties

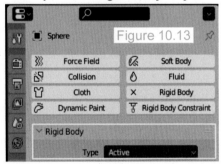

Scene Properties   Figure 10.12

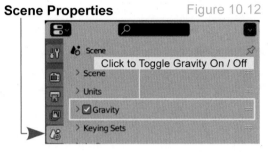

To have the Sphere fall and roll down the Plane, add **Ridged Body Physics** to both the Sphere and the Plane **AND** in the **Rigid Body Tab** set **Type: Active** for the Sphere (Figure 10.13) and **Type: Passive** for the Plane (Figure 10.14) . The Sphere will fall, the Plane remains stationary.

UV Sphere – Rigid Body Physics

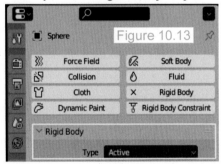

Plane – Rigid Body Physics

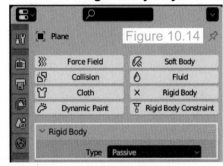

Click **Play** in the **Timeline Editor Header** to see the Sphere fall and roll down the Plane

Note: Rigid Body Physics automatically includes Collision Physics hence the reaction between Sphere and Plane.

Figure 10.16

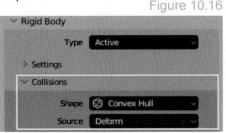

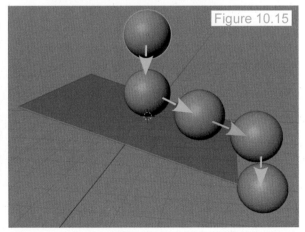

Figure 10.15

Rigid Body and Particles

With a Particle System added to the UV Sphere and combinations of Physics applied to the Plane and the UV Sphere you control how the Sphere and Particles react with the Plane.

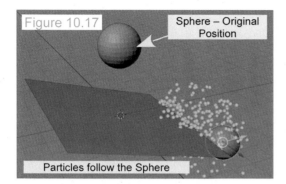

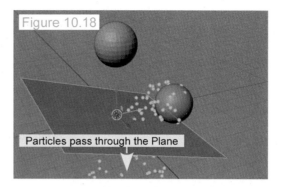

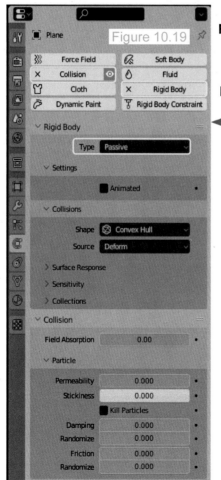

UV Sphere
Rigid Body Physics

Plane
Rigid Body Physics

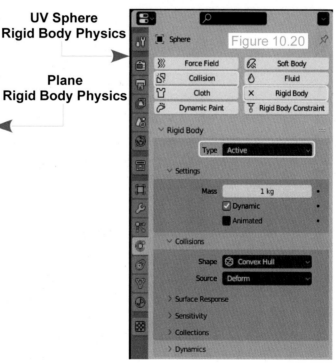

The Sphere falls, rolls down the Plane and over the edge. Particles follow (Figure 10.16).

By removing the **Collision Physics** from the Plane the Sphere still rolls down the incline on impact but the Particles being Emitted pass through the Plane (Figure 10.18).

10.3 Force Field

An example of a Force Field is a Wind Force which influences the direction of flow of Particles. The Wind Force may be assigned to an Empty Object in the Scene which enabled the Force to be positioned for effect.

A Wind Force may be applied to any Object. The Empty Object is used since it doesn't Render in the Scene. Figure 10.21 shows a Force Field – Type Wind applied to a Cone Object which is directed to blow the Particles being emitted from the UV Sphere used in the previous exercise.

Figure 10.21

Properties Editor

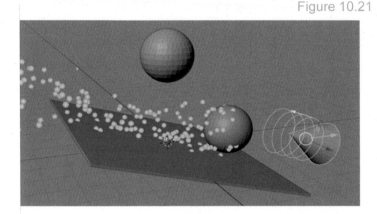

Physics Properties →

The Particles being emitted from the Sphere as it falls and rolls to the right down the Plane are blown to the left back up the incline

Note: the negative **Strength** value for the Wind Force.

10.4 Collision Physics

in **Real World Physics** Section 10.2, applying **Collision Physics** to an Object causes it to interact with other Objects in the Scene.

10.5 Cloth Physics

Figure 10.22

With **Cloth Physics** applied, an Object exhibits the characteristics of different types of fabric.

Consider a **Plane Object** in the 3D Viewport Editor in Object Mode, **Subdivided ten times** (in Edit Mode). With the Plane selected in **Object Mode**, click **Cloth** in the **Physics Properties** (Figure 10.22).

If you click on the **Modifier Properties** in the Properties Editor you will see that a Cloth Modifier has been added to the Plane referring you to the controls in the Physics Properties (Figure 10.23). The controls for Cloth Physics display in the Properties Editor (Figure 10.24).

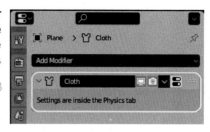

Figure 10.23

Physics Cloth Properties

Properties Editor – Physics Properties

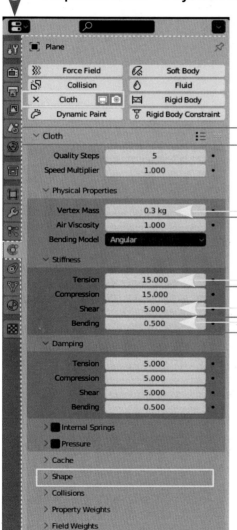

The default Cloth settings in the Physics buttons give the Plane the characteristics of a cotton fabric.

As a guide the following setting changes may be made for other **fabric materials**.

Default

Figure 10.24

	Cotton	Leather	Rubber	Denim	Silk
Vertex Mass	0.300	0.4	3.000	1.000	0.150
Tension	15	80	15	40	5
Shear	5	25	25	25	0.0
Bending	0.5	150	25	10	0.05

To see the Plane acting as a cotton fabric leave the default settings in place.

With the Plane selected in the 3D Viewport Editor, Tab into Edit Mode, deselect all vertices then select two corner vertices and create a **Vertex Group.** The Vertex Group is names **Group.**

In the **Properties Editor, Physics Properties** expand the **Shape Tab** (way down the bottom Figure 10.24). You are about to fix (Pin) the two Vertices in space, something like pegging the corners of a sheet on a clothes line, **without the line**.

Enter the name of the Vertex Group in **Pin Group**.

183

Play the Animation in the Timeline editor.

Figure 10.25

The Plane cotton fabric swings down pinned at the two corners.

Pinned Vertices

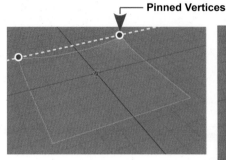
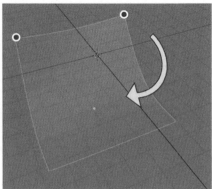

Cloth Interaction

Cloth may be made to interact with other Objects in a Scene (Figure 10.26).

Figure 10.26

As an example of interaction, in the previous example (Figure 10.25), position a UV Sphere below the Plane **before playing the animation**. Create a second Vertex Group for the Plane, this time, including all Vertices on the Plane.

Select the **UV Sphere and in the Physics Properties** activate **Collision Physics** maintaining the default settings.

With the **Plane selected**, in the **Cloth Physics Properties, Collisions Tab** (Figure 10.27), have **Object Collision** checked with **Collision Collection: Collection** entered. Also have **Self Collision** checked with **Vertex Group: Group.001** entered.

Replay the animation to see the Cloth droop over the Sphere (Figure 10.28 over).

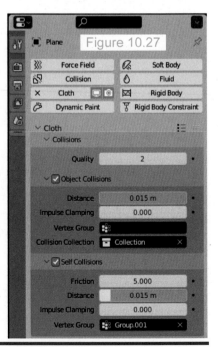

Figure 10.28

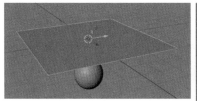

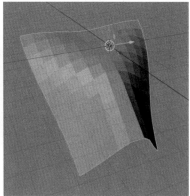

> **Note:** Dynamic Paint is the next entry in the Physics list. This is detailed in Chapter 11.

10.6 Soft Body Physics

Figure 10.29

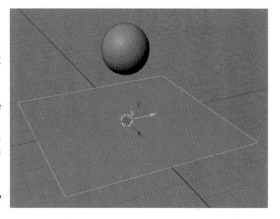

Soft Body Physics, when applied to an Object, causes it to act like dough or clay or anything that is soft and pliable.

As an example, set up a UV Sphere Object above a Plane (Figure 10.29). The Sphere is a good object for the demonstration since it has a reasonable number of Vertices forming its mesh surface.

With the Sphere in Object Mode add **Soft Body Physics** to the UV Sphere .

Playing an animation in the Timeline Editor at this point sees the UV Sphere remain in situ and bounce up and down slightly.

In the **Properties Editor, Physics Properties**, **Soft Body Tab**, **uncheck Goal** (Figure 10.30) to have the Sphere fall in the animation. The Sphere falls straight through the Plane.

Select the Plane and in the Properties editor, Physics buttons, **enable Physics for: Collision**.

Playing the animation again, shows the UV Sphere crumpling when it makes contact with the Plane (Figure 10.32). Initially the crumpling will be hesitant and the animation will hesitate due to the time for the computer to calculate the deformation. Let the animation run its course.

Figure 10.30

The deforming data will be written to the Cache (memory) then on replay the Sphere will squish into a blob and settle on the Plane.

Figure 10.31

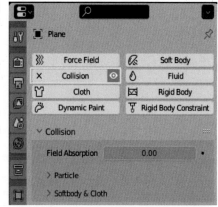

The amount of hesitation in the initial animation will depend on how fast the computer can perform the calculation.

The speed and deformation of the Sphere on impact may be controlled by adjusting values in the **Edges Tab** with the Sphere selected.

Figure 10.32

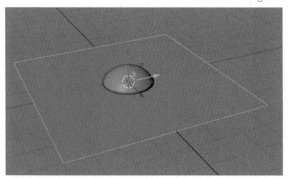
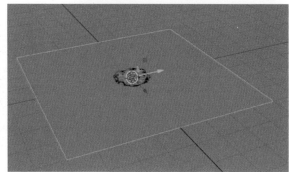

10.7 Fluid Simulation

Fluid Simulation, replicates how fluid behaves in the real world. How a fluid behaves depends on its environment which comprises physical obstacles and physical forces such as gravity and pressure. The physical composition of the fluid also has an effect on its behaviour. As you can guess, the laws of physics have a great deal to do with how a fluid behaves.

In Blender, a fluid simulation means, a graphical display is generated on the computer screen tricking the observer into believing they are seeing a fluid react to an environment. It should be remembered that this is an illusion and what you think you see is a clever bit of trickery.

In Blender an extensible framework called **Mantaflow** has been incorporated in the program for the execution of fluid and gas simulations.

Mantaflow is an open-source framework targeted at fluid simulation research in Computer Graphics. Its parallelized C++ solver core, python scene definition interface and plugin system allow for quickly prototyping and testing new algorithms.

In a **Fluid Simulation**, the Fluid you see on the computer Screen, is initially represented by Particles. The Fluid is generated from a series of Particle Systems which represent the Fluid itself and may incorporate, Spray, Foam and Bubbles. The Particles are eventually Rendered as as a Mesh which has Materials applied reacting to Scene Lighting produce a realistic Fluid Flow Effect.

In a nutshell, the procedure for creating a Fluid Simulation is to create a space in the Scene in which the Fluid Flow it to take place (the Domain), insert an Object in the Domain to act as a Fluid Inflow Source and to insert other Objects which act as obstacles and controls for directing the flow. The Fluid Inflow Source is a Particle Emitter Object.

To demonstrate the basic concept of Fluid Simulation work through the following, not so simple, exercise beginning with the default Blender Scene containing the Cube Object.

Place the 3D Viewport Editor in **Wireframe Display Mode**.

Figure 10.33

In the default Blender Scene, Scale the default Cube up twice on the Z Axis. Deselect the Cube and add a second Cube scaling it down in size (S Key + 0.173). Both Cubes will be located at the center of the 3D World. Move the second, smaller Cube, up towards the top of the default Cube (Figure 10.33). The default Cube will be the **Domain** (the mini artificial World) and the second smaller Cube will be the **Fluid Emitter**.

Note; it is very important to keep all Objects participating in the Fluid Simulation entirely inside the Domain (nothing protruding outside) (Figure 10.33).

When setting up a **Domain** containing a Fluid Emitter, the scale of the Emitter relative to the Domain is important. A large Emitter will produce a large amount of fluid in a short time.

In the **Outliner Editor** rename the small Cube, **Fluid** and the default Cube, **Domain** (Figure 10.34).

┌─ **Outliner Editor**   Figure 10.34

Fluid Emitter

Domain

Preview

Fluid

187

Fluid Flow

In this simple demonstration Fluid will be generated by the Emitter Object and delivered as a continuous stream. The stream will initially be directed along the Y Axis where it will contact the side of the Domain before descending and filling the Domain as if it were a container. In Figure 10.33 the direction of flow is shown by the blue arrows.

Simulation Controls

Properties Editor

Figure 10.35

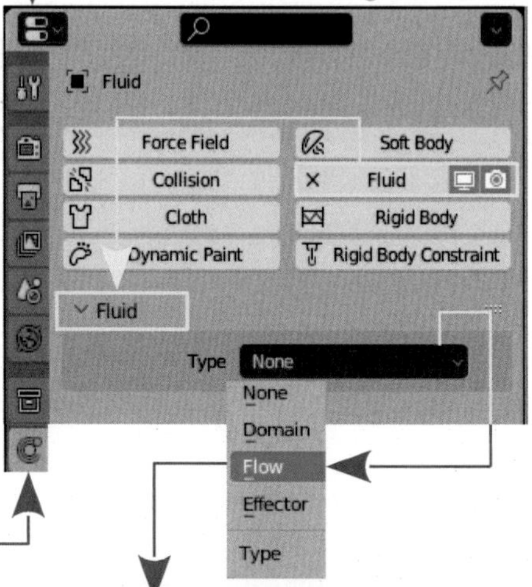

Controls for Fluid Simulation are found in the **Properties Editor, Physics Properties** (Figure 10.35). You have to set both **Fluid Emitter Controls** and **Domain Controls**.

Fluid Emitter Controls

Deselect the Domain and select the **Fluid Emitter Cube**.

In the **Properties Editor, Physics Properties** click on **Fluid** (Figure 10.35) to display the **Fluid Tab.**

In the **Fluid Tab** click where you see **Fluid Type: None** and select **Flow** in the menu that displays.

Fluid Settings display in the Editor, **Physics Properties**

In the Fluid **Settings Tab** change **Flow Type**: Smoke to **Liquid** and **Flow Behaviour: Geometry** to **Inflow** (Figure 10.36).

Check that **Use Flow** is checked (ticked).

Figure 10.36

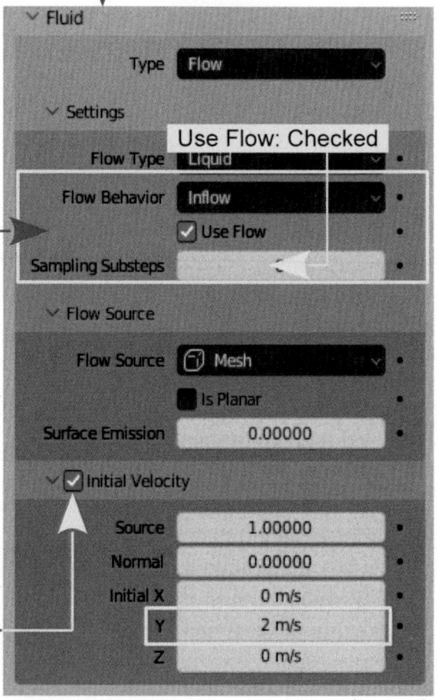

Flow Behaviour

Flow Behaviour: Inflow sets the Emitter Object Cube to deliver a continuous flow of fluid. The flow of fluid is generated when an animation is played in the Timeline Editor.

Note: At this point nothing would occur if the animation were to be played.

Figure 10.33 shows the fluid inflow direction, starting along the Y Axis of the 3D World. You set this by giving the fluid an initial velocity. In other words give the fluid a kick start in the Y direction. To do this check (tick) the **Initial Velocity Tab.**
Set the **Initial Y** value to **2 m/s** (Figure 10.36).

The completed set up for the **Emitter Object** in the **Properties Editor** is shown in Figure 10.36.

Domain Object Controls

The **Domain Control** set up is similar to the Emitter Control. With the Domain Cube selected, in the 3D Viewport Editor open the Physics Properties in the Properties Editor, click **Fluid**. This time change Fluid Type None to **Type: Domain**. In the **Settings Tab** change Domain Type from the default Gas to **Liquid** (Figure 10.37).

Playing the Animation

By playing the Animation in the **Timeline Editor** you will see Particles being Emitted from the Fluid Cube. The Particles initially move on the Y Axis until affected by Gravity when the fall and splash at the bottom of the Domain as if it were a container. As the animation continues to play Particles are continually Emitted from the Fluid Cube.

Physics Properties

Particles splashing in the Domain appear to rise as they accumulate with the impression that they are the **upper surface of the liquid** in the Domain (Figure 10.38).

Properties Editor

Figure 10.37

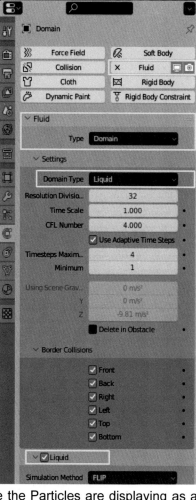

Figure 10.38

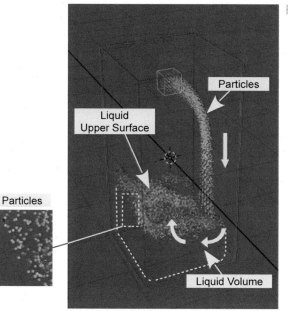

Particles

At this stage the Particles are displaying as a representation of the Fluid Flow only, not an actual display of Fluid. They merely give an indication of Fluid Flow.

The Fluid Simulation relies on **Particles** being generated by a Particle System (Chapter 9) which obeys the Gravitational affect in the Scene and interact with Objects acting as obstacles or receptacles.

Remember: Particles Do Not Render.

At this point you may make adjustments to the control settings, reconfigure the Domain shape and resize and reposition the Fluid Flow Object to modify the Particle display. With each change you can replay the Animation to see the effect.

Animation Length

Note: When playing the Animation in the Timeline Editor the default Animation Length is set by the End Frame value, 250 Frames. You may rest the End Frame to something less to speed up the simulation when adjusting Flow controls or increase the length to suit your final simulation. Bear in mind that, in playing the Animation, you are generating Data which is being stored on the computer's hard drive.

Memory Computer Power and Baking

As the simulation is developed, revisions and modifications can generate a considerable amount of Data. At each replay of the Animation the Data is stored in the computer's memory (RAM).

This is not significant with the relatively simple Animation produced so far but when complex simulations are underway a significant amount of memory can be consumed which may hamper the computers ability to process information.

This being the case, in Fluid Simulation, the **Particle Display Data** is written to the hard drive in a **Cache Folder** to free memory for future processing.

Figure 10.39

Properties Editor, Physics Properties

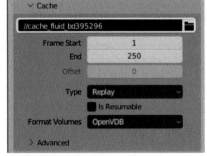

Initially a Cache Folder is automatically created in the Folder where the simulation Blender File is being saved. This Data may be viewed as temporary while the simulation is being developed. For the final simulation the Data will be written to a permanent File for future use.

Writing data to a permanent Folder is called **Baking**.

When you **Bake**, you should designate where on your hard drive to save the data.

With the Domain selected in the 3D Viewport Editor, scroll way down to the bottom of the **Properties Editor, Physics Properties** to the **Cache Tab**. Blender automatically creates a folder for saving named **\cache_fluid** (Figure 10.39) with a File Path something like that shown here.

Cache File Path

Obviously the **Cache File** (cache_fluid_b395296\) is not that easily accessed when searching for it on the computer. It is better to create a new Folder in a more accessible location.

Cache Folder created in the **C: Drive**   Click to open the **File Browser**

Figure 10.40

Baking Controls

In the **Domain Properties**, **Cache Tab** you will see **Type: Replay.**

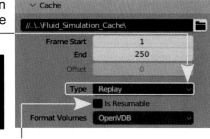

Figure 10.41

Replay: is one of three Modes which determine if you can Bake or how you Bake. With **Replay** there are no Bake Buttons. **You cannot Bake**.

Modular: provides individual Bakes for Baking **Settings Data, Particle Data and Mesh Data**.

All: Bakes everything at the same Time.

Is Resumable

When **Type: Replay** is active you may make adjustment to controls, reconfigure the arrangement and replay the Animation as previously mentioned but you **Can Not Bake**. To Bake you have to select **Type: Modular** or **Type All**.

Fluid Simulation Framework

Blender incorporates a Fluid Simulation Framework (Fluid Processing System) called **Mantaflow**.

Mantaflow is the new physically-based fluid simulation framework in Blender for gas (smoke & fire) and liquid simulations.

Note: Mantaflow allows a Bake to be paused and restarted but only with **Is Resumable** checked (Figure 10.41). If **NOT** checked you see a warning.

> ℹ Non Resumable Cache: Baking mesh or particles will not be possible   Figure 10.42

With **Is Resumable** checked you may pause the Bake by pressing **Esc**. In which case **Resume and Free** buttons display. Resume continues the Bake, Free clears the Cache.

Click **Bake Data**   Figure 10.43

Bake Data

Press **Esc** to pause the Bake

Resume   Free

Click **Resume** to continue Baking

With the Bake paused you change back to Replay Mode to rerun the Animation when adjustments have been made.

Baking in Practice

To put Data Storage and Baking in perspective the following exercise is offered in relation to the Fluid Simulation, previously set up and shown in Figure 10.38. The simulation length is the default 250 Frames in the Timeline Editor.

With the Domain selected the **Cache Tab** in the **Properties Editor, Physics Properties** shows Folder automatically created named: **//cache_Fluid_4b85f272**.

Note: This **Cache Folder** has been created in the directory: Figure 10.44

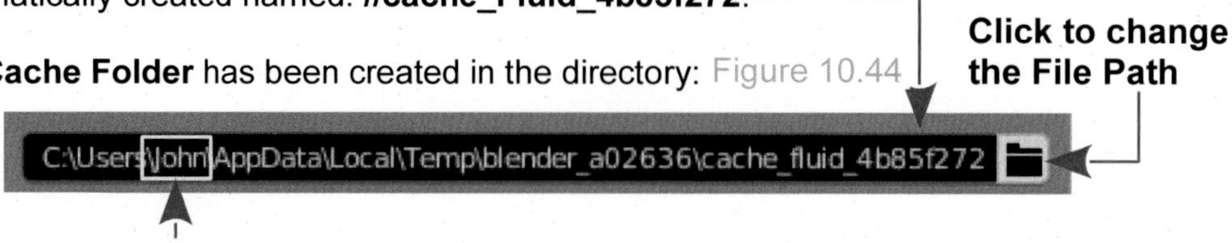

Click to change the File Path

C:\Users\John\AppData\Local\Temp\blender_a02636\cache_fluid_4b85f272

User Name

Note: In the **Properties Editor, Physics Properties, Cache Tab** for the Domain , the **Cache Type** is **Replay** and **Note: Is Resumable** is unchecked (inactive).

Type: Replay allows pausing and replay of the Animation Timeline when Particles are being generated. In this state **Is Resumable** is not required to be active.

Having the Cache Folder located in the C:\Users Directory is not a convenient place to access. You may create a new Folder and change the File Path in the Cache Tab. When the File Path is changed to the new Folder sub Folders, config and data are automatically created which in turn contain a single .uni and .vdb File.

Windows: C (C:)

Figure 10.45

∨ Fluid_Simulation_Cache

config   config_0001.uni

data   fluid_data_0001.vdb

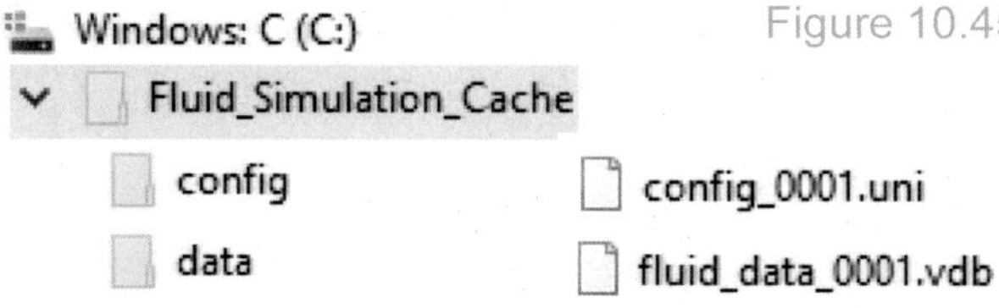

When the Animation is played in the Timeline Editor multiple **config** and **data** Files are generated.

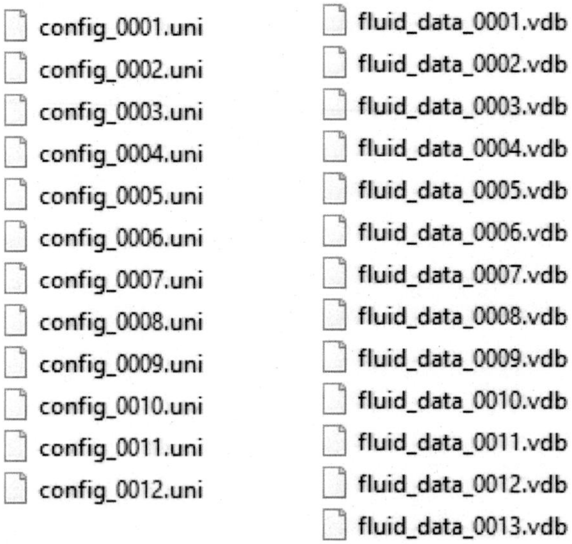

config_0001.uni	fluid_data_0001.vdb
config_0002.uni	fluid_data_0002.vdb
config_0003.uni	fluid_data_0003.vdb
config_0004.uni	fluid_data_0004.vdb
config_0005.uni	fluid_data_0005.vdb
config_0006.uni	fluid_data_0006.vdb
config_0007.uni	fluid_data_0007.vdb
config_0008.uni	fluid_data_0008.vdb
config_0009.uni	fluid_data_0009.vdb
config_0010.uni	fluid_data_0010.vdb
config_0011.uni	fluid_data_0011.vdb
config_0012.uni	fluid_data_0012.vdb
	fluid_data_0013.vdb

The .uni and .vdb Files contain the information which allows you to replay the Animation showing the Fluid Flow.

Note: At this point there is no facility allowing you to Bake the simulation. The .uni and .vdb are temporary Files which allow you to replay the simulation and make adjustments.

Figure 10.46

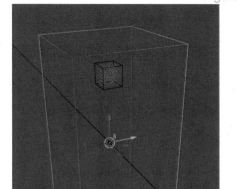
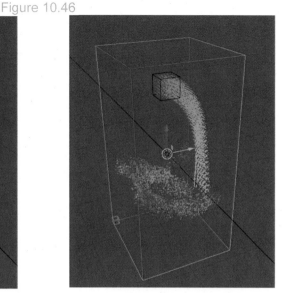

| **Particles at Frame 1** | **Particles at Frame 100** |

By changing the **Type** value to **All** in the **Properties Editor, Physics Properties, Cache Tab** displays a **Bake All** button.

Note: Changing to **Type: All** deletes the **config** and **data** Folders with the .uni and .vdb files. Replaying the Animation at this point does nothing. To regenerate the simulation you have to Bake. Changing to Type: All also removes the display of Particles (Fluid Flow) from the 3D Viewport Editor.

Remember: Mantaflow allows a Bake to be paused and restarted but only with **Is Resumable** checked (Figure 10.41). If **NOT** checked you see a warning.

Bake All

Figure 10.47

Bake All means you will Bake (regenerate) the information for the Fluid Flow Simulation. This information (Folders and Files) is segregated into categories: **Bake Data** (in the Settings Tab), **Bake Particles** (in the Particles Tab) and **Bake Mesh** (in the Mesh Tab).

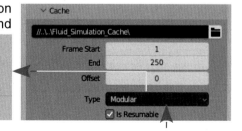

Click to display the Cache Type Menu

To see the Bake buttons for each category you have to select **Modular** in the **Cache: Type**.

With **Bake Type: All** selected, clicking the Bake All button starts the Bake process. A progress bar appears in the Timeline Editor and the Bake All button becomes displays instruction to **Pause Bake** (Figure 10.48).

Figure 10.48

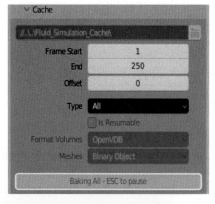

Bake Progress Bar

On completion of the Bake, the Bake button displays as Free Bake which will delete all data generated.

The 3D Viewport shows the Fluid as a Mesh which Renders.

Figure 10.49

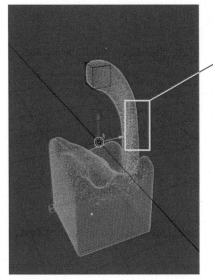

Mesh
Particles Inside

Mesh – Wireframe Display Mode   **Rendered Viewport Display**

Bake Modular

With **Modular** selected in the Cache Type the Bake button disappears from the Cache Tab. In its place you will find Bake buttons for separate categories as previously described.

Note: You are required to **Bake Data** before you can Bake Particles or Mesh and you must have Is Resumable checked in the Cache Tab. Also, to Bake Particles you are required to select (check) at least one of the **Spray, Foam** or Bubbles categories in the Particles Tab.

Selecting Spray, Foam and or Bubbles generates Particles within the Mesh Particles to create these effects.

At this point the Rendered View shows the Fluid Mesh as a gray color. Since the demonstration began by using the default Cube Object as the Domain the default gray Material is displayed. With a few tweaks in the Material Properties (Figure 10.50) you can have nice cool green.

Figure 10.50

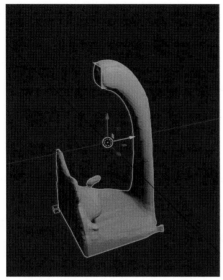

Rendered Viewport Display

Domain Material Properties

Remember: If your Domain is not created from the default Cube Object you will have to apply a New Material.

Rebaking with Cache Type: Bake All

You may pause a Bake at any time by pressing the **Esc Key.** Pausing allows you to preview the Fluid being generated in the 3D Viewport Editor. If it looks OK you can continue the Bake **providing you have Is Resumable checked**. The Bake buttons in the Properties Editor will display a **Resume** button to allow you to restart the Bake. **Note:** As soon as you start a Bake the Physics button Controls become grayed out. At this point you can not change settings.

If you have forgotten to check **Is Resumable**, Free the Bake and start over.

To change settings, press **Esc** to stop the Bake, alter settings then Resume the Bake.

Rebaking with Cache Type: Modular

The Bake Data and Bake Mesh buttons change to **Free Data** and **Free Mesh** after baking. Clicking either of these cancels the data saved to memory in the Cache and makes the controls active. You may then adjust settings and Rebake. You may Rebake the Mesh without Rebaking the Data.

As previously stated, **Baking** writes Data to the Cache Folder on the hard drive to save RAM. When you save the Blender File the Data written to the Cache Folder is not saved with the Blender File. When you close the Blender File the Data remains in the Cache on the hard drive. If you create a new simulation using the same Cache Folder the Data will be overwritten, therefore, the simulation in the original Blender file will not play when the file is reopened. **Therefore, create a new Cache Folder for a new simulation**.

Adding Spray Foam Bubbles

Figure 10.51

So far Particles have been generated which simulate a Fluid Flow. These were created when the Data was Baked. In the Properties Editor, Particle Properties, with the Domain selected. You will see that a **Particle System named Liquid** has been automatically applied to the Domain.

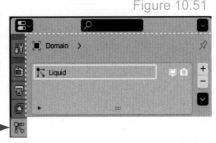

Particle Properties ———▶

Note: You can not edit this Particle System in the Particle Properties.

Select (check) either or Spray, Foam, Bubbles ————

Spray Particles Selected ——————

Figure 10.52

Additional Particles may be created to act as **Spray**, **Foam** or **Bubbles**. To create these Particles you check either one or all of the buttons in the **Properties Editor, Fluid Physics buttons, Particles Tab** (Figure 10.52). The controls in the Particles may be adjusted to affect the selection as a whole.

Making a selection adds a **Particle System.** Figure 10.53

Domain Physics Properties

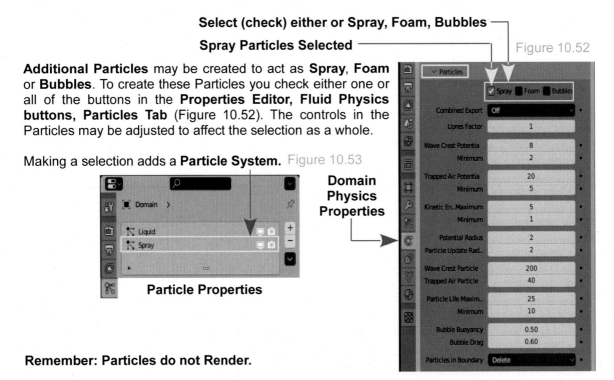

Particle Properties

Remember: Particles do not Render.

To have the Spray display amongst the fluid in the 3D Viewport Editor you add an Object to the Scene and set the Particle System to Render the Particles (display) as that Object (an Instance Object).

Instance Object

Figure 10.54

Add an Icosphere to the Scene, scaled down and parked to one side. Give the Icosphere a nice bright Material (color).

Leave the Subdivisions for the Icosphere, when in Edit Mode, as the default value (1). The objective being to have an Object with a minimal number of vertices. This minimises the number of calculations for the computer when Baking Data.

When Spray Particles were selected in the Domain Physics Properties a Spray Particle System is introduced (Figure 10.54).

In the render Tab set Render As to Object and in in the Object Tab set Instance Object as Icosphere. In the Viewport Display Tab, Display As – Rendered.

Rebake the Simulation to see Spray Particles (tiny Icospheres) dispersed amongst the Fluid Mesh (Figure 10.55).

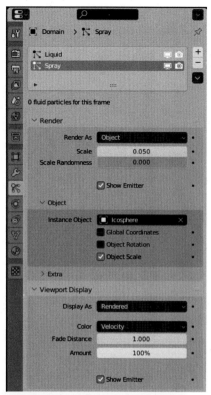

Figure 10.55

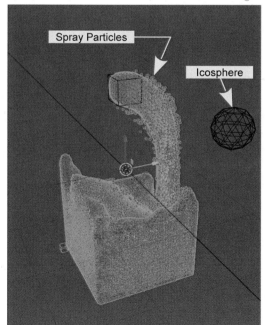

Wireframe Display Mode

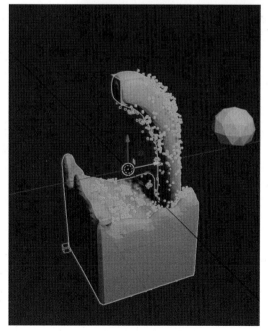

Rendered Display Mode

Summary

In following this exercise you may be in danger of loosing your way, therefore, a summary follows.

The default Cube Object has been assigned as the Domain.

A second Cube has been scaled down relative to the Domain and positioned inside the Domain. This Cube has been designated as the Inflow Object.

In the Properties Editor, Physics buttons, with the Domain selected, Fluid Data and Mesh Data were Baked.

In Baking the Data the length of the animation is the default 250 Frames, therefore, the time to Bake is relatively short. With a lengthy Animation the Bake time could be exponentially longer, therefore, it is not advised to have Is Resumable checked in the Domain, Physics Properties, Cache Tab. Is Resumable allows replaying the simulation after Baking but with the generation of additional data.

In the Cache Folder you will find sub folders have been created containing a variety of File Formats which are data Files for the simulation.

Remind yourself that this is fun and when you become conversant with the settings you will produce fantastic results.

You could have **Bubbles Particles** and **Foam Particles** set up and Baked at the same time.

In this exercise settings have been kept to a minimum. Obviously there are many many settings with which to experiment, but the foregoing should help in understanding the basic procedure for Fluid Simulation.

Before you go! Look at **Effector – Collision and Outflow Objects.**   Figure 10.56

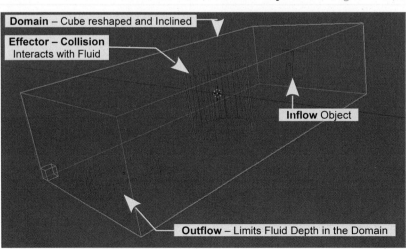

Properties Editor, Physics Properties, Fluid settings for the components in the simulation.

Inflow Object Cube.001

Figure 10.57

Domain Cube

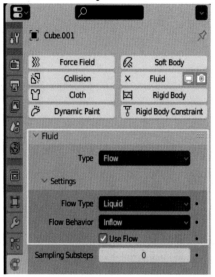

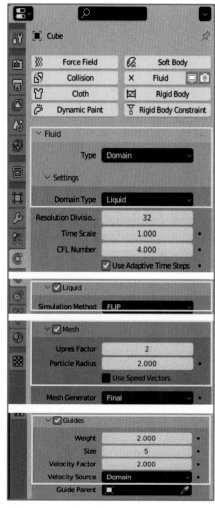

Effector Collision Cylinder

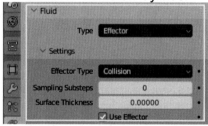

Outflow Effector Guide Cylinder.001

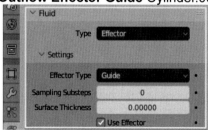

Fluid issues from the Inflow Object (Cube) into the Domain and flows down the incline, separating as it contacts the Effector Collision Cylinder. The Outflow Effector Guide (Cylinder) limits the depth of Fluid in the Domain.

Fluid Simulation after Baking Figure 10.58

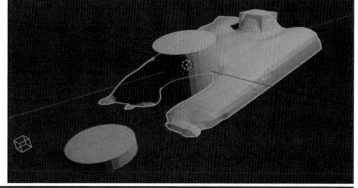

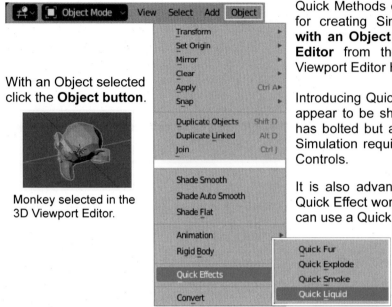

With an Object selected click the **Object button**.

Monkey selected in the 3D Viewport Editor.

Quick Methods or **Quick Effects** are shortcuts for creating Simulations. They are activated **with an Object selected in the 3D Viewport Editor** from the **Object button** in the 3D Viewport Editor Header (Figure 10.59).

Introducing Quick Methods at this juncture may appear to be shutting the door after the horse has bolted but activating the replay in Physics Simulation requires a knowledge of Simulation Controls.

It is also advantageous to understand how a Quick Effect works, in a practical sense, so you can use a Quick Effect by adding to it.

Consider a Quick Effect for a Fluid Simulation. The Quick Effect for Fluid Simulation is labelled **Quick Liquid**.

As an example, delete the default Cube in a new Blender Scene and add a Monkey Object. **With the Monkey selected** click on **Quick Liquid** in the Quick Effects menu.

The Monkey is entered in the 3D Viewport Editor with the Editor in Solid Viewport Shading Mode. Activating the Quick Liquid Effect changes the 3D Viewport Editor to Wireframe Display Mode and the Monkey is surrounded by a Cuboid.

A Fluid Simulation has been created with the Cuboid being the **Domain** and the **Monkey is now a Fluid Flow Object, Flow type Liquid with Flow Behaviour: Geometry**.

Controls have been set in the Properties Editor, Physics Properties.

Flow Behaviour **Geometry** sets the Liquid in the Simulation to be delivered as a Mass inside the Domain.

Figure 10.60

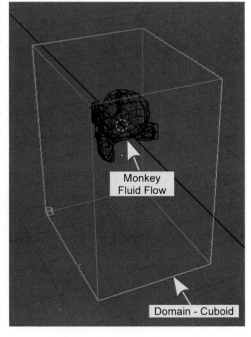

Monkey Fluid Flow

Domain - Cuboid

Press the **Play Button** in the **Timeline Editor** to see a volume of fluid drop from the Monkey into the Domain (Figure 10.61).

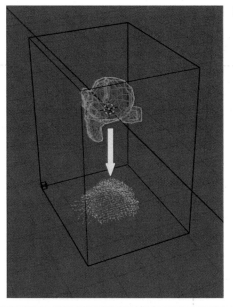

Figure 10.61

Note: With Cache Type Replay, when setting up any Simulation, allows you to Play the Animation and preview the action before performing a Bake. This is very useful in determining if the Simulation will perform correctly.

Properties Editor – Physics Properties

Suzanne – Fluid Flow Object

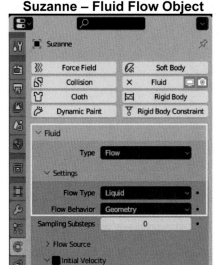

Cube - Domain

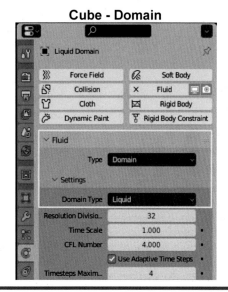

10.9 Fluid Simulation Continued

The Fluid Simulation setup in section 10.7 has demonstrated a basic configuration using a Fluid Flow Type: **Flow** with Settings, **Flow Type: Liquid** and Flow Behaviour: **Inflow**.

Flow Behaviour: Inflow produces a continuous delivery of Fluid over the length of the animation. To expand on the topic, examine the difference in Fluid Behaviour when **Type Geometry** is employed. Instead of a continuous flow, Type Geometry delivers the Fluid in a mass. An example of this type of delivery was demonstrated by using the **Quick Liquid** method (Section 10.8).

Filling a Cup

In this example **a volume** of fluid will be generated to fall into a cup.

Figure 10.62

The arrangement in Figure 10.62 shows the 3D Viewport Editor in Wireframe Viewport Shading Mode. The Scene has been constructed with a fluid Emitter (UV Sphere), a Domain Cube (the default Cube scaled up), and an Obstacle Object (a Cup). For the Cup see Chapter 3 – 3.17.

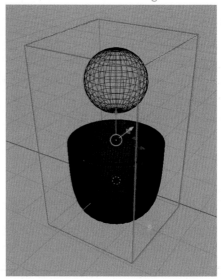

Note: Providing you have saved a Blender file containing the Cup you will be able to append into a new Blender Scene. **Important: When using the Cup developed in Chapter 3, Apply the Modifiers.**

Domain Object Setup

The Domain is a Cube that has been scaled to enclose the Sphere and the Cup. For this demonstration default Physics settings will be used.

With the Cube selected, in the 3D Viewport Editor (Figure 10.62). Go to the **Properties Editor, Physics Properties** and click on **Fluid** to display the Fluid Tab. Change the Fluid Type to **Domain**. In the Settings tab set **Domain Type** as **Liquid**.

Scroll down and check **Mesh**.

In the **Cache Tab** change the default **End Frame** to **50**.

In the **Timeline Editor** set the **End Frame** to **50**.

Generator Object Setup

The fluid will be emitted by the Sphere that has been placed in the Domain immediately above the Cup. The convention of calling this type of Object the **Generator** is adopted.

It is tempting to call the Sphere simply the Fluid Object, since it controls the fluid generation, but all Objects included in the simulation which have Fluid Physics applied, are Fluid Objects.

Select the UV Sphere. In the **Properties Editor, Physics Properties** set values; **Flow Behaviour: Geometry** (sets the Fluid inflow to take the form of the Generator Object). This means the Fluid will be generated as a spherical mass rather than the continuous flow seen in Section 10.7.

Obstacle Object Setup

Objects included in the simulation which interact with the fluid are called **Effectors**. The Obstacle to the fluid flow inside the Domain will be the Cup.

Select the Cup. Set values; **Fluid type: Effector** and **Settings Effector Type : Collision**.

Note: The Effector Object is named **Cylinder** in the Outliner Editor since the Cup Model has been constructed from a default Cylinder Object and hasn't been renamed. Note also, the **Effector Type: Collision**.

Scale and Proportion

When creating a Fluid animation you should consider the proportion (size relationship) of Objects. In this particular simulation the Sphere Flow Object has been scaled relative to the Effector Cup. The volume of the Sphere determines the volume of Fluid generated, therefore, it has been scaled to produce a volume of Fluid that will reasonably fit into the Cup.

As it is, the Cup is 1.94m in diameter which is a very large Cup. If this were to be placed in a Scene with other Objects the scale of everything would have to be relative.

Another factor to consider is Time. Look at the arrangement and think about how long you want this huge drop of Fluid to take to drop into the Cup. So that you can see what happens when this occurs, perhaps two seconds is appropriate.

The animation length has been set at 50 Frames. The output Frame Rate, by default, set in the Properties Editor, Output Properties is 24 fps (Frames Per Second).

50 Divided By 24 = 2.08333 seconds

If you want exactly Two seconds change the Frame Rate to 25.

Viscosity

Yet another factor to consider is **Viscosity**. The viscosity refers to the "thickness" of the fluid and actually the force needed to move an object of a certain surface area through it at a certain speed. Blender uses the kinematic viscosity which is dynamic viscosity.

The table following gives some examples of fluids together with their dynamic and kinematic viscosities.

Figure 10.63

Fluid	Dynamic viscosity (in cP)	Kinematic viscosity (Blender, in $m^2.s^{-1}$)
Water (20 °C)	1.002×10^0 (1.002)	1.002×10^{-6} (0.000001002)
Oil SAE 50	5.0×10^2 (500)	5.0×10^{-5} (0.00005)
Honey (20 °C)	1.0×10^4 (10,000)	2.0×10^{-3} (0.002)
Chocolate Syrup	3.0×10^4 (30,000)	3.0×10^{-3} (0.003)
Ketchup	1.0×10^5 (100,000)	1.0×10^{-1} (0.1)
Melting Glass	1.0×10^{15}	1.0×10^0 (1.0)

Blender viscosity unit conversion.

Check Diffusion

Viscosity is entered in the **Properties Editor, Physics Properties**, with the **Domain** selected. The entries are found in the **Diffusion Tab**.

Figure 10.64

By default the Viscosity for Water is set which is;
    Base: 1.000 and Exponent: 6.

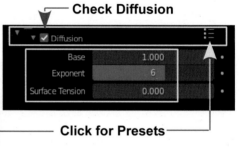

1.002×10^{-6} (0.000001002)

Click for Presets

Note: The Diffusion Tab only displays when the Domain Type is **Liquid** and under Viscosity Presets the default display is **Fluid Presets.** Clicking the Fluid Presets button displays a selection menu for Honey, Oil and Water (Figure 10.64). Selecting an option changes Fluid Presets to the option selected.

With these very basic settings in place, **Bake Data** then **Bake Mesh**. How the Bake performs will depend on your computer power. The fantastic video demonstrations on the internet tend to breeze over this process so be warned and be prepared to wait during Baking. On my PC, for this demonstration, Data Bake and Mesh Bake takes several seconds.

Remember: In the **Cache Tab**, the default Type is Replay. Check **Is Resumable** and change to **Type: Modular**. **Change the Cache Folder to an empty Folder.**

Bake Data then **Bake Mesh** (expand the Mesh Tab).

When Baking Data is complete the Sphere displays with a blue mesh overlay. When Mesh is Baked the Domain consolidates and takes on the shape of the Sphere.

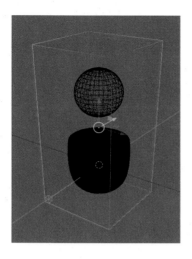
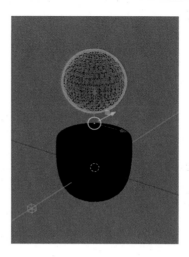

Figure 10.65

Play the Animation in the Timeline Editor. Figure 10.66

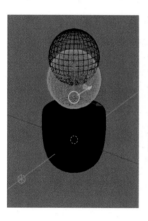
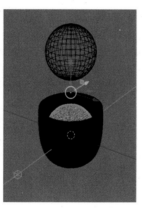
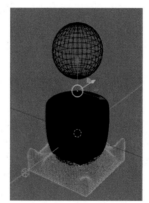
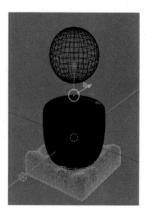

The consolidated Domain is now the Fluid which descends into the Cup **BUT** as you see it breaks through the Cup Mesh and ends up sitting in what was the profile of the Domain. This is obviously not what you want. A modification is required followed by a Re-bake.

Figure 10.67

In the 3D Viewport Editor, select the Cup. In the Properties Editor, Physics Properties, Fluid Tab you will see Surface Thickness: 0.00000. This value determines the distance around the Effector Object to be used when calculating the Collision. The default value is: 0.00000

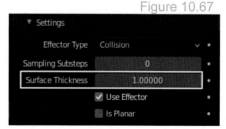

A suggestion for a correct value is; 1.0000

Select the Domain Cube in the Outliner which is consolidated as a sphere on the Flow Sphere. Free the Data and Mesh Bakes. Change the Surface Thickness value, clear the Cache Folder then Rebake Data and Mesh. Play the Animation to see the Fluid descend and fill the Cup (depending on the Sphere size).

Figure 10.68

Note: If the Bake is not performing as expected, it can be terminated by pressing the **Esc Key** or the Cancel button in the Header. Settings can be adjusted to correct the action. To REBAKE the simulation, select the Domain by clicking on Cube in the Outliner Editor (which is now the blob attached to the sphere) and press Resume to continue the Bake. Alternatively, Free the Bake and Bake a second time.

Note: If the demonstration does not perform as expected you could have made an error in the set up. Check your settings and change values accordingly, BUT Note; having changed a setting you will have to Free Data and REBAKE the simulation. Simply changing settings will not correct the action.

Note: Before setting up a new Fluid Simulation clear the data from the Cache file or set a new location for saving the Bake. If data exists in the Cache when a new Domain is created, Blender will attempt to use the existing data.

10.10 Fluid Simulation Experiment (The experiment will show Fluid filling a Bowl.)

Modeling a Bowl

A simple method of creating a Bowl is the delete the upper part of a UV Sphere Object by selecting Vertices in Edit Mode (Figure 10.69). With the Vertices deleted and with the remaining Vertices selected, press the E Key to Extrude (duplicates the Vertices) then immediately press the S Key (Scale) and move the Mouse Cursor towards the center, scaling the Extrusion down, forming a inner surface for the Bowl. Finally move the inner selection up to align the rim.

The Bowl will be an **Effector Object** in the Fluid Simulation and as such must have thickness or be a solid Object. An Object such as a Plane will not work as an Effector.

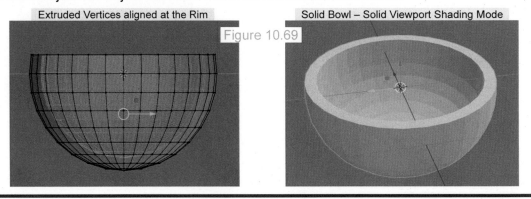
Extruded Vertices aligned at the Rim   Solid Bowl – Solid Viewport Shading Mode
Figure 10.69

Arrange the model of the Bowl inside a Cube Domain and have a smaller second Cube positioned above the Bowl (Figure 10.70). The smaller Cube will be the Fluid Inflow Object.

Fluid Physics Setup

Figure 10.70

3D Viewport Editor Wireframe Display Mode

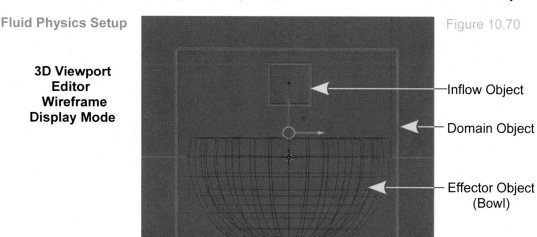

Inflow Object

Domain Object

Effector Object (Bowl)

Select each Object to be included in the simulation and apply the following settings in the Properties Editor, Physics Buttons.

Domain: Fluid – Fluid Type: Domain – Settings Domain Type: Liquid.

Have the Liquid tab checked.

Have the Mesh tab checked.

Enter the File Path to the Cache Folder.

Emitter: Fluid – Fluid Type: Flow – Flow Type: Liquid – Flow Behaviour: Geometry. (Flow Behaviour Geometry delivers the Fluid as a Mass)

Effector: Fluid – Fluid Type: Effector- Effector Type: Collision.

Note: Apart from the above settings default settings are employed.

Timeline Editor: In the Timeline Editor set the Animation End Frame to 50 to correspond to the end Frame value in the Properties Editor, Cache tab for the Domain settings.

With the above in place, **Bake Data**. Press Bake in the Properties Editor, Physics Properties with the Domain selected.

It is not necessary to Bake Mesh at this juncture. You can play the animation and see the Particles generated to check the Flow in the Domain.

When you play the animation or step through the animation frames in the Timeline Editor, in all probability, you will see the Fluid Particles generated by the Emitter descend and pass straight through the Bowl splashing into the domain (Figure 10.71).

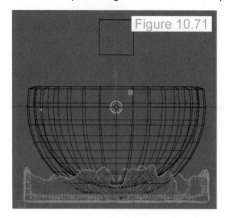
Figure 10.71

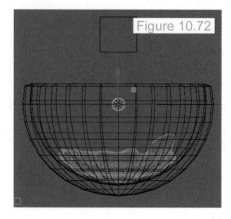
Figure 10.72

To correct the Flow, with the Domain selected press **Clear Data** in the Physics Properties to delete the Data in the Cache Folder. In the 3D Viewport Editor, select the Bowl and change the **Surface Thickness** to **1.00000** in the Properties Editor Fluid, Settings Tab.

Note: The correction instructions are purposely repeated to reinforce the concept.

Select the Domain and Rebake Data. Replay the Animation (Figure 10.72). With the correct Fluid Flow, **Bake Mesh** to see the Fluid as a Mesh with the 3D Viewport Editor in Material Preview or Rendered Viewport Shading Mode.

The experiment has been using a **Fluid flow Type Liquid** with **Flow Behaviour: Geometry applied to the Emitter Cube.**

With the identical arrangement, clear the Data to remove data from the Cache Folder then change the **Flow Behaviour** to **Inflow**. Changing to Inflow will deliver the Fluid in a continuous stream instead of a Mass (Figure 10.73). The stream will descend into the Bowl and continuously fill the bowl, eventually overflowing and filling the Domain (Figure 10.74).

Figure 10.73

Figure 10.74

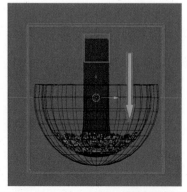

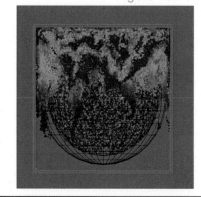

With Fluid Simulation the effects are limitless. To discover the possibilities you will have research tutorials on the internet and experiment by yourself. Some effects will be fairly obvious but when you have an idea to create an animation, in the beginning you may find the techniques required to perform the operations required are allusive. The following example will show another variation on what has already been describe.

Ball Dropping into a Cup

This example will demonstrate how to set up an Object (Sphere) to drop into a Cup containing a Liquid. The first task is to model a Cup. This new Cup Model will allow an exact volume of Fluid to just fill the Cup. Start with a **Cylinder Object** and tab into Edit Mode. In Edit Mode change Vertex Select Mode to Face Select Mode and delete the top Face of the Cylinder.

Change back to Vertex Select Mode, select the upper rim of Vertices and Scale out slightly forming a thin walled Cup. The Cup will become an **Effector Type Collision Object** in the Fluid Simulation. **Remember**; simple planer objects will not work as Effectors.

To give the Cup wall thickness, select all Vertices, Press the E Key (Extrudes – Duplicates selected Vertices), press the S Key (Scale) and move the Mouse Cursor towards the center, scaling the selected (duplicated) Vertices. While remaining selected move the selection up forming a flat rim (Figure 10.75).

Figure 10.75

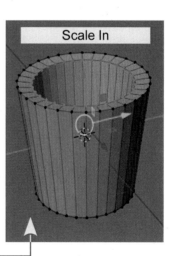

Tab to Edit Mode ———⌐   **Extrude All Vertices** ———⌐

Arrangement

The arrangement of Objects for this simulation is shown in Figure 10.76. A Cube has been scaled on the Z Axis forming the Domain. The Cup is scaled to fit inside the Domain and positioned at the bottom.

A Cylinder Object is Scaled to fit inside the Cup and positioned just above the bottom of the inner surface of the Cup. In Figure 10.77 Data has been Baked, therefore, Fluid Particles can be seen (blue dots) attached to the Cylinder while at Frame 1 in the animation.

A UV sphere Object is Scaled down and positioned towards the top of the Domain immediately above the Fluid Inflow Object.

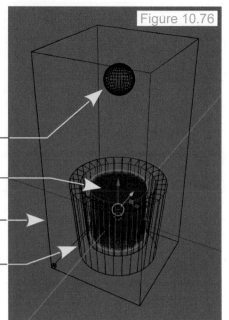
Figure 10.76

Settings: In the **Property Editor, Physics Properties**, default settings are employed with the Objects participating in the Simulation as follows:

UV Sphere – Fluid Type: Effector – Collision
Surface Thickness: 1.0000

Inflow Object Cylinder – Fluid Type: Flow
Flow Type: Liquid – Flow Behavior: Geometry

Domain Cube – Fluid Type: Domain
Domain Type Liquid

Cup – (Figure 10.75) Fluid Type Effector
Effector Type: Collision

In the Domain settings the **Liquid** and **Mesh Tabs** are checked. The File path to the **Cache Folder** is entered in the Cache Tab. The End Frame in the **Cache Tab** and in the **Timeline End Frame** is **50** (Figure 10.77). **Note:** In the **Cache Tab** the default **Type** is **Replay**. Check: **Is Resumable**.

Before Baking Fluid the **UV Sphere Effector Object** is animated to fall into the Cup starting at Frame 10 and ending at Frame 30.

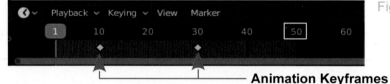
Figure 10.77

————— Animation Keyframes

With the Domain selected, change the **Type** in the **Cache Tab** to **Modular** and ensure you check **Is Resumable**. **Bake Data and Mesh**. Rendered Viewport Shading Mode sees the Sphere splashing into the Liquid when the Animation is played.   Figure 10.78

10.11 Smoke and Fire Simulation

By analysing the Properties Editor, Physics and Material Properties for the **Quick Smoke** method you will gain an appreciation of the settings required for a simulation. Revisit the **Quick Smoke Method** for **Fire**.

The arrangement in the 3D Viewport Editor is simply two Cube Objects, one Scaled down and positioned inside the other. Figure 10.80 shows the arrangement in Wireframe Display Mode. The Physics Properties are shown in Figure 10.79.

Figure 10.79

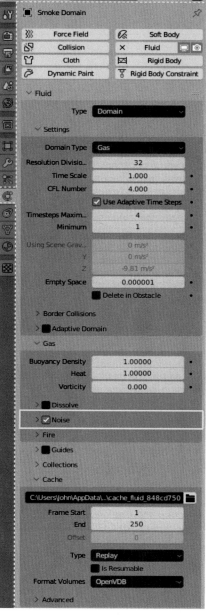

Figure 10.80

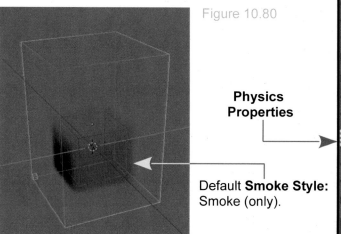

Physics Properties

Default **Smoke Style:** Smoke (only).

Note: Activating **Smoke Style – Smoke and Fire** in the **Last Operator panel** automatically checks **Noise**.

Figure 10.81

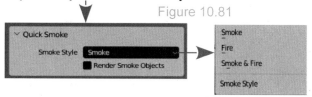

Note: If you perform an operation in the 3D Viewport Editor the Quick Smoke options panel disappears.

Losing the Quick Smoke options emphasises the need for knowing what settings the Quick Smoke method has automatically generated.

When apply the Quick Smoke tool you are designating the selected Object as a smoke **Emitter**. Blender automatically applies Physics settings to the Object. Blender also creates a cubic volume of 3D Space in which the simulation will take place ; the **Domain**. Physics settings are also applied.

Smoke can be generated using any Mesh Object in a scene as an **Emitter (Flow Object).**

There are basically only two objects required in a scene for a smoke simulation, a **Domain** and an **Emitter**. This is similar to the principles for setting up **Fluid Simulation**. Both the Domain and the Emitter have Physics applied.

Scene Setup

If you are starting from scratch the default Screen background is dark gray and is not the best when viewing gray smoke. It is, therefore, suggested you change the color of the background.

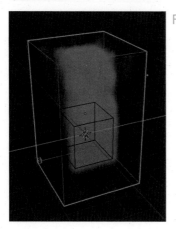
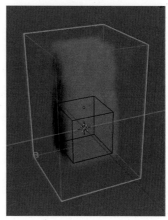

Figure 10.82

World Background

Figure 10.82 shows the 3D Viewport Editor background in Solid Viewport Shading Mode. If you switch to Rendered Viewport Shading Mode you will be back to a gray background color. Rendered Viewport Shading is previewing what you see when the Scene is Rendered. You change this background in the **Properties Editor, World Properties, Surface Tab, Color bar**.

Lighting

The default Blender Scene contains a single **Point Light**. Smoke, being what it is, can be very thin and wispy in nature which makes it difficult to see at times. It is suggested that you, at least, change the Point Light to an **Area Light.**

With the Point Light selected go to the **Properties Editor, Object Data Properties,** select **Area in the Light Tab** and ramp up the **Power setting to 3000w**. You could also consider duplicating the lamp a number of times and positioning the duplicates around the Scene.

To demonstrate setting up a Smoke Simulation from scratch a Plane Object will be used as an Emitter with a Cube Object as the Domain.

Scene Setup

Figure 10.83

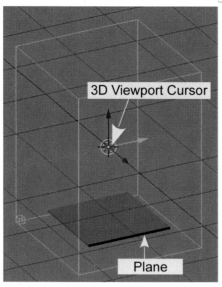
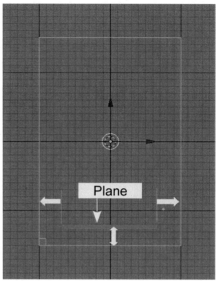

Set the Scene as shown in Figure 10.83. A Plane Object will be used as the **Emitter** (source of the smoke) and a Cube Object will be used as a **Domain**. Scale the Cube and the Plane as shown making sure the **Plane** is totally inside the **Domain** (Check in **Front Orthographic view**). For the demonstration keep the Objects in proportion with the Domain Cube approximately 1.5 Blender units high.

You can use Wireframe Viewport Shading to position the Objects then change to Solid Viewport Shading. In Solid Mode the Plane is inside the Cube, therefore, you only see the Cube.

To use the Objects in a Smoke simulation **Physics** has to be applied.

Figure 10.84

The Domain Object (Cube)   **Properties Editor** ➤

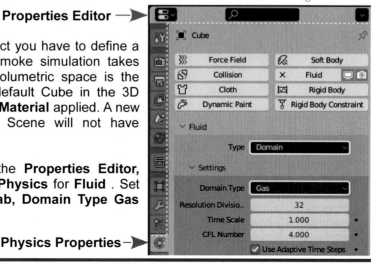

To emit smoke from a Mesh Object you have to define a volume of space in which the smoke simulation takes place. In Blender Physics this volumetric space is the **Domain**. **Note:** If you use the default Cube in the 3D Viewport, this Cube has a default **Material** applied. A new Cube Object introduced to the Scene will not have Material.

With the Cube selected go to the **Properties Editor, Physics Properties** and enable **Physics** for **Fluid** . Set **Fluid Type:Domain, Settings Tab, Domain Type Gas** (Figure 10.84)**.**

Physics Properties ➤

213

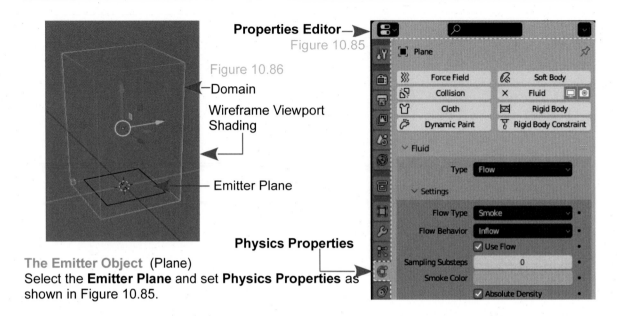

Properties Editor —▶

Figure 10.85

Figure 10.86

— Domain

Wireframe Viewport
Shading

◀—

— Emitter Plane

Physics Properties

The Emitter Object (Plane)
Select the **Emitter Plane** and set **Physics Properties** as
shown in Figure 10.85.

Play the Animation

Figure 10.87   Figure 10.88

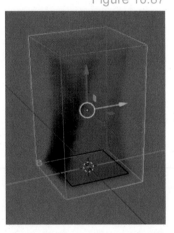

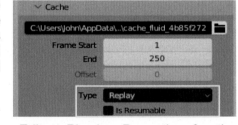

At this stage playing the
Animation in the
Timeline Editor shows
Smoke being Emitted
from the Plane and
rising in the Domain.

Note: In the Properties Editor, Physics Properties for the
Domain, Blender has assigned a Cache Folder. The **Cache
Mode is: Replay** and **Is Resumable** is NOT checked.

Note: The default **End Frame** values are being used (250
Frames).

Smoke will issue from the Plane and rise in a column towards the top of the **Domain** Cube
(Figure 10.87). This simulation will play for the default 250 Frames as set in the Timeline Editor
and then repeat. Press **Esc** to quit or press the **Pause** button in the Timeline Editor and then the
Return to Start button.

Note: At this point the 3D Viewport Editor is in **Wireframe Viewport Display Mode** and with the
animation paused in the Timeline you will see smoke as shown in Figure 10.87. If you switch to
Rendered Viewport Shading Mode you will be disappointment to find that the Smoke doesn't
show. If you press F12 to render the Scene all you see is the domain as a solid Object.

To display Smoke in Rendered Viewport Shading Mode and in a Render, Nodes have to be
configured in the **Shader Editor**.

Viewport Display

Figure 10.89

How a Smoke simulation displays in the Viewport is dependent on the Material Nodes for the Domain Object. If you have created the Domain using a new Cube Object, the Cube will not have a material applied, therefore, the Material buttons in the Properties Editor will only contain the **New** button and the Shader Editor will be empty (NO Nodes).

When using a New Cube Object click the New button to display Material controls. If you have used the default Cube for the Domain, Material controls will be displayed and a default Node arrangement will be in the Shader Editor (Figure 10.89).

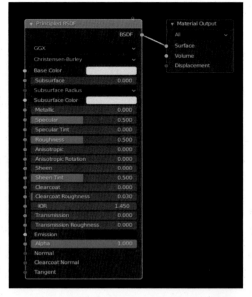

The Node arrangement consists of a Principled BSDF Node connected to a Material Output Node. Smoke does **NOT** show in Rendered Viewport Shading Mode.

Replace the Principled BSDF Node with a **Principled Volume** Node and connect as shown (Figure 10.90).

Figure 10.90

With the Node arrangement reconfigured Smoke will display in Rendered Viewport Shading Mode and in a Render when you press F12.

Note: The Render will take a few seconds to load.

Figure 10.91

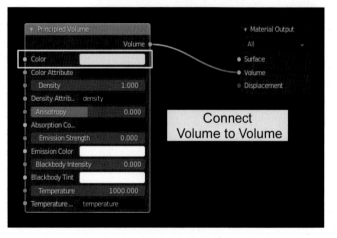

Connect
Volume to Volume

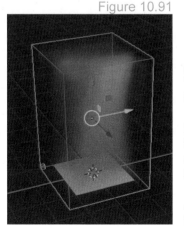

At this point you can control the **Smoke Color** in the Principled Volume Node **with the Viewport in Rendered Viewport Shading Mode.**

Note: There are other Smoke controls in the Physics buttons for the Emitter Plane. The Smoke Color control in these controls will allow you to change the Smoke color when in Solid Viewport Shading Mode.

At this stage only Smoke Simulation has been considered. Its time to look at **Fire** which is a little different.

Note: Figure 10.91 shows the Scene with a single Area Light (1000 W).

Fire Simulation

Figure 10.92 **Emitter Physics**

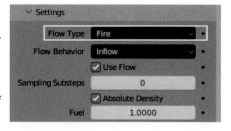

Using the previous Object, Node and settings for the Emitter and the Domain make one change in the Emitter Plan Physics. In the **Settings Tab** change the **Flow Type to Fire**. Play the animation in the Timeline while the Viewport is in **Solid Viewport Shading Mode** to see Fire instead of Smoke.

Figure 10.93

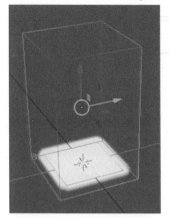

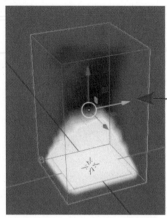

Domain Physics   Figure 10.94

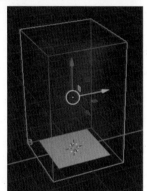

Increase the **Temperature: Max**. in the **Domain Physics, Fire Tab.**

You guessed it! When you change to Rendered Viewport Shading Mode there is no Fire, maybe just a little bit of Smoke (Figure 10.95).

Figure 10.95

With the Domain selected add and connect Nodes as shown in Figure10.96 and **replay the Animation in the Timeline.**

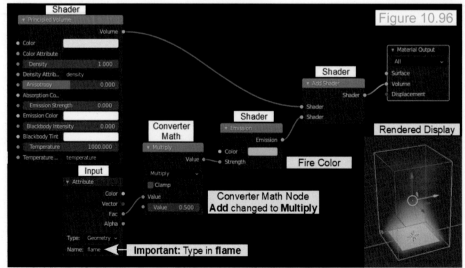

Note: The Fire displays in different ways depending on the Viewport Shading Mode. The inset in Figure in Figure 10.96 is in Material Preview Rendered Viewport Shading.

Figure 10.97

Solid Viewport Shading

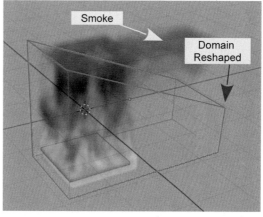

With the Node arrangement in Figure 13.96 for the Domain you may select the Emitter Plane and change the Settings, **Flow Type** to **Fire + Smoke**. When the Animation is replayed the Smoke will intensify and fill the Domain (Figure 10.97).

Domain Bounds

How the Fire and Smoke accumulates in the Domain is determined by the **Domain Bounds**. Every Object in Blender has a Bounding Volume which is a cubic volume of space in the Scene which it occupies for the purpose of calculation. By Scaling the Domain in the demonstration, along the Y Axis and repositioning such that the Emitter Plane is to one side you will see the Smoke and Fire being generated as shown in below.

Figure 10.98

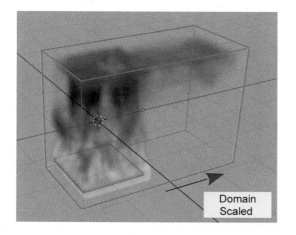

Domain Scaled

Smoke

Domain Reshaped

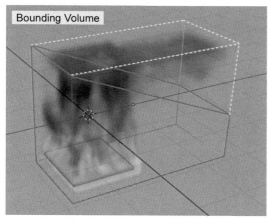

Bounding Volume

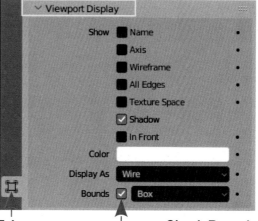

Domain Object Properties, Viewport Display Tab

Check Bounds

Dynamic Paint

Introduction

Dynamic Paint is the process of using one Object to color (paint) or deform the surface of another Object.

When coloring the process is much like painting on a canvas using one Object as a **Brush**. The Object being painted is called the **Canvas**.

Although named **Dynamic Paint** the process can also deform the surface of an Object by displacing Vertices in a permanent displacement or by simulating a wave formation as one Object moves through the surface of another in a dynamic effect.

The following will demonstrate the basic setup when using Dynamic Paint and is intended to show you the method of setting the Physics for the basic operation. By adjusting settings in the Properties Editor, Physics Properties and creating Node arrangements in the Node Editor the final outputs are infinite.

Caveat: The following procedure has been developed through experimentation and describes one method only.

Understanding the procedure involved in creating a Dynamic Paint effect will allow you to research and follow detailed tutorials.

11.1 Dynamic Paint - Painting

To demonstrate **Dynamic Painting** a UV Sphere Object will be used as a **Brush** to paint a Material Color onto the surface of a Plane Object, the **Canvas**. You may use any Object as Brush and paint on to the surface of any Object. A Plane gives a nice flat surface on which to work.

The word Dynamic in the title refers to the fact that, in this process, painting takes place when an animation sequence is being run in the Timeline Editor. The Brush is moved on the surface of the Canvas while the animation sequence is running. This introductory demonstration will employ **Format Type: Vertex** which means that where the Brush Object coincides with the Canvas Object, the Vertices of the Canvas at the intersection, will have color applied.

Set up a Scene as shown in Figure 11.1 with a UV Sphere Object off to the side of a Plane Object. The Plane is scaled up six times and subdivided, in Edit Mode, **eighty times** producing plenty of Vertices. The Plane has a Material color applied (blue).

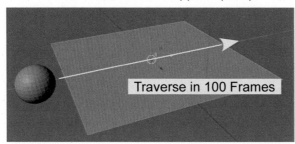

Figure 11.1

Traverse in 100 Frames

For convenience when testing the procedure, animate the UV Sphere to traverse the Plane on the Y Axis in 100 Frames.

With the Plane selected Subdivide in Edit Mode eighty times to create plenty of Vertices.

Last Operator Panel   Figure 11.2

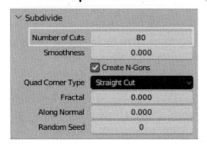

Plane – Edit Mode

Note: The **3D Viewport Editor** is in **Solid, Viewport Shading Mode.**

As stated in the introduction the UV Sphere Object will be used as a **Brush** to paint color on to the Plane Object which acts as a **Canvas**. The terms, **Brush** and **Canvas** are used in the **Properties Editor, Physics Properties**.

Properties Editor ——▶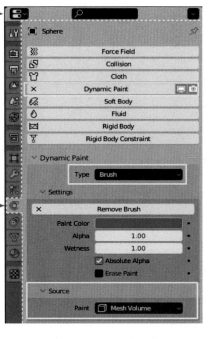

Select the **UV Sphere** (at Frame 1 in the Animation). **Note:** The Sphere **Does Not** have a Material applied but is displaying in the viewport with the default Blender gray color.

Figure 11.3

In the **Properties Editor, Physics Properties** (Figure 11.3), click **Dynamic Paint** then in the **Dynamic Paint Tab** set the **Type** to **Brush** and click **Add Brush** to display **Settings** (**Add Brush** becomes **Remove Brush**).

Physics Properties ——▶

Note: When selecting Physics – Dynamic Paint the arrangement of Physics Type Selection buttons changes from two columns to a single vertical stack.

Make Note: Paint Color is dark blue and in the **Source Tab, Paint** is type **Mesh Volume**. These settings will be revisited later.

Viewport Shading Settings   Figure 11.4 **Solid Viewport Shading** ——┐ **Click**

The default Viewport Shading Mode for the 3D Viewport is Solid Viewport Shading. To demonstrate Dynamic Painting change to Rendered Viewport Shading in the Viewport Header.

Rendered Viewport Shading ——┘

Canvas Configuration

Select the **Plane** and Tab to **Edit Mode** and ensure that the Mesh is subdivided with plenty of Vertices (80 Subdivisions).

Figure 11.5

Important: Add a Material to the Canvas with **Use Nodes active**. The default gray will be fine.

Tab back to Object Mode and activate **Physics, Dynamic Paint** in the **Properties Editor**, this time with **Dynamic Paint Type: Canvas** (the default). Click **Add Canvas** to display the **Dynamic Paint Properties** (Figure 11.6).

Figure 11.6

In the **Surface Tab**, make note that the **Surface Type** is **Paint**.

Expand the **Output Tab** (way down the bottom). You will see **Paintmap** and **Wetmap Layers** highlighted red.

Click the plus sign next to **Paintmap Layer**. Clicking the plus sign changes the red highlight to black. This indicates that a paint layer has been created named **dp_paintmap**. If you click on the name you will display a panel showing **dp_paintmap** as the single entry.

Physics Properties

Withe the Canvas (Plane) selected open the Shader Editor showing a Principled BSDF Node connected to a Material Output Node. Add an **Attribute Node** and connect as shown in Figure 11.7. Enter (type) **dp_paintmap** in the Attribute Node Name bar.

Figure 11.7

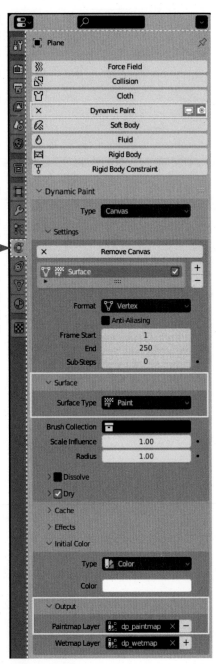

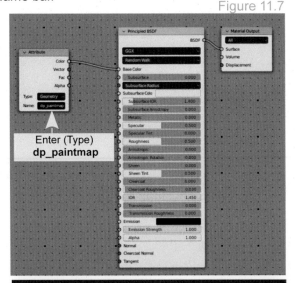

Enter (Type)
dp_paintmap

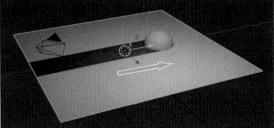

Playing the Animation in the Timeline sees the Sphere traverse the Plane painting a blue stripe.

Figure 11.8

Paint Settings in the **Dynamic Paint, Source Tab** for the
Brush (Sphere) control the Brush Stroke.

Figure 11.9

Mesh Volume

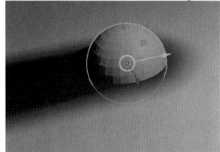

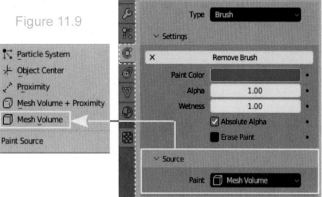

Mesh Volume + Proximity

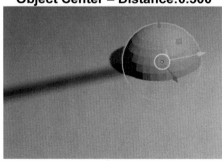

Proximity – Distance:3.400

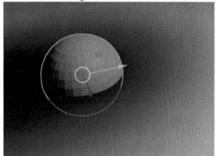

Object Center – Distance:0.500

(image of object center)

Particle System

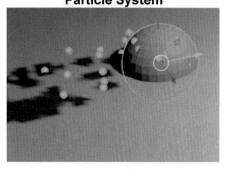

Note: With **Particle System** a Particle System has to
be created for the UV Sphere in the Properties Editor,
Particle Properties and entered in the Brush Settings,
Source Tab. When the Animation is played Particles
Emitted from the Brush (UV Sphere) contact the Plane
causing the application of color.

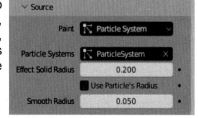

Figure 11.10

Figure 11.11

Brush Paint: ParticleSystem with the Brush elevated above the Canvas Plane (Raindrop Effects).

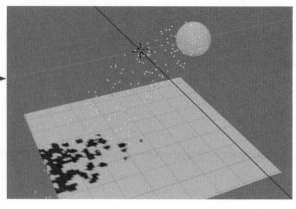

Sphere Brush descending as it transitions.

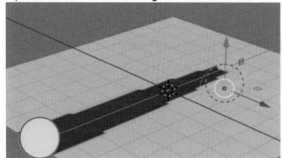

Figure 11.12

Freehand translate the Brush while playing the Animation in the Timeline or Add a Follow Path Constraint with a Curve Path.

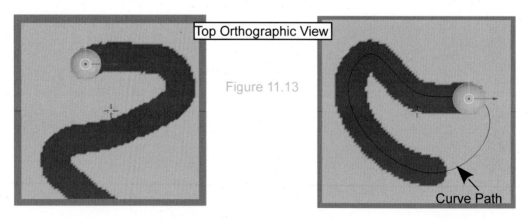

Top Orthographic View

Figure 11.13

Curve Path

Configure Nodes in the **Shader Editor.**

With the Node arrangement shown in Figure 11.7 the Base Color (default gray) of the Plane Object is set by the Principled BSDF Node. A Paintmap Layer is introduced by the Attribute Node allowing the blue paint color in the Brush Settings to be applied by the UV Sphere Brush or Particles emitted by the Brush.

The different color scheme shown in Figures 11, 12 and 13 above are produced by configuring the Node arrangement in the Shader Editor.

Remember: Since Nodes are being employed the 3D Viewport must be in Material Preview or Rendered Viewport Shading Mode.

To produce different color schemes in Dynamic Paint you may replace the Principled BSDF Node with a Diffuse BSDF Node and add connect a **Converter - Color Ramp Node** as shown in Figure 11.14.

Figure 11.14

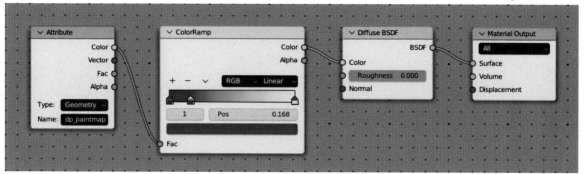

With the Nodes configured, **in this particular instance**, the Plane displays yellow. When the Animation is played in the Timeline a red stripe is painted where the UV Sphere coincides with the surface of the Plane (Figure 11.15)

The color of the Plane and the Paint Color are determined by the settings in the **Color Ramp Node**.

Figure 11.15

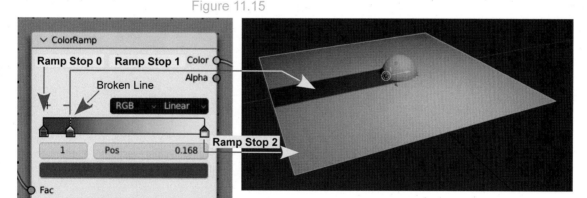

In the Color Ramp Node click on a Ramp Stop and select a color in the color bar. (Ramp Stop 1 is selected as indicated by the broken line above the Stop). Click, hold and drag Stops to see the affect on colors with the Animation paused.

With the Nodes configured the Paint Animation displays in Material Preview and Rendered Viewport Shading Modes. In Solid Viewport Shading the Plane continues to display gray and the Paint color does not show.

Besides painting, the Brush may also be used to deform the surface of the Canvas. **Wave** and **Displace** Options are found in the **Dynamic Paint Physics** buttons for the Canvas in the Surface Tab, **Surface Type**.

12

Geometry Nodes

Geometry Nodes in Blender may be considered as a system for generating Arrays or Patterns which are used for visual effects or for creating complex geometric shapes. The Arrays may be rendered as still images or animated creating a video file

Geometry Nodes are accessed in the **Geometry Node Editor** which is part of the **Geometry Node Workspace.**

Assumptions

This chapter assumes that readers have a working knowledge of Blender, and are conversant with the Graphical User Interface and how the different Editors (panels) are arranged into Workspaces. In particular it is assumed that the readers know how to Model in Blender, apply Materials (colors) use Shader Nodes and perform Keyframe Animation.

12.1 Geometry Node Workspace

Geometry Nodes are accessed in the **Geometry Node Editor** which is part of the **Geometry Node Workspace.**

Geometry Node Workspace   Figure 12.1

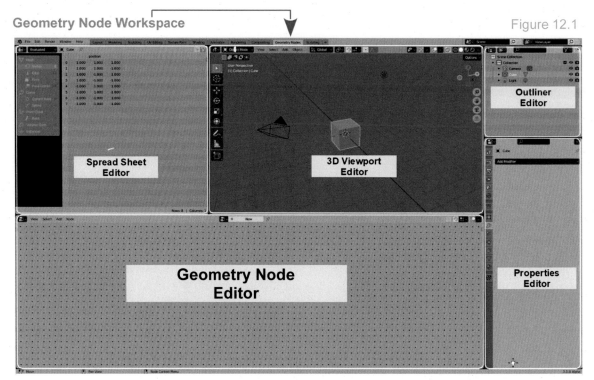

The **Geometry Node Workspace** is accessed by clicking **Geometry Nodes** in the selection menu in the Blender Graphical User Interface Screen Header (Figure 12.1). Alternatively the Workspace may be configured by dividing and arranging Editors in the default Blender Screen.

What are Geometry Nodes? To answer this question, begin by asking, **What is a Node?**

In Blender and other computer graphics programs a **Node** may be considered a point in a pipeline of information which contributes to a result. In the case of **Material Shader Nodes** the result is the appearance of the surface of an Object in the 3D Viewport Editor. There are usually numerous Nodes connected together producing the result, each of which may be disconnected, rearranged or replaced to vary the final display.

The **Node** is a graphical representation of computer data or instruction which is arranged in a **Pipeline**. Think about mixing colors. The primary colors are Red, Green and Blue, which when mixed in equal proportions produce White (Figure 12.2).

In a **Node System** this would look like: Figure 12.2 R + G + B = White

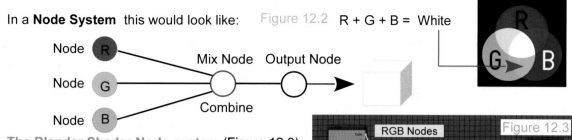

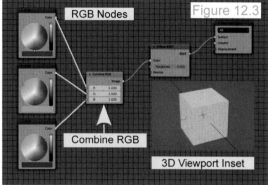

The Blender Shader Node system (Figure 12.3)

Note: Figure 12.3 is conceptional only (not strictly correct). The RGB Nodes are NOT connected and are represented instead by the **Combine RGB Node**. Red, Green and Blue values all 1.000.

A Simple Shader Node Arrangement.

```
  Computer Code
shader simple_material(
    color Diffuse_Color = color(0.6, 0.8, 0.6),
    float Noise_Factor = 0.5,
    output closure color BSDF = diffuse(N))
{
    color material_color = Diffuse_Color * mix(1.0, noise(P * 10.0), Noise_Factor);
    BSDF = material_color * diffuse(N);
}
                                        Text Editor
```

Computer Code written in **Python**, is represented by the **Diffuse BSDF Node**, which outputs data to the **Material Output Node.** This in turn applies Material (color) to the surface of the **Cube** Object in the 3D Viewport Editor.

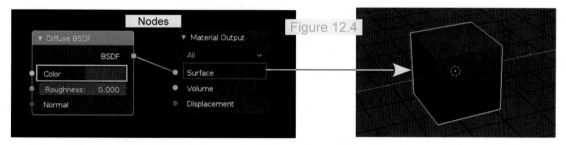

Individual Geometry Nodes are similar to Material Shader Nodes in appearance and the way in which they are arranged and connected in a **Pipeline.** To produce an effect Material Shader Nodes are arranged in the Shader Editor and affect an Object (model) which is selected in the 3D Viewport Editor. **Geometry Nodes** also affect an Object which is selected in the 3D Viewport Editor but they are arranged and connected in the **Geometry Node Editor**.

A reference to the similarities with Shader Nodes may be somewhat misleading. The reference may infer that Geometry Nodes are a different method of modeling and applying Materials but this is not the case. Geometry Nodes are methods for creating visual effects.

It has been said that Geometry Nodes change the way environments are made, procedural effects are generated and the way things are scattered around. Procedural assets can be generated for a current project and then reused in future work since a non-destructive workflow is utilised. This means the assets can be modified for new projects. The assets in a current project are easily adjusted when the results are not satisfactory.

Figure 12.5

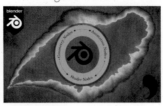
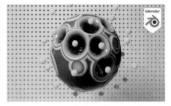

12.2 The Geometry Node Pipeline

The Geometry Node Pipeline may be considered as, using an Object's Geometry as a basis for generating an **Array**.

A Node in the Pipeline may position an Object in 3D Space as a whole which determines where the Array is placed in the Scene.

A Node may control the position in 3D Space of each of the Objects Vertices which determines the shape of the Array.

The Node may provide a method of adding Vertices to an Object which alters its shape or it may display additional Vertices on the surface of an Object to create an Array.

The Node may provides a method of displaying Vertices as other Objects   (instances) which serves to create an **Array of Objects**. ⟶

Figure 12.6

Vertices

Individual Nodes generally contain values which may be edited to affect the display in the 3D Viewport Editor. Individual Nodes are connected in a Pipeline to produce an effect. **Note**; a Pipeline is sometimes referred to as a **Tree**.

Starting a Pipeline

In the default Blender Screen, with the default Cube Object selected in the 3D Viewport Editor, select the **Geometry Nodes Workspace** in the Blender Screen Header. ⟶

Blender Screen Header   Figure 12.7

Selecting **Geometry Nodes** in the Header changes the default Screen arrangement to the Geometry Nodes Workspace (Figure 12.1).

Note that the default Cube Object is selected in the 3D Viewport Editor as indicated by its orange outline. The Geometry Node Editor is empty except for the **New Button** in the Header. The **Spread Sheet Editor** is showing data which is the location in 3D Space of each Vertex making up the Cube Object (more on this to follow).

The procedure in creating a **Node Pipeline** is to click the **New Button** in the Geometry Node Editor Header to introduce a default Node arrangement, then Add Nodes and connect the Nodes to the Pipeline.

A Node Pipeline may be associated with any Object which is selected in the 3D Viewport Editor.

Note: If the default Cube Object In the default Blender Scene is deleted, and the Geometry Node Workspace is entered, you will find that the New Button in the Geometry Node Editor Header does not display. The New Button displays when an Object is added to the Scene. A new Object entered in a Scene, by default, **is selected** when entered. In other words, an Object must have been selected in the 3D Viewport Editor before the New Button displays and is active.

To demonstrate; In a new Blender Scene **delete the default Cube**. Open the Geometry Node Workspace. The **New Button** is not in the Geometry Node Editor Header. In the 3D Viewport Editor, add a **Cone Object**. The New Button is reinstated in the Geometry Node Editor Header.

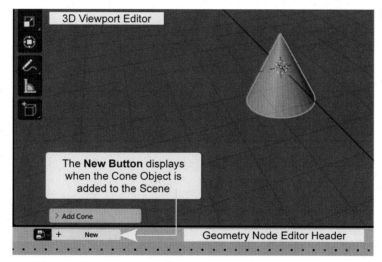

Figure 12.8

Deselect the Cone then add a **UV Sphere** followed by a **Monkey** (Suzanne) separating each along the Y Axis and deselecting each in turn.

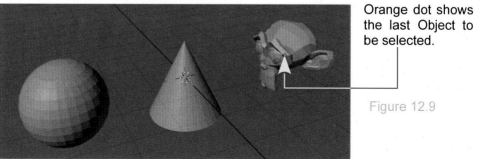

Orange dot shows the last Object to be selected.

Figure 12.9

With all three Objects deselected, click the **New Button** in the Geometry Node Editor Header to introduce a **Node Pipeline**.

The Pipeline will consist of a **Group Input Node** and a **Group Output Node**. The two Nodes are connected by a **Noodle** (green line) from the Group Input, Geometry Socket to the Group Output Geometry Socket. **Note:** The name **Geometry Nodes** where the New button displayed.

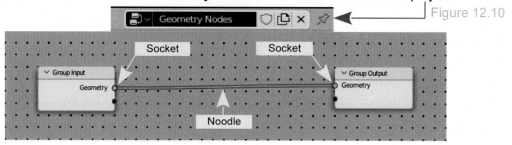

Figure 12.10

Note: None of the Objects are selected in the 3D Viewport Editor. In the Geometry Node Editor Header, click **Add,** to display the Node Selection Menu. Mouse over on the **Geometry** category then in the sub menu click **Transform**.

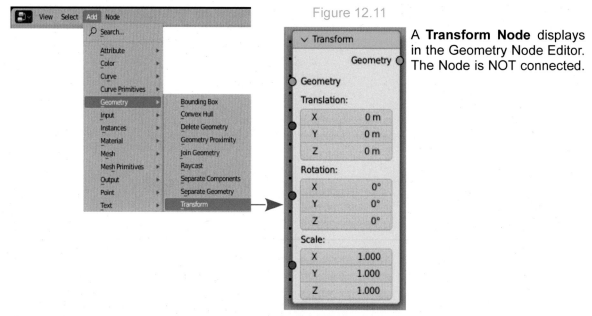

Figure 12.11

A **Transform Node** displays in the Geometry Node Editor. The Node is NOT connected.

Click on the Node, hold and drag the mouse, placing the Node over the green Noodle, between the Input and Output Nodes. This automatically connects the Transform Node in the Pipeline.

Note: If the new Node were incompatible in the Pipeline the Noodle would display red.

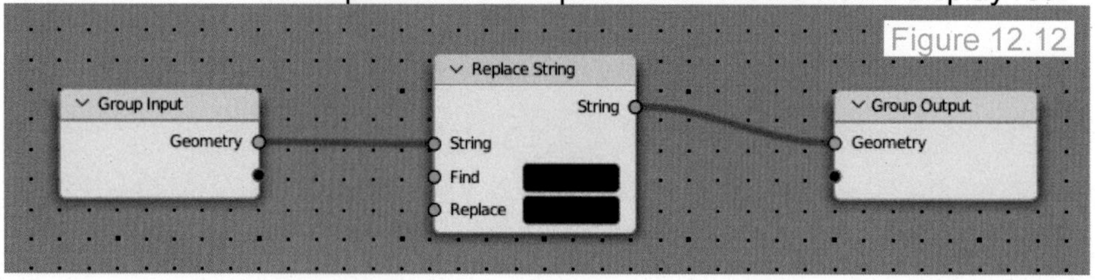

Figure 12.12

In the Transform Node you will see **Translation**, **Rotation** and **Scale** values.

Figure 12.13

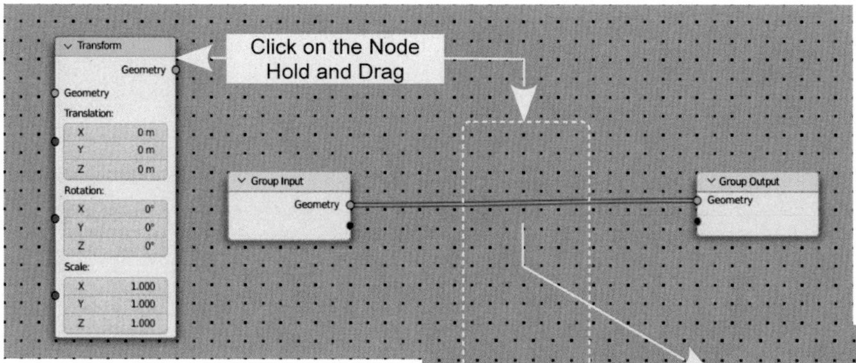

The Value bars are sliders on which you may click, hold and drag right or left (positive – negative) to adjust the values. You may alternatively double click a value, delete and retype a new value.

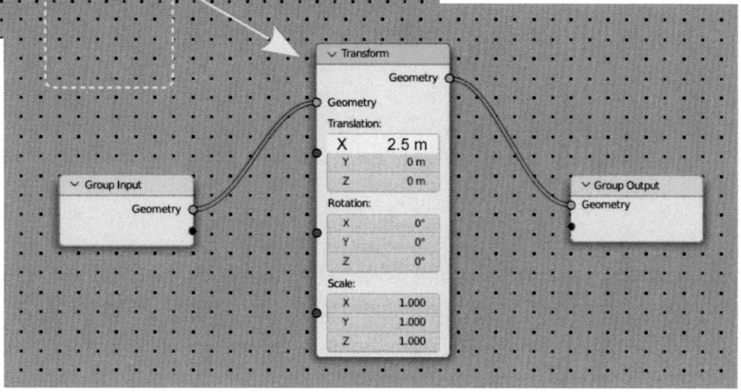

Click on the Node
Hold and Drag

In this particular instance changing the **Translation X** Value will show the Monkey Object in the 3D Viewport Editor displace on the X Axis of the Scene.

This demonstrates that the New Pipeline is applicable to the last Object selected in the Scene.

Note: The last Object that was **selected**, is not necessarily the last Object **entered**.

Figure 12.14

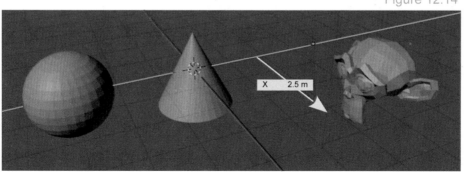

Note: In the Geometry Node Editor Header, when the New Button was clicked, the **New Button** was replaced by the name **Geometry Nodes**. This is the name of the Pipeline affecting the Monkey Object.

Selecting one of the other Objects in the 3D Viewport Editor shows the name **New Button** again.

With the very basic **Node Pipeline** consisting of the **Group Input Node** connected to the **Group Output Node,** the Input Node represents the data for displaying the selected Object. This data is transmitted to the Group Output Node which affects the display of the Object in the 3D Viewport Editor. Introducing the **Transform Node** and connecting it in the Pipeline allows that original Input Data to be modified thus affecting the display in the 3D Viewport Editor.

12.3 Arranging Nodes

It has been demonstrated that Nodes will automatically be connected when they are dragged over a connecting Noodle (Figure 12.13). Nodes may be arranged to suit user preferences by clicking on the Node to select it (a thin red outline is displayed) then holding LMB and dragging the Node to the desired location. If you wish to connect a Node between two other Nodes and the space on the Screen is too small, the space automatically adjusts. At times you may wish to delete a Node in which case, with the Node selected (red outline) press **X Key**.

If you delete the **Transform Node** shown in Figure 12.13 you will be left with the Group Input Node and the Group Output Node **disconnected**. With the Nodes disconnected, Suzanne (the last Object selected in the 3D Viewport Editor) disappears from view.

Figure 12.15

To reconnect the Input and Output Nodes, click on the green Group Input, Geometry Socket, hold and drag over to the Group Output green Geometry Socket.

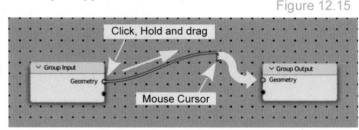

To disconnect Nodes there are two options:

Figure 12.16

Click on the **Input Socket** of a Node (right hand end of the Noodle) hold and drag away from the Socket.

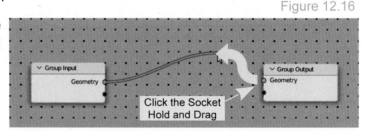

Figure 12.17

Hold **Ctrl** on the Keyboard, **click RMB,** hold and drag the **Knife** tool over the Noodle.

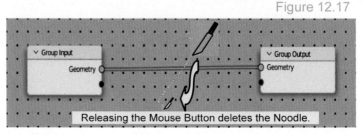

Note: If you hold **Shift** on the Keyboard, **RMB click** and drag the Mouse Cursor over the Noodle a new connection Socket is created on the Noodle.

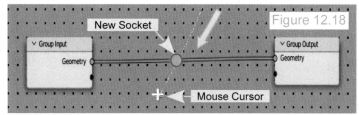

Figure 12.18

New Socket

Mouse Cursor

Adding and arranging Nodes creates a Node Tree. Figure 12.19 shows a **Simple Node Tree**. The adjective **Simple** must be emphasised since Node Trees can be very complex and have to be organised.

Nodes in the Pipeline - Node Tree   Figure 12.19

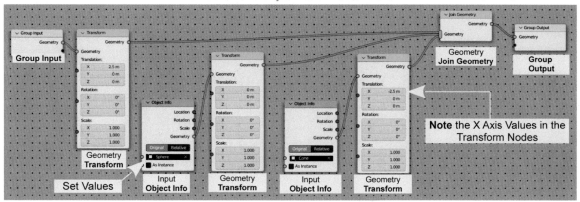

Remember: The objective in creating a Geometry Node system is to use an Object for creating arrays or effects. The Pipeline created generates an Array around Suzanne (last Object selected).

In Figure 12.19 the **Group Input Node** transmits data pertaining to the last Object selected (Suzanne) to the **Transform Node** where the data may be modified before being sent on to the **Group Output Node**. Two **Object Info Nodes** have been added connected to additional **Transform Nodes**. The **Object Info Nodes** have been set to gather data from the UV Sphere and Suzanne respectively. This data is transmitted to the additional Transform Nodes. All three Transform Nodes are connected via a **Join Geometry Node** to the **Group Output Node**. The X Axis values in the Transform Nodes determine the position of Objects in the Array.

Figure 12.20

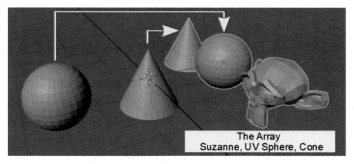

The Array
Suzanne, UV Sphere, Cone

Click the **Eye Icons** in the **Outliner Editor** to hide the original Sphere and Cone.

A complex Pipeline can consume Screen space, therefore, individual Nodes may be collapsed to minimise space. Nodes can be grouped to make it easier to distinguish components of the Tree and the **Groups** themselves may be minimised.

Minimising Node Display

In Figure 12.21 the **Transform** and **Object Info** Nodes may be minimised by clicking the chevron adjacent to the Node Name.

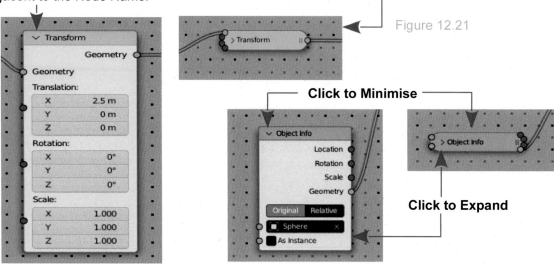

Figure 12.21

Click to Minimise

Click to Expand

Grouping Nodes   Figure 12.22

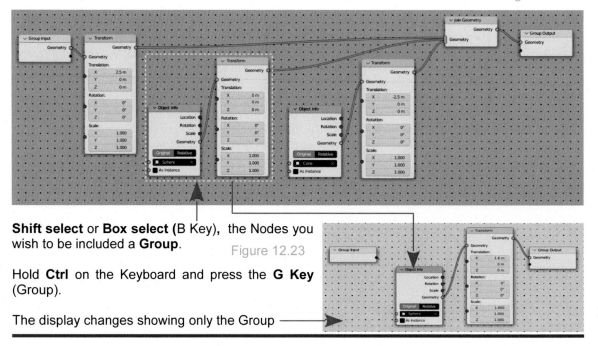

Shift select or **Box select** (B Key), the Nodes you wish to be included a **Group**.

Figure 12.23

Hold **Ctrl** on the Keyboard and press the **G Key** (Group).

The display changes showing only the Group ———

The **Group Input** and **Output** Nodes remain displayed as does the **Join Geometry** Node. All Noodle connections remain in situ.

Remember: The Node Pipeline is associated with the last Object selected in the Scene.

Select either of the Objects in the **Outliner Editor** followed by **Suzanne** to see the Node Group minimised in the Node Tree.

Figure 12.24

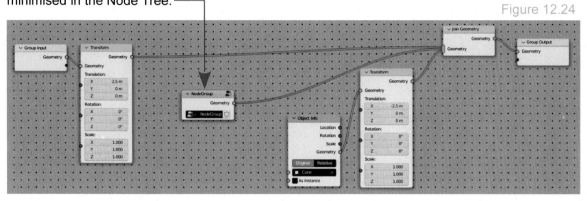

In minimising the Node Group you lose the ability to amend values in the Transform Node. Select the minimised Node Group, RMB click and select **Ungroup** in the menu that displays. The Nodes are reinstated where you adjust values then RMB click and select Group again.

12.4 Multiple Pipelines

Multiple Pipelines may be created by selecting each Object in the Scene and pressing the New Button in the Geometry Node Editor Header. UV Sphere and Cone in turn. The automatic Pipeline Names will be **Geometry Nodes.001** and **Geometry Nodes.002**.

By clicking the **Node Tree to be Linked Button** you will see the three Node Pipeline names. The data for each Pipeline is stored in a Cache.

Figure 12.25

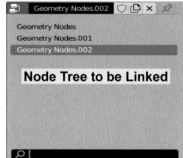

If you add a fourth Object to the Scene, then click the New Button in the geometry Node Editor Header, then click the Browse Node tree to be linked button and select (click) one of the stored Pipelines, you apply an instance of that Pipeline (tree) to the new Object.

Note: You may rename the Pipelines to something meaningful to your project.

The foregoing is intended to convey the basic process for creating an Array using the Geometry Node Editor. Understanding the method will assist when following demonstrations.

Before studying examples it should be realised that creating a Node Tree or Pipeline adds a Modifier to the selected Object.

12.5 The Geometry Node Modifier

Figure 12.26

When a Pipeline is created in the Geometry Node Editor a Modifier is added in the Properties Editor, Modifier Properties. It follows that, Geometry Nodes are, therefore, Modifiers and that they modify the Geometry of the selected Object.

Note: The Pipeline is applicable to the selected Object in the 3D Viewport Editor (the Cube).

In the first instance the name of the **Modifier** is **Geometry Nodes.**

Note: Geometry Node Modifiers, unlike traditional Modifiers are not Applied directly to an Object.

Modifier Properties →

Geometry Node Modifiers are, however, transferable to other Objects which are entered in the 3D Viewport Editor.

For example: Consider the arrangement of the Cone, UV Sphere and Monkey Objects previously described.

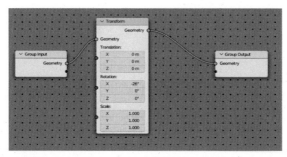

Figure 12.27

Selecting Suzanne (Monkey) and creating the Pipeline shown above (Figure 12.27) adds the **Modifier** named **GeometryNodes** (Figure 12.26). The Modifier is added in the Properties Editor, Modifier Properties immediately on selecting Suzanne and pressing the New Button in the Geometry Node Editor Header. Adjusting the X Axis Rotation value in the Transform Node causes Suzanne to rotate in the 3D Viewport Editor. The Cone and the UV Sphere are not affected.

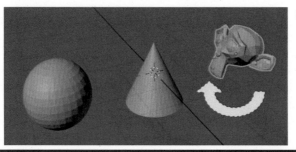

Figure 12.28

Clicking the **Browse Node to be Linked button** in the Geometry Node Editor Header or in the Modifier Properties shows the single Modifier named **Geometry Nodes.**

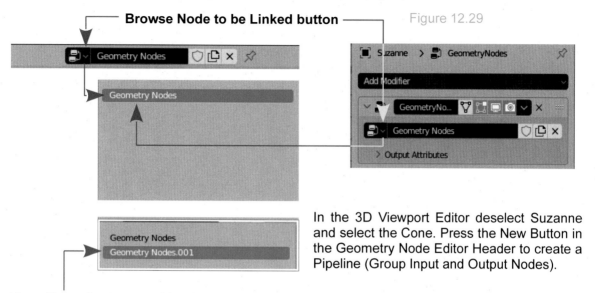

Figure 12.29

Browse Node to be Linked button

In the 3D Viewport Editor deselect Suzanne and select the Cone. Press the New Button in the Geometry Node Editor Header to create a Pipeline (Group Input and Output Nodes).

You will now have a new Modifier named **Geometry Nodes.001** in the Modifier Properties and in the Geometry Node Editor Header. Instead of adding Nodes to the Pipeline, click the **Browse Node Tree to be Linked button** and select **Geometry Nodes** in the drop down menu to assign the Modifier named **Geometry Nodes** to the Cone. The Cone is rotated in the 3D Viewport.

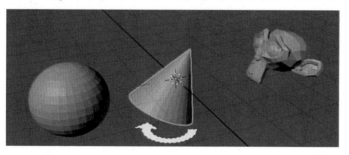

Figure 12.30

12.6 Spread Sheet Editor

When introducing Geometry Nodes it has been shown how a Pipeline is created in the Geometry Node Editor which affects the Object in the 3D Viewport Editor. Objects included in the Scene are listed in the Outliner Editor where they may be selected and hidden from view (Figure 15.19). The Geometry Node Modifier is shown in the Properties Editor. The fifth Editor in the Geometry Node Workspace is the **Spread Sheet Editor** (Figure 12.31).

The Spread Sheet Editor displays coordinates for different aspects of the selected Object in the 3D Viewport Editor i.e. the position in 3D Space of Vertices, Edges, Faces and Face Corners.

Note: You **Cannot** edit coordinate values in the Spread Sheet.

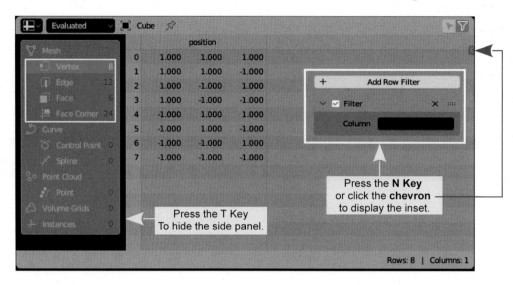

Figure 12.31 shows the default **Spread Sheet Editor** when the Cube Object is selected in **Object Mode** in the **3D Viewport Editor**.

Note: the **Geometry Node Editor** is empty.

The **Spread Sheet Editor** has a column headed **position** containing the location of each of the Cube's Vertices in 3D Space. Note: The Cube in the 3D Viewport Editor is in Object Mode. Changing the 3D Viewport Editor to Edit Mode shows the Cube's Vertices which relate to the values in the Spreadsheet.

Spread Sheet Editor Figure 12.32 **3D Viewport Editor – Edit Mode**

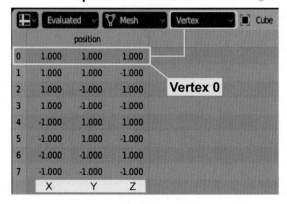

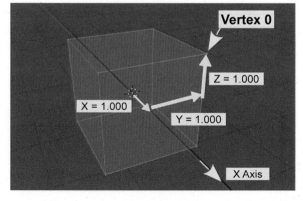

The Spread Sheet Editor shows the XYZ coordinates of the Cube's Vertices in 3D Space. Eight Vertices numbered 0 to 7. Note: In Geometry Nodes, Vertices are considered to be **Points**.

When an Object is Transformed in the 3D Viewport Editor by editing values in the Transform Node in the Node Editor you see the Point coordinates change in the Spread Sheet Editor. You see the Transformation of the Object in the 3D Viewport Editor in Object Mode. By changing the 3D Viewport Editor to Edit Mode you will see the Object in its original state.

To clarify this concept consider the following:

In a new Scene in the Geometry Node Workspace with the default Cube selected in the 3D Viewport Editor add a Geometry Transform Node to the Pipeline in the Geometry Node Editor.

In the Transform Node change the X Translation value to 3m and the Y Rotation to 25°.

Figure 12.33

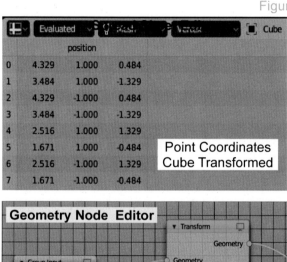

	position		
0	4.329	1.000	0.484
1	3.484	1.000	-1.329
2	4.329	-1.000	0.484
3	3.484	-1.000	-1.329
4	2.516	1.000	1.329
5	1.671	1.000	-0.484
6	2.516	-1.000	1.329
7	1.671	-1.000	-0.484

Point Coordinates
Cube Transformed

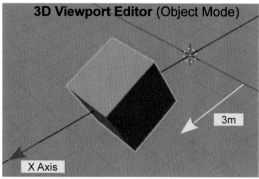

3D Viewport Editor (Object Mode)

3m

X Axis

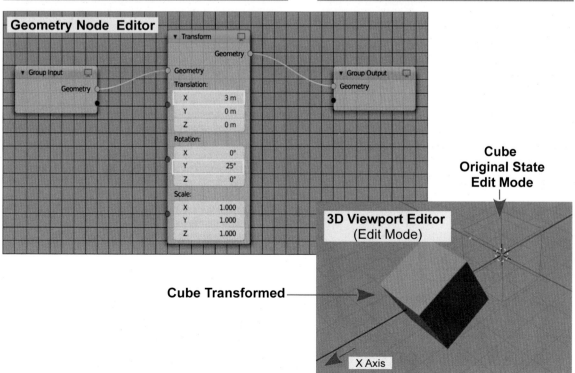

Geometry Node Editor

Cube
Original State
Edit Mode

3D Viewport Editor
(Edit Mode)

Cube Transformed

X Axis

241

With the 3D Viewport Editor in Edit Mode, select a single Vertex (Vertex Point 0 – Figure 12.34). Translate the Vertex on the X Axis. You see the translation occur on the Rotated Cube and you see the Coordinate Values change in the Spread Sheet Editor.

Figure 12.34

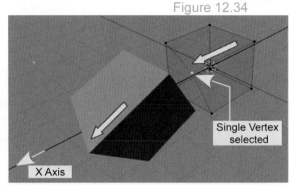

	position			
0	5.009	1.000	0.167	Vertex selected
1	3.484	1.000	-1.329	
2	4.329	-1.000	0.484	
3	3.484	-1.000	-1.329	
4	2.516	1.000	1.329	
5	1.671	1.000	-0.484	
6	2.516	-1.000	1.329	
7	1.671	-1.000	-0.484	

Single Vertex selected

X Axis

With the single Vertex selected in the 3D Viewport Editor you may check (tick) **Selected Only** in the upper RH corner of the Spread Sheet Editor to isolate the Point coordinates for the selected Vertex.

Figure 12.35

Evaluated Coordinates for the selected Vertex **Point 0**

In the **Spread Sheet Header** change **Evaluated** to **Original** to see the Point Coordinates for the Vertex prior to Translating on the X Axis.

Figure 12.36

Note: In the Spread Sheet Editor Header you may select the options, **Vertex, Edge, Face** and **Face Corners** to view coordinates for each. These correspond to the selection modes in the 3D Viewport Editor in Edit Mode.

Spread Sheet Header   Figure 12.37   **3D Viewport Edit Mode Header**

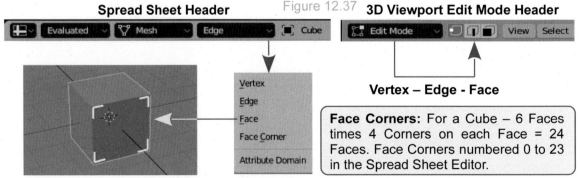

Vertex – Edge - Face

Face Corners: For a Cube – 6 Faces times 4 Corners on each Face = 24 Faces. Face Corners numbered 0 to 23 in the Spread Sheet Editor.

The **Geometry Transform Node** has been employed to demonstrate the basic concept of the Node Editor being used in conjunction with the Spread Sheet Editor and the 3D Viewport Editor.

4.0 Node Selection Menu

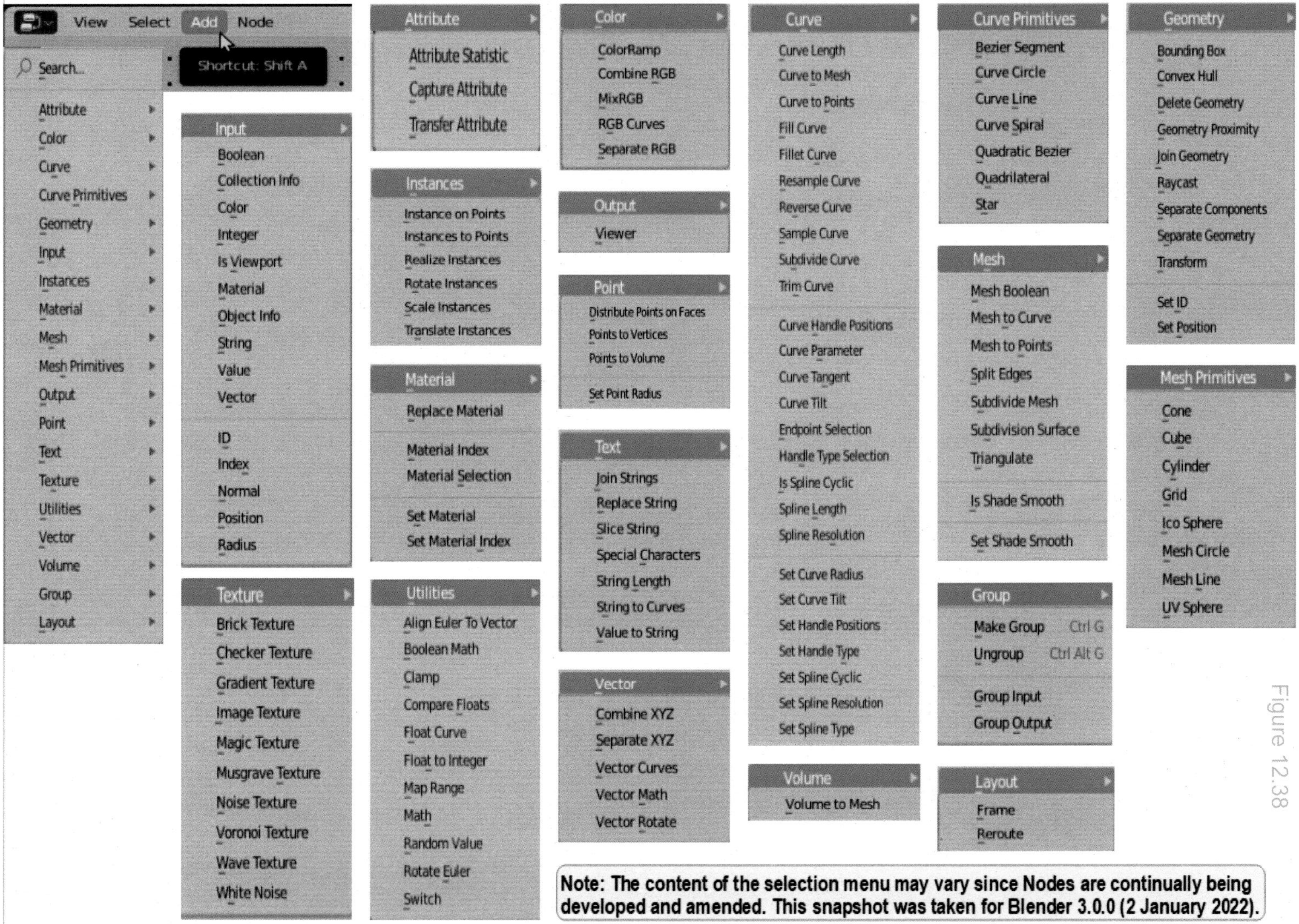

Add Node — Shortcut: Shift A

View | Select | Add | Node

Search...

- Attribute
- Color
- Curve
- Curve Primitives
- Geometry
- Input
- Instances
- Material
- Mesh
- Mesh Primitives
- Output
- Point
- Text
- Texture
- Utilities
- Vector
- Volume
- Group
- Layout

Attribute
- Attribute Statistic
- Capture Attribute
- Transfer Attribute

Color
- ColorRamp
- Combine RGB
- MixRGB
- RGB Curves
- Separate RGB

Curve
- Curve Length
- Curve to Mesh
- Curve to Points
- Fill Curve
- Fillet Curve
- Resample Curve
- Reverse Curve
- Sample Curve
- Subdivide Curve
- Trim Curve
- Curve Handle Positions
- Curve Parameter
- Curve Tangent
- Curve Tilt
- Endpoint Selection
- Handle Type Selection
- Is Spline Cyclic
- Spline Length
- Spline Resolution
- Set Curve Radius
- Set Curve Tilt
- Set Handle Positions
- Set Handle Type
- Set Spline Cyclic
- Set Spline Resolution
- Set Spline Type

Curve Primitives
- Bezier Segment
- Curve Circle
- Curve Line
- Curve Spiral
- Quadratic Bezier
- Quadrilateral
- Star

Geometry
- Bounding Box
- Convex Hull
- Delete Geometry
- Geometry Proximity
- Join Geometry
- Raycast
- Separate Components
- Separate Geometry
- Transform
- Set ID
- Set Position

Input
- Boolean
- Collection Info
- Color
- Integer
- Is Viewport
- Material
- Object Info
- String
- Value
- Vector
- ID
- Index
- Normal
- Position
- Radius

Instances
- Instance on Points
- Instances to Points
- Realize Instances
- Rotate Instances
- Scale Instances
- Translate Instances

Material
- Replace Material
- Material Index
- Material Selection
- Set Material
- Set Material Index

Mesh
- Mesh Boolean
- Mesh to Curve
- Mesh to Points
- Split Edges
- Subdivide Mesh
- Subdivision Surface
- Triangulate
- Is Shade Smooth
- Set Shade Smooth

Mesh Primitives
- Cone
- Cube
- Cylinder
- Grid
- Ico Sphere
- Mesh Circle
- Mesh Line
- UV Sphere

Output
- Viewer

Point
- Distribute Points on Faces
- Points to Vertices
- Points to Volume
- Set Point Radius

Text
- Join Strings
- Replace String
- Slice String
- Special Characters
- String Length
- String to Curves
- Value to String

Texture
- Brick Texture
- Checker Texture
- Gradient Texture
- Image Texture
- Magic Texture
- Musgrave Texture
- Noise Texture
- Voronoi Texture
- Wave Texture
- White Noise

Utilities
- Align Euler To Vector
- Boolean Math
- Clamp
- Compare Floats
- Float Curve
- Float to Integer
- Map Range
- Math
- Random Value
- Rotate Euler
- Switch

Vector
- Combine XYZ
- Separate XYZ
- Vector Curves
- Vector Math
- Vector Rotate

Volume
- Volume to Mesh

Group
- Make Group — Ctrl G
- Ungroup — Ctrl Alt G
- Group Input
- Group Output

Layout
- Frame
- Reroute

Figure 12.38

Note: The content of the selection menu may vary since Nodes are continually being developed and amended. This snapshot was taken for Blender 3.0.0 (2 January 2022).

12.7 Node Selection Menu

By navigating through the Add Menu in the Node Editor Header you will discover a selection of Nodes (see diagram included). This paper is intended to demonstrate the basic concept of using Geometry Nodes not to provide instruction in the use of every Node. With an understanding of the basic concept you will be better placed to follow the many video tutorials available on the internet. As you experiment with the use of Geometry Nodes you will discover Node Systems for particular applications. As you discover a system save a Blender file with the Node arrangement for future use thus compiling a library. The systems may be suitable for future applications or may be a starting point for modifications and used in your work.

12.8 Editing Shapes

Editing the shape of an Object in the 3D Viewport Editor when using Geometry Nodes is performed to create a shape for an Array or Pattern. How you shape the Object determines how the Array displays in the 3D Viewport Editor. Bear in mind, what you see in the 3D Viewport Editor, should be considered with respect to Camera View. After all, Camera View shows what will be the final result and this is the ultimate goal. A shape for an Array can be a shape for a complex model such as plant leaves or flower petals.

As an example the simple Array of Monkey Heads shown in Figure 12.6 is created by instancing Objects on the Vertices of a Circle Object. The Circle could be reshaped to represent a plant stem and in place of Monkey Heads you would use a model of a leaf.

To continue; you should be aware that the different Nodes affect the display of the Object in the 3D Viewport Editor in different ways. The Geometry Transform Node has been shown affecting the Cube Object as a whole. To modify the Cube's shape, Vertices in the 3D Viewport Editor were shown to be manipulated in the 3D Viewport Editor in Edit Mode.

Another factor to consider is; to use Geometry Nodes a Mesh Object or a Curve Object must be entered in the 3D Viewport Editor as a starting point. You can not create a Node Tree without the base Object. Objects such as Empty Objects, Surfaces, Cameras and Armatures will not work.

When employing Mesh Objects in conjunction with Geometry Nodes there are two types of Objects to be considered; Procedural Objects and Non-Procedural Objects.

Explaining Procedural Objects will be limited to purely describing the mechanics of using an Object with Nodes in relation to the Graphical User Interface.

To understand what a Procedural Object is you would have to understand Procedural Generation in Computer Graphics and its application when developing Computer Games. This is beyond the scope of this discussion but in a nutshell "procedural" and "generation" imply that you are dealing with computer procedures, or algorithms, that create something and perhaps incorporate AI (Artificial Intelligence). Such procedures are particularly applicable when creating Computer Games.

At this point consider that the use of Geometry Nodes in conjunction with Procedural Mesh Objects as employing computer procedures through the use of Geometry Nodes.

12.9 Procedural Mesh Objects

When using Geometry Nodes it important to distinguish between **Procedural** and **Non-Procedural** Mesh Objects.

Non Procedural Objects

Geometry Nodes have been demonstrated, thus far, using a Mesh Object by employing one of the Blender's Primitives.

The basic procedure has been to enter an Object in the 3D Viewport Editor and with the Object selected, generate a Node Pipeline in the Geometry Node Editor.

With the Node Pipeline generated the **Group Input Node** obtains data from the selected Object and creates the display in the 3D Viewport Editor, secretly superseding the original display.

Nodes are added and connected in the Pipeline which modifies the display of the Mesh Object.

Figure 12.39

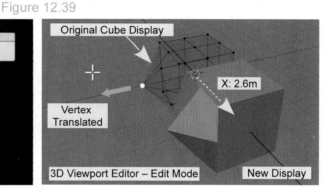

Figure 6.1 shows the Node Pipeline in the Geometry Node Editor producing the display in the 3D Viewport Editor. The Transform Node has moved the new Cube display 2.6 m on the X Axis. The data for the original Cube displays in the 3D Viewport Editor (in Edit Mode) in the original position. The Cube has been subdivided. Translating a single Vertex on the original alters the new display which demonstrates that **Non-Procedural Objects** may be edited in Edit Mode.

Disconnecting or deleting the Node Pipeline will show the edited Cube in its original default position at the center of the Scene.

Procedural Objects

A **Procedural Object** is introduced to a Scene by adding one of the **Mesh Primitive Nodes**.

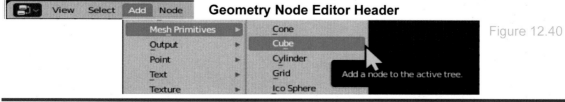

Figure 12.40

Placing a **Cube Mesh Primitive Node** in the Pipeline will not produce a display in the 3D Viewport Editor until the red Noodle is disconnected. A red Noodle indicates that the connection is invalid.

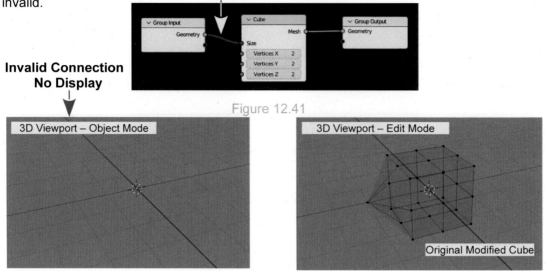

**Invalid Connection
No Display**

Figure 12.41

3D Viewport – Object Mode

3D Viewport – Edit Mode

Original Modified Cube

Following on from the previous example (Figure 12.41) shows that the original modified Cube Object remains with the 3D Viewport Editor in Edit Mode. There is no display in Object Mode and consequently nothing Renders. This demonstrates that the data for the original Cube Object remains.

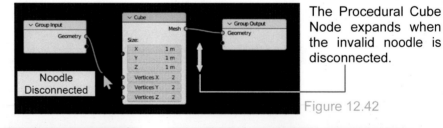

The Procedural Cube Node expands when the invalid noodle is disconnected.

Noodle Disconnected

Figure 12.42

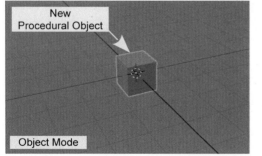

New Procedural Object

Object Mode

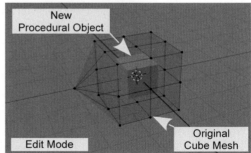

New Procedural Object

Edit Mode

Original Cube Mesh

Disconnecting the invalid connection displays the new Procedural Object (Cube) in the 3D Viewport Editor in Object Mode and in Edit Mode. In Edit Mode the new Cube is encapsulated by the original Cube Mesh which again demonstrates that the original Cube data remains in the Scene.

The new Procedural Cube display is being generated by the computer code contained in the Mesh Primitive, Cube Node. The original Non Procedural Cube display is generated by Blender's internal coding. The Procedural Cube supersedes the original.

Note: Editing the original Cube, in Edit Mode, has no effect on the new Procedural Cube. A rendered view of the Scene captured by the Camera only displays the Procedural Cube.

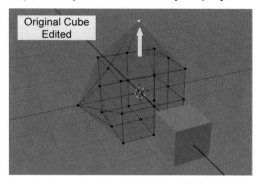

Figure 12.43

To edit the Procedural Cube, Nodes are entered in the Node Pipeline in the Geometry Node Editor.

Figure 12.44

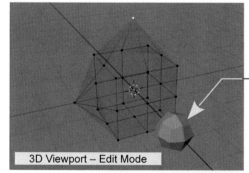

3D Viewport – Edit Mode

In Figure 12.44 the new Procedural Cube is Translated on the X Axis by the transform Node entered in the Pipeline. **The new Procedural Cube is subdivided by the Subdivision Surface Node.**

Note: Not all Nodes work as you may expect. For example, substituting a **Subdivide Mesh Node** in place of the **Subdivision Surface Node** has no effect on the Cube (Figure 12.45).

Node Pipeline in the Geometry Node Editor

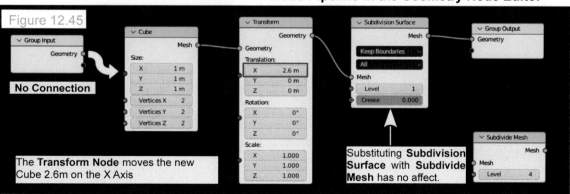

The foregoing will allow you to more easily understand the following examples. By following examples and experimenting you will create your own Node Systems.

12.10 Naming and Color Coding

Nodes Minimised

Figure 12.46

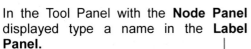

Nodes Color Coded

Figure 12.47

To conserve Screen space when a Node Pipeline becomes complicated Nodes may be collapsed (minimised) by clicking the **chevron** adjacent to the Node Name.

To color code and name Nodes, with the Mouse Cursor in the Geometry Node Editor, press the **N Key** to display the **Tool Panel** at the right hand side of the Editor.

In the Tool Panel with the **Node Panel** displayed type a name in the **Label Panel.**

Figure 12.48

To color code Nodes, check (tick) **Color**.

Click on the **color bar** and select a color in the color picker circle that displays.

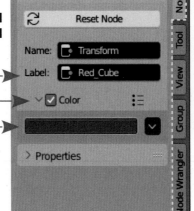

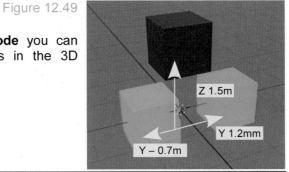

Red Cube Z Axis value adjusted to 1.5m.

12.11 Arranging Objects

Figure 12.49

By adjusting the values in the **Transform Node** you can manipulate and arrange the Array of Objects in the 3D Viewport Editor.

In Figure 9.1 the Translate values are:

    Red Cube: Z 1.5m
    Green Cube: Y 1.2m
    Blue Cube: Y minus 0.7m

12.12 Subdivision Surface Node

Adding a Subdivision Surface Node to the Pipeline will affect a single Cube Object or all Cube Objects depending on where the Node is placed.

Figure 12.50

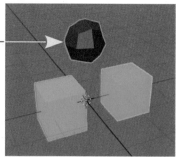

Subdivision Surface Node affects the Red Cube only

Figure 12.51

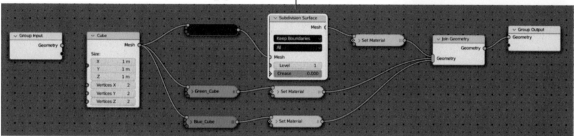

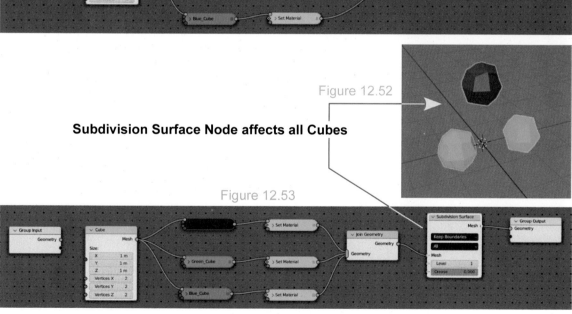

Subdivision Surface Node affects all Cubes

Figure 12.52

Figure 12.53

A Node placed in a Pipeline affects the Nodes preceding when read from left to right. In Figure 12.53 the **Subdivision Surface Node** could be placed between the **Set Material Node** for the Red Cube and the **Join Geometry Node** to produce the same effect.

12.13 Add Convex Hull

Placing a Convex Hull Node in the Pipeline between the Subdivision Surface Node and the Group Output Node wraps the Array in a tight Mesh.

Remember, you are producing a visual effect not necessarily a model of a particular object. This wrapping may or may not be what you want displayed.

Figure 12.54

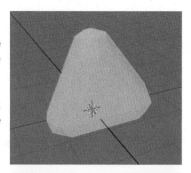

Figure 12.55

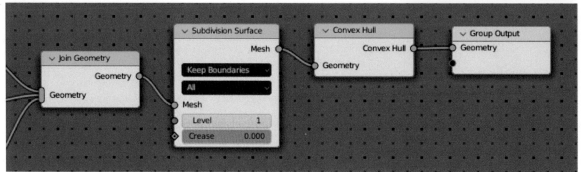

Placing the Convex Hull Node as shown in Figure 12.55 and adding a second Join Geometry Node into the Pipeline will wrap only the Red Cube and the Green Cube. This again demonstrates that a Node affects the preceding Nodes.

Figure 12.56

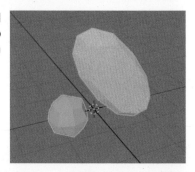

Figure 12.57

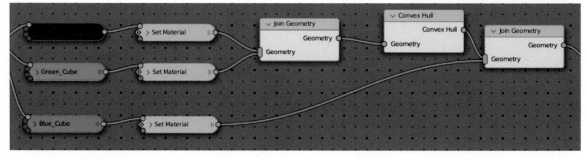

A further variation on this effect would be to convert the solid mesh wrap to a **Wireframe Display**.

Wireframe Display

Figure 12.58

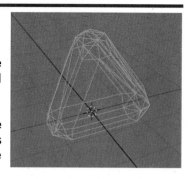

Placing a Mesh to Curve Node in the Pipeline between the Convex Hull Node and the Group Output Node converts the solid mesh wrap to Wireframe.

You now have the original Cubes with Subdivided Surface producing the shape of the Array, wrapped in a Mesh which has been converted to a Wireframe. The Cube Array shapes the Wireframe Mesh.

Figure 12.59

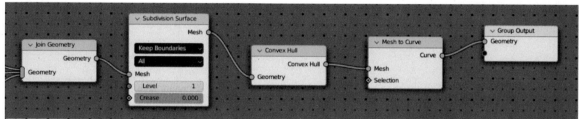

A Wireframe does NOT Render, therefore, perhaps you would prefer that the Wireframe should have a solid appearance.

Figure 12.60

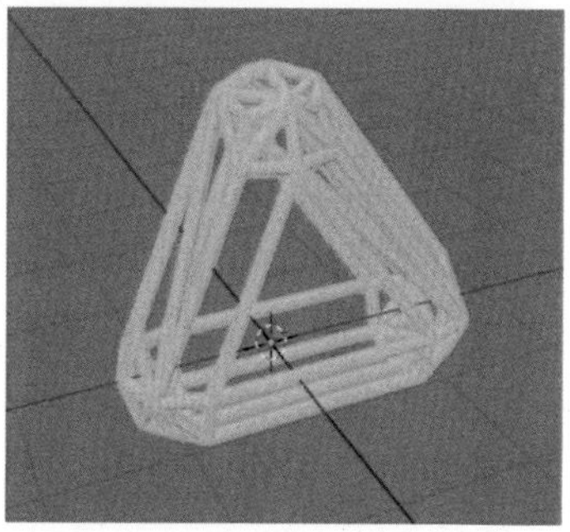

Convert the Wireframe (the Curve) back to a Mesh giving it a solid profile. To do this place a Curve to Mesh Node between the Mesh to Curve Node and the Group Output and connect a Curve Circle Node to provide the profile.

Instead of a Curve Circle Profile try a Curve Primitive-Star. You have to play with the settings in the Nodes to obtain the look you want.

Figure 12.61

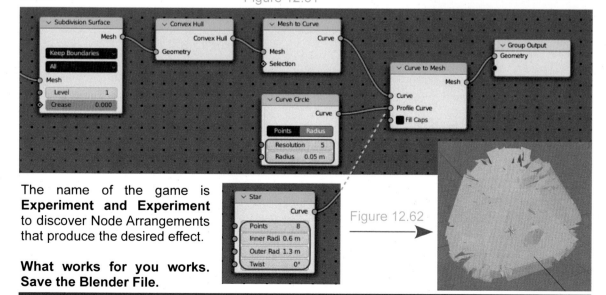

The name of the game is **Experiment and Experiment** to discover Node Arrangements that produce the desired effect.

What works for you works. Save the Blender File.

Figure 12.62

12.14 Materials (Color) for Geometry Nodes

In examples where **Set Material Nodes** are used, the Material is entered in the Node. The Material entered is selected from Materials pre-generated in **Properties Editor, Material Properties.**

To generate Materials you may have Blender opened in the General Layout Workspace or in The Geometry Node Workspace. The default Cube Object in the 3D Viewport Editor has a default gray Material pre-applied.

You see this Material in the **Properties Editor, Material Properties.**

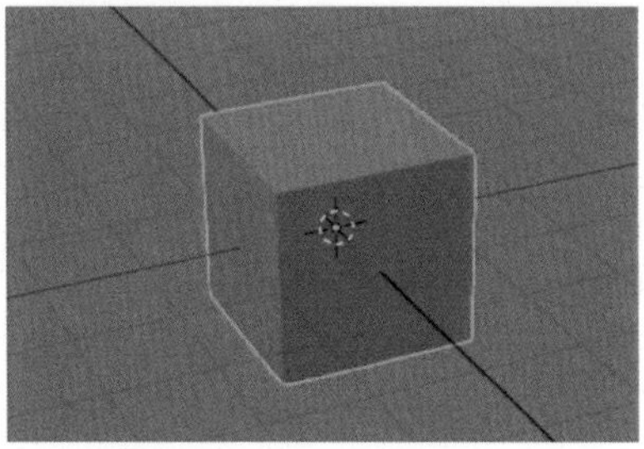

Figure 12.63

Cube Object – 3D Viewport Editor

The default Material is named **Material.**

By clicking the **Browse Material to be linked** button you see the Material named Material stored in the **Material Cache**.

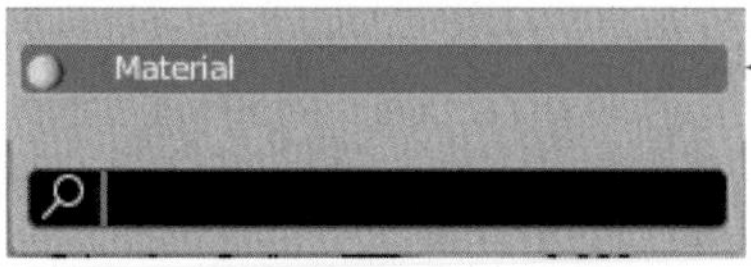

Figure 12.64

Material Properties →

Note: The Material Properties has Use Nodes activated and the 3D Viewport Editor by default is in Solid Viewport Shading Mode. To see new Materials being generated change the 3D Viewport Editor to Material Preview or Rendered Viewport Shading Mode.

Figure 12.65

To generate a new Material click the plus sign in the Properties Editor then click the New Button that displays. This creates a new **Material Slot**. The Properties Editor, Material Properties expands. Click on the **Base Color Bar** and select a color in the Color Picker Circle to assign the color to the new Material Slot.

Repeat the procedure creating new Materials. The Materials are added to the Material Cache.

252

Figure 12.66

Properties Editor

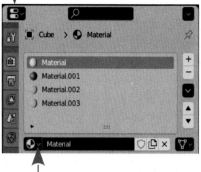

The **Materials** display in the top panel of the **Properties Editor** and by clicking the **Browse Material to be linked button** you see them stored in the **Material Cache**.

Clicking the Material bar in the Set Material Node displays the Material Cache where you select one of the pre-generated Materials to be assigned to the selected Object in the 3D Viewport.

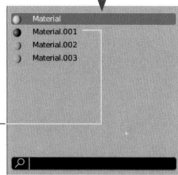

Browse material to be linked

3D Viewport Editor

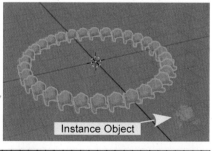

Geometry Node Editor

12.15 Instance Objects

Creating an Array by arranging Objects whether they are Procedural or Non-Procedural is one method. Another method, as shown in Figure 1.6 is to **Instance Objects** on the **Vertices of an Object**. Add a Material to the Instance.

Figure 15.6 replicated

Instance Object

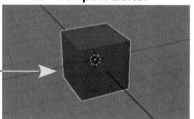

Figure 12.67

Non-Procedural Object

Procedural Object

The **Object Info Node** provides the **Instance Object** information to the **Instance on Point Node**.

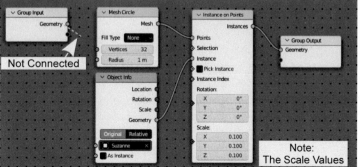

Note: The Scale Values

By substituting the Mesh Circle with an **Icosphere** you will appreciate that the shape of the Array is infinite.

Figure 12.68

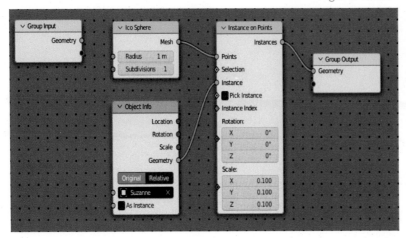

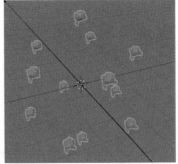

Note: The Instance Object (Suzanne) has been hidden from view by clicking the **eye icon** in the **Outliner Editor**

12.16 Bloom - Object Glow

Figure 12.69

By making the Instance Object glow against a dark background the effect may be further advanced.

To set the background, go to the **Properties Editor, World Properties, Surface Tab** and set the Surface Background making it black, Strength: 0.000.

With the Instance Object (Suzanne) selected go to the **Properties Editor, Material Properties** and add a Material with Use Nodes active.

Figure 12.70

In the Surface Tab, set Surface to Type **Emission** and make Strength: 3.000.

Type: Emission makes the Object emit light (glow) when viewed in the 3D Viewport Editor in Rendered Viewport Shading Mode.

Even with a static display as shown in Figure 12.69 the display begins to show signs of becoming impressive.

Remember, the Instance Objects are assigned to the Vertices of an Icosphere. The Icosphere may be animated to rotate and change in size which would see the Array of Monkey Heads rotate and change position in 3D Space as the animation is played.

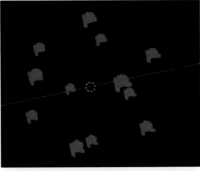

12.17 Spiral

Using a Spiral to create an Array can produce impressive displays.

Start with the default Cube Object selected in the 3D Viewport Editor and in the Geometry Node Editor click the New Button in the Header to create a Pipeline. Have an Instance Object in the Scene (UV Sphere scaled way down with a Material added). Add a **Spiral Node** and connect together with an **Instance on Point Node** and an **Object Info Node**. The UV Sphere is entered in the Object Info Node as the **Instance Object**.

Figure 12.71

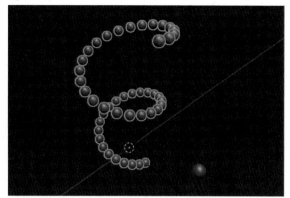

Figure 12.72

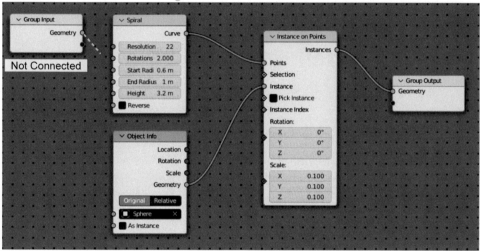

Disconnect the Group Input Node to see the spiral. Adjust the values in the Spiral Node to achieve the effect you want. Note: In Figure 12.71 an Area Light or Sun Light added to the Scene will add to the effect.

Figure 12.73

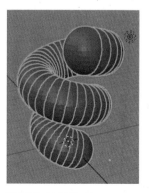

12.18 Point Cloud and Fields

At this point, Arrays have been demonstrated by manually arranging Objects in the 3D Viewport Editor or shaping a single Object and Instancing a secondary object (the Instance Object) to Vertices. Geometry Nodes allow the creation of **Point Clouds** or **Fields** which automate the manual process.

Point Clouds and Fields are treated as separate subjects but at a basic level they are very similar with Instance Objects being displayed on Points which have been designated as the Faces or Vertices of the selected Object.

In the previous example (12.17 Spiral) Instance Objects (UV Spheres) have been displayed on the Points (Vertices) of a Spiral (Figure 12.71).

Point Cloud

To demonstrate a Point Cloud, start with a Plane Object selected in the 3D Viewport Editor.

Create a Pipeline in the **Geometry Node Editor** by clicking the **New Button** in the Header.

Add a **Distribute Points on Faces Node** (Figure 12.74).

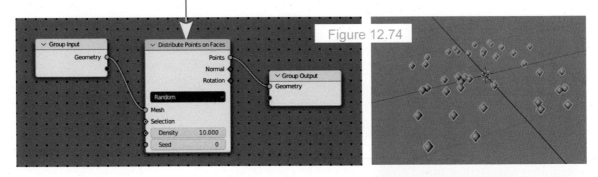

Figure 12.74

With the **Distribute Points on Faces Node** connected Points are scattered over the Face of the Plane Object.

Figure 12.75

Note: The Plane Object has only four Vertices (Figure 12.75). Points are distributed on the Face of the Plane in accordance with the **Density** value set in the Distribute Points on Faces Node (Figure 12.74).

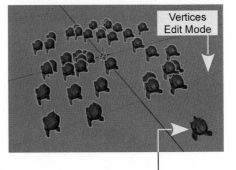

By introducing an **Instance Object** to the Scene (Monkey – Suzanne) and Instancing to the Points you generate an Array of Monkey Heads.

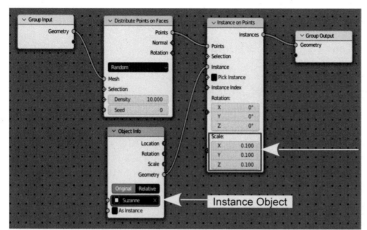

Figure 12.76

With the 3D Viewport Editor in Edit Mode you will see the Plane with its four Vertices (Figure 12.75).

Note: The Instance Monkey Object has been Scaled down in the 3D Viewport Editor and importantly the X, Y and Z Scale Values in the **Instance on Points Node** have been reduced to 0.100.

Figure 12.77

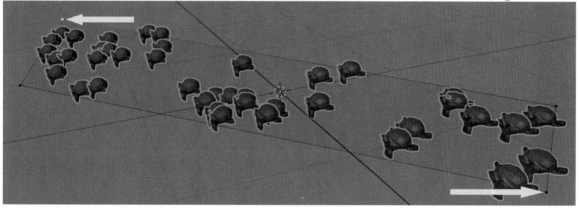

Manipulating the Plane's Vertices in Edit Mode shapes the Monkey Array (Figure 12.77).

From the perspective of **Camera View** the Array constitutes a **Point Cloud**. The 3D shape of the Point Cloud will be governed by the selected Object.

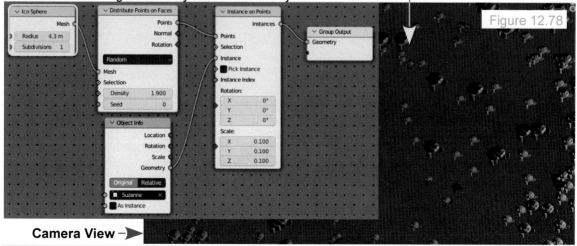

Fields

Fields, at a basic level, are similar to **Point Clouds** in that they are concerned with distributing Points in a formation to generate an Array.

By comparing Figure 12.78 with Figure 12.79 you see that the **Procedural Icosphere** Object is replaced by a **Grid Object** which displays similar to a Plane in the 3D Viewport Editor. The **Distribute Points on Faces Node** and the **Instance on Points Nodes** are retained but instead of the **Object Info Node** being employed a **Procedural Cube Node** is connected directly as the Instance Object.

The Scale of the Cube in the **Cube Node** (3m x 3m x 3m) is being overridden by the values in a **Random Node** (Min 0.000 – Max 1.000) connected the Scale in the **Instance on Points Node**.

A **Set Position Node** is included in the Pipeline which at this point allows positioning of the display in the 3D Viewport Editor on the X, Y and Z Axis.

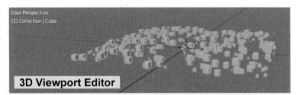

Figure 12.79

3D Viewport Editor

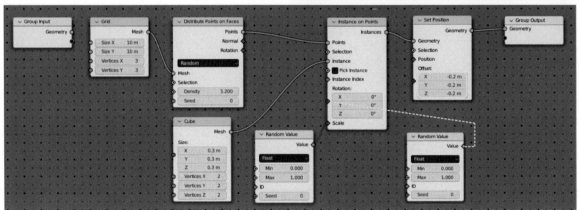

By connecting a **second Random Value Node** to the Rotation value in the Instance on Points Node you will randomly Rotate each Instance Object in the 3D Viewport Editor.

Note. In the 3D Viewport Editor all Instance Cubes are aligned on the XY Plane (Figure 12.80).

Figure 12.80

Maths and the use of Maths Nodes were described in Section 10 and it was explained that to control the shape of the Array you may connect **Maths Nodes to perform calculations** which affects an Object selected in the 3D Viewport Editor.

To affect the display shown in Figure 12.79 the following Nodes will be used and added to the Pipeline (Figure 12.81).

Noodle connecting the Instance on Points Node

Figure 12.81

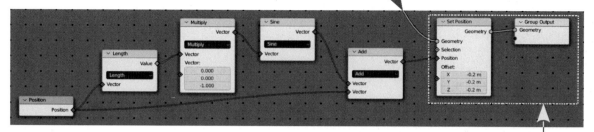

Set Position and Group Out Nodes (Figure 12.79)

The **Position Node** outputs the vector of each **Point** of the geometry that the Node is connected to. In this case the Node being the **Grid** and more precisely, the **Points assigned to the Grid**.

The **Multiply Node** is a **Vector Math Node** changed from the default Add configuration to Multiply. The **Sine Node** is a **Vector Math Node** changed from the default Add configuration to Sine.

Finally, the **Add Node** is a **Vector Math Node** which, in this case, is combining the outputs from the three previous Nodes and the data from the **Position Node**.

Figure 12.82

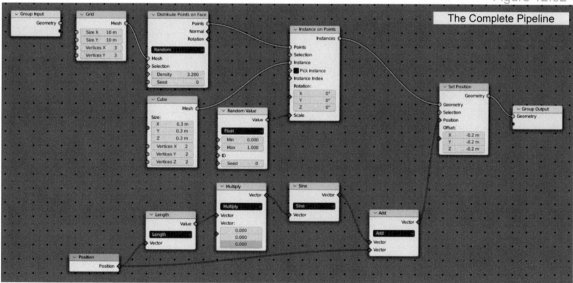

By Animating the **X Vector** value in the **Multiply Node** from 0.000 to 1.300 over 100 frames in the Timeline the display oscillates in the 3D Viewport Editor following a Sine Wave form. Set the Animation **End Frame** to 100 Frames for a continuous oscillation as the Animation plays.

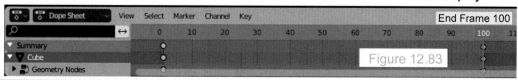

12.19 Creating a Landscape

There are many ways to create a Terrain or Landscape for a Scene. Geometry Nodes in conjunction with **Foliage Assets Packs** provide a quick method.

Assets Packs , in this context, are collections of pre-constructed models of plants, rocks, trees and stumps which you would find in a landscape.

There are many sites on the internet which offer Assets Packs or individual models, some free and others require a payment.

One site is: https://www.motionblendstudio.com/blender-vfx-assets

Figure 12.84

Ground Foliage Pack

This particular **Assets Pack** downloads as a ZIP file name **blenderGroundFoliage.zip**

Unzipping the file produces two Folders:

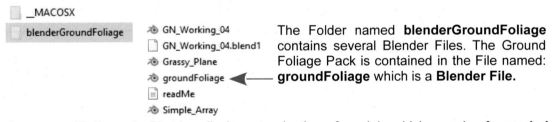

The Folder named **blenderGroundFoliage** contains several Blender Files. The Ground Foliage Pack is contained in the File named: **groundFoliage** which is a **Blender File.**

Opening **groundFoliage**, in Blender, displays a selection of models which may be **Appended** into a Blender File in which you create your landscape.

Separate Models

Figure 12.85

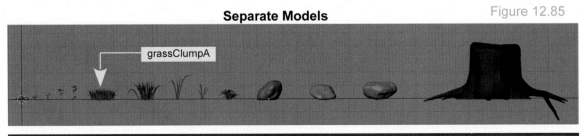

grassClumpA

260

Before starting an exercise it's nice to know where you are heading. Figure 12.86 shows the final result.

Sand Duns covered in Grass

Figure 12.86

The Ground Plane for the Scene is simply a Plane Object, Scaled and Subdivided in Edit Mode with Vertices manipulated with Proportional Editing activated and Set Smooth.

Figure 12.87

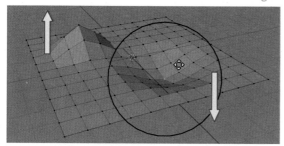

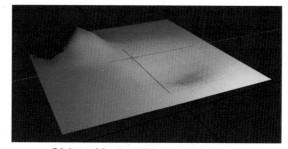

Proportional Editing Circle of Influence   **Object Mode – Material Applied**

Figures 12.87 is shown for method only. You may configure your ground plane to suit the Scene you are creating. To achieve something like the Figure 12.86 above, a gently undulating plane is preferable.

The method to be employed in generating the Landscape will be the **Point Cloud** procedure previously described with a similar Node arrangement to that shown in Figure 16.3. A Node Pipeline is generated for the ground Plane with a **Distribute Points on Faces Node** being added. A Foliage model is then used as an **Instance Object** which is applied to each of the Points. Bear in mind that once **Cloud Points** are generated the Plane on which they are generated disappears from view in the 3D Viewport Editor. Obviously you want the Ground Plane to remain in view, therefore, before adding the Distribute Points on Faces Node make a duplicate of the Ground Plane complete with Material.

To **Instance Foliage Objects** to the Points in this exercise you **Append** one of the Models from **Ground Foliage Pack**.

Appending Objects

To **Append**, click **File** in the Blender Screen Header and navigate to the Model.

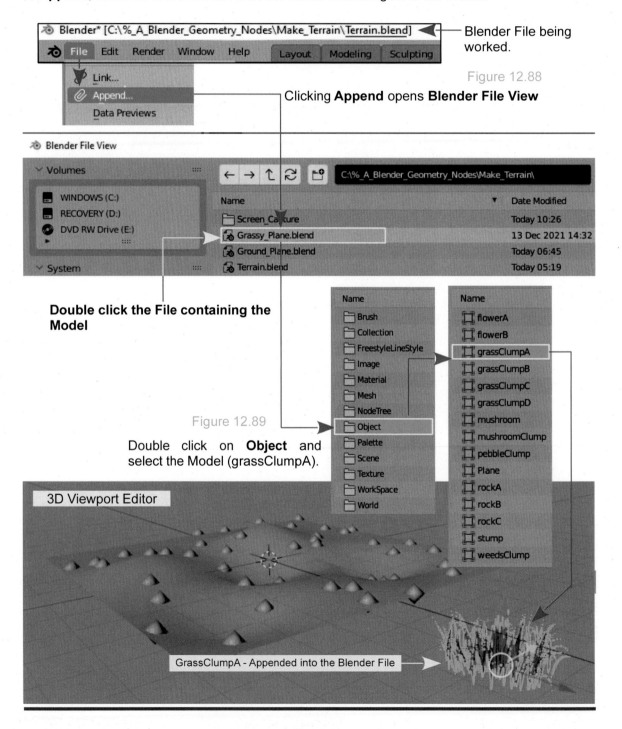

Blender File being worked.

Figure 12.88

Clicking **Append** opens **Blender File View**

Double click the File containing the Model

Figure 12.89

Double click on **Object** and select the Model (grassClumpA).

3D Viewport Editor

GrassClumpA - Appended into the Blender File

Remember there are two ground planes in the Scene, one is named simply **Plane** the other is named **Plane.001**.

Figure 12.90

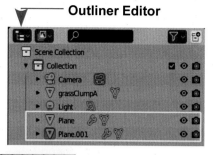

Outliner Editor

Plane has a pale green Material Applied.

With **Plane.001** selected create the **Node Pipeline** shown in Figure 12.91 which generates a Point Cloud on the Plane and Instances the Grass Model, **grassClumpA** at each Cloud Point.

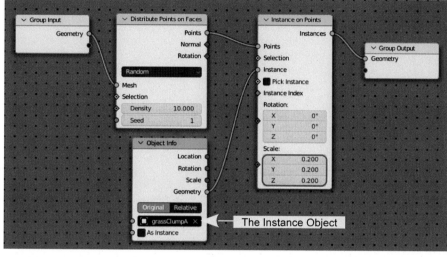

Figure 12.91

The Instance Object

Note: The Scale Values

In this particular case, Plane and Plane.001 are **Non-Procedural Objects**, therefore, with the **Node Pipeline** created for **Plane.001** the **Group Input Node** remains connected to the **Distribute Points on Faces Node.**

By giving the World Background a nice blue Material Color and changing the default Point Light in the Scene to an Area Light the Scene Renders as shown in Figure 12.92.

Figure 12.92

12.20 The Assets Library

The **Assets Library** is not a component of Geometry Nodes but, when set up, it is very useful for entering Objects to be used as Instance Objects. The Assets Library may be used to enter Objects into any Blender File once you have stocked the Library with Assets (Models). By default the Library is empty.

To demonstrate stocking the Library, that is, setting up the Assets Library it will be assumed you have downloaded and saved the **Ground-Foliage_ZIP** file and have unzipped to a folder on your PC. Models from the Ground Foliage Pack will be added to the Assets Library.

On my PC **Ground-Foliage_ZIP** is unzipped to a Folder named **Ground_Foliage**:

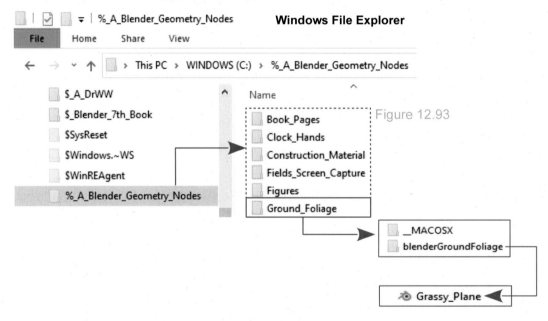

Figure 12.93

When Ground-Foliage_ZIP is unzipped the **Ground_Foliage** Folder contains two sub Folders (_MACOSX and blenderGroundFoliage) The sub Folder named **blenderGroundFoliage** contains the Blender File **groundFoliage.** This file contains the Foliage Models (Flowers, Grass Clumps, Rocks etc.) which are the **Assets**.

Creating the Assets Library

Using Windows Explorer or File Browser create a new Folder on your PC's Hard Drive and name it **Assets_Library**. In this Folder create sub Folders for different categories of Assets i.e Foliage Models, Human Models, Cartoon Models etc.

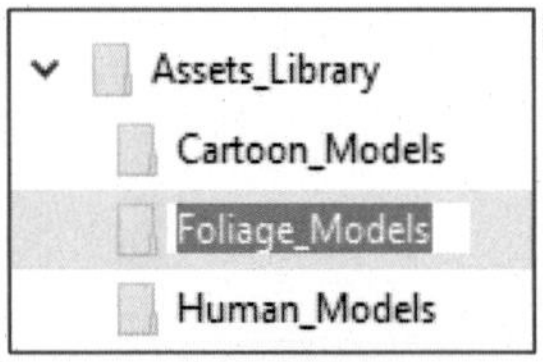

Copy and paste the Blender file **groundFoliage** from blenderGroundFoliage to the Folder named Foliage_Models in the Assets_Library.

Figure 12.94

- Assets_Library
  - Cartoon_Models
  - Foliage_Models
  - Human_Models

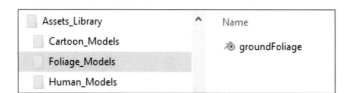

Blender File **groundFoliage** pasted into the sub Folder named **Foliage_Models**

Figure 12.95

In Blender open **groundFoliage.blend**, and divide the 3D Viewport Editor. Make one part the **Assets Browser Editor**. In the **Outliner Editor** expand the **groundFoliagePack**.

Figure 12.96

In the upper left hand corner of the Assets Browser change **Current File** to **Asset_Library.**

Warning: If a message displays stating that the Path to the Library does NOT exist you add the **File Path** in the **Preferences Editor.**

Figure 12.97

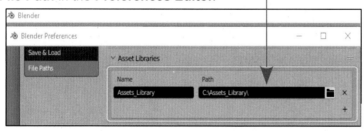

Outliner Editor

At this point you add Assets to the Library by marking entries in the **Outliner Editor**.

Figure 12.98

By expanding the entries in the Outliner Editor for the groundFoliagePack you display the separate entries for each of the Models displayed in the 3D Viewport Editor.

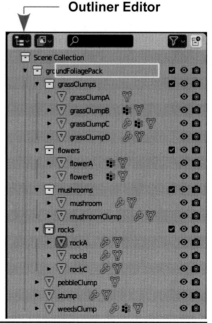

grassClumpA

Figure 12.99

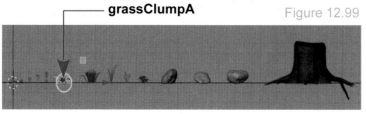

The orange triangle in the Outliner Editor gives an indication that the entry is suitable for marking as an Asset.

To add the Asset (Model) to the Assets Library, right click on the entry in the Outliner Editor and select Mark as Asset in the menu that displays.

In the Asset Browser Editor you will see a Thumbnail Image display for the entry selected in the Outliner Editor.

Figure 12.100

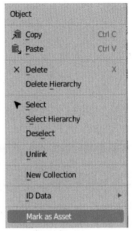

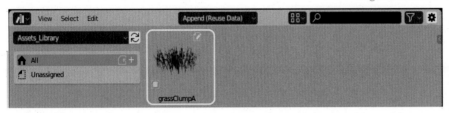

Mark Assets for each Model you wish to add to the Library.

To add more Assets to the Assets Library you copy Blender Files containing Models to the Assets_Library sub Folders then open each Blender File, open the Assets Browser Editor and mark the Model in the Outliner Editor as an Asset.

Figure 12.101 shows, **grassClumpA**, **rockA** and **stump** as Assets from the File **groundFoliagePack.blend**, **Cube** is a character named **Chibi** from a **Chibi.blend** File and **Make_Human_Figure** is a model of a Human created in the **Make Human Program** and imported into a Blender File named **Make_Human_Figure.blend**.

Figure 12.101

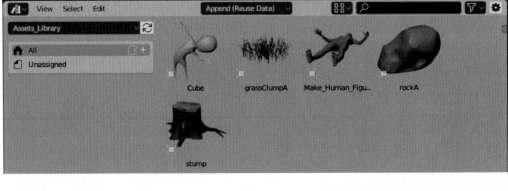

With Assets (Models) entered in the Assets Library you may open the Assets Browser in a new Blender File, select the Assets Library then click, hold and drag an Asset (Model) into the 3D Viewport Editor.

When Models are entered in the new File they will require Translating, Rotating and Scaling.

12.21 Animation

As with many features in Blender, values in Geometry Nodes may be animated to create an animation in the 3D Viewport Editor and then Rendered.

To demonstrate, values in the **Transform Node** will be animated.

With the default Cube Object selected in the 3D Viewport Editor change the Screen Display to the Geometry Node Workspace. To demonstrate Animation divide the Geometry Node Editor horizontally and change the lower part to the **Timeline Editor**.

Click the New Button in the Geometry Node Editor Header to create a Node Pipeline for the Cube Object and insert a **Transform Node** in the Pipeline.

Figure 12.102

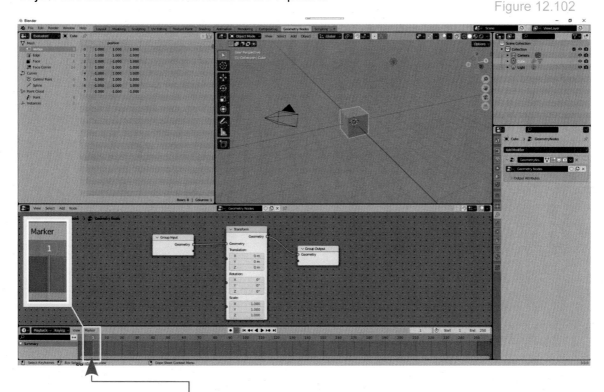

In the Timeline Editor the Cursor (blue line) will be at Frame 1.

Remember: The Cube is selected in the 3D Viewport Editor, therefore, the Node Pipeline is applicable to the Cube. The values in the Transform Node control the Translation, Rotation and Scale of the Cube.

To demonstrate Animation the X Axis value in the Transform Node will be Animated to affect the X Axis translation (movement) of the Cube in the 3D Viewport Editor.

In the Transform Node, right click on the **X Translation** value and select **Insert Single Keyframe**. This inserts a single Keyframe at Frame 1 in the Timeline Editor. At this point the Translation X value bar is _colored yellow_ indicating that a Keyframe has been inserted.

Figure 12.103

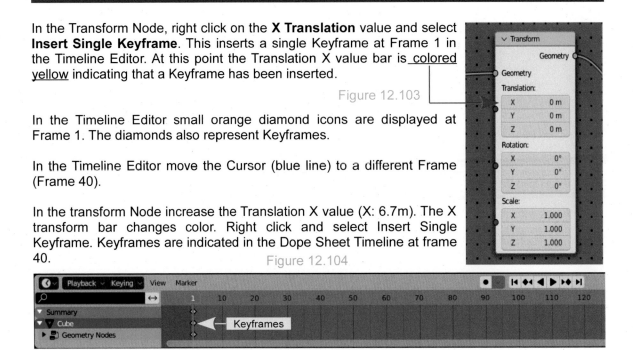

In the Timeline Editor small orange diamond icons are displayed at Frame 1. The diamonds also represent Keyframes.

In the Timeline Editor move the Cursor (blue line) to a different Frame (Frame 40).

In the transform Node increase the Translation X value (X: 6.7m). The X transform bar changes color. Right click and select Insert Single Keyframe. Keyframes are indicated in the Dope Sheet Timeline at frame 40.

Figure 12.104

In the 3D Viewport Editor the Cube has relocated 6.7m along the X Axis of the Scene.

Move the Cursor in the Dope Sheet Editor back to Frame 1. Scrub the Animation (Drag the Cursor) to see the Cube move in the 3D Viewport Editor. Alternatively, press the **Play Button** in the Header to see the Cube move as the Animation is played.

Figure 12.105

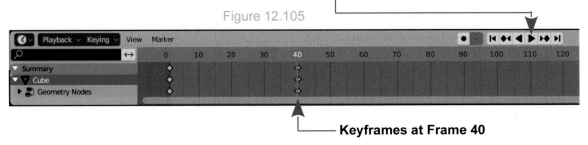

Keyframes at Frame 40

Note: When the Animation is played the Cube moves in the 3D Viewport Editor from the center of the Scene and stops at 6.7m along the X Axis. The Animation continues to play with the Timeline Cursor travelling on to Frame 250 where the Animation replays. Frame 250 is set as the length of the Animation.

The foregoing has demonstrated the Animation of a single value. By adjusting multiple values at different Frames you select **Insert Keyframes** instead of **Single Keyframe**.

12.22 Maths

Maths in Geometry Nodes refers to the use of Nodes to perform calculations which affect an Object which is selected in the 3D Viewport Editor. By stepping through the following exercise you will gain an appreciation of how this is performed and the power of using Nodes.

Figure 12.106

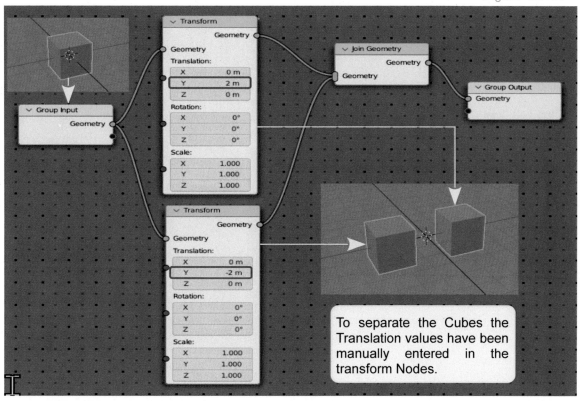

To separate the Cubes the Translation values have been manually entered in the transform Nodes.

The **Node Pipeline** shown above is applied to the default Cube Object in the 3D Viewport Editor. The Node arrangement with two **Transform Nodes** creates two Cubes spaced 2m either side of the X Axis of the Scene.

Note: Translation plus 2m value in the upper transform Node and Translation minus 2m value in the lower Transform Node. Both values are for the Y Translation.

Manually entering values in the Nodes is fine but were you to Animate the Translation (movement) of the Cubes you would have to Animate the plus and minus values separately. For a simple Scene this is a legitimate method but for complicated Scenes with multiple Objects all moving at the same time you may wish to arrange a Node System such that only one value needs to be Animated.

To employ a single value you add a Value Node to the Pipeline. Bear in mind that all Nodes do not output the same type of value and that although they may connect legitimately, the result may or may not be what you require.

Simple Node Value Rule

Figure 12.107

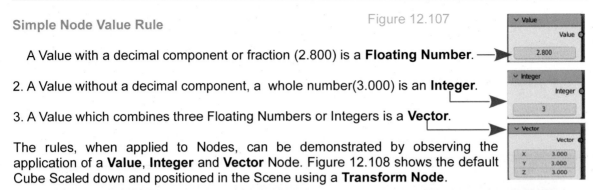

A Value with a decimal component or fraction (2.800) is a **Floating Number**. ➤

2. A Value without a decimal component, a whole number(3.000) is an **Integer**. ➤

3. A Value which combines three Floating Numbers or Integers is a **Vector**. ➤

The rules, when applied to Nodes, can be demonstrated by observing the application of a **Value**, **Integer** and **Vector** Node. Figure 12.108 shows the default Cube Scaled down and positioned in the Scene using a **Transform Node**.

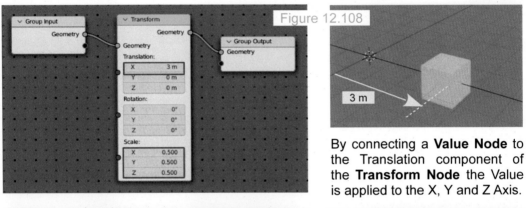

Figure 12.108

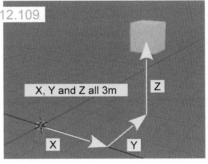

By connecting a **Value Node** to the Translation component of the **Transform Node** the Value is applied to the X, Y and Z Axis.

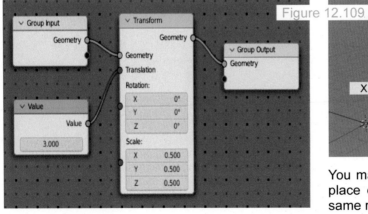

Figure 12.109

You may use an **Integer Node** in place of the **Value Node** for the same result.

Note: The value 3.000 in the **Value Node** is a **Floating Number** value. The value could be amended to 2.8. In contrast if you enter value 2.8 in an **Integer Node** the value will be rounded up to 3.

Figure 12.110

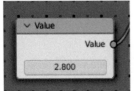

270

Connecting a **Vector Node** to the **Translation Input Socket** of the Transform Node maintains control of the X, Y and Z Values external to the Transform Node.

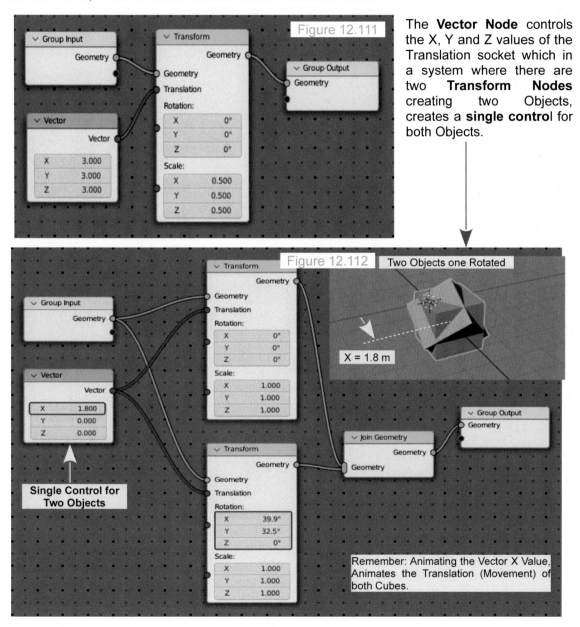

Figure 12.111

The **Vector Node** controls the X, Y and Z values of the Translation socket which in a system where there are two **Transform Nodes** creating two Objects, creates a **single control** for both Objects.

Figure 12.112

Two Objects one Rotated

X = 1.8 m

Single Control for Two Objects

Remember: Animating the Vector X Value, Animates the Translation (Movement) of both Cubes.

Sockets and Noodle Colors

In the above, you will observe that sockets and noodles are connected green to green, blue to blue which indicates that the connections are valid. A **red noodle** means; connection is invalid.

At this point you may well be asking; what has any of this to do with Maths? Well, the Nodes actually perform Maths calculations according to the values you enter. Different Nodes perform different calculations, therefore, you have to select the correct Node for the right job. The colored sockets give an indication only but when connected may not produce the correct result.

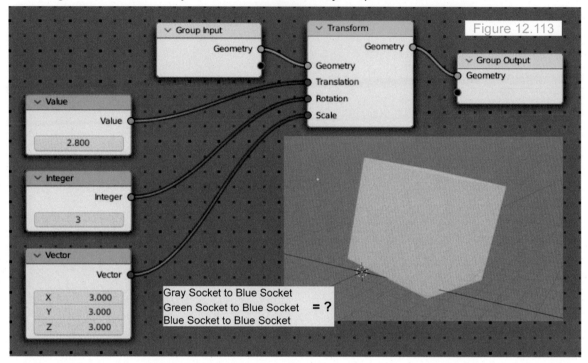

Figure 12.113

Gray Socket to Blue Socket
Green Socket to Blue Socket   = ?
Blue Socket to Blue Socket

Consider the **Vector – Math Node** shown above to comprise three Float Values. This may be represented as:

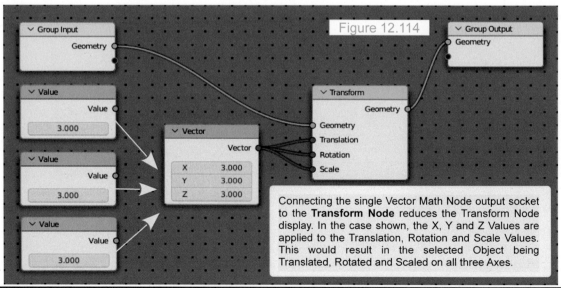

Figure 12.114

Connecting the single Vector Math Node output socket to the **Transform Node** reduces the Transform Node display. In the case shown, the X, Y and Z Values are applied to the Translation, Rotation and Scale Values. This would result in the selected Object being Translated, Rotated and Scaled on all three Axes.

Using Maths

Reciprocating Cubes   Figure 12.115

Maths or rather Maths Nodes may be used to generate effects. As a demonstration, two elongated Cube Objects will be Animated to display reciprocated motion. Imagine the Cubes as pistons in an engine. When one piston moves up the other moves down.

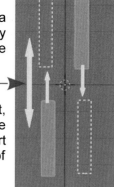

Reciprocating Motion ⟶

When considering machine components dimensions are very important, therefore, the physical dimensions of the elongated Cubes determine the length of the motion. The dimensions of the default Cube in the 3D Viewport Editor are 2m x 2m x 2m and the Scale is X, Y and Z = 1.000. The divisions of the Grid Floor in the default Scene are 1m x 1m.

Set the Dimensions of the Piston (Cube)   Figure 12.116

With the default Cube selected press **S + 0.5 + Enter** to reduce the Cube to 1m x 1m x 1m. Press **S + Z + 4 + Enter** to elongate the Piston to 4m.

With the elongated Cube (piston) selected and with the Mouse Cursor in the 3D Viewport Editor, press the **N Key** to display the Object Properties and see the dimensions of the Piston.

In the Object Properties panel the Dimensions correspond to the values that have been set but the Z Axis Scale value is 2 **NOT** the value 4 that was entered?

This occurs since the original default dimensions of the Cube were 2m x 2m x 2m, therefore, 2m x Scale 2 = 4m.

This may seem obvious but is emphasised since setting dimensions in relation to Object Properties is important.

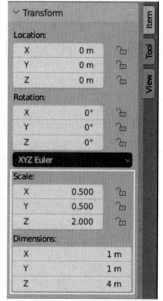

Duplicate the Piston   Figure 12.117

To duplicate the Piston use the Transform Nodes in the Geometry Node Editor.

3D Viewport Editor – Edit Mode

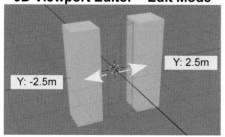

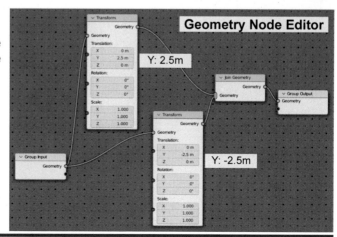

From the foregoing, the elongated Cube is 4m in length. To set the Translation (movement) shown in Figure 12.118 the Value is **1m + A. Assume A = 0.3m**

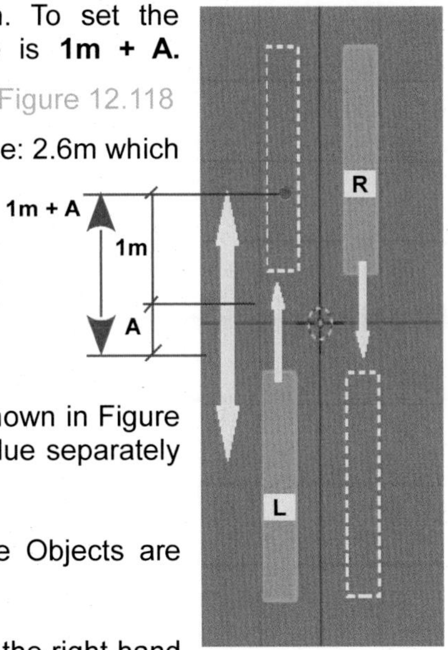

Figure 12.118

The total movement from the upper to the lower positions will be: 2.6m which will be from +1.3m to -1.3m.

The total movement has to be considered with respect to the length of the Animation. Assuming the total Animation length is 100 Frames the movement will be from +1.3m to -1.3m over 100 Frames.

With the Node Pipeline containing two Transform Nodes as shown in Figure 12.117 you would have to Animate each Z Transformation Value separately to create a reciprocal motion.

To simplify the Animation process, especially where multiple Objects are involved, you add Nodes as shown in Figure 12.119.

The **Value Node** contains the value which sets the position of the right hand piston at Frame 1 in the Animation.

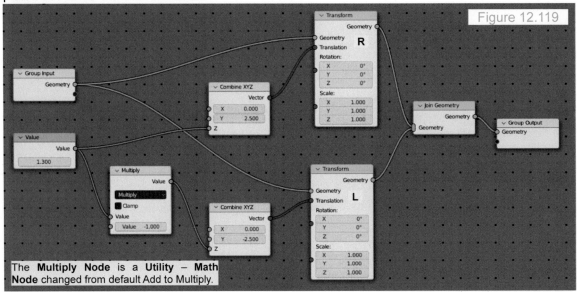

Figure 12.119

The Multiply Node is a Utility – Math Node changed from default Add to Multiply.

The value in the **Value Node** is a **Floating Number** which does not give a **Vector Value** required for the **Translation values in the Transform Node**, therefore a converter **Combine XYZ Node** is inserted. The Value Node is connected to the **Z input Socket** on the converter then the Vector output socket is connected to Translation input socket on the Transform Node. This allows the value from the Value Node to be conveyed as the **Translation value** and at the same time retain the Y Axis control for the right hand piston.

To produce a reciprocal Translation for the left hand piston the **Multiply Node** with a **minus 1** value converts the plus 1.3 value from the Value Node to a minus 1.3.

To Animate the reciprocal motion right click on the value in the **Value Node** and select Insert **Keyframe**. Keyframes are inserted in the Timeline at Frame 1.

Note: With the Timeline Editor displayed you may NOT see the Keyframes. If this is the case change to the **Dope Sheet Editor Timeline** and click the **Only Show Selected** button.

Move the Timeline Cursor to Frame 50. Change the value in the **Value Node** to minus 1.3 and insert a second Keyframe.

Move the Timeline Cursor to Frame 100, change the value back to plus 1.3 and insert a Keyframe.

Playing the Animation at this point will see the pistons reciprocate from Frame 1 to Frame 100 then stop as the Animation plays on to Frame 250 (the default End Frame) before the Animation replays.

Change the **End Frame** in the **Timeline Editor** to 100 and play the Animation to see continuously reciprocating pistons.

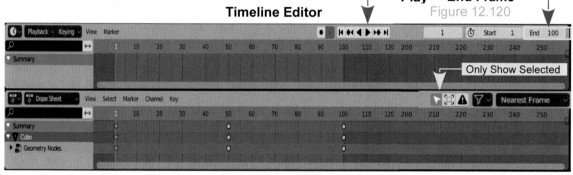

Figure 12.120

Dope Sheet Editor

12.23 Summary

This brief introduction to **Geometry Nodes** is intended to get you started. The subject is extensive and is continually being developed, therefore, it is felt that with a basic knowledge, following instruction provided in the many video tutorials on the internet will be a little easier.

There are many tutorials available but be aware that some of the instruction contained in the tutorials has been superseded as development have been applied. Always check the date the tutorial was published and the version of Blender for which the tutorial was written.

Most importantly, be prepared to experiment and record your findings.

Geometry Nodes are a fantastic tool for creating a multitude of effects. It is hoped you will be enthused to pursue a study and develop skills allowing the creation of fantastic effects.

13

Drivers

Drivers are functions or scripts which use properties (values) to affect other properties. This is particularly applicable when animating. Drivers are used to control the animation of one property based on the value of another.

For example, the Translation (movement) of one Object may be used to control the Rotation of another Object. This means that the Object's animated value is not controlled by the Frame number interpolated from Keyframes, but rather by the data in a specified animation channel. Drivers can take their effects from single properties, differences in rotation or scripted Python expressions which may be edited inside the User Interface controls.

Drivers are not limited to simple animated movements. You may use the X location of a Driver of an Object to control the Material color (RGB curves) of another Object's Material, or use the rotation of a Driver to control the Scale of an Object, or use the Scale of a Driver to control the shape (through Shape Keys) of a Mesh/Curve/etc., use a Python function to control a constraint's influence, and much much more.

One key usage of Drivers is in Character Animation: for example, you can add Object Drivers to the relative Shape Keys of a Face. Then, you manipulate the expressions of your character just by moving these Drivers' Objects.

To explain Drivers in detail would require a dedicated publication. This chapter will simply demonstrate, in practical terms, what a driver is and where the controls are located in the interface. This will provide a starting point for a detailed study.

13.1 Blender Drivers

To understand the basic concept of using Drivers work through the following example.

A Driver will be set, causing a Monkey to rotate on its Z axis when a Cube is translated on its Y axis. The Driver will be applied to the Monkey Object (Suzanne).

Open Blender with the default Scene containing the Cube object. Deselect the Cube and add a Monkey object. Move the Monkey to one side as shown in Figure 16.1.

Split the 3D Viewport Editor in two and make one part the **Driver Editor**. With the cursor in the Driver Editor press **N key** to display the **Drivers Properties panel**.

Drivers Editor　　　　　　　　　　**3D Viewport Editor**　　　Figure 13.1

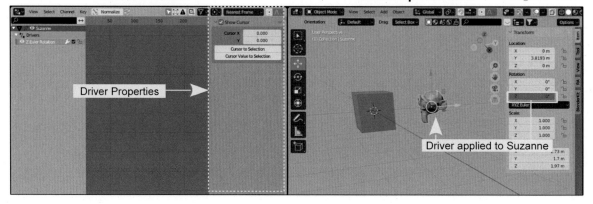

With the cursor in the 3D Viewport Editor press the **N key** to display the **Transform Properties Panel**. You now have a properties panels in the 3D Viewport and in the Drivers Editor. With the Mouse Cursor In the 3D Viewport Editor press the **T Key** to close the Tools panel and remove clutter from the left hand side of the Scene.

With the **Monkey Object** selected right click on the **Z Axis Rotation Slider** in the **Transform Properties Panel** (press N key). Select (click) **Add Driver.** The slider will turn purple showing that a driver has been added and the **Driven Property** panel displays (Figure 13.2).

Transform Properties Panel in the 3D Viewport　　　Figure 13.2

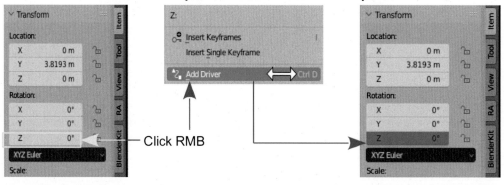

Note: Moving the **Mouse Cursor** out of the panel, causes the panel to disappear from view.

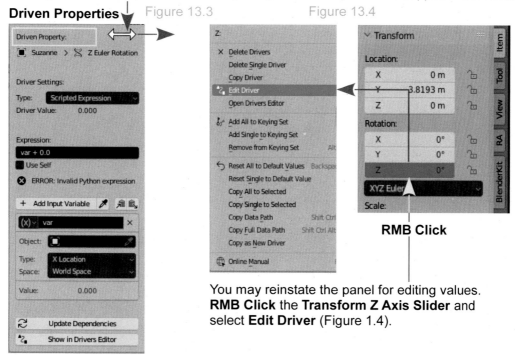

Figure 13.3   Figure 13.4

You may reinstate the panel for editing values. **RMB Click** the **Transform Z Axis Slider** and select **Edit Driver** (Figure 1.4).

Adding a **Z Axis Driver** with the **Monkey** selected means that a change in the property values of a secondary Object, yet to be specified, will control the Z Axis Rotation of Suzanne. Specifying the secondary Object takes place in the **Drivers Editor**.

13.2 The Drivers Editor

The secondary action is defined in the **Drivers Editor** (Figure 13.5). The Drivers Editor (at this point) is showing the **Z Euler Rotation Driver** applied to **Suzanne** (the Monkey Object).

Figure 13.5

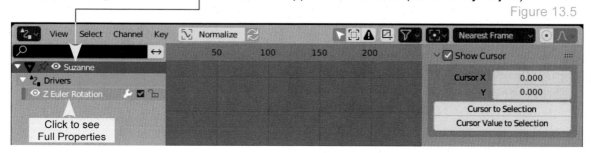

Where you see **Show Cursor** checked at the right hand side of the Editor is a copy of the **Driven Property View Tab**. To see the full Properties Panel for Driver Properties , click on **Z Euler Rotation**.

Figure 13.6

Clicking **Z Euler Rotation** expands the view showing Driver **Properties Tabs** with **F-Curve** selected. The center panel is the **Graph Editor**.

Figure 13.7

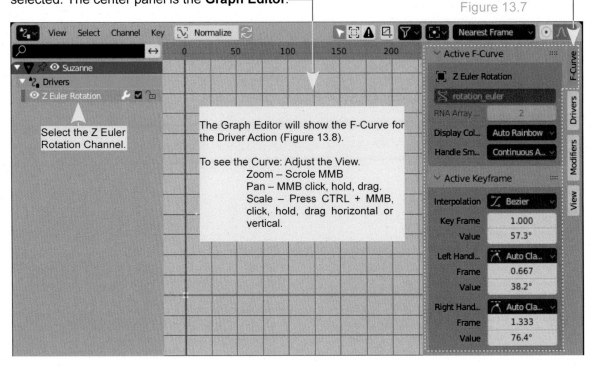

Select the Z Euler Rotation Channel.

The Graph Editor will show the F-Curve for the Driver Action (Figure 13.8).

To see the Curve: Adjust the View.
    Zoom – Scrole MMB
    Pan – MMB click, hold, drag.
    Scale – Press CTRL + MMB, click, hold, drag horizontal or vertical.

To set **Z Euler Rotation Drivers for Suzanne**, defining the secondary Object, change from the **F-Curve Tab** to the **Drivers Tab** (Figure 13.8).

Figure 13.8

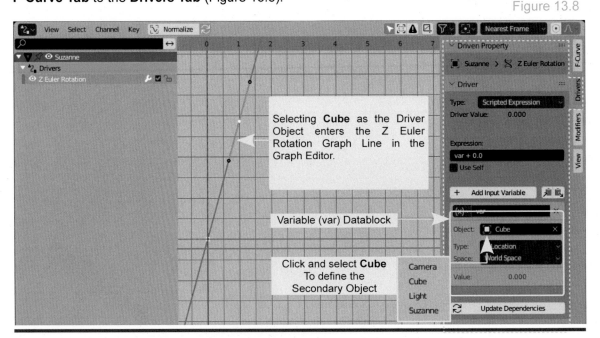

Selecting **Cube** as the Driver Object enters the Z Euler Rotation Graph Line in the Graph Editor.

Variable (var) Datablock

Click and select **Cube** To define the Secondary Object

By selecting the Cube in the 3D Viewport Editor and using the Move Tool, Translating the Cube along the X Axis of the Scene, Rotates Susanne about her Z Axis.

Figure 13.9

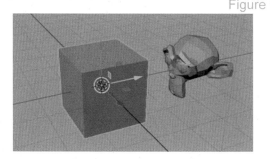
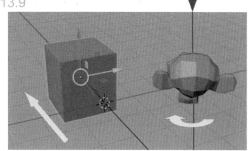

This simple demonstration is the tip of the iceberg in understanding Drivers and merely shows that Drivers are a way to control values of properties by means of a function, or a mathematical expression.

The Blender Manual: The Blender 3.0.0 Manual provides an in depth discussion of Drivers with some excellent examples.

https://docs.blender.org/manual/en/latest/animation/drivers/introduction.html

Excellent Tutorial: One of many excellent tutorials on the internet describing the basic use of Drivers is:

https://www.youtube.com/watch?v=N8GR9icb51w

13.3 Expanding the Demonstration

Go back to the Transform Properties Panel in the 3D Viewport Editor with Suzanne selected and add a Driver for the Z Location Channel. In the Driver Editor set Cube as the driver Object.

With the second driver added to Suzanne, Translating the Cube Object along the X Axis causes Suzanne to move up or down an the Z Axis while at the same time Rotating on about the Z Axis.

Figure 13.10

A **Z Location Graph Line is** inserted in the Graph Editor.

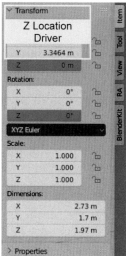

Note: In the **Driven Property** the **Driver Type** by default is; **Scripted Expression.** Figure 13.11

The Driver Type determines how the variables are used. The type can be:

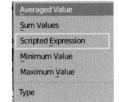

- ⬚ a built-in function: for example, the **sum of the variables**' values, or

- ⬚ a **scripted expression**: an arbitrary Python expression that refers to the variables by their names.

Without going into a whole heap of Python scripting, for the moment, consider that when **var** is entered as the name of the variable value the Expression **var + 0.0** is executed by the driver causing Suzanne to Rotate when the Cube is moved on the X Axis of the Scene.

To gain an understanding of how the different settings and values affect the movement of Objects study the following which has been copied from the Blender 3.0 Manual.

13.4 Workflow & Examples

Simple Drivers can be configured from the pop-over that appears when adding a new Driver. When adding multiple Drivers or for more advanced configurations, it is useful to have open the Drivers Editor.

13.5 Transform Driver

Control a property with an object's transform. In this example, the Y rotation of Object 2 will be driven by the X position of Object 1. Starting from a simple setup with two objects:

Add a Driver to the Rotation Y property of the second object via the context menu or with Ctrl-D.

3D Viewport Editor   Figure 13.12

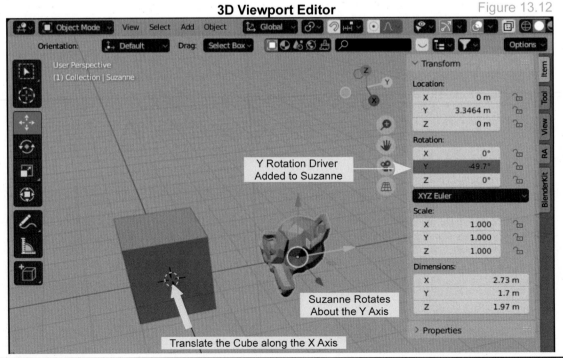

Driver Editor

Figure 13.13

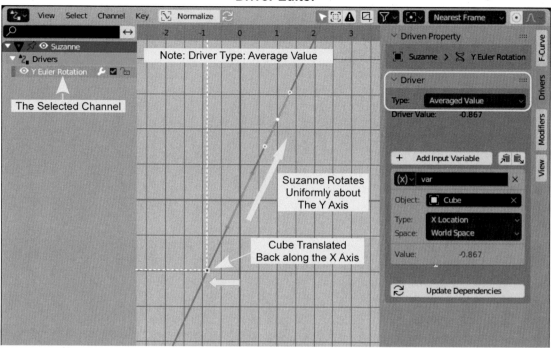

Figure 13.14

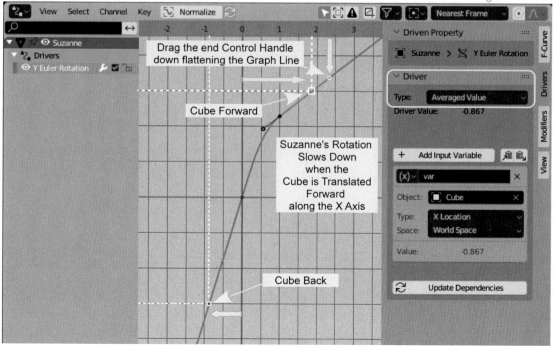

13.6 Scripted Expression – Orbit a Point

Orbit an Object's position (a Cube Object) around a point with a custom **Scripted Expression**. The Object's position will change when **scrubbing the timeline**. Circular motion can be defined in 2D using the **sine** and **cosine** functions. In this example, the current frame is used as the variable that induces the motion.

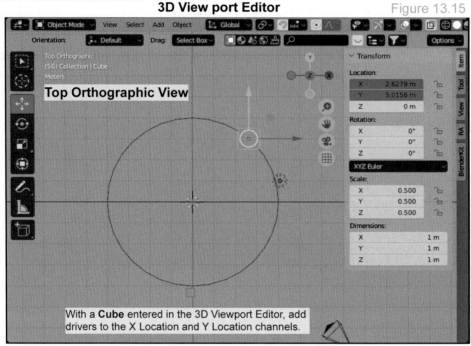

3D View port Editor   Figure 13.15

Adding Drivers in the 3D Viewport Editor for the X and Y Location Transform Properties of the Cube creates Drivers Driven Properties for the X Location and the Y Location of the Cube. You see these Properties displayed in the Drivers Editor.

Drivers Editor

X Location Channel   Figure 13.16   **Y Location Channel**

To set the Driven Properties to have the Cube Orbit around the center of the Scene when the Timeline Editor Cursor is scrubbed you set values in the Driven Property Panels for both X and Y Location Channels.

Pay careful attention to the values. The slightest error, especially to the Expression value, will result in a failure.

Figure 13.17	Figure 13.18	Figure 13.19
Default Driven Property	**Modified X Location**	**Modified Y Location**

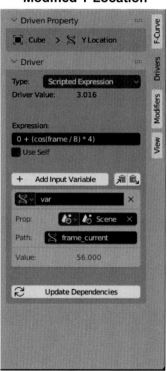

Figure 16.17 shows the default Driven Property when a Transform Driver is added to the Cube.

The procedure fore editing values for the X Location Driver and the Y Location Driver is identical except for the Expression. For X Location Driver change the Expression: var + 0.0 to:

$$0 + (sin(frame / 8) *4)$$

Important: Type the Expression exactly as shown. **Type sin NOT sine**.

For the Y Location Driver the Expression is: 0 + (cos(frame / 8) *4)

When the Expression is entered the Error message in the default Driver display remains in the panel.

Figure 13.20

There is a little more setup to do before the expression will take effect.

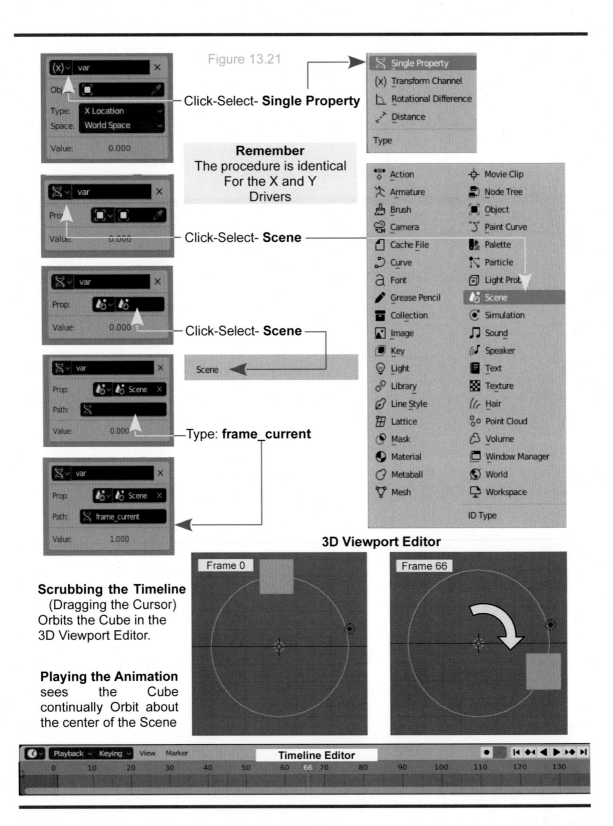

Figure 13.21

Click-Select- **Single Property**

Single Property
(x) Transform Channel
Rotational Difference
Distance
Type

Remember
The procedure is identical
For the X and Y
Drivers

Click-Select- **Scene**

Click-Select- **Scene**

Scene

Type: **frame_current**

Action   Movie Clip
Armature   Node Tree
Brush   Object
Camera   Paint Curve
Cache File   Palette
Curve   Particle
Font   Light Prot.
Grease Pencil   Scene
Collection   Simulation
Image   Sound
Key   Speaker
Light   Text
Library   Texture
Line Style   Hair
Lattice   Point Cloud
Mask   Volume
Material   Window Manager
Metaball   World
Mesh   Workspace
                      ID Type

3D Viewport Editor

Frame 0

Frame 66

Scrubbing the Timeline
(Dragging the Cursor)
Orbits the Cube in the
3D Viewport Editor.

Playing the Animation
sees the Cube
continually Orbit about
the center of the Scene

Playback ~ Keying ~ View Marker   **Timeline Editor**

0   10   20   30   40   50   60 66 70   80   90   100   110   120   130

The Scripted Expression: 0 + (sin(frame / 8) *4)

(frame / 8) is the current frame of the animation, divided by 8 to slow the orbit down.

(sin(   ) *4) multiplies the result of sin(frame /8) by 4 for a larger orbit circle.

0 + controls the offset to the obit center point.

The forgoing is intended to wet your appetite for using Drivers. With an understanding of Drivers and perhaps a little bit of Python the results are limitless. To entice you further the following exercise will show how a **Python Script** is used.

13.7 Randomise Object Properties

The objective in this exercise is to set up a Blender file which may be used to create a Random Array of Objects, that is to create a number of similar objects which vary in their characteristics. To be specific, say you want to create a bunch of cubes with each cube slightly different in size, rotated and located in a different position in a scene. You do not require and specific differences, in fact you want a **Random Array of Objects**.

There are several ways in which you could create the array. You could simply duplicate the Cube in the 3D Viewport Editor then Scale, Rotate and Translate and change the Material. Keep on doing this until you have sufficient Cubes. To help with changing the Objects size you could set up **Shapes Keys**. To help with duplicating the Cubes you could use an **Array Modifier** or multiple **Array Modifiers**. Needless to say these methods are somewhat tedious.

The following instructions will demonstrate how to set up a **Blender File** including a **Python Script** which may be used with **Drivers** to create an **Array**.

Create the Blender File

In creating the Blender File you register a **Python Script** in the File. This means that this particular Blender File, when saved, will contain the Python Script. The File will then be available to be used for creating Random Arrays at a later date.

Create a Python Script

A Python Script is a piece of code written in the **Python Computer Language** and is simply a text file. In this exercise the script shown in Figure 13.22 will be used.

Figure 13.22

```
rand.py - Notepad
File  Edit  Format  View  Help
import bpy
import random

# Random floating point number between lo and hi

def randf(lo, hi):|
        return random.uniform(lo, hi)

# Random integer from lo (inclusive) to hi (inclusive)

def randi(lo, hi):
        return random.randint(lo, hi)

# Random values given mean and standard deviation

def gauss(mean, stdev):
        return random.gauss(mean, stdev)

bpy.app.driver_namespace["randf"] = randf
bpy.app.driver_namespace["randi"] = randi
bpy.app.driver_namespace["gauss"] = gauss
```

Type the text shown in the diagram into a Text Editor such as Notepad or Wordpad and **save the text file**. You will copy and paste this into a Blender file. You can type it directly into the Blender text editor but having it saved as a text file gives you a back up. Make sure the text is copied **exactly** as shown. The slightest error will cause an error when running the script.

The Python Script will be used in conjunction with the **Blender Driver Functions**. Remember where you have saved the Text File and the name of the File. The name of the File in this exercise is **rand.py**.

In simple terms **Drivers** are functions which affect the attributes or properties of an Object. Refer to the demonstration at the beginning of this paper where the translation of one Object controls the rotation of another. In that instance the position of one Object in the Scene controlled the rotation of the other. Instead of using the translation of an object the **Python Script**, will be introduced to the **Driver** to control properties of Objects.

The first step is to **Enter** and **Register** the **Python Script** in a Blender file. This will create a Blender file which you can save for future use.

Open a new Blender file and open the **Text Editor**. Create a new **Text Block** by clicking **New** in the window header or by clicking **Text - Create New Text Block**. Figure 13.23

The default name of the new text block is show simply as **Text**. Rename this to something more significant. Since you are about to work with random properties and a Python Script, **ran.py**. is appropriate. Note the suffix **.py** is very important, therefore make sure you include this in the name. Figure 13.24

With the text block created go get your Python Script. That is, go to the text file you previously created. Open the file in the Text Editor you used and select (highlight) the text and copy it to the clipboard. Paste the text into the newly created text block in the Blender **Text Editor.** Figure 13.25

```
1   import bpy
2   import random
3
4   # Random floating point number between lo and hi
5
6   def randf(lo, hi):
7       return random.uniform(lo, hi)
8
9   # Random integer from lo (inclusive) to hi (inclusive)
10
11  def randi(lo, hi):
12      return random.randint(lo, hi)
13
14  # Random values given mean and standard deviation
15
16  def gauss(mean, stdev):
17      return random.gauss(mean, stdev)
18
19  bpy.app.driver_namespace["randf"] = randf
20  bpy.app.driver_namespace["randi"] = randi
21  bpy.app.driver_namespace["gauss"] = gauss
```

In the Text Editor Header click **Run Script** then check **Register**.　　**Run Script**

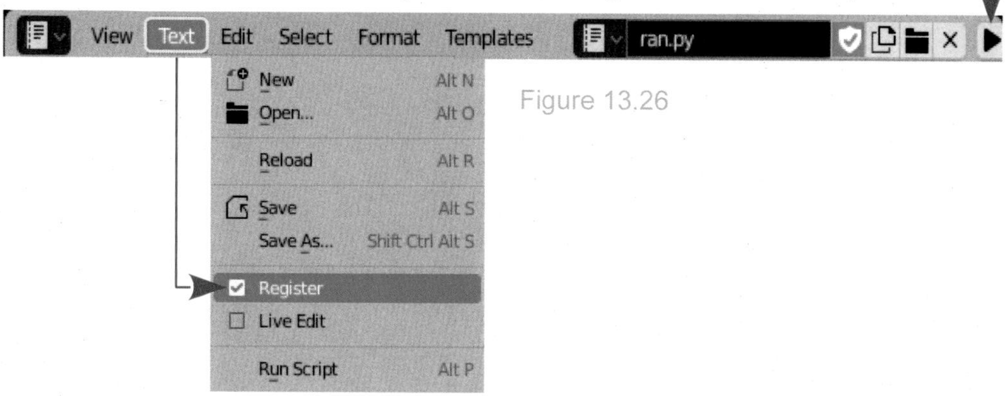

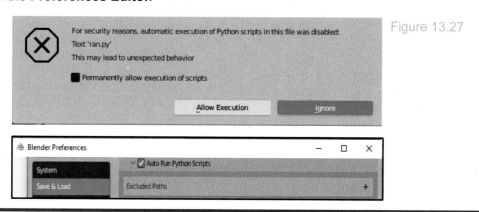

Figure 13.26

Run Script will make the functions contained in the Script available to the Driver. The functions in the Python Script are the **randf, randi and gauss** bits (functions). Register means that the next time you open the Blender file it will run the script and register automatically.

Save the Blender File with the name **RandomPy.blend**.

Registering the Python Script makes functions in the script (**randf, randi** and **gauss**) available for use by the Blender Drivers. Either of these functions can be called (entered into Blender) for use by a driver. Saving the **RandomPy.blend** file means you now have a Blender file available for generating random properties. How the **randf (lo, hi)** part of the Python Script works will be demonstrated. This is the only part being used in this demonstration. Including the **randi (lo, hi)** part and the **gauss (mean, stdev)** parts merely makes them available should you wish to use them in the future. To understand these statements you will have to undertake a study of the Python programming language.

OK! with the **RandomPy.blend** file open you can close the **Text Editor** and return the **3D Viewport Editor.**

Note: If you close the RandomPy.blend file and reopen it at a later date a notice may display in the Info window header stating **For security reasons, automatic execution of scripts in this file was disabled**. This occurs if **Auto Run Python Scripts** is disabled in the **Preferences Editor**.

Figure 13.27

At this point it will be assumed that you previously save the Blender File named RandomPy.blend and now wish to use the File to create a Random Display of Objects. With the Array created you can Append the Array into other Blender Files.

Arrange the 3D Viewport Editor and Driver Editor

Have BlenderPy.blend opened with the Blender Screen arranged as shown in Figure 13.1 with the Driver Editor and 3D Viewport Editors side by side. Note: This arrangement is purely a matter of choice and will depend on your Screen size and preference.

With the mouse cursor in the 3D Viewport press the **N Key** to display the **Transform Properties Panel**. **Note:** This Properties Panel displays the same information as the **Object Properties** in the **Properties Editor, Object Properties Tab**. Drivers may be added to an Object in either Panel.

Save the File, that is save the current version of RandomPy.blend, as (Save As) a new File with a name of your choice relevant to the Array you are creating, For example; **Random_Cubes.blend**.

Saving a new File leaves the original File (RandomPy.blend) intact, for future use.

OK you have **Random_Cubes.blend** opened ready to go.

Note: The Array to be created will be constructed in stages by Adding Property Drivers and Expressions for different facets of the Array. To begin a **Rotation Driver** will be engaged.

Rotation Driver Properties

Begin by setting a driver for the X Rotation Property of the default Cube Object in the 3D Viewport. Make sure your Object, the Cube, is selected. In the **Object Properties panel of the 3D Viewport Editor**, right mouse click on **X Rotation** and select **Add Driver** (Figure 13.28).

Figure 13.28

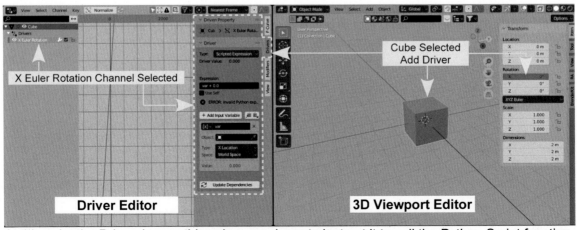

At this point the Driver does nothing since you have to instruct it to call the Python Script function.

Remember: The Blender File named **RandomPy.blend** has been created with the Python Script named **ran.py** entered and registered. You have then copied the File and saved it as **Random_Cubes.blend**. Since it is a copy of RandomPy.blend it also has the Python Script ran.py entered and registered.

Attempting to create an Array in a new Blender File without the Python Script entered and registered will fail.

Enter the Python Script Function

You are using a **Scripted Expression** (Python Script) which has been entered and registered in the Blender File named Random_Cubes.blend (a copy of RandomPy.blend). The Python Script contains several functions.

Figure 13.29

```
1  import bpy
2  import random
3
4  # Random floating point number between lo and hi
5
6  def randf(lo, hi):
7      return random.uniform(lo, hi)
8
9  # Random integer from lo (inclusive) to hi (inclusive)
10
11 def randi(lo, hi):
12     return random.randint(lo, hi)
13
14 # Random values given mean and standard deviation
15
16 def gauss(mean, stdev):
17     return random.gauss(mean, stdev)
18
19 bpy.app.driver_namespace["randf"] = randf
20 bpy.app.driver_namespace["randi"] = randi
21 bpy.app.driver_namespace["gauss"] = gauss
```

You have Added an **X Axis Rotation Driver** to the Cube Object. The Driver Type is: **Scripted Expression**. The objective in this first stage of creating an Array is to generate a Random Rotation of the Cube. This means that a change to the status of the Cube, such as, it's location in the Scene will cause the Cube to randomly Rotate.

To have the Driver execute this Random Rotation you call a function in the Python Script, in this instance, **def randf(lo, hi)**.

Read this as, **rand** [random], **f** [function], **(lo, hi)** [lower value to higher value] which you enter in the **Driver Property Panel** as the **Expression: randf(-pi, pi)**

Expression:
randf(-pi, pi)

Figure 13.30

+180°

-180°

pi (in Python) = π = 3.142. There are 2 π Radians in 360°, therefore, (-pi, pi) = -180° to +180°.

Immediately you enter the Expression you will see the Cube Rotate about the X Axis in the 3D Viewport. Each time you click **Update Dependencies** in the **Driver Property** panel the Cube Rotates to a new orientation. With the Cube selected in the 3D Viewport, pressing the G Key and dragging the Mouse sees the Cube Rotate to a new orientation.

Entering the function is in effect telling Blender to use **randf** expression of your Python Script with the arguments **-pi** and **+pi** to recalculate a random value of rotation about the Cubes X Axis within the range minus π to pluss π. In other words pick a rotational value about the X Axis between 0° and 360° since there are 2 π radians in a circle (Arguments are values that an expression uses in its calculation).

By adding Drivers to the Y Axis and Z Axis Rotation Channels and entering randf(-pi, pi) as the Expression in the Driver Property Panel the Cube will Rotate Randomly about all three Axis.

Note: When using the **randf(hi, lo)** Expression the **hi lo** values are not limited to Rotational values. If you are using the Expression to affect the Scale of an Object you would use numeric values.

> When entering values in the Expression be careful when pressing the . (period) Key and , (comma) Key. Its too easy to press the wrong Key.

Re-evaluating Drivers

With Drivers set , in the 3D Viewport, pressing G key (Grab) and dragging the Mouse moves the Object in the Scene. Blender constantly re-evaluates the Driver and produces random values for the properties values. Note: This will affect any Driver which has the "randf", "randi", or "gauss" Python expression inserted. This function can be negated by unchecking the **F-Curve Contribution button** in the Driver Editor. You will want to negate this function if you require to manually reposition the cube without it Rotating.

Figure 13.31

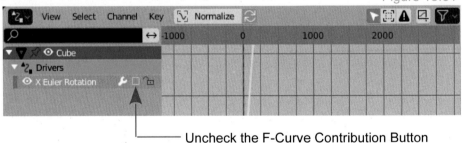

────── Uncheck the F-Curve Contribution Button

Scale Properties Driver

Up to this point Rotation Drivers have been evaluated but, in fact, any Object Property can have a Driver added and use a Python Script Expression.

You can create Scale Drivers and set up a process where the X, Y and Z Axis all Scale in proportion to each other. To show how this works a different process will be demonstrated for each axis. You may however use any one of the processes on each axis.

X Axis Scale Driver (Scripted Expression)

Start by adding the **X Axis Scale Driver** using Scripted Expression. In the 3D Viewport, Object Properties panel, RMB click on **Scale: X Axis**, select Add Driver etc. as before. A new Driver Channel is entered in the Driver Editor and again, clicking on the Channel displays the Driven Property Panel. The Tabs displayed are now applicable to the X Axis Scale of the Cube in the 3D Viewport (Figure 13.32).

Figure 13.32

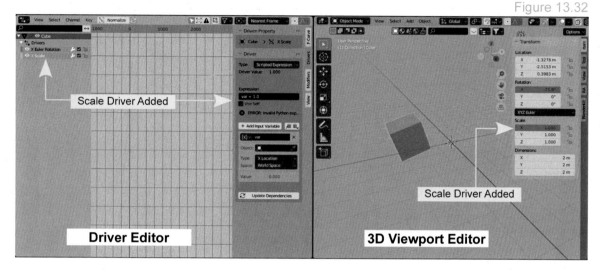

Driver Editor   3D Viewport Editor

This set up is the same as you used for the X Axis Rotation with the exception that you insert the values 0.8 and 1.8 instead of -pi and pi in the randf Expression

The X Scale value will now be randomly re-evaluated between 0.8 and 1.8 Blender units when you click **Update Dependencies**. You can set any values you like but don't get carried away.

Figure 13.33

Y Axis Scale Driver (Max, Min, Sum, Average values with Variable)

On the **Y Axis Scale** values, Right click **Add Driver.** Instead of selecting **Scripted Expression** in the Driver Editor, Driven Property Panel, choose either **Max, Min, Sum or Average** Driver types. Use **Average Value** (Figure 13.33).

This is where the **Variable Data-block** in the **Driven Properties Panel** is used. **Note:** An error message displays until data is entered in the Variable Datablock and you click Update Dependencies (Figure 13.33).

Variable Datablock ⟶

OK! You are setting up the Y Axis Scale Driver but you want to use the X Axis Scale Data via the Variable Datablock to control the scaling of the Cube on the Y axis.

Enter the following in the Variable Datablock with the **Cube** selected (The cube object being used) in the Specific Property I.D. block.

Use: **Transform Channel**. Type: **X Scale**. Space: **Transform Space** (Figure 13.34).

At this point clicking **Update Dependencies** produces a random Scale change along the X Axis of the Cube with a corresponding change on the Y Axis

Figure 13.34

Figure 13.35

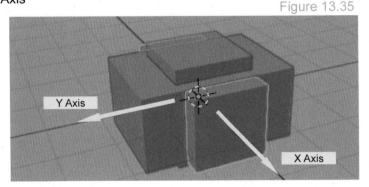

Z Axis Scale Driver

Repeat the identical process for the Z Axis as that used for the Y Axis.

Clicking **Update Dependencies** recalculates random scale values and all Axis Scale in proportion. Translating the Cube in the 3D Viewport will do the same thing.

OK! Take a deep breath. You are not finished.

Material properties can be randomized using Python Script just as you did with the Rotation and Scale properties for the X Axis Driver. For the Rotation you used a value range of **-pi** to **pi** (2π radians in a circle, therefore -π to +π) and for the Scale the range was 0.8 to 1.8 Blender units).

Remember: For the Cube's X Axis Scale randomizing was performed using Scripted Expression randf(lo, hi). For the Y Axis Scale randomizing was dependent on the Average Value of the X Axis Scale.

Figure 13.36

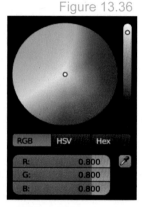

When using the **randf(lo, hi)** Expression to generate random colors on the Object, when dependencies are updated, you use the numeric values in the RGB Color Scheme range where 1.000 = White and 0.000 = Black.

The values between these maximum and minimums produce the spectrum of visible color between white and black. To randomize Material within the spectrum all that is required is to use the expression **randf(0.000, 1.000)**.

Remember: The Blender File must have the Python Script Entered, Run and Registered. Use the File named **RandomPy.blend** previously created.

Figure 13.37 — **Properties Editor**

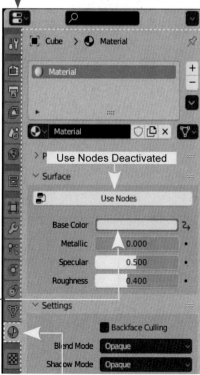

The first step in randomizing Materials (colors) is to Add Drivers. Previously Drivers have been Added in the Transform Properties Panel in the 3D Viewport Editor which displays when you press the N Key. This Panel does not include Material settings. To Add Drivers for Materials you right click on the **Base Color bar** in the **Properties Editor, Material Properties** and select **Add Drivers**.

Note: To demonstrate Randomizing Materials by Adding Drivers in the Properties Editor, Material Properties will be employed with Blender Nodes **deactivated**.

RMB Click, Add Drivers

The Drivers Editor will display Driver Channels for the RGB Materials and the A (Alpha or Transparency value).

Material Properties

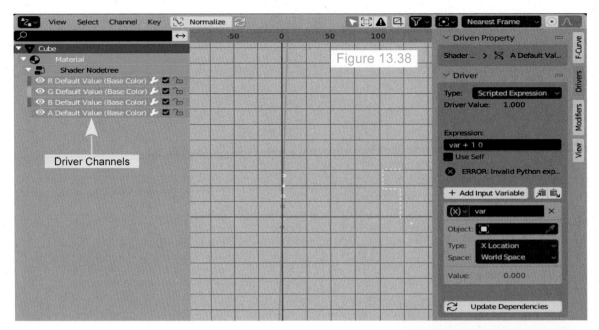

Figure 13.38

Driver Channels

Select each **Driver Channel** in turn and in the corresponding **Driven Property Panel** enter the Expression: **ranf(0.000, 1.000)**

Figure 13.39

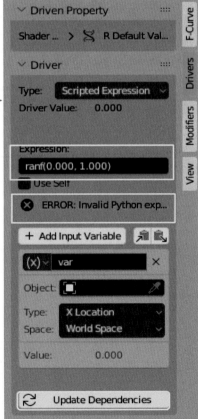

You may disregard the **A Alpha Channel** if you are not concerned with having the selected Object fade in the view.

When Enter is pressed to enter the script the Error Message changes to [i] **Slow Python expression**

Each time Update dependencies is pressed the Material (color) changes randomly.

Figure 13.40

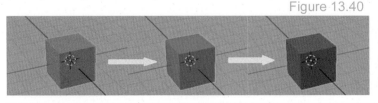

Duplicating the Object

In the 3D Viewport, by default, there is only have a single Cube Object in the Scene. Remember, at the beginning of the chapter, the objective was to create a bunch of Cubes scattered about the Scene.

It will be assumed that **Material Drivers** have Added as well as **Rotation Drivers** (see Figure 13.41)

All you do is simply duplicate the Cube. With the Cube selected press **Shift + D key** to duplicate.

A duplicate is created and placed in Grab Mode ready to be Translated. Drag the mouse to relocate and observe that the original and the duplicate are both re-evaluated by the Drivers and the properties change.

There are now two Cube Objects in the Scene which are identical and appear to be separate. The duplicate Cube (Cube.001) is however linked to the original (Cube) in that it is sharing Properties Data-Blocks of the original. If you translate **Cube.001, Update Dependencies** is activated and the properties of the Cube change. If you translate **Cube** the properties of both Cubes are changed.

Shift select both Cubes and you will see two sets of Drivers in the **Graph Editor window** (Figure 13.41).

Figure 13.41

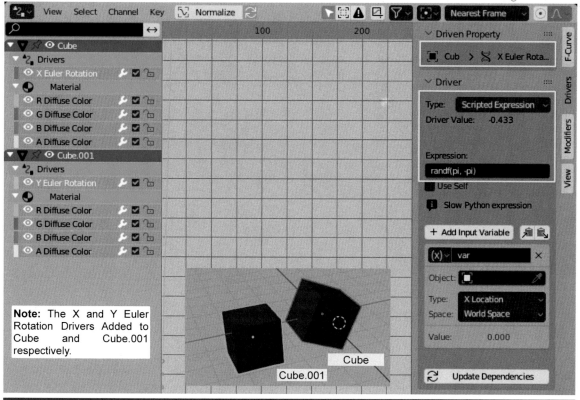

Note: The X and Y Euler Rotation Drivers Added to Cube and Cube.001 respectively.

Note: The Euler Rotation Drivers have been Added separately to Cube and Cube.001 following the Cube being duplicated. If the X Euler Rotation Driver were Added to Cube, before duplication, then both Cube and Cube.001 would have an X Euler Rotation Driver.

Anomaly: The above being the case, selecting either Cube and pressing G Key (Grab Mode) and moving the Mouse sees the selected Cube, Translated and randomly Rotated but the Material remains the same. Shift selecting both Cube and Cube.001 and Translating sees both Cubes randomly Rotated with the Material unchanged. Clicking Update Dependencies in any Driver, Driven Property Panel sees both Cubes randomly Rotate with the Material changing but the Material on both Cubes is identical.

To have the Material and Rotation randomly change when Update Dependencies is pressed, select all Cubes in the 3D Viewport Editor then in the Header click **Object – Relations – Make Single User - Object & Data & Material.**

Figure 13.42

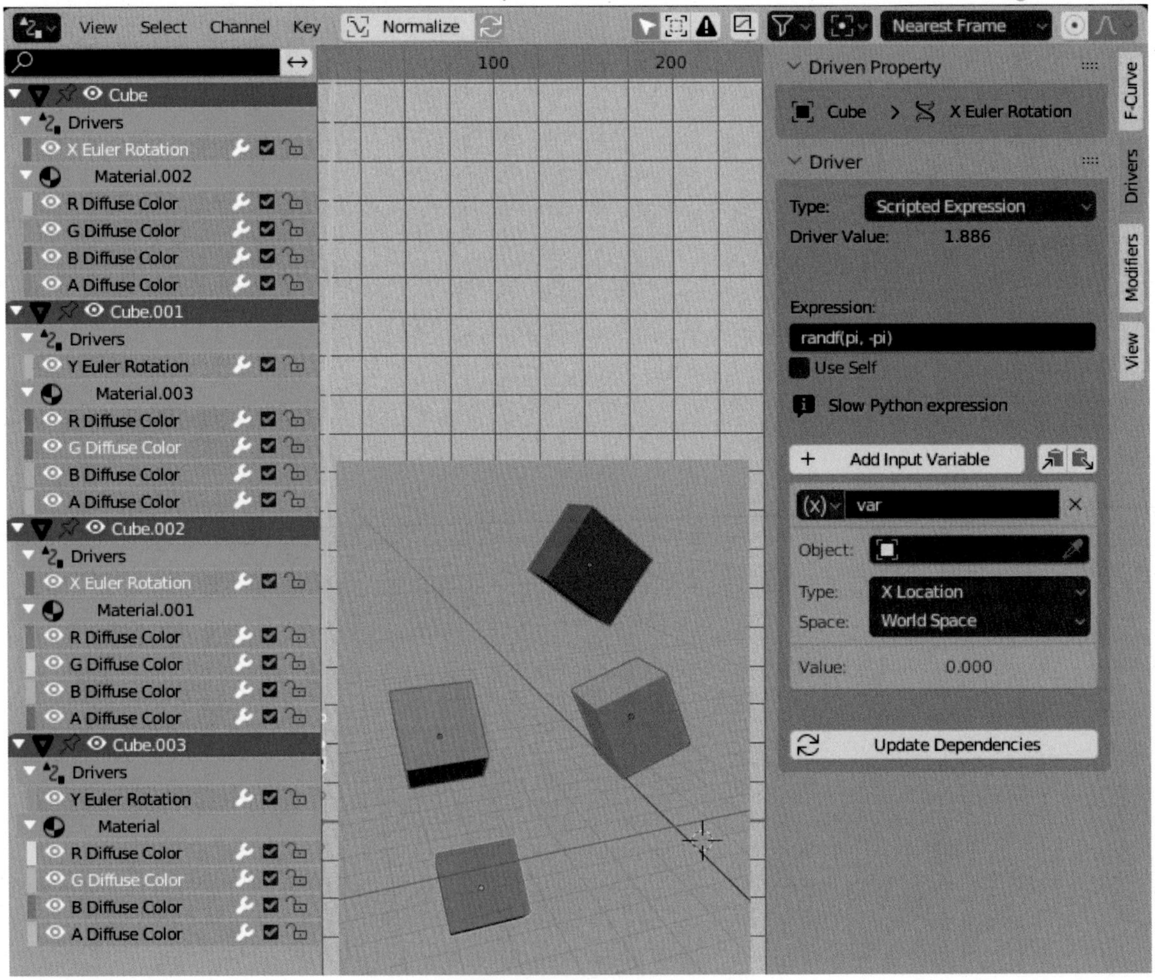

Select all Cubes and continue duplicating as many times as you like (Figure 13.43).

Figure 13.43

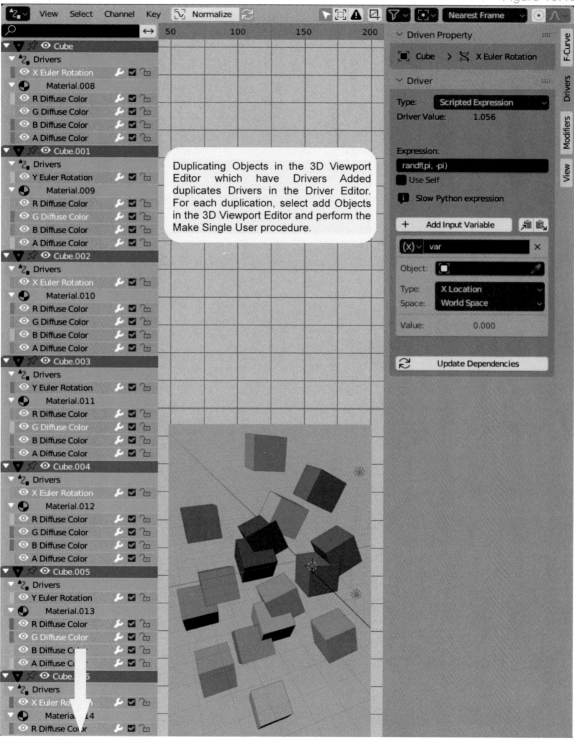

Duplicating Objects in the 3D Viewport Editor which have Drivers Added duplicates Drivers in the Driver Editor. For each duplication, select add Objects in the 3D Viewport Editor and perform the Make Single User procedure.

Animating the Properties

The simplest way to demonstrate the Animation of the Properties is to select all the Cubes in the 3D Viewport Editor (Press A Key), press the I Key and select Location, Rotation, Scale & Custom Properties. Do this at several Frames in the Timeline Editor. Play the Animation in the Timeline to see the randomly Rotate and change color.

In Conclusion

The forgoing description of **Randomizing Properties** is based on material in a Video Tutorial presented by **David Miller**. For an in depth understanding of this fantastic application in Blender the Tutorial is highly recommended.

Video: https://vimeo.com/40389198

David Writes: I found it easy to work with drivers on object and mesh properties. But I found it surprisingly difficult to get drivers to work on properties in material, texture, and node datablocks. This video will show you the secrets to coercing drivers to work anywhere:

- ☐ learn multiple ways to create a driver; when one method fails, another will work
- ☐ learn how to fix broken drivers after copying an object workflow tips for managing many drivers, objects, and datablocks

There is a multitude of Tutorials available on the Internet specific to the application of Drivers but bare in mind, many have been written and presented as the Blender program continues to develop. You will, therefore, encounter anomalies between the instruction provided and the current Blender release.

You are encouraged to pursue this topic and experiment with new and current information.

Non Linear Animation

14.1 Non Linear Animation Workspace
14.2 An Action
14.3 The Animation
14.4 Armature Actions
14.5 Parenting
14.6 Practical Application

Non Linear Animation allows manipulation and re-purposing Actions without the tedium of handling Keyframes. It is often used to make broad, significant changes to a Scene's animation, with relative ease. It can also re-purpose or chain together a sequence of motions and "layered" actions, which make it easier to organise and version-control your animation.

Non Linear Animation is a technique somewhat akin to RVK used to merge different, simple, Actions in complex, fluid Actions

While you may create animation clips in a specific order with a specific storyline in mind, nonlinear animation refers to **the process of moving, rearranging, manipulating, and blending those clips to produce a new series of motions**.

Non Linear Animation is performed in the **NLA Editor**.

Figure 14.1

 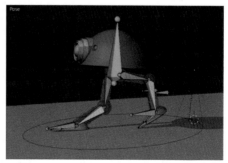

Screen captures from: **CBaileyFilm**

301

14.1 Non Linear Animation Workspace

Reconfigure the Blender Screen to create a Workspace for Non Linear Animating as shown in Figure 14.2.

Blender – Graphical User Interface

Figure 14.2

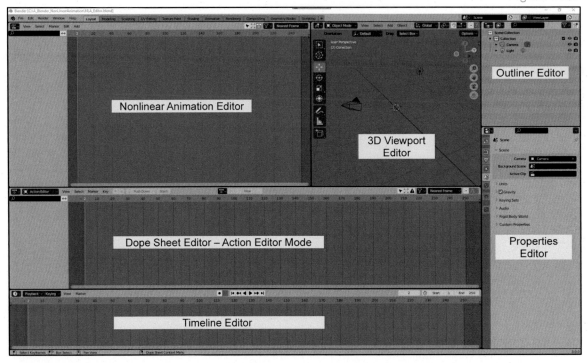

Save the Workspace in a Blender file with the 3D Viewport Editor, the Dope Sheet Editor in Action Editor Mode, the Timeline Editor and the NonLinear Animation (LNA) Editor displayed. Also have the Outliner Editor and the Properties Editors open (Figure 14.2).

14.2 An Action

When an Animation is created in the 3D Viewport Editor the data generating the Animation is called an **Action**. The data is saved in the Blender (.blend) file when the file is saved. The Action is pertaining to an Object which is Animated in the 3D Viewport Editor but by utilising the **Dope Sheet – Action Editor**, the Action (data) may be assigned to other Objects in the Scene.

The same Action may be manipulated and Edited in the **Nonlinear Animation Editor**.

These two features allow new Objects entered into a Scene to be Animated without the tedious process of creating Keyframes.

14.3 The Animation

To demonstrate the assignment of an **Action** created for one Object which is Animated in the 3D Viewport Editor to a second Object entered in the Scene using the **Dope Sheet Editor – Action Editor Mode**, create the simple Animation shown in Figure 14.3.

3D Viewport Editor   Figure 14.3

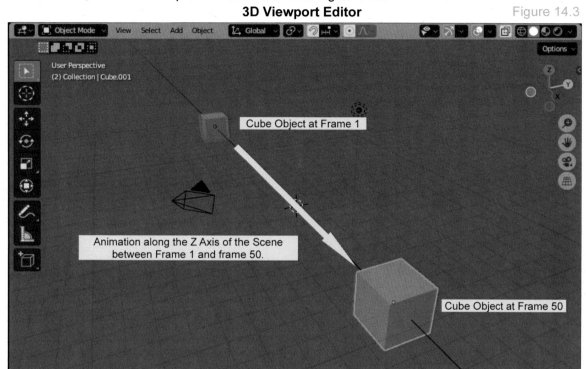

The Cube in the 3D Viewport Editor is Animated to Translate along the X Axis of the Scene in 50 Frames.

When the Animation is created the **Dope Sheet – Action Editor** displays the **Keyframes** inserted at Frame 1 and Frame 50 (Figure 14.4).

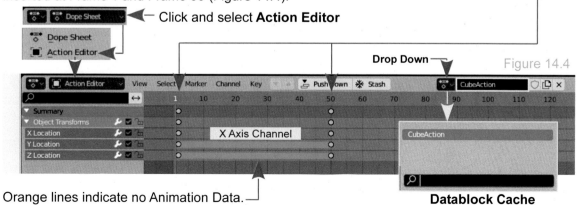

Note: When the Animation is created the name **CubeAction** displays in the Action Editor Header. This is the name of the Action (datablock) of the Animation Data. By clicking the **Browse Action to be Linked** drop down you see this as the single item entered in the Datablock Cache.

Note: There is no Animation data for the Y and Z Location Channels as indicated by the orange highlights.

Note: In creating the Animation, **CubeAction** has been entered in the **NLA Editor** (Figure 14.5).

NonLinear Animation Editor (Figure 14.2)

Figure 14.5

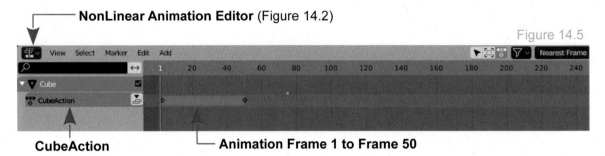

CubeAction   **Animation Frame 1 to Frame 50**

Deselect the Cube in the 3D Viewport Editor and enter an **IcoSphere,** positioning it adjacent to the Cube offset on the Y Axis Figure 14.6.

Figure 14.6

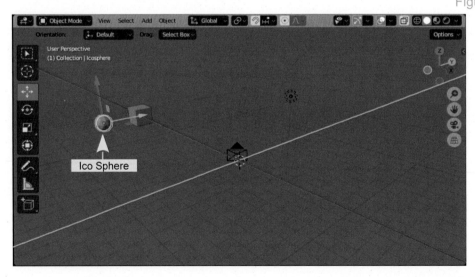

At this point with the IcoSphere selected in the 3D Viewport Editor there are no Keyframes displayed in the **Dope Sheet – Action Editor** but you will see that Cube Action remains displayed in the **NLA Editor**.

In the Action Editor you see a **New Button** in the Header. Click on the **Browse Action to be Linked** button adjacent to the **New Button,** then click on **CubeAction** in the drop down menu. This assigns **CubeAction** to the **Ico Sphere. Icosphere** with **CubeAction** is added to the **NLA Editor** and CubeAction Keyframes display in the Action Editor.

Note: In the 3D Viewport Editor the Ico Sphere has relocated to the center of the Cube. This means that both Objects are occupying the same region in 3D Space and playing the Animation sees both the Cube and the Ico Sphere move on the X Axis of the Scene.

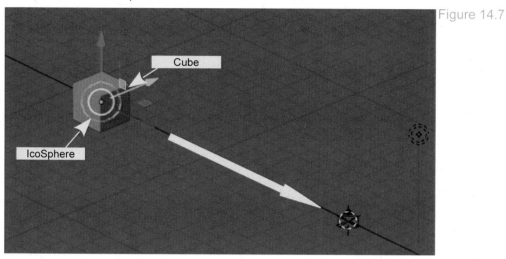

Figure 14.7

In the **NLA Editor** you see **Channels** with Cube having **CubeAction** applied and Icosphere with **CubeAction** applied.

Only Show Selected – only show Action Channels for the Object that is selected in the 3D Viewport Editor

Figure 14.8

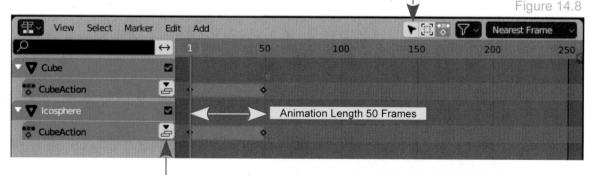

Note: The Push Down Action Button.

Clicking the **Push Down** button in the NLA Editor or in the Action Editor Header creates a new **NLA Track** Channel in the NLA Editor and cancels the display in the Action Editor. With the NLA Track in the NLA Editor you may edit the CubeAction. That is, you may edit the Animation in the 3D Viewport Editor.

Figure 14.9

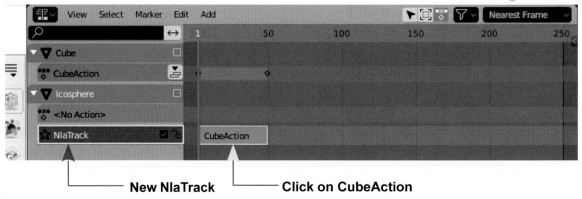

New NlaTrack   Click on CubeAction

Click on **CubeAction** to select (white outline displays). At this point you may click on **Edit** in the **NLA Editor Header** and select from a variety of **Editing Options**.

Selecting **Transform – Move** allows you to reposition the CubeAction in the Animation Timeline.

Figure 14.10

Alternatively; LMB click, hold and drag CubeAction left or right (changes to- 1) **Temp-Meta** and turns purple).

Edit	Add	
Transform		▶
Snap		▶
Duplicate	Shift D	
Linked Duplicate	Alt D	
Split Strips	Y	
Delete Strips	X	
Delete Tracks		
Toggle Muting	H	
Apply Scale	Ctrl A	
Clear Scale	Alt S	
Sync Action Length		
Make Single User	U	
Swap Strips	Alt F	
Move Strips Up	Page Up	
Move Strips Down	Page Down	
Track Ordering...		▶
Remove Empty Animation Data		
Start Editing Stashed Action	Shift Tab	
Start Tweaking Strip Actions	Tab	

Move
Extend
Scale

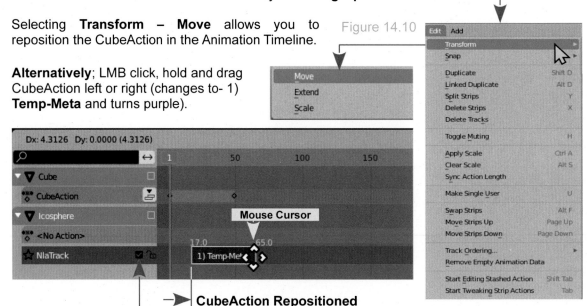

➤ **CubeAction Repositioned**

Make sure Channel Muting **is checked(ticked).**

Playing the Animation will see the Cube move along the X Axis with the IcoSphere following when the Timeline Cursor reaches the beginning of the relocated CubeAction strip.

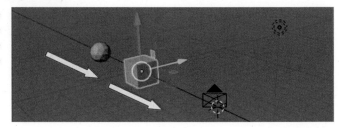

Example

You will have to experiment with combinations of settings to become proficient with the use of the NLA Editor but one example is as follows:

Figure 14.11

Properties Editor

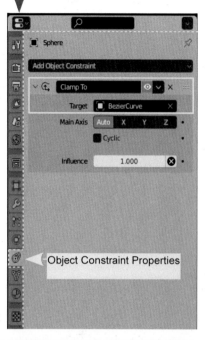

To have several colored Spheres follow each other along a track (**Bezier Curve**) have a single **UV Sphere** in the **3D Viewport Editor** and a Bezier Curve. Scale the Bezier Curve to suit the Scene. Select the UV Sphere and add a **Clamp To Constraint** in the **Properties Editor, Object Constraint Properties** setting the **Target as BezierCurve**.

With the UV Sphere selected in the 3D Viewport Editor and with the Constraint Applied, press Shift + D Key to duplicate the Sphere. Duplicating the UV Sphere duplicates the Constraint.

In the **NLA Editor** you will see **NLA Tracks** are automatically created for each Sphere.

Stagger the NLA Tracks to offset the Animation of each UV Sphere.

Note: Assigning Actions in the Action Editor does not duplicate the Sphere's Animation when the Sphere has a Constraint Applied.

Figure 14.12

The foregoing has shown the very basics of creating Actions (Animation Data) in the Dope Sheet – Action Editor and manipulating Actions in the NLA Editor. Up to this point each Action has been for the Animation of a single Object.

There will be occasions when you wish to Animate multiple Objects or components of an Object and combine the Animation Data for each Object or component into a single Action. This is achieved by using Armatures, Parented to the Objects or components.

14.4 Armature Actions

To understand **Armature Action** step through the following:

Consider a Cube Object and a Cone Object, two separate Objects in the 3D Viewport Editor (Figure 14.13).

By Animating the Cube to Rotate and the Cone to Translate up on the Z Axis you create two separate **Actions**.

Figure 14.13

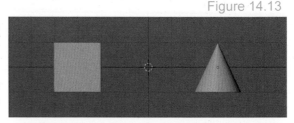

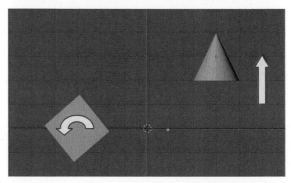

NLA Editor   Figure 14.14

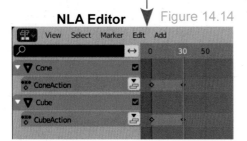

Dope Sheet – Action Editor   Figure 14.15

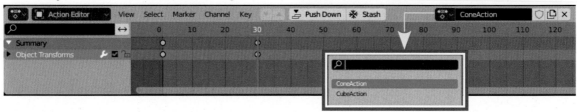

An alternative method to produce the same Animation effect is to Parent Armature Bones to each Object and Animate the Bones such that the Objects follow the Bone.

An important concept to understand when performing the above is that the **individual Bones must be part of the same Armature.**

To create Bones as part of the same Armature, with the 3D Viewport in Object Mode, select **Add - Armature - Single Bone** in the Viewport Header, with the single Bone Armature in the Viewport, Tab to Edit Mode. Click (select) the Armature (single Bone) and press Shift + D to duplicate the Bone. You may drag the new Bone to one side but the important thing is, the new Bone is part of the Armature not a separate Bone. You see this in the **Outliner Editor.**

Figure 14.16

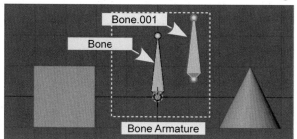

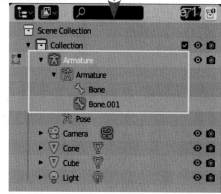

14.5 Parenting

In **Edit Mode** select each Bone in turn and position relative to each Object (Figure 14.17).

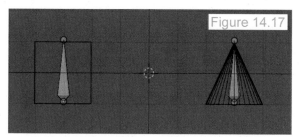

Figure 14.17

3D Viewport Editor – Wireframe Display

Tab to Object Mode.

Select the **Cube**. Shift select **Bone**. Press **Ctrl + P Key** and select **Set Parent to: With Automatic Weights**.

Select the Cone. Shift select Bone.001. Press Ctrl + P Key and select Set Parent to: **With Automatic Weights.**

With both Objects Parented and with the 3D Viewport Editor in Pose Mode, you select either of the Armature Bones to manipulate the Parented Object.

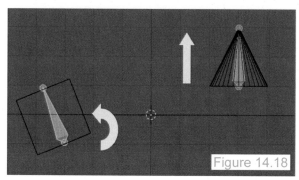

Figure 14.18

In Pose Mode, select Bone and Rotate to Rotate the Cube. Select Bone.001 and Translate to Translate the Cone.

Before manipulating the Objects add Keyframes at Frame 1 in the Animation Timeline (Loc, Rot, Scale).

Move the Timeline Cursor (to frame 30). Manipulate the Objects by moving the Armature Bones separately in Pose Mode and add a second Keyframes.

By Playing the Animation in the Timeline or scrubbing the Timeline Cursor you see both Objects Animated. **Note:** Animating both Objects has created a single Action in the Dope Sheet Action Editor. You see this in the NLA Editor.

NLA Editor

Figure 14.19

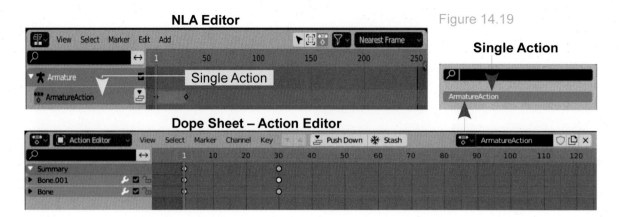

Single Action

14.6 Practical Application

Creating a single Action for Animating multiple Objects or components of an Object comes into its own when Animating Characters.

NLA Editor Figure 14.20

My little friend **Chibi** has been Animated to give you a wave and say **Hi!**

Chibi"s arm (mesh) has been Parented to Bones.

Dope Sheet – Action Editor Figure 14.21

The Bones are Rotated in Pose Mode with Keyframes added at Frame 1 and frame 30.

Figure 14.22

By using a Multi Bone Armature a single Action is created in the Dope Sheet – Action Editor. The Action may then be manipulated or modified in the NLA Editor to affect the Animation.

For Example: Splitting the Action in the NLA Editor and separating the parts will pause the wave mid way in the Animation, adding realism.

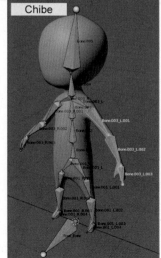

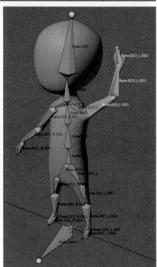

15

Rigging – Rigify – Animbox

The title, **Rigging – Rigify – Animbox** represents the progression when Rigging a humanoid Character and Animating the Character to walk using the Blender Add-ons**, Rigify** and **Rigify Animbox**.

Note: The Add-on named **Rigify Animbox** has been designed to be used with the Add-on named **Rigify**. When activated, Rigify provides several preconstructed **Armature Assemblies** with the Bones in the Armatures linked in **Child Parent Relationships** resembling a bone skeleton. Rigify will automatically create **Control Handles** for the Armature Assembly which is then known as the **Armature Control Rig**. Rigify Animbox automatically generates an **Animation** of a **Walk Cycle** for the the Character. When the Animation is played the Character is seen to walk.

Since an Armature Control Rig is specific to the original Armature Assembly, to use Rigify Animbox with a custom Armature Assembly, the custom assembly must conform to Armature Assemblies provided by Rigify.

Important: The Add-on **Rigify Animbox** is designed to be used with an Armature assembly provided by the Add-on, **Rigify**.

Animation Walk Cycle   Figure 15.1

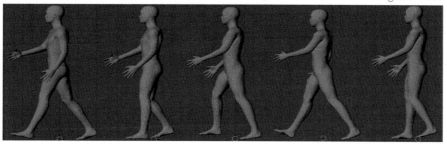

15.1 Prerequisites

The prerequisites to using the Add-ons are: You must have a **Model** of a humanoid figure and you must have the Add-ons **Rigify** and **Rigify-Animbox** installed on your computer **and activated**. If you are not conversant with installing and activating Add-ons in Blender, see the instructions at the end of this chapter.

Important: The Add-on **Rigify Animbox** is designed to be used with an Armature assembly provided by the Add-on, **Rigify**.

15.2 Rigify

Rigify provides a collection of pre-constructed **Armature** assemblies with the Bones connected in Child-Parent Relationships.

Rigify and **Rigify Animbox** will be demonstrated using the **Human Armature**.

Figure 15.2

The Human Armature is named **Human (Meta-Rig).**

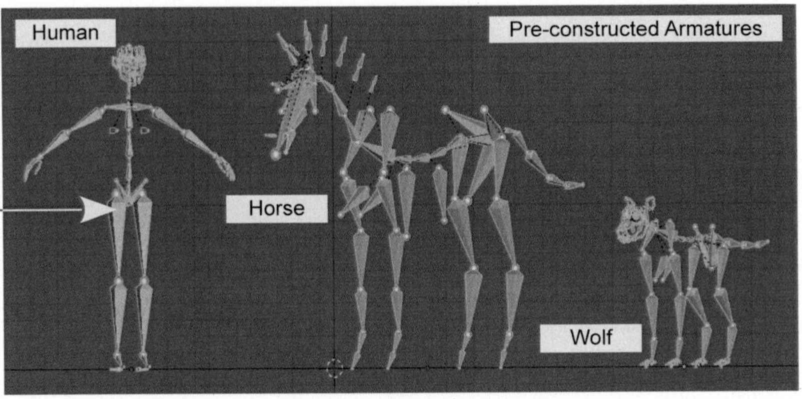

Remember: The objective is to demonstrate the process of Rigging a humanoid Character and Animating the Character to walk using the Blender Add-ons **Rigify** and **Rigify Animbox**.

15.3 Models for Animating

You may construct your own Model of a Human Figure or Character bearing in mind, the Model has to be a Mesh Model with the Mesh inclusive of an adequate number of Vertices in the Mesh.

You may also download Models from the internet but again the Model has to be a Mesh Model with sufficient Vertices.

One source of downloads is: **TURBOSQUID**

https://www.turbosquid.com/Search/3D-Models/free/human/blend

Another Source is: **Free3D**

https://free3d.com/3d-models/blender-human

15.4 Preparing a Model

If you elect to download a Model be aware that all models are NOT equal. For example;

Base Mesh sculpt 2 from TURBOSQUID   Figure 15.3   **Man2.5 from FREE 3D**

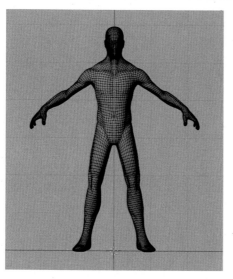 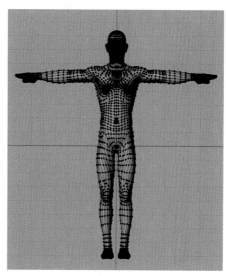

In Figure 15.3 **Man2.5**, you may experience difficulty in Rigging the mesh for Animation due to the lack of Vertices in the Mesh.

Another source for a Human Model is the Program, **Make Human** (open source). By exporting the default Human Model from the Make Human Program as a **Wavefront .obj** file you can import the Model into Blender (**see how at the end of the chapter**).

http://www.makehumancommunity.org/content/downloads.html

Figure 15.4

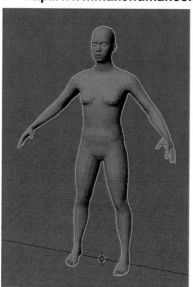 

The Model imported from the **Make Human** program (Figure 15.4) has less Vertices in the Mesh than the **Base Mesh sculpt 2** but is adequate for Rigging and Animating. You may modify the Figure while in the **Make Human Program** if you wish, but for this demonstration the default Model, as shown in Figure 15.4, will be used.

15.5 The Armature Assembly

Remember; An Armature can be a single Bone or have multiple Bones.

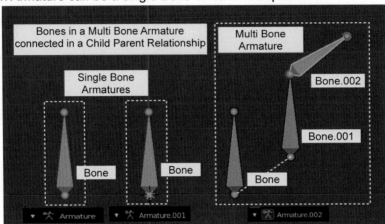

Figure 15.5

The **Rigify Armature Assembly** is a **Multi Bone Armature** pre-configured to suit a Humanoid Model. To enter a Rigify Armature Assembly in the Scene, click **Add – Armature – Human Metarig** in the 3D Viewport Header. The Armature Assembly is named **Metarig**.

The Human Metarig (Armature Bone Skeleton) displays nestled between the Model's legs (Figure 15.6). With the Armature selected, in Object Mode, Scale the Armature up to suit the Model (Figure 15.7).

Figure 15.6

Figure 15.7

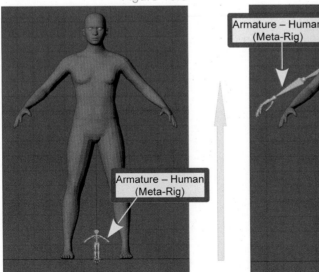

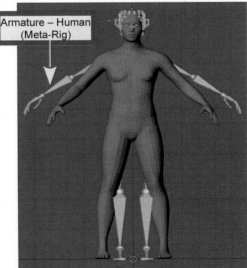

As you see the Armature is partially hidden inside the Model. To see the full Armature, go to the **Properties Editor, Object Data Properties** for the **Metarig** and in the **Viewport Display Tab**, <u>check **In Front.**</u>

Figure 15.8

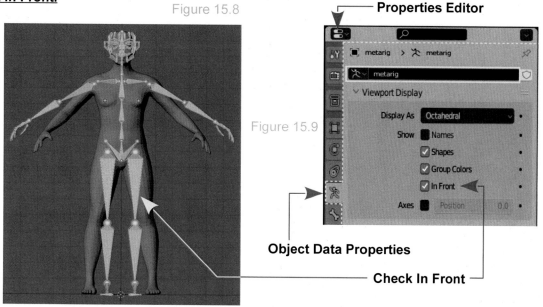

Figure 15.9

Properties Editor

Object Data Properties

Check In Front

Armature Scale Alignment

Figure 15.10

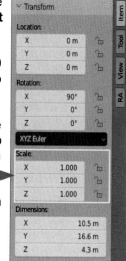

Important: When the Model was Imported into the Scene its Scale Value was 1.000. You see the value by pressing the **N Key** to display the **Object Properties Panel** (Figure 15.10)

When the Metarig is entered in the Scene it also has a Scale Value: 1.000 even though it displays as a minute size. When the Metarig is Scaled up to fit the Model its Scale Value will increase to something like 8.345.

Both the Model and the Metarig must have the same Scale Value. With the Metarig selected press **Ctrl + A Key** and select **Apply – All Transforms** to reset the Metarig"s Scale to 1.000. All transforms = Translation, Rotation and Scale.

Alternatively; you could manually change the **X, Y and Z Scale Values** in the Object Properties Panel.

Clarification: The Armature Assembly obtained from Rigify is named Metarig. The Armature Assembly is a Multi Bone Armature. Armatures in Blender may be displayed in the 3D Viewport Editor in Object Mode, Edit Mode and Pose Mode.

Align the Armature Assembly with the Model

The Armature has to be aligned with the Model such that the Bones are placed inside the Mesh.

With the Armature selected **Tab to Edit Mode**. To assist in the alignment activate **X Axis Mirror** in the upper right hand corner of the 3D Viewport (Figure 15.11). Click on **X**.

Figure 15.11

With **X Axis Mirror** activated (highlighted blue), when a right hand **Bone** in the Armature is positioned the left hand **Bone** automatically follows.

The Bones in the Armature are connected in **Child Parent Relationships** such that when Parent Bones are moved Child Bones follow. The Child Parent Relationship is only applied with the Armature in **Pose Mode**.

Positioning Bones to fit the Model is performed in **Edit Mode**. Bones are selected and moved to fit inside the Model's Mesh. Moving Bones in Edit Mode does not disconnect the Bones from the Armature. The Bones remain connected and the Child Parent Relationship is retained which is active when the Armature is in Pose Mode.

Armature Bones may be Parented to Vertex Groups in the Mesh but when using the Armature Assembly obtained from Rigify, a **Control Rig** is generated and Parented to the Mesh utilising the position of the Armature Bones to make the association.

The Armature Assembly (Metarig) provided by Rigify has detailed Bones for the face, ears and hands. To simplify the demonstration these will be deleted.

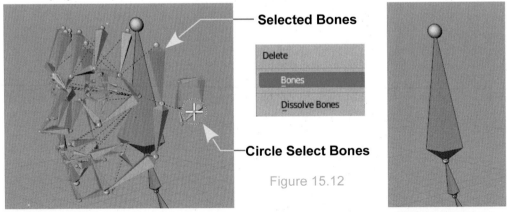

Figure 15.12

Zoom in and Rotate the Viewport. With **Circle Select**, select Bones and **X Key, Delete**.

Repeat the procedure, deleting Hand Bones (both Hands).

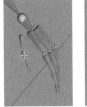

While remaining in Edit Mode select Bones and position them inside the Mesh Model. Press Num Pad 1 and 3 to see front and side views Num Pad 7 for top view.

The following Figures show the alignment of the Upper Left Arm Bone. In Edit Mode select the **Tip** and the **Base** of the Bone separately and G Key (Drag) to position relative to the Model. You may also select a Bone Body and Translate, Rotate and Scale.

Upper Arm Bone Before Positioning   **Upper Arm Bone After Positioning**

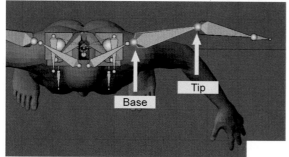 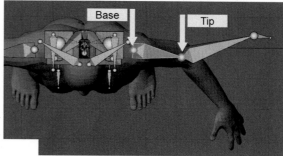

Figure 15.13

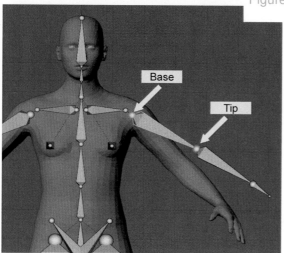 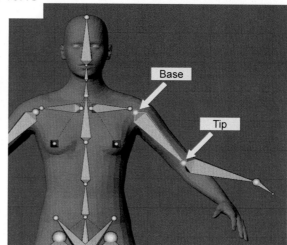

Go over the whole Model, aligning the Armature Bones. You do not have to create an anatomical skeleton. The aim is to position Bones inside the Mesh Model such that the Mesh may be Parented to the Control Rig (see following) using the Bone alignment. The Face and Hand Bones may be deleted to simplify the alignment since your objective is generating a Walk Cycle. Hand and facial Animation will certainly add character and realism but require detailed alignment.

With the Bones aligned, Tab to Object Mode, press **Ctrl + A Key** and **apply All Transforms again**.

Cleaning Up

Figure 15.14 **Outliner Editor** ───➤

An anomaly which can cause an error when generating a **Control Rig** is a Bone named **face** residing inside the Head Bone, **spine.006**. This is a residual after deleting Face Bones

Figure 15.15

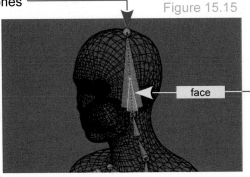

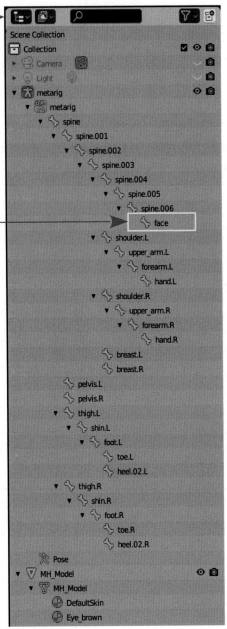

You will see the Bone listed in the Outliner Editor when the **Metarig** entries are expanded.

Select **face** in the **Outliner Editor, X Key, Delete**.

Figure 15.16

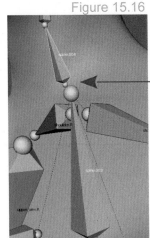

Another anomaly which occasionally occurs and is apt to cause an error is the misalignment of Bones.

The base of Bone spine.004 may not be aligned with the tip of Bone spine.003.

To correct the issue, Tab to Edit Mode, select spine.004, delete, then select the Tip of spine.003 and Extrude a new Bone up to the Base of spine.005. The new Bone will be automatically named spine.004.

With the Bones aligned, Tab to Object Mode, press **Ctrl + A Key** and apply **All Transforms** again.

15.6 Generate the Armature Control Rig

To clarify the foregoing procedure; a Model has been entered in the Scene and an Armature named Human Metarig has been aligned with the Model.

Note: At this point the Mesh Model has not been Parented to the Armature. Moving a Bone in Pose Mode will not cause the Mesh to follow. Instead of Parenting the Armature Bones to the Mesh Model a Control Rig will be generated for the Armature Metarig and Parented to the Mesh using Bone positions. Posing (Moving) Control Handles in the Rig will cause components of the Mesh to follow.

With the Metarig Armature selected in **Object Mode** click **Generate Rig** in the **Properties Editor, Object Data Properties, Rigify Buttons Tab.**

Armature Metarig (human)-Object Mode Figure 15.17

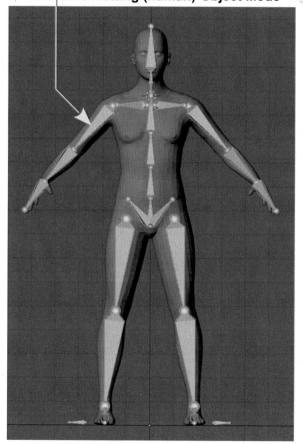

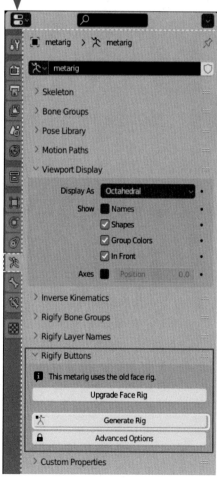

Blender will probably take time to compute the Rig, depending on your PC, and all being well you will see the Control Rig shown in Figure 15.18 (following).

If an Error Message displays (Figure 15.18). Bone misalignment has occurred as previously described.

Figure15.18

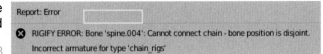

Report: Error

❌ RIGIFY ERROR: Bone 'spine.004': Cannot connect chain - bone position is disjoint.
Incorrect armature for type 'chain_rigs'

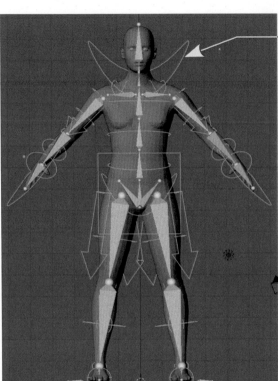

Figure15.19

The Control Rig is generated and displays in Object Mode.

Note: The Control Rig with Control Handles is arranged in accordance with the position of the Bones in the Armature Metarig.

The Armature Metarig and the Control Rig are NOT Parented to the Mesh Model.

You select individual Control Handles with the 3D Viewport Editor in **Pose Mode** but at this point, moving a Control Handle will have no effect on the Mesh.

Deselect the Control Rig (LMB Click in the Viewport).

Figure 15.20

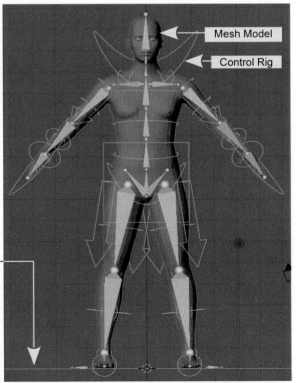

Mesh Model

Control Rig

To **Parent the Control Rig** to the Mesh Model, remain in Object Mode, select the **Mesh Model** then Shift Select the **Control Rig** (Figure 15.20).

Press, **Ctrl + P Key** and select **Set Parent To: With Automatic Weights**.

Figure 15.21

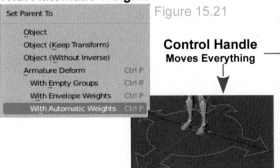

Set Parent To

Object
Object (Keep Transform)
Object (Without Inverse)
Armature Deform   Ctrl P
  With Empty Groups   Ctrl P
  With Envelope Weights   Ctrl P
  With Automatic Weights Ctrl P

Control Handle
Moves Everything

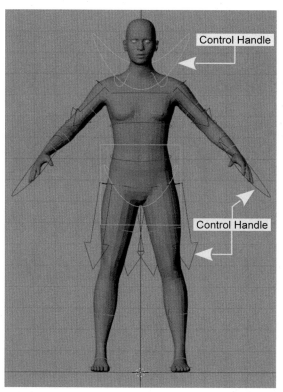

Control Handle

Control Handle

Figure 15.22

In **Pose Mode** the Control Rig Handles display in the 3D Viewport Editor in different colors.

In Object Mode go to the Outliner Editor and hide the Armature Metarig. You may also hide the Camera and the Light (Lamp) (Figure 15.23).

Figure 15.23

Click the Eye Icons to Hide

By selecting (LMB Click) Controls Handles they display blue. Press G Key (Grab), S Key (Scale) or R Key (Rotate) manipulating the Handles, to Pose the Mesh Model (Figure 15.24).

You would normally Pose the Figure (Mesh Model) in different Poses at different Frames in the Animation Timeline to produce an Animation but with the magic of **Animbox** the Figure can be automatically Animated to walk.

Something Strange? Figure 15.24

Figure 15.24

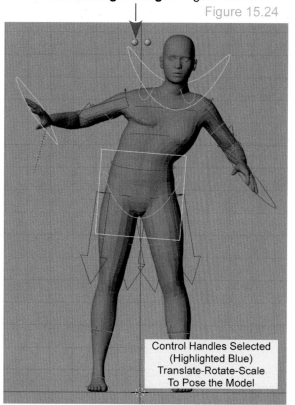

Control Handles Selected
(Highlighted Blue)
Translate-Rotate-Scale
To Pose the Model

Figure 15.25

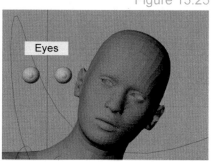

Eyes

It appears the Make Human Model is Imported into Blender without the Eyes being Parented. Also, by activating X-Ray in the 3D Viewport Editor while in Object Mode it appears that the model has a Pallet built into the mesh.

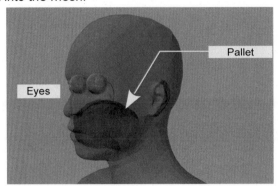

Figure 15.26

The anomalies in regard to the Eyes and Pallet are mentioned here to make you aware that such occurrences may be present when Importing from other programs.

15.7 The Magic of Animbox

Animbox is a Blender Add-on designed to be used in conjunction with Metarigs supplied from the Add-on **Rigify**.

Remember: A **Metarig** supplied by **Rigify** is a multi Bone Armature assembly with Bones connected in Child Parent Relationships.

The **Animbox Add-on** generates a Control Rig similar to that previously described but also provides the facilities to generate Rigs for Animal Metarigs. At the same time, Animbox will also generate a Walk Cycle Animation sequence. The Add-on includes a variety of options such as the RigBox Eye Controls and Motion Paths. In the following exercise a Model of a Human Figure will be Animated in a Walk Cycle . This is intended as a starter only. Once familiar with the basic sequence to implement the Add-on, you will have to experiment to discover the full potential of Animbox.

Figure 15.27

The first step, in using Animbox is to ensure that Rigify and Animbox are activated in the Preferences Editor. Animbox must be activated in the Preferences Editor, Add-ons to display the Controls in the 3D Viewport Editor (Figure 15.27).

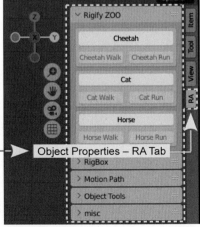

Note: The 3D Viewport Editor Controls for Animbox display in the **RA Tab** of the **Object Properties Panel** in the upper RH corner of the 3D Viewport Editor (Press the N Key to Toggle the Object Properties Panel On/Off). The **RA** (Rigify Animbox) Tab only displays when **Rigify Animbox** is activated in the Preferences Editor.

The second step in using Animbox is to have a Mesh Model in the 3D Viewport Editor with a Metarig added from Rigify, scaled up and positioned to suit the Mesh (Figure 15.28).

Don't forget to Apply Transforms after scaling the Metarig.

For simplicity delete Face and Hand Bones and the hidden face bone inside the Head Bone. To prevent an error occurring delete the spine.004 Bone and extrude a new Bone. (see previous instruction).

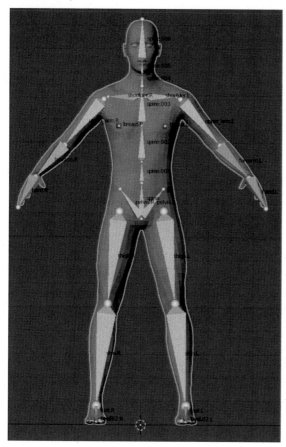

Figure 15.28

In Object Mode deselect the Metarig and the Model. In the 3D Viewport Editor, in Object Mode press N Key to display the Object Properties Panel (Figure 15.29). In the Panel Click the **R.A.** Tab – Click the **misc** Tab followed by **Test Rig**

Figure 15.29

(**Note:** The Armature disappears from view).

The Test Rig displays between the feet, selected in Pose Mode.

Figure 15.30

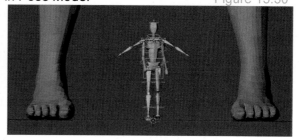

The Test Rig is very small in comparison to the Model but as you will see with the 3D Viewport Editor in Object Mode, the Scale Values for both are; 1.000.

In Properties Editor, Object Data Properties, Viewport Display Tab for the Rest Rig, Check **In Front.**

Zoom Out on view

With **Test Rig** selected in **Object Mode**, Scale the Rig up to fit the Model (Figure 15.31). **Deselect the Rig.** There is no need to Apply Transforms.

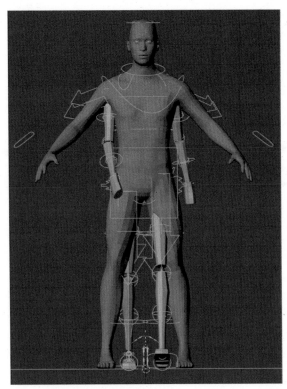

Select Model – Shift select Rig – Press **Ctrl + P** – **Parent to With Auto Weights** – Wait awhile for the computer to perform calculations.
Figure 15.31

The Model is Posed at the start of the Walk Cycle (Figure 15.32).

Figure 15.32

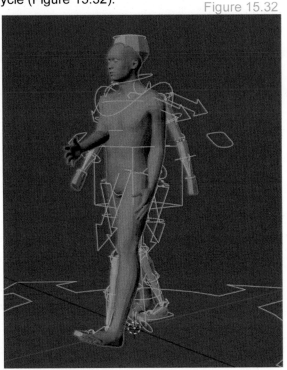

Remember the Parenting is being calculated based on the position of the Bones in the Armature Metarig which has disappeared from view.

Change to **Pose Mode** and press **A Key** to select the entire Test Rig (Turns blue) - Scale and Grab to fit Model (If required).

Press **Ctrl + A** (**Apply Visual Transforms** to the Pose).

At this point the 3D Viewport Editor is cluttered with Controls and Rigs. To unclutter the Scene, hide **metarig.001**, and **Rig_Mesh** in the Outliner Editor.
Figure 15.33

Click Eye Icons to Hide

Outliner Editor

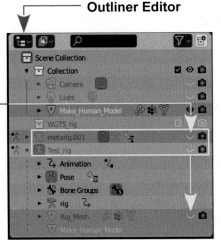

Animate the Model to Walk

In the **Outliner Editor** right click on Test_rig and click **Select**.

Have the 3D Viewport Editor in **Pose Mode**.

Press the **A Key** to have the entire **Test_rig** selected (highlighted blue).

Figure 15.34

In the **Object Properties Panel** in the 3D Viewport Editor have the **RA Tab** selected and expand **Rigify Walk / Run** (Figure 15.34).

Under **Rigify Walk Run** you will see the options to have the Model Walk or Run. In either case you select a number to play the Animation for a prescribed number of Frames, i.e. 18 Frames will see the Animation play for 18 Frames then repeat over and over.

In the **Timeline Editor** the Animation **End Frame** will be 18.

You may now hide **Test-rig** in the **Outliner Editor** to see the Model walk (Figure 15.35) when you press the Play button in the Timeline Editor.

If you wish to change the Animation from Walk to Run or alter the Animation Length, unhide Test_rig in the Outliner Editor to display the Rig in the 3D Viewport Editor. With the Mouse Cursor in the 3D Viewport Editor (Pose Mode), press A Key to select the Test_rig (highlights blue). Doing this reactivates the options in the Object Properties Panel.

Make your changes and hide Test_rig.

Replay the Animation.

Animation Walk Cycle   Figure 15.35

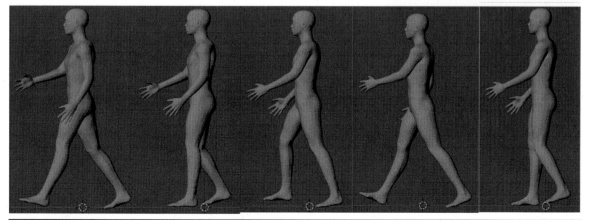

15.8 Installing Add-ons in Blender

Installing an Add-on is as simple as ABC. To explain how, the Add-on named **Rigify Animbox** created by VALANGDANCE will be used,

Congratulations to VALANGDANCE for this fantastic addition to Blender.

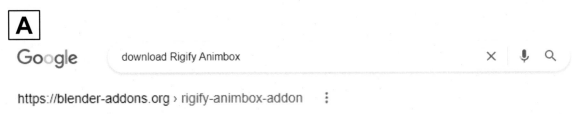

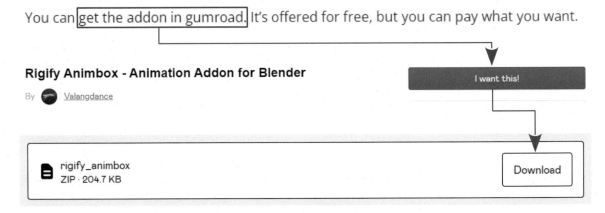

The download process is a little convoluted but you will eventually get the ZIP file rigify_animbox

rigify_animbox
DO NOT UNZIP THE FILE

B

Open **Blender** to install the Add-on. In the Blender Screen Header select **Edit – Preferences**.

Select **Add-ons** in the **Preferences Editor** and click the **Install** button in the Header.

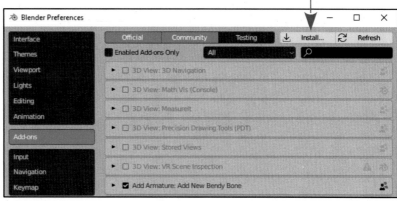

Clicking the Install button opens **Blender File View** where you navigate and find the **rigify_animbox.zip** File.

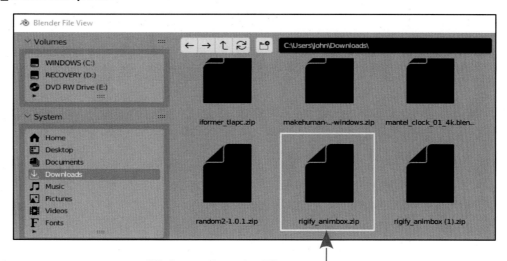

Click to select the File ⸺

C

Click Install **Add-ons**.

Important: To use the Add-on, don't forget to **Activate** it in the **Preferences Editor.**

15.9 Make Human Export

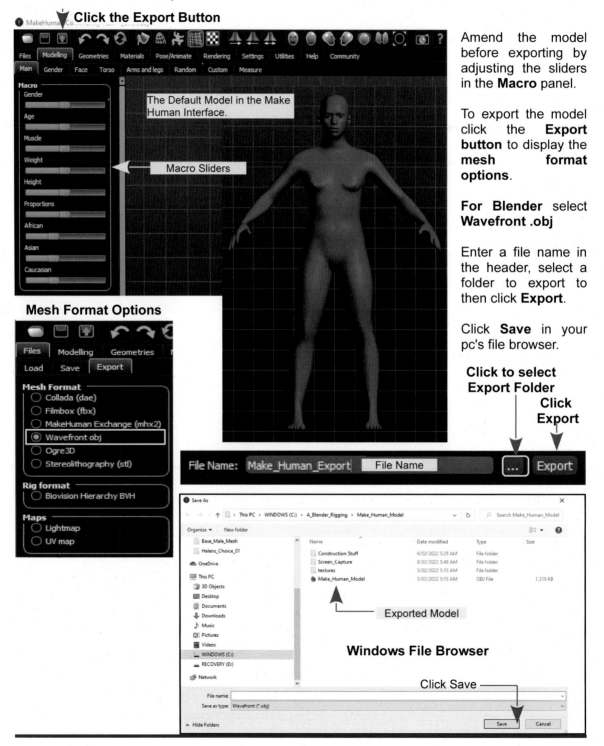

Click the Export Button

The Default Model in the Make Human Interface.

Macro Sliders

Mesh Format Options

Amend the model before exporting by adjusting the sliders in the **Macro** panel.

To export the model click the **Export button** to display the **mesh format options**.

For Blender select **Wavefront .obj**

Enter a file name in the header, select a folder to export to then click **Export**.

Click **Save** in your pc's file browser.

Click to select Export Folder

Click Export

File Name: Make_Human_Export   File Name

Exported Model

Windows File Browser

Click Save

16

Blender Render Engines

The Render Engine

The software that converts a Blender Scene into an Image or Movie File is the **Render Engine**. there are three **Render Engines** built into Blender named; **Eevee, Cycles** and **Workbench**. There are alternative Render Engines external to the program which may be used with Blender but for practicality instruction will be limited to using the internal systems.

Eevee is the default Engine which shows what is produced in a final Render, when the 3D Viewport is in **Rendered Viewport Display Mode**.

The **Cycles** Rendering system, built into Blender, is designed to produce photo realistic images and to provide an interactive workspace where you see a rendered view as a Scene is developed.

Photo realism and high definition in images, including animation frames comes with a demand on computer power and render time. The **Eevee Render Engine** gives an excellent result but there are situations where **Cycles** will provide added benefit.

All the Blender tools and controls for generating a Scene are applicable to both Render processes although there is a difference in the Node Systems.

Workbench Render provides a simplified process for previewing Scenes in the construction process before implementing a final Render.

In this Chapter instruction will outline the use of the **Cycles Render Engine**.

16.1 Cycles Render

Cycles Rendering simulates many effects that have to be specifically added to other methods of rendering such as soft shadows, depth of field, motion blur, caustics, ambient occlusion and indirect lighting.

The **Cycles Render Engine** is described as being a raytracing based engine with support for interactive rendering. Being interactive means you see a rendered view of your work as it progresses in the 3D Viewport Editor when in **Rendered Viewport Shading Mode**. Cycles incorporates a Shading Node system, a different material and texture work flow and it utilises **GPU** acceleration.

Computer Specifications for Cycles

Before using Cycles, be aware that you will require a reasonable computer processor and a graphics card which meets the specifications to handle this advanced process (refer to the Blender Wiki – Hardware Requirements).

In essence, to fully utilise **Cycles** you need a fast processor, heaps of memory (RAM) and a graphics card with **Open GL** (graphics card with built in memory **GPU** and **CUDA** enabled).

> **Note:** Cycles Rendering is activated from the main Blender interface but CUDA and GPU acceleration require a secondary activation similar to an Add-on.

If you are new to Blender these terminologies and specifications may be slightly on the technical side but just be aware that, to utilise the full effects of **Cycles** you computer has to meet the requirements. The following will show you how to activate Cycles and discover if your system is up to speed.

16.2 Starting Cycles

To activate Cycles change **Eevee** to **Cycles** in the Properties Editor, **Render Properties** (Figure 16.1).

Render Properties

Figure 16.1

To demonstrate Cycles Rendering set up a Scene in the 3D Viewport Editor as shown in Figure 16.2.

Figure 16.2 shows a UV Sphere positioned just above a Plane (ground plane). A second Plane (Plane.001) is placed above and behind the UV Sphere opposite the Camera. The ground plane is scaled to fill the Camera aperture as shown in the Camera View inset, while Plane.001 is positioned outside Camera View. The UV Sphere is scaled up and set to Smooth. There is a single Point Lamp in the Scene.

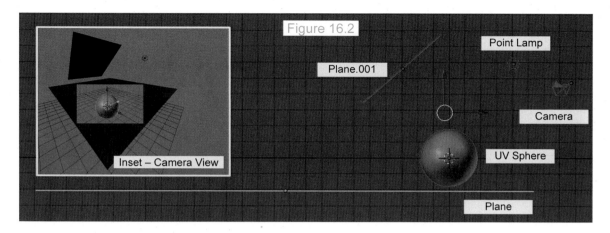

Figure 16.2

Point Lamp

Plane.001

Camera

UV Sphere

Inset – Camera View

Plane

To see **Cycles** in action place the 3D Viewport Editor in **Rendered Viewport Shading Mode**.

The 3D Viewport Editor will change showing the Objects with a dark gray background (Figure 16.4). If you rotate the Scene you will see the Objects being re-rendered as you rotate.

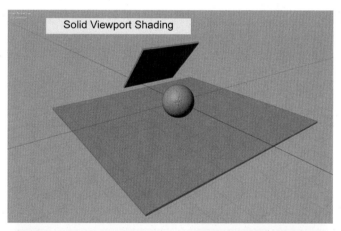

Solid Viewport Shading

Figure 16.3

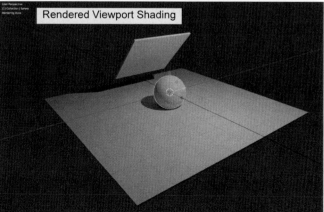

Rendered Viewport Shading

Figure 16.4

Unless you have a reasonably fast processor the Render will be very blocky and grainy and may take a considerable time. With **Rendered Viewport Shading** the 3D Viewport Editor re-renders at each change made to the Scene. The longer you wait the clearer the render becomes, **up to a point**. You wouldn't want your computer stuck in an infinite rendering loop so Blender incorporates time-out settings to limit the Render. When the Scene is altered i.e. rotated, the **Render** process is activated.

In the upper LH corner of the 3D Viewport Editor you will see a progress display giving the number of Render Samples. When a Render is completed this displays, **Rendering Done**.

Figure 16.5

The **Properties Editor, Render Properties, Sampling Tab** sets the quality of the Render which is expressed in terms of how much noise displays in the view. Noise means how speckled or clear the view looks.

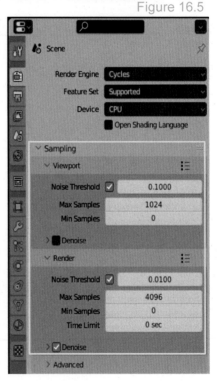

Speckled   Figure 16.6   Clear

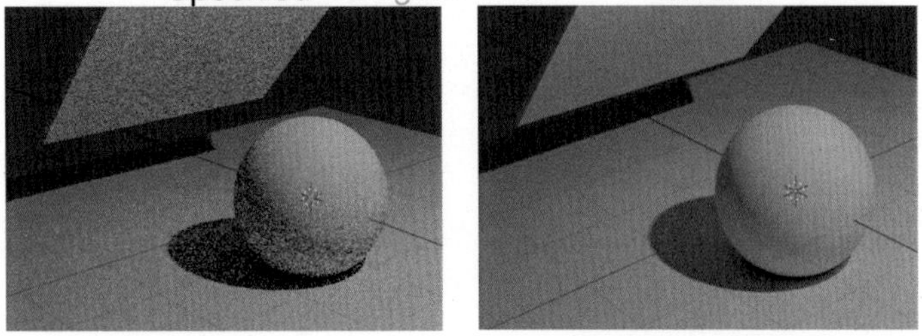

Samples: 5   **Samples: 44**

The Sampling Tab (Figure 16.5) allows you to set the quality of the Render of the display in the Viewport and the display in the final Render. You should be aware that Rendering can take a considerable time, therefore, in the process of constructing a Scene you may wish to minimise the Render time.

There are several method for setting Render limits:

       Noise Threshold – sets a limit for Noise.
       Max Samples   – Maximum number of Samples.
       Min Samples   – Minimum number of Samples.

Figure 16.7

In the default settings the **Noise Threshold** is controlling the Samples.   Noise Threshold ☑   0.1000

Adaptive Sampling Threshold
Noise level step to stop sampling at, lower values reduce noise at the cost of render time. Zero for automatic setting based on number of AA samples, for viewport renders.

To set Maximum and Minimum Sample settings **uncheck Noise Threshold**.

What Render Settings you use will depend on the quality of the display in the Viewport and the quality of the final Render. A higher quality in both cases incurs a higher Render Time and this will be dependent on your computers capability.

16.3 Cycles vs Scene Content

The content of the Scene also affects the Render time. For example, on a machine, with the Default Blender Scene containing the single Cube Object the elapsed time for the Viewport Render in Rendered Viewport Shading Mode is 00.09.40 seconds. The full image Render, pressing F12 times out at 01.20.21 seconds. Scaling the Cube X 2 increases the preview time to 01.12.61 seconds and a full render time out at 01.36.82 seconds. Note: These Render Times are approximate on my PC. Yours will be different.

There are numerous factors which will affect Render Times, therefore, what to expect from Cycles will depend on your computer and your operating system, your display adaptor (Graphics Card) and the drivers (Software) that have been installed for the card.

Before proceeding it will help to understand some terminology.

NVIDIA graphics: NVIDIA is one of many suppliers of graphics chipsets used in graphics cards. At the time of writing Blender is configured to use NVIDIA with Open CL and CUDA or OptiX enabled for GPU rendering.

Open CL is a set of graphics standards used world wide which is designed to give maximum performance on the GPU.

GPU (Graphics Processing Unit) is the processing device built into the graphics card which performs computations in parallel with the computer's central processing unit (CPU).

CUDA™ (Computer Unified Devise Architecture) is a parallel computing platform and programming model that enables dramatic increases in computing performance by harnessing the power of the graphics processing unit (GPU).

OptiX is **a domain-specific API designed for accelerating ray tracing**. It provides a complete package with programmable ray generation, intersection and shading while using RT Cores on NVIDIA RTX GPUs for accelerating Bounding Volume Hierarchy (BVH) traversal and ray/triangle intersection testing.

To summarize, the GPU performs computations in conjunction with the CPU which significantly speeds up the changing graphics display that is required for **On the Fly** graphics rendering. BUT! whether the GPU is faster than the CPU depends on your computer configuration. It could be your CPU is faster for some aspects of the process.

If you have a NVIDIA GPU you can use either CUDA or OptiX. OptiX is specifically built for ray tracing and is probably faster than CUDA, which is built for general compute. Blender OptiX option uses NVIDIA RT tech, which is only available on the newer NVIDIA cards (NVIDIA GeForce, Quadro and Tesla products with Maxwell and newer generation GPUs.) Another factor in this technicality is the **Compute Capability** rating of your graphics card. Cards are rated through a range something like 1.1 to 3.5. At the time of writing, Blender only supports graphics cards rated at 1.3 and above for GPU processing (Rendering), so again, unless your system meets the requirements you will not realize the full capability of **Cycles**.

OK! Cycles has been turned on and there is a display on the Screen but at this point the ancillary architectures are not activated. CUDA, OptiX and OpenCL require a secondary activation.

Also be aware that what you see in the Blender controls will depend on your system configuration. Blender takes a look at your system and displays controls accordingly.

To activate CUDA, OptiX or OpenCL, in the **Blender Screen Header** click on **Edit** and open the **Preferences Editor**. Select **System** in the LH column to see **Cycles Render Device** (Figure 16.8).

Figure 16.8

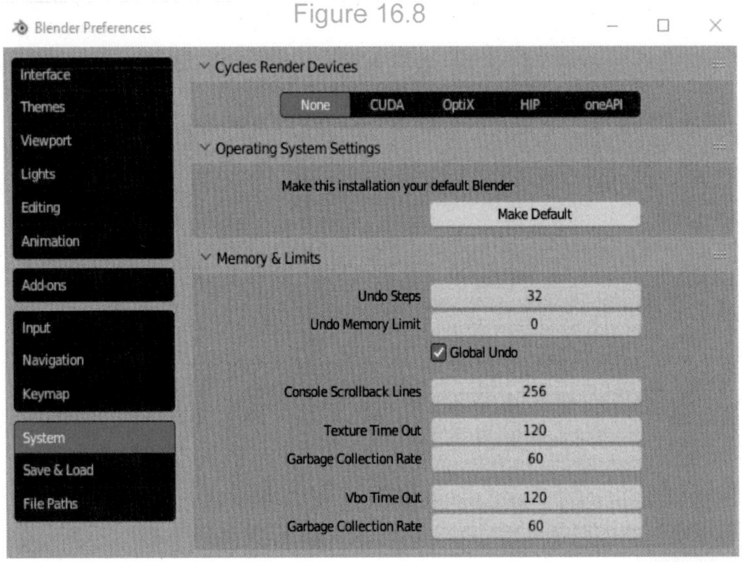

If you do not have a NVIDIA graphics chipset or your drivers for the card are outdated then you will see a message stating **No compatible GPUs** found and, therefore, the Cycles rendering process will be performed entirely by the CPU.

Select CUDA

Figure 16.9

Providing you have the correct graphics chipset you may click on **CUDA** and the **Cycles Render Devices** Tab will show the name of your graphics card (Figure 16.9).

This display is specific to your PC

Figure 16.10

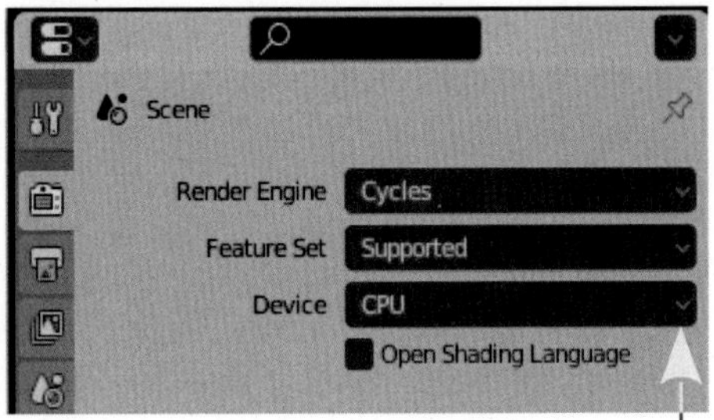

In the **Properties Editor, Render Properties** you will have the option to select **GPU Rendering** (Figure 16.10).

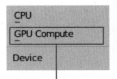

Click to select GPU Compute

With Cycles activated it's time to see what it can do.

16.4 Create an Object Light Source

Figure 16.11

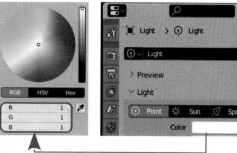

With Cycles Render active Objects can act as a light source. In the Scene previously created (Figures 16.1, 16.2, 16.3) none of the Objects have a Material applied. They all display in the 3D Viewport Editor with Blender's default gray color when the Point Light in the Scene is set to the default white (RGB: all 1) (Figure 16.11).

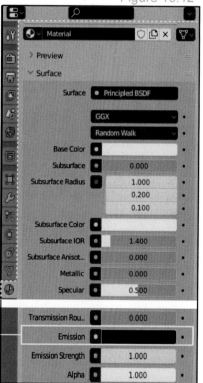

Figure 16.12

By selecting a different Color for the Point Light the Objects in the Scene will reflect that Light Color.

In the Scene, select the inclined Plane (Plane.001). In the Properties Editor, Material Properties, click the New button to add a Material. Note: The Base Color is the default Gray.

Scroll down to the Surface, Emission Tab. The Emission color bar shows black. Click on the black color bar to display the color picker. Increase the Brightness Slider and select a nice bright color.

Increase the Emission Strength value.

With the 3D Viewport in Rendered Viewport Shading Mode you will see Plane.001 Emitting Light which illuminates the Objects in the Scene (Figure 16.14).

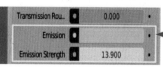

Figure 16.13

By changing the default Point Light color you mix the Scene color (Figure 16.15).

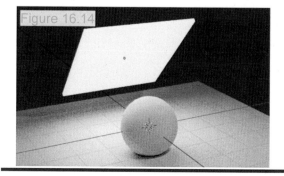

Figure 16.14

Figure 16.15

16.5 Cycles Using Nodes

An Object Light Source may be created using the Node System in Blender. You will be aware that the **Materials Properties** in the **Properties Editor** are replicated in the **Shader Editor** by the **Principled BSDF Node**. In the case of an Emission Object the Principled BSDF Node may be replaced by an **Emission Node**.

Nodes in the Shader Editor   Figure 16.16

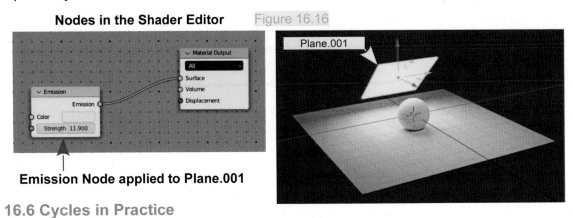

Emission Node applied to Plane.001

16.6 Cycles in Practice

To demonstrate the practical application of Cycles Render, the following demonstration which will show a comparison between Eevee and Cycles. **All Render Properties are default values.**

Set up the Scene

Arrange a **UV Sphere**, a **Cube** and a **Monkey** Object to sit just above a **Plane** such that the Objects are captured in **Camera View**.

Figure 16.17

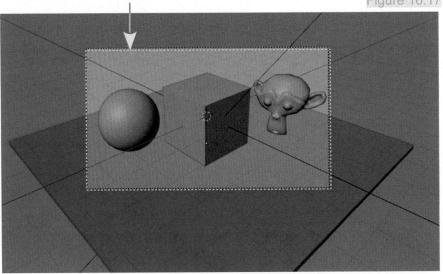

In the **Material Properties** for each Object set the values shown in Figure 16.18.

UV Sphere

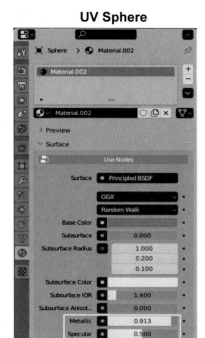

Cube   Figure 16.18   **Monkey**

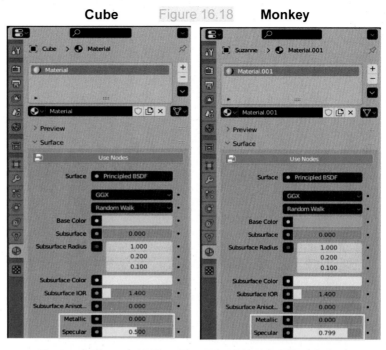

Plane

Eevee – Camera View Render Viewport Shading

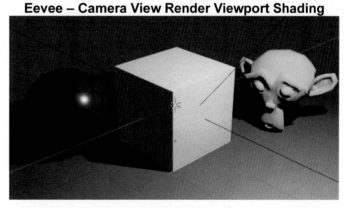

Cycles – Camera View Render Viewport Shading

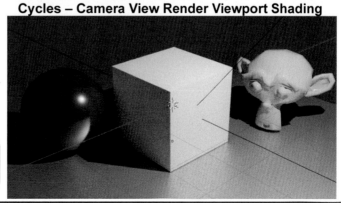

Pay attention to the **Metallic** and **Specular** values for each Object.

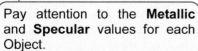

Cycles and Nodes

In the preceding example the Materials assigned to each Object in the Scene have been set in the Properties Editor, Material Properties. By opening the Shader Edit and selecting Objects in turn you will see that each Object's Material Properties are replicated by a Principled BSDF Node connected to a Material Output Node (Figure 16.19).

Figure 16.19 **Nodes for the UV Sphere**

A different Node arrangement may be configured for each Object to replace the Principled BSDF Node and produce different Material effects.

For example, by selecting the UV Sphere and replacing the Principled BSDF Node with the Nodes shown in Figure 16.20 and mixing Materials, color effects may be varied.

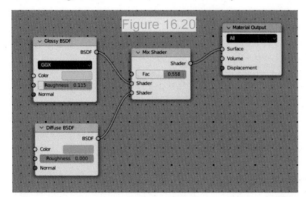

Figure 16.20

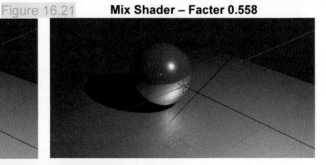

Mix Shader – Facter 0.075   Figure 16.21   **Mix Shader – Facter 0.558**

Mix Shader – Facter 0.917

Note: The Material colors being mixed are those shown in the **Glossy BSDF** and **Diffuse BSDF** Nodes

16.7 Cycles Lighting Effects

The preceding examples have been generated with the default single Point Light producing the Lighting in the Scene. You may change the Light Type, color, intensity etc. in the Properties Editor to create different lighting to generate a mood for the Scene or use **World Properties** in the Properties Editor to create effects (Figure 16.22).

Figure 16.22

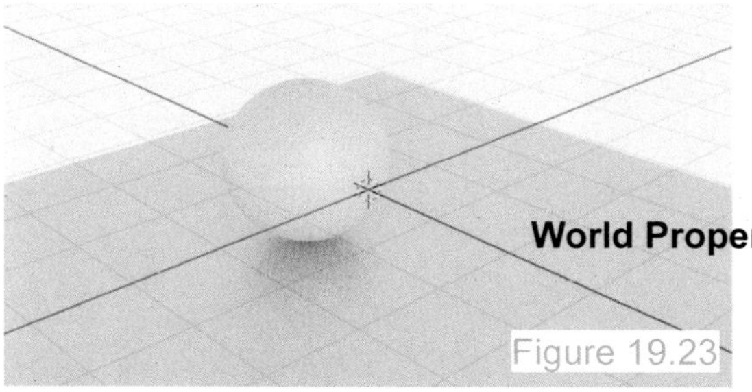

World Properties

Figure 19.23

Click to select Sky Type options.

Lighting effect using World Properties shown in Figure 16.22 with the default Point Light removed from the Scene.

Click, hold and drag the trackball to alter effects. Trackball only available with Preetham and Hosek / Wilki

Sky Type Options

Preetham
Hosek / Wilkie
Nishita
Sky Type

World Properties are also employed to create external Lighting.

Figure 16.24

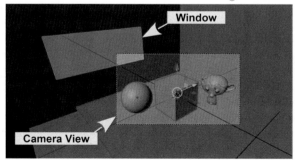

Window

Camera View

Note: The Camera has been located inside the new Cube which creates a Scene in Camera View, inside a room.

Outside View

By adjusting settings in the **Properties Editor, World Properties** (Figure 16.26) you create an **Ambient Lighting Effect** casting light into the room.

The Objects shown in Figures 16.24, 16.25 are positioned inside a Cube Object which is subdivided in Edit Mode and has Vertices deleted creating a window. The Point Light in the default Scene has been deleted.

Figure 16.25

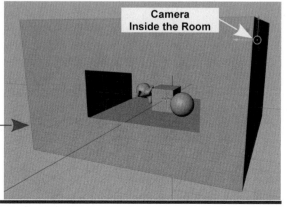

Camera Inside the Room

Figure 16.26

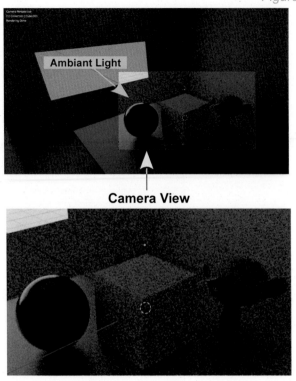

Note: With the Scene using Cycles Render the default Sampling Render will take a considerable time (depending on your computer) and with default Render settings the result will appear grainy as shown above. Fantastic results can be obtained with extended Render Times.

Rendered View : 1024 Samples   Figure 16.27

16.8 Workbench Render

This introduction to the **Workbench Render Engine** is intended to make you aware of its existence and its features. The following description is taken from the Blender Wiki.

General Description

The Workbench Engine is a render engine optimized for fast rendering during modeling and animation preview. It is not intended to be a render engine that will render final images for a project. Its primary task is to display a scene in the 3D Viewport when it is being worked.

Workbench also has an X-ray mode to see through objects, along with cavity and shadow shading to help display details in objects. Workbench supports several lighting mechanisms including studio lighting and MatCaps.

Lighting

The Workbench engine does not use the lights of the scene. The lighting conditions that will be used can be set in the Lighting panel (Tab).

Figure 16.28

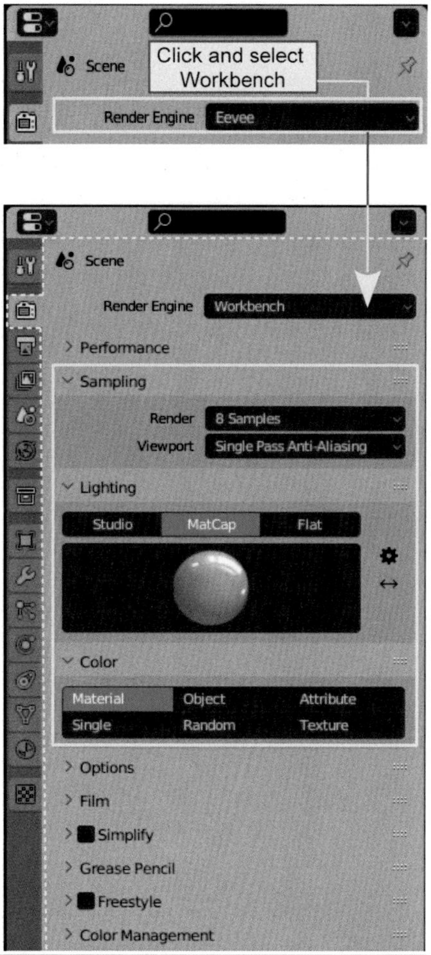

Workbench Render is accessed in the Properties Editor, Render Properties (Figure 16.28).

With Workbench opened the Render Properties display with the Sampling Tab, Lighting Tab and the Color Tab open. Settings in these tabs will directly control the display in the 3D Viewport Editor and supersede normal controls.

For example: With Workbench active the Viewport Display Modes are limited.

Figure 16.29

Eevee   **Workbench**

You will also find the Materials Properties in the Properties Editor limited or appear to be. More on this later.

Figure 16.30

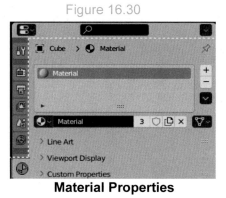

Material Properties

The display in the 3D Viewport Editor is controlled from the Properties Editor Render Properties. To use Materials as an example, a Material applied to the default Cube in the default Scene with Eevee Render active does not display in the Viewport when you switch to Workbench Render.

Workbench is designed to present a complicated Scene in a simplified display for modeling, and at the same time provide a preview only of color and lighting effects.

The Scene shown in Figure 16.31 is far from being complicated but it will serve to demonstrate Workbench controls.

Figure 16.31

  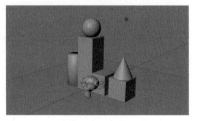

Eevee Material Preview Mode

Eevee Rendered Mode

Workbench Solid Mode

With Materials added to the Objects the colors display in Eevee Render in Material Preview and Rendered display Modes. Changing to Workbench Render sees the Objects in the default Gray. In Figure 16.31 the Workbench Solid Mode shows a green Screen background. Changing to Workbench Render with Rendered Viewport Shading shows a gray World background (Figure 16.32). This is the starting point for exploring the Properties Editor, Render Properties for Workbench Render.

Figure 16.32

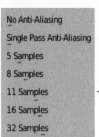

Click for Options

Sampling

The first thing to note is the **Sampling** setting in the Sampling Tab. The default value is **8 Samples**. Click to display options. Higher values improve the display. Lower values reduce the resolution.

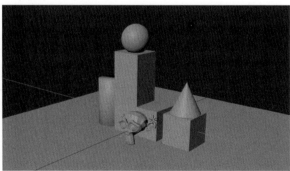

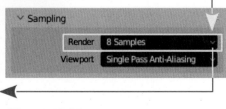

Figure 16.33

16.9 Workbench Lighting

Figure 16.34

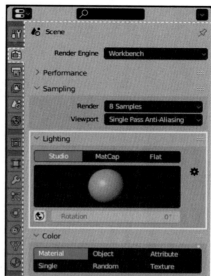

Note: In Workbench Render the default Point Lamp in the Scene or any Lamps placed in the Scene have no effect on lighting. The lighting is controlled by the settings in the Workbench Properties Editor, Render Properties (Figure 16.34).

Studio Lighting: The default Lighting display.

Flat Lighting: Shows all Objects without color in a flat gray.

MatCap Lighting: Provides a variety of options which show the Scene with an overall lighting effect. It should be remembered that the effects are a preview only to allow you to see how the Scene will look after you set the lighting effects in Eevee or Cycles render.

Click to select MatCaps

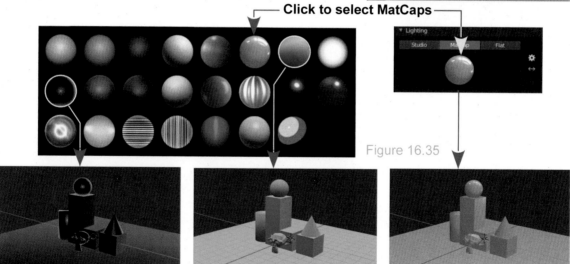

Figure 16.35

16.10 Workbench Materials

The Color Tab allows you to preview Materials and Textures applied to Objects.

Figure 16.36

The default Color option is **Material** (Figure 16.36). This is perhaps the trickiest option to explain since it relates to the Material applied to an Object and at the beginning of the chapter it was stated that the Material Properties in the Properties Editor were limited.

Material: Assume that you would like to see how Suzanne (Monkey) would look with a different Material, in the Scene, before actually making a change.

Figure 16.37

Suzanne as viewed in Eevee

The Scene is displayed in Eevee, in Rendered Viewport Shading Mode (Figure 16.37).

Switch to Workbench Render in **Solid Viewport Shading Mode** and select Suzanne in the Viewport.

At this point everything in the Scene displays gray. With the limited display in the Material Properties (Figure 16.38), open the Viewport Display Tab and click the Color bar to display the Color Picker Circle. Select a color and adjust the Metallic and Roughness settings (Figure 16.39). When satisfied switch back to Eevee and make the changes.

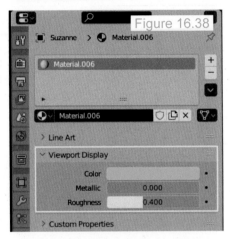
Figure 16.38

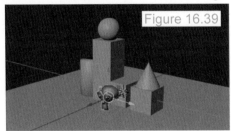
Figure 16.39

Object:

The Object Color option is similar to the Material option. Select an Object in the Viewport in Solid Viewport Shading Mode then in the Properties Editor, Object Properties, Viewport Display tab, select a Color for preview.

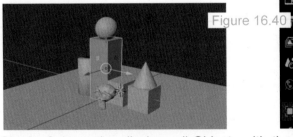
Figure 16.40

Single: The **Single** Color option displays all Objects with the same color in rendered Viewport Shading Mode.

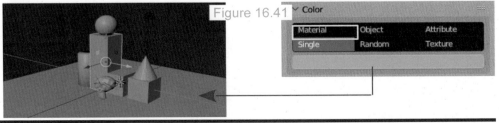
Figure 16.41

Random: Random applies a different color to each Object in the Scene making it easier to distinguish one object from another when the scene becomes really congested.

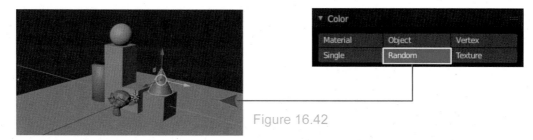

Figure 16.42

Texture: Displays textures which have been applied to Objects in a Scene.

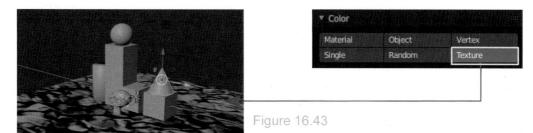

Figure 16.43

Attribute:

Attribute allows you to **Paint** Objects as a preview before making changes to a Scene. Have the Attribute option selected. Select an Object in the 3D Viewport. Change the 3D Viewport (in Rendered Display Mode) from Object Mode to **Vertex Paint Mode**. RMB click in the Viewport for the Color Picker. Select a color. The Mouse Cursor is a circle which you click , hold and drag over the Object to paint color.

Figure 16.44

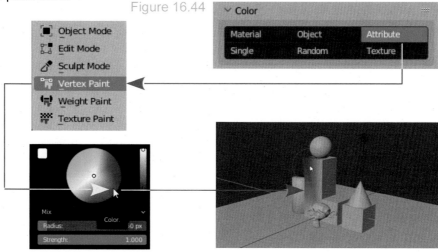

16.11 The Options Tab

Finally a few of the settings in the **Options Tab**. Figure 16.45

Backface Culling: Allows you to see through the rear Face of Objects.

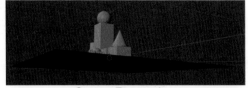

Scene Rotated

Backface Culled

Shadows:

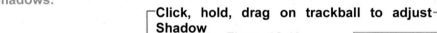

Click, hold, drag on trackball to adjust Shadow

Figure 16.46

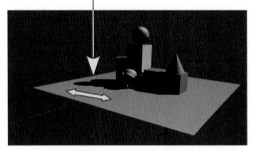

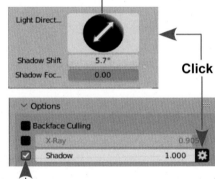

Click

Check Shadows

X-Ray: Displays Objects in the Scene transparent **IN A RENDERED VIEW** when you press **F12**.

Figure 16.47

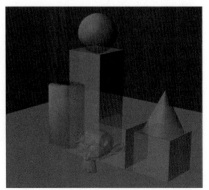

Index

I

Icosphere 25
Individual Geometry Nodes 229
Inflow 202
Inflow Object 210
Input Socket 234
Insert Keyframes 268
Inserting Keyframes 120
Install Add-on 16
Installing Add-ons 326
Instance Foliage Objects 261
Instance Modifier 142
Instance Object 153,173,174,197,253-256
Instance on Point Node 253,255,258
Integer Node 270
Is Resumable 191,193-195,204,210

J

Join Geometry Node 235,237,249

K

Key Slider 118,119,120
Keyed Particles 175
Keyed Physics 175
Keyframe 117,121,124
Keyframe 120
Keys 122
Knife Tool 234

L

Laplacian Deform Modifier 58,59
Laplacian Smooth Modifier 66
Last Operator Panel 7,21
Lathing 84
Lattice 59
Lattice Modifier 59,60
Lattice Object 60,61
Lifetime Randomness 131
Lighting 212,341
Lighting Effects 89
Limit of Movement 122
Liquid 204,208,210

Locked Track 110
Lofting 84
Loops 79

M

Make Human   14,313,314
Make Human Export 328
Make Human Program 266
Mantaflow 191,186,193
Map From 108,109
Map To 107-109
Mark as Asset 14
Mask Modifier 37
Master Key 118
MatCap Lighting 343
Material 12,89
Material Assets 18
Material Assignment 89
Material Assignment 90
Material Cache 94-97,101,159,252,253
Material Color 92,101
Material Datablock 94,95,161
Material Drivers 297
Material Icon 12
Material Index 94,95
Material Node System 90,92
Material Nodes 100
Material Preview 100,165
Material Properties 91,93,94
Material Property Drivers 295
Material Shader Nodes 228
Material Slot 100,252
Material Slot 95-98
Materials 95,254
Materials Texture and Lighting 89
Maths 269,273
Maths Nodes 258
Maths in Geometry Nodes 269
Memory Computer 190
Mesh Deform Modifier 62,67
Mesh Extra Object 22
Mesh Primitive 2
Mesh Primitive Node 245,246
Metarig 18,314
Mirror Modifier 38
Mirror Object 39